A League of His Own

A League of His Own

A. G. Spalding and the Business of Baseball

Mark A. Stein

Essex, Connecticut

An imprint of The Globe Pequot Publishing Group, Inc.
64 South Main Street
Essex, CT 06426
www.GlobePequot.com

British Library Cataloguing in Publication Information available

Library of Congress Cataloging-in-Publication Data available

ISBN 978-1-4930-7765-6 (cloth : alk. paper)
ISBN 978-1-4930-9086-0 (electronic)

∞™ The paper used in this publication meets the minimum requirements of American National Standard for Information Sciences—Permanence of Paper for Printed Library Materials, ANSI/NISO Z39.48-1992.

For Alina,
Ben, and Gabriel

Contents

Preface

A Place in the Pantheon

Cooperstown's Community Band struck up "Take Me Out to the Ball Game" shortly after midday on June 12, 1939, all 30 members blowing as hard as they could to try to be heard over the buzzing multitudes milling on Main Street. More than 10,000 visitors—the local weekly newspaper, the *Otsego Farmer*, later estimated as many as 15,000—packed into the remote lakefront village 150 miles northwest of New York City, quintupling its population virtually overnight.

Earlier in the morning, a special train with 13 Pullman passenger coaches had brought hundreds of celebrities and fans from New York to Cooperstown station, the first passenger train to stop at the modest wood-frame structure since the Depression killed regular service in 1933. Smaller special trains arrived from Chicago and Boston, bearing additional players and celebrities, including the retired Metropolitan Opera soprano and devoted baseball fan Geraldine Farrar, as well as dozens of other lifelong followers of the game. Men and boys swarmed each train as it arrived, eager to collect autographs of the active and former baseball gods who were assembling in this unlikely Olympus.

Legendary Philadelphia Athletics manager Connie Mack had come, as had the Pittsburgh Pirates shortstop Honus Wagner, and Tris Speaker, anchor of Boston's vaunted "Million Dollar Outfield." Pitching greats Cy Young, Walter Johnson, and Grover Cleveland Alexander strolled down the sidewalks, posing for photos and scratching their signatures on anything thrust before them. So did Napoleon Lajoie, the slugging second baseman who was so revered in Ohio that Cleveland renamed its club the Naps after his first season there. And there was the Babe, George Herman Ruth Jr., who had retired four years earlier but remained a wildly popular, instantly recognizable celebrity.

Altogether, 12 of the greatest players in the game's history were in town, joined by more than 30 current stars, including Hank Greenberg of the Detroit Tigers, Ruth's heir as the home-run king. Greenberg, too, declined the offer of a car and driver, preferring to walk from the station through the ocean of fans, signing autographs and shaking hands.

At one point, 10 of the greatest names in baseball history obligingly posed together for the newspaper photographers: "Cocky" Eddie Collins, second baseman for the A's and Chicago White Sox; Ruth, without a tie but sporting two-toned shoes; Mack, as stiff and uncomfortable-looking as a preacher at a burlesque show; and the 72-year-old Young sat on folding chairs. Behind them stood Wagner, hulking but looking friendly, as always; Alexander, the shutout ace; Speaker, the outfielder nonpareil; Lajoie, the first player in the modern era to be intentionally walked with the bases loaded; "Gorgeous George" Sisler, who set the record for hits in a 154-game season; and Johnson, the hard-throwing Washington Senators pitcher, who appeared to be uncharacteristically bashful.

The setup produced an image for the ages, one never to be duplicated because this was a one-time-only gathering of immortals. The players, some active, others aging, had assembled in Cooperstown to open a new baseball "hall of fame" and museum, and to commemorate what organizers said was the centennial of the game's invention by Civil War hero and one-time Cooperstown resident Major General Abner Doubleday. Publicity men pointed out the dusty lot a block south of the business district where they claimed the miraculous birth had occurred.

The Doubleday connection had persuaded Major League Baseball to cooperate on the creation of a hall of fame and museum in out-of-the-way Cooperstown, a pleasant but ordinary home to 2,500 souls on the shores of Lake Otsego. Until the hall arrived the village was best known—if it was known at all—for its founder, William Cooper, father of the 18th-century novelist James Fenimore Cooper, and for producing exceptional hops until Prohibition outlawed beer in 1920 and put many local growers out of business.

Cooperstown also had the good fortune to be the town where an heir to the Singer Sewing Machine fortune had grown up.[1] Stephen Carlton Clark, a grandson of Singer cofounder Edward Cabot Clark, offered to organize, underwrite, and promote the entire Hall of Fame enterprise, as long as it was located in his hometown.

Clark wasn't particularly interested in baseball; he was a publisher, philanthropist, and collector of modern art. In addition to owning three newspapers in Albany, New York State's capital, he was a founding trustee of the Museum of Modern Art in New York City, and would become chairman of MoMA's board of trustees not long after the Hall opened. He also owned a country estate in Cooperstown, loved the village, and wanted to revive its fortunes.

When a local resident found a stuffed lump of leather in his attic, Clark bought it for $5 and displayed it in the village library, calling it a relic of the early days of the game.[2] Some people came to accept it as a baseball that Doubleday himself had used. As Clark added artifacts, the idea of a museum took root.

The effort to establish a national baseball museum in Cooperstown—and later a Hall of Fame for the game's greatest players—was aided by a report issued about a quarter of a century earlier by a blue-ribbon commission of baseball grandees led by a different Civil War veteran, a Chicago lawyer, and a former National League president named Abraham G. Mills. At the end of two years of sporadic, lackadaisical research—most of it conducted by Mills, alone, in his spare time—the so-called Mills Commission had concluded in 1908 that baseball was a wholly American sport, not descended from any of the similar stick-and-ball games played in foreign lands for millennia but invented by Doubleday on a sandlot near his family's home in Cooperstown in 1839.

From that report—as well as Clark's ample generosity—sprang the celebration that came to overwhelm Cooperstown on that fine, sunny late-spring day. "Nowhere else than at its birthplace could this museum be appropriately situated," Judge Kenesaw Mountain Landis, the commissioner of baseball, told the fans in attendance, some of whom had climbed atop parked cars and hung out of open windows so they could see the show. And what a show it was. After presenting inductees chosen before the hall was ready, National League President Ford C. Frick cut a red ribbon across its entrance, American League President William Harridge cut a white ribbon, and President William G. Bramham of the National Association of Professional Leagues, which governed the minor leagues, cut a blue ribbon.

A parade down Main Street followed, led by a 30-piece band from the American Legion Post No. 4 in Syracuse and followed at regular intervals by three more marching bands of similar size: a drum and bugle corps from Abraham Lincoln Kellogg High School in nearby Treadwell, New York, another representing the Veterans of Foreign Wars in nearby Oneonta, and an encore for the Cooperstown Community Band. A clutch of Cooperstown High School students strutted in fashions from a century earlier, while soldiers from Fort Jay in New York Harbor marched in baseball uniforms from the 1850s. Bringing up the rear were the 12 living members of the Hall of Fame and the professional players who would play a demonstration game at Doubleday Field, a ballpark built on what was said to be the very spot where Doubleday had invented the game.

The show continued at the park, with local boys dressed "like so many Huckleberry Finns," according to one account, demonstrating "town ball," a stick-and-ball game credited as an antecedent of baseball.[3] The Fort Jay soldiers then took the field to show how the game was played back in Doubleday's time. Finally, at the conclusion of what event promoters called a "Cavalcade of Baseball," the contemporary stars took the field for seven innings played for fun. The highlight of the game was when Babe Ruth was called out of the stands and put to work as a pinch-hitter for a pickup team Wagner had organized. Spectators whooped and hollered for the Babe to belt one, but he popped out weakly to the catcher, his former Yankees teammate Art Jorgens. "Don't catch it!" the crowd shouted to Jorgens, but he did.

It was a swell ceremony, a terrific promotion for a down-on-its-luck farm town, and a nice day out for the crowd, but it was all just so much baloney—publicity for a fairy tale. Abner Doubleday didn't invent baseball; he is not even known to have ever played the game. In 1839, the year he purportedly invented "base ball," as the sport was then spelled, he was a cadet confined to the campus of the US Military Academy at West Point, 100 miles from Cooperstown. He never mentioned baseball in the voluminous diaries he left behind when he died in 1893. The general came to be feted as baseball's inventor largely through the work of one man, a wealthy, willful, proud, and patriotic sporting goods magnate who had died 24 years before that pleasant afternoon in Cooperstown. Coincidentally, he was one of the 12 "pioneers of the game" who were posthumously inducted into the Hall of Fame on the day it opened.

Albert Goodwill Spalding was that magnate and, arguably, professional baseball's first star player. He was certainly the first player to get extraordinarily rich off the game, not so much from his salary as a pitcher—although he was the first player to receive a percentage of ticket sales as well as an ample paycheck—but from the mighty sporting goods empire he built from scratch with his brother and brother-in-law after retiring from the game at the age of just 27. While he played professional ball for only seven years, Spalding won 252 games, an average of 36 wins each season; he recorded 65 losses in all, for a career-long winning percentage of .795.

This was back in the 1870s, when pitchers really pitched—they threw underhand, as if pitching a horseshoe—but young Spalding pitched so fast and accurately that he had built a national reputation long before he threw his first ball for pay: He had drawn interest from the biggest amateur clubs on the East Coast while still a teenager working part-time in a grocery store in Rockford, Illinois, a frontier town on the Rock River near Wisconsin.

As a paid player, Spalding led his first team, Boston's Red Stockings, to four straight championships of the first professional league, the National Association of Professional Baseball Players. The Red Stockings so dominated the competition that players in other cities began to grumble about baseball being "the Boston game." A pugnacious western coal merchant named William Ambrose Hulbert sought to change that in the most direct way he could think of: by luring the league's best pitcher—Spalding—back to Illinois to play for Hulbert's Chicago White Stockings.

His tools for tempting the young player were as simple as his plan to revive the team. He offered Spalding an enormous pay raise, a percentage of ticket sales, stock in the team, and enough money to attract other established stars. Hulbert even conspired with Spalding to avoid a National Association rule that forbade players to sign contracts with other teams before the end of a season. The rule could have led the National Association to ban Spalding from the sport, as well as the three other Boston players and two Philadelphia Athletics whom he persuaded to bolt to Chicago with him. Hulbert and Spalding evaded the rule by creating the National League, the same organization that comprises half of Major League Baseball today.

Spalding went on to become the controlling partner of the White Stockings and unofficial leader of the league, and when a players' union revolt in 1890 challenged the owners' iron-fisted authority over the game, league officials and team owners enlisted Spalding as their field general in what came to be known as the Brotherhood War. Using detectives, compliant newspaper reporters, moxie, and mendacity, Spalding broke the union, formally the Brotherhood of Professional Baseball Players, destroyed their "Players' League," and restored the National League's monopoly on major-league baseball.

Despite his authority over pro ball at all levels, Spalding was silent about the color line that excluded Black players from the major leagues. While a semipro league adopted the first explicit ban of Black players in 1867, when Spalding was still a schoolboy, there is no evidence that he resisted discrimination after becoming the most powerful man in pro ball. As the largest stockholder of the Chicago White Stockings, he did nothing to rein in the truculent racism of Adrian Constantine "Cap" Anson, his team's manager for 18 seasons, a Hall of Fame member, and arguably the most visible advocate of the color line. Instead, he appeared to be more interested in avoiding any issue that might hurt his club's revenue.

* * *

Innovation drove Spalding as much as money and power. In baseball's barehanded era, he was the first player to openly wear a glove in the field—a black leather, fingerless design that looks more like a work glove than the amply padded and hinged baseball gloves common today. While a few other players had previously experimented with tan-colored gloves that they hoped fans would not notice (they were noticed, attracting spectators' condemnation), Spalding consciously chose black leather; his reputation enabled him to wear it without being mocked. Not coincidentally, gloves provided a lucrative new product line for his sporting goods business.

As a team owner, he established baseball's first permanent spring training facility, in Hot Springs, Arkansas. As a businessman, he made the first volleyball and first basketball shoes. He did not make the first basketball, as some have said, but the sport's inventor, James Naismith, did personally ask Spalding to be the first to mass produce them. Spalding had a factory complex in Chicopee, Massachusetts, when Naismith worked at the YMCA in nearby Springfield.

In every part of his life, Spalding—known as "A. G." to business associates, "Al" to his friends, and "Albert" to his family—sought not only to win but to dominate. When he left baseball to focus on the "baseball emporium" he and his brother, J. Walter Spalding, had opened in Chicago, the company quickly became the largest brand in the nascent sporting goods industry. It was the first to integrate vertically by making its own branded products in its own factories, and the most aggressive in buying up rivals—and keeping the rivals' names after acquiring them, to maintain the appearance of thriving competition in the field.

He used his influence as a cofounder of the National League to have Spalding brand baseballs declared the league's "official ball"—initially paying the league $1 a dozen for the privilege of providing balls to teams at no cost and reaping invaluable advertising in return. When Ban Johnson founded the rival American League in 1901, the Spalding-controlled A. J. Reach & Co. of Philadelphia became the sole source of "official" balls to the junior circuit.

Similarly, Spalding launched a lucrative publishing empire. He obtained exclusive rights to publish the National League's official yearbook, a publication that quickly blurred into the authoritative and perennial best-selling *Spalding's Official Base Ball Guide* and begat a publishing house, the Spalding-owned American Sports Publishing Co. of New York. The company not only cashed in on the increase in leisure time and growing interest in sports and fitness in the 1880s and '90s by publishing how-to guides and rule books for activities from archery to wrestling, it hired the leading experts of the day to write them, making the publications de facto official guides that earnest young athletes felt they had to have.

Walter Camp, the Yale coach celebrated as the "father of American football," penned the *Spalding Guide* on that sport. Bill Tilden, then the world's number one player, explained how to win at tennis. Luther Halsey Gulick Jr., chair of the Amateur Athletic Union's basketball committee and James Naismith's boss, wrote the guide on that game. Equally authoritative experts were retained to write authoritative instruction guides about boxing, fencing, field hockey, gymnastics, lacrosse, tennis, track and field, and dozens of other sports, all under Spalding's name.

To oversee the publishing empire, Spalding made a shrewd choice: James E. Sullivan, a sportswriter who had founded the Amateur Athletic Union and would eventually create the American Olympic Association, the forerunner to the US Olympic Committee. Sullivan continued to control the AAU—serving variously as secretary, president, and secretary-treasurer—while running Spalding's publishing company. Not surprisingly, Spalding's firm published the official AAU handbook as well as the official rule books for every sport it oversaw, essentially every sport then being played by organized amateurs. Between American Sports Publishing's founding, in 1892, and sale in 1941, the firm published about 200 titles, most of them perennials like *How to Play Basketball*, *Indian Club Exercises*, *The Art of Fencing*, and *Tennis for the Junior Player, the Club Player, the Expert*.

Sullivan's dual roles as the rule maker for amateur sports and a senior employee of the dominant supplier of sporting goods gave Spalding's empire unprecedented influence. It was not always welcome, or healthy. In the early 1900s, muckraking journalists and aggrieved athletes were accusing Spalding's company of corrupting amateur sports in America, exploiting athletes, and crushing competitors. The AAU, for example, disregarded a collegiate discus record because it had been achieved with a discus the Union had not approved; remarkably, at the time, the AAU under Sullivan recognized results only if they were achieved with Spalding gear. On another occasion, Sullivan used his considerable authority to enforce amateurism in collegiate sports when he revoked the amateur status of University of Chicago football star Walter Eckersall after he led the Maroons to a national championship. Sullivan accused Eckersall of having accepted expense money while playing in a summer baseball league—a league sponsored by Spalding. Eckersall's teammates and friends said Sullivan's true motive for punishing the quarterback was that he had declined to wear Spalding brand football boots.

Spalding and Sullivan's control of amateur sports at the end of the 19th century went far beyond college teams. They led a national campaign to introduce and expand sports programs in elementary and high schools, drawing up programs, lobbying school boards and politicians, and providing trophies to the most outstanding schools. They arranged exhibition games between retired professional ballplayers and college teams. Each initiative ended in the same way: with an increase in participation in organized leagues, a rising demand for sporting goods, and a Spalding contract to supply them. The company's ubiquity in 1908 was such that the *Boston Herald* sarcastically declared:

> *Next to Abraham Lincoln and George Washington the name of A. G. Spalding is the most famous in American literature. It has been blazoned forth on the covers of guides to all sorts of sports, upon bats and gloves and all the various accoutrements of the same sports for many years. Young America gets his knowledge of the past in the world of athletics from something that has Al Spalding on it in big black letters, and for that reason as much as any other, he is one of the national figures of the times.*[4]

Spalding's influence extended beyond America. He and Sullivan were leaders early in the Olympics movement, choosing, training, and managing the US teams at the Olympic Games in Paris in 1900 and St. Louis in 1904. As the head of America's sporting delegation in Paris, Spalding persuaded his French hosts to avoid scheduling churchgoing American athletes to compete on Sundays. Sullivan, meanwhile, was a close confidant of Pierre de Frédy, Baron de Coubertin, the founder of the modern Olympic movement.

The two men even played a decisive role in having the 1904 Olympic Games moved to St. Louis from Chicago, the first choice of the International Olympic Committee, even though St. Louis had only about one-third as many residents and Chicago was still basking in favorable worldwide admiration for its staging of the Columbian Exhibition world's fair in 1893. Moving the Games to St. Louis, where the AAU had already scheduled the national championship meet, put amateur athletics firmly in the control of Sullivan and Spalding.

As the manic spread of baseball throughout America in the decades after the Civil War, in which men who had played ball for fun in New York and Massachusetts taught the game to soldiers and prisoners from all parts of the country, allowed Spalding to build his sporting goods empire from Boston to San Francisco, it also got him thinking about so many other large markets waiting to be tapped: Britain, Ireland, Australia, and beyond. The natural entrée to these markets was the same one he used so skillfully at home: baseball. So Spalding took it upon himself to make America's national pastime—the *New York Mercury* had awarded the game that title in 1856—a pastime for the rest of the world, too.

He led two international tours of American ballplayers, including a six-month around-the-world tour in 1888 and 1889 that included exhibition games around Australia, beneath the Great Sphinx of Giza near Cairo, in the Villa Borghese gardens in Rome, the Bois du Boulogne of Paris, and the great cricket grounds of England. The tour was followed in the United States courtesy of newspaper reporters whom Spalding had shrewdly invited along for the ride, all expenses paid. The tourists, as the players and press were known, left the country after a lavish nine-course feast (a "meal in nine innings") in San Francisco, and upon the teams' return to the country they—and Spalding—were again feted like royalty at another sumptuous banquet, this one at the Gilded Age landmark Delmonico's restaurant in New York; the author Mark Twain was among those toasting the tourists' success.

The excursion was a commercial success for Spalding, who left behind a trail of stores from Honolulu to High Holborn in London, but it was a cultural flop. The exhibitions did not persuade Britons to give up on cricket, nor did it encourage

Egyptians to build ballparks in the desert; it also did nothing to stymie the newer game of soccer from becoming the first true world sport. Their failure in this regard didn't discourage other baseball players from mounting similar promotional tours well into the 20th century.

Spalding—Goodwill was his mother's family name—was thoroughly a product of his era, when scientific and industrial advances promised a utopian future, and soon. While he built his sporting goods business, railroads cut the continent down to size, accelerating the transportation of coal, oil, steel, and lumber, and opening the interior of the United States to habitation, farming and development. Factories churned out goods at unimaginably low prices. After developing the germ theory of illness transmission, scientists began to deliver miraculous vaccines that checked the spread of a terrifying litany of death-dealing diseases: cholera, anthrax, rabies, tetanus, diphtheria, and typhoid. The telephone made instant voice communication possible; two years after Alexander Graham Bell invented it, the country's first telephone company was founded in Chicago, Spalding's hometown, with 75 subscribers. Electric lights were supplanting gas lamps in America's cities. Phonographs made it possible to capture and reproduce evanescent phenomena from a human voice to an orchestral crescendo.

Such developments fed the faith that Spalding and other Victorian era businessmen, politicians, and scholars shared in the inexorable advance of science and the perfectibility of humanity. Added to that was a conviction—not unique to Spalding, certainly, but firmly embraced by him—that the United States was an exemplar to the world. He was a Gilded Age entrepreneur who summered with sugar barons and Wall Street financiers on the Jersey Shore and, like them, believed fervently in free markets—if trusts, reserve clauses, and other behind-the-scenes arrangements were made to keep the marketplace "efficient," which was to say, more stable and profitable for him and his colleagues. When Spalding's big bet on the bicycle boom of the 1890s began to sour as production greatly exceeded demand and prices plummeted amid an historic recession, he did what John D. Rockefeller, J. P. Morgan, and other business barons of the era did: He formed a trust to reduce supply, cripple competitors, and drive up prices.

Spalding also introduced the business idea of "vertical integration" into sporting goods. Rather than sell gear made by others, he acquired his suppliers or erected his own factories to stock his retail stores; he also bought timberland to secure wood for baseball bats, croquet mallets, and tennis racquets.

Later he sponsored leagues and encouraged participation in sports to increase the number of people throwing, running, paddling, and pedaling, thus assuring himself of a growing market. By the turn of the 20th century, his company, A. G. Spalding & Bros., was making equipment for—and actively promoting the spread of—more than a hundred different sports and outdoor pursuits, from badminton to boating and squash to skating.

As his influence and his fortune grew, Spalding, like other successful capitalists of the time, invested heavily in land. He bought properties at the conjunction of several new railroads south of Chicago, musing publicly and privately about founding an "ideal" town called Spalding, Illinois. He eventually threw in his lots with another new industrialist, a lumber baron named Turlington W. Harvey, a close friend and financial backer of the Bible-thumping evangelist Dwight Moody. The combined properties became Harvey, Illinois, a factory town where saloons and liquor stores were banned and factories were required to hire local residents first.

Spalding's alliance with a temperance zealot like Harvey was not a surprise. As a player and later manager and team owner, Spalding was consistently a vocal moralizer who campaigned against liquor and gambling at a time when they threatened his desire to make baseball a socially acceptable form of entertainment. He scolded, fined, and eventually sold players—even such stars of the era as the boozy batsman Michael "King" Kelly—who did not meet his standards. Spalding hired Pinkerton agents to shadow players and report back on their after-hours drinking and carousing.

High-minded moralizing and public attacks on the vices of others, however, did not prevent Spalding from conducting a prolonged extramarital affair with a married woman or fathering a son by her while appearing to be a happily married paragon of virtue.

Spalding displayed his approach to life, baseball, and business on a desk plaque that read: "Everything Is Possible to Him Who Dares," a slogan he cribbed from *The Seamy Side*, a popular novel of the 1890s. It was a lesson he had learned early. His father died when he was nine, and three years later Albert's mother, Harriet, sent him from their hometown, a wide spot on the Rock River called Byron, to Rockford, a larger town about 14 miles away. She and her two younger children, Walter and Mary, remained in Byron to settle affairs while Albert lived with an aunt and started school in the new town.

He also took a job, the first of many fated to end with his employer going out of business. The litany of failed employers—grocers and insurance agents, newspapers and banks—made an impression on the young man and taught him some fundamental lessons that served him well: Be your own boss. Make your own luck. Create your own opportunity. Think for yourself and act on your own. These principles helped him to create great things and amass great wealth; they also led him to acts that tarnished his reputation later in life.

Close friends, notably the White Stockings' player-manager "Cap" Anson, publicly scolded him for sharp business dealings. Child-welfare advocates in New York criticized him for his role in transporting 11 Cuban orphans to a utopian commune in California run by the Theosophical Society, a pan-religious philosophical group he had embraced at the urging of his second wife. Like-minded Republican progressives were puzzled when, in 1909, he agreed to be the US Senate candidate representing the mainstream Republican Party, which was then openly dominated by the corrupt Southern Pacific Railroad political machine.[5] Spalding finished first among three candidates in most of California's legislative districts but trailed Judge John D. Works of Los Angeles, a candidate from the party's reformist Lincoln-Roosevelt faction, by a few thousand ballots in the statewide popular vote. Spalding's candidacy ended in a bitter fight among Republicans in the state capital, Sacramento, early in 1910.

Denied public office, the indomitable Spalding pursued public service in his own way, becoming a leading advocate for better public highways. Ironically, his support of good roads worked against the interests of the Southern Pacific Railroad, his erstwhile political patron. But Spalding's devotion to smooth streets, kindled when he was a major bicycle manufacturer, did serve his interests as a budding land developer in San Diego, where he had moved after retiring.

He was at the time president and chief executive of the San Diego Securities Company, which owned several miles of harbor frontage on San Diego Bay and more than 1,000 acres of land overlooking the Pacific Ocean at Point Loma. Working with other San Diego millionaires—the newspaper magnate E. W. Scripps and sugar and streetcar baron John D. Spreckels, who also had considerable real estate holdings in the area—Spalding successfully lobbied for federal road-building funds and endorsed the sale of government bonds that raised enough money to build 500 miles of roads in San Diego County. The roads passed by each man's properties, considerably raising their value.[6]

Spalding devoted much of his time to a task that was vitally important to him, writing a definitive history of baseball, and his role in it. He had long urged his friend and mentor, the seminal sportswriter Henry Chadwick, to write the book, but Chadwick was too old and ill to take on such an ambitious project; after he died in the spring of 1908, Spalding took over the task and his American Sports Publishing Company published the book *Baseball: America's National Game*, in 1911.

Even after filtering out Spalding's considerable self-aggrandizement and self-promotion—reflexive traits he took to his death, by stroke, in 1915—the book gives ample evidence to support the description of him that Major League Baseball cast in the bronze plaque installed in the Hall of Fame on the day it opened:

Organizational genius of baseball's pioneer days.

Chapter 1
An Unbaked Country Boy

Albert Goodwill Spalding was born on September 2, 1850, to a prosperous land-owning family in the primitive frontier village of Byron, Illinois, about 85 miles west of Chicago. The settlement was not long past its founding, when pioneers slept on their wagons, using their boots as a pillow and their coat as a blanket. Even when Albert arrived, Byron was little more than a collection of log cabins, some of which did double duty as a tavern or a general store as well as the proprietor's home. Settlers insulated their rough living quarters with prairie grass to protect themselves from the plains' brutal subzero winters; some cabins were only 10 by 14 feet and used blankets for doors.[1]

Albert was the second son born to James Lawrence Spalding and the former Harriet Irene Goodwill Wright but the first son to survive infancy. The couple's first child, Henry Clinton Spalding, died one year to the day before Albert arrived; he was eight months old.

Spalding's father was a descendant of one Edward Spalding, who had emigrated to America from Lincolnshire, England, in the earliest days of the Massachusetts Bay Colony, arriving between 1630 and 1633, and settling in Braintree, Massachusetts. At least four Spaldings served in the Continental Army during the Revolutionary War, including James's great-grandfather, Simon, and grandfather, John. James's branch of the family had moved to Pennsylvania from New England around 1771, arriving in 1810 in Towanda, on the Susquehanna River near the border with New York about 175 miles northwest of Philadelphia. James was born three years later. His father, John, who ran a store and a tavern, became treasurer of Bradford County when it was created from parts of Lycoming and Luzerne Counties.[2]

James was one of four brothers who had left their hometown in the 1830s to seek their fortunes in the West. They were part of a wave of Easterners who doubled Illinois's population in the first half of that decade and doubled it again in the second half. James and his older brother, Asa, settled first in Madison County, Illinois, across the Mississippi River from St. Louis, in the winter of 1836.[3] In that year of frenzied land speculation, the US government sold three million acres in Illinois, compared with just 133,372 acres five years earlier.

The Spalding brothers bought 46 acres northwest of Alton, Illinois, for $57.49 in February. President Andrew Jackson burst the speculative bubble that summer by requiring that purchasers buy public lands only with gold or silver, not with private banknotes of dubious value. The order rendered bank reserves worthless, triggering a string of bank failures as far away as New York in what came to be called the Panic of 1837. In April, three months before the speculators' reckoning, Asa migrated 250 miles north, to the village of Byron, Illinois, which was then little more than one log cabin nestled in an oxbow of the Rock River roughly a day's ride from the Wisconsin Territory. James followed in May and younger brother Simon arrived in October.

The brothers waited for the economy to recover before they staked claims to hundreds of acres of public land north and west of Byron in 1842. Until recently, the land had been home to indigenous people—most of them in the Pottawatomie and Winnebago nations—whom the US government relocated west of the Mississippi River to make way for white settlers.[4]

In June 1842, James and Simon rode 27 miles to Dixon, Illinois, the location of the closest branch of the General Land Office, to pay for the public land they had staked out. James acquired 240 acres for the statutory minimum of $1.25 an acre, or $300.[5] He inherited the capital from his father, Harry, a Revolutionary War veteran who died in 1822. Simon bought 129 acres on the same trip. James added 20 acres for $77.40 in July 1844, and another 160 acres for $200 in October 1846, bringing his total to 420 acres. He and Asa also were among five partners who acquired the land on which the village was being built, giving James several "town" plots where he erected houses, one for his family and others to rent to pioneers pouring into the area.[6]

The Spaldings were not just prosperous; they were leading citizens of both Byron and Ogle County. Brother Asa Spalding was Byron's first postmaster, once the Frink, Walker and Co. stage company added the village to its network around 1845. That relieved residents of having to ride to Dixon once a week to collect mail. Asa also oversaw elections. Simon was a marshal for the Claim Protection Society, a citizens' group that adjudicated land disputes; his wife, Lydia-Ann, was Byron's first schoolteacher.

James focused on managing his properties and training his horses as if they were show ponies. His family and friends, however, were seeking another way for the 34-year-old bachelor to fill his days: They were looking for a suitable wife.[7]

Harriet Irene Goodwill was born in Genesee County, New York, on March 19, 1820, the third of four children of Johnson Goodwill, a prominent lawyer and local politician, and his wife, the former Ruth Durkee Tiffany, a relative of Charles Lewis Tiffany, the jeweler, and his son, the artist Louis Comfort Tiffany. The Goodwills owned a 20-acre estate in Batavia, a town founded by a large developer, the Holland Land Co., in 1801 to facilitate the sale of homesteads to pioneers moving west from New England to the wilderness between Rochester and Buffalo.[8] When Harriet was nine years old, her mother died from injuries suffered in a carriage accident. Before passing away, Ruth asked her husband to send Harriet to live with her sister's family in Clarence, New York, about 20 miles west of Batavia. He did so and dispatched his other children to live with relatives or attend boarding schools.[9]

Harriet's guardians, Amos and Lucinda Wright, welcomed the remarkably tall and skinny girl into their home, arranged for her to attend a private school, and made sure she had many advantages, including instruction in art, writing, dance, and music. Always quick to smile, Harriet befriended the Wrights' son, Henry, who was five years younger than she, and Amos's brother Austin, who was seven years older. "I was very fond of him," she said of Austin, her second cousin; "in fact, it grew into more than friendship as he grew older. . . . I began to realize that I thought a great deal of him." While out for a ride one day in 1839, Austin, then 25 years old, asked Harriet, 18, if she would accompany him to the Wisconsin Territory, where he had invested in property. Harriet eagerly accepted, and only then, she recalled, did Austin think to ask her to marry him. They exchanged vows in Uncle Amos's house on September 30 and then drove a carriage 20 miles west to Buffalo, where they spent their wedding night. The next morning, they boarded a steamship headed west.

Arriving in Chicago by way of Detroit, they found the six-year-old Illinois city to be disagreeably marshy and many of its 4,000 settlers suffering fevers and ague, a flu-like illness. Harriet's recollection that "we were not favorably impressed," seems to be an understatement. After a week, they left to visit acquaintances in the Rock River area about 85 miles to the west, where they found the promised land they expected: "Rivers so clear, banks so high and dry, and the prairies covered with wildflowers in abundance," Harriet wrote. But during the extended stay with their friends, the couple's enthusiasm was tested by the hard labor required to plow dense prairie soil, manually harvest a crop, and use horse-drawn wagons to get it to market.

Austin and Harriet thought the hospitality business might be more to their liking, so when they arrived in Wisconsin the following summer, Austin rented a log-cabin tavern in East Troy, a tiny settlement 30 miles southwest of Milwaukee. A local historian approvingly noted that the tavern's founder, Austin McCracken, ran the business "on strictly temperance principles"—that is, he did not sell alcohol. He added with evident disdain that under Wright, the inn "was run . . . *not* on strictly temperance principles."[10] The Wrights added a dry-goods store in 1842.

Harriet bore her first child, Austin Jr., a year later, but the couple's joy was cut short when the boy's father developed an alarming fever. Doctors summoned to the tavern treated him as best they knew how, by opening a vein and allowing him to bleed to balance the fluids in his body. The millennia-old procedure, still common at the time, was for naught. Austin Wright Sr. died on Saturday, August 16, 1845. Not long after, Austin Jr. developed croup and died.

Emotionally shattered and alone, Harriet accepted a friend's invitation to grieve with her in Rockford, Illinois, a three- or four-day journey away.

When she arrived, Harriet became reacquainted with James Spalding, to whom she had been introduced when she and her late husband arrived in western Illinois. She recalled the very eligible bachelor, who was seven years her senior, as "tall and straight, of dignified bearing and a very fine-looking man." He resided in Byron, about 15 miles south of Rockford, where he owned a home, rental houses in town, and two nearby farms he leased to tenant farmers, giving him a comfortable income. Encouraged by friends and relatives, James and Harriet began a friendship that grew more intimate over time. They wed on June 6, 1848, in Byron and spent their honeymoon in Chicago, traveling by carriage.

Since Harriet's introduction to the city a decade earlier, Chicago had grown to more than 20,000 residents and become home to many fancy stores on its unpaved, often muddy streets. And Harriet was happy to take advantage of all those shops had to offer, buying fine carpets, gold-banded tableware, mahogany furniture, and other goods to decorate the house James had built for her in

Byron—a "good-sized" log cabin with a wood-frame extension at the intersection of Second and Chestnut Streets.[11]

Anxious that she was spending too much, she asked her new husband if he was comfortable with her purchases. "You are paying out with your own money; do just as you wish with it," he replied. "I think you are using very good judgment." After returning to Byron, she realized that she had forgotten to buy some items on her list, including two mahogany footstools and a white spread. Such items were not essential in their home, which was a log cabin with a wood-frame addition, but James good-naturedly said, "I don't see how we can live without them. We ought to send right off and get them."

The aging couple—James was almost 35 years old and Harriet was 27 in the summer of 1848, when lifespans averaged 37 years—quickly set about starting a family. After their first son Henry died at eight months of age in 1849, Albert arrived in the summer of 1850, followed by Mary Lorette on October 14, 1854, and James Walter on July 28, 1856. Over the same period, Harriet's foster parents, Uncle Amos and Aunt Lucinda, passed away in Clarence, as did their only child. Harriet stood to inherit part of their estate, making the Spaldings even more financially comfortable.

Despite the relatively luxurious living situation, Harriet was no Byron booster. Her antipathy toward the hamlet surfaced the day she arrived there with James in 1848: Her first impression of the primitive village was that it was "rather quiet." This contrasted with Rockford, which had three times as many residents as Byron and which she described as "quite lively."[12] The Spaldings were not religious but the fact that church services were conducted in log-cabin homes was, to Harriet, a measure of Byron's backwardness; there would be no dedicated church building in town until 1855. In Byron, she disapprovingly noted, local men could often be found sitting on kegs in the general store, wasting time by swapping witless jokes and idle chatter. "I was not entirely satisfied with the surroundings in Byron so far as my children were concerned," she wrote years later.[13]

The rudimentary level of health care also concerned her. Albert Spalding contracted typhoid fever when he was 10 and was "very ill indeed."[14] At the time, typhoid was a feared killer on the frontier. Doctors were at a loss about how to heal it, sometimes settling to treat the worst symptoms—fever, muscle pain, gastrointestinal distress, and pneumonia—while the disease ran its course.

Byron had no trained nurses, so Harriet stayed with her son night and day, giving him coffee to drink until his fever broke, sparing her the death of another child.

Byronites' envy of the Spaldings' affluence was a thorn in Harriet's side. Inherited wealth, shrewd land acquisitions, and hard work had made James Spalding one of Byron's wealthiest residents. The family stood out in the village not only for its fancy wardrobe but for having a live-in servant, an Irish immigrant named Ann Ryan; the 1870 Census estimated Harriet's real estate was worth $20,000, the equivalent of $500,000 in 2024.[15] She spoke of James as "a man of sufficient means to enable us to have every comfort," and said, "he took life leisurely and was prosperous in every way." Her pride in her family and disdain for Byron did not sit well with her neighbors, and her children sometimes paid for it.

Harriet once saw her older son scrape his feet together after returning home from Byron's jerry-built log cabin school, scuffing up the leather shoes she had polished just that morning. When she asked why, he shot back: "I ain't going to have the boys call me stuck up!" Spalding's younger sister, Mary, told similar stories. A neighbor girl once followed her home from Sunday school, calling her "stuck up" and making fun of the elaborate silk dress and ribboned hat Harriet had dressed her in that morning.

Her joy was her family. "I had the reputation of being a very indulgent mother, and possibly this was true," she later wrote, "but I lived entirely for my children and my one desire was to grant their every wish, where it would do them no harm." She was particularly proud of her oldest, Albert, and particularly protective of him. When he began spending summer hours idling with friends doing who knows what, Harriet instructed him to spend more time with her at home. The boy objected, but his mother insisted. As soon as he grudgingly capitulated, Harriet offered a compromise: mornings at home, afternoons with his friends.

She knew from experience that her older boy would do as he was told. Years earlier, when James and Harriet were invited to dine at the home of one of Byron's leading citizens, Judge Henry Wheelock, Harriet allowed four-year-old Albert to accompany them—but only if he agreed that he would not sit at the table with the adults, would wait for his supper, and would not cry or make a fuss. "If you let me go, I will wait," he promised. Harriet said: "We took him and he lived up to his word, and that gave me an idea that I could rely on any promise he might make me."

Later in his life, others would not say the same about him.

In the autumn of 1858, there were signs that James's health was beginning to falter; the Spaldings were invited to a town dance at the two-story Pacific House, Byron's only hotel. Organizers asked James, an enviable dancer, to lead the Money Musk, a popular contra dance, but he demurred, saying, "I don't dance much anymore." Harriet found that odd, as she had always admired his dancing. Not long after that, a neighbor rapped on a window of their house to warn that a drove of stray cattle was trampling one of his cornfields. James set out for the farm on foot but had to turn back before getting halfway there. After returning home struggling to breathe, he told Harriet: "Did you ever run, as a child, against the wind, with your mouth a little open and then feel almost strangled? I had that sensation." He sought the counsel of the sole physician in Byron, Dr. Clinton Helm, and returned with some worrying news: "The doctor did not tell me, but from what he said I think there is something wrong with my heart."

With the country doctor at a loss about how to treat him, James spent the summer of 1858 in Kenosha, Wisconsin, taking a "water cure" offered by Dr. H. T. Seeley. It may have been a fashionable new "Electro-Chemical Bath" that the doctor had advertised.[16] Such baths were promised to cure any number of ailments, from rheumatism to syphilis, by allegedly removing mercury, lead, and other minerals in the body. James returned to Byron in October, looking and feeling better but soon resumed his decline. In January, Dr. Helm urged Harriet to summon his mentor, Dr. Lucius Clark, from Rockford, 15 miles away. "I cannot see this man die without some other physician seeing him," Dr. Helm said, "although I do not think we can do him any good."[17] The Rockford doctor arrived in Byron several days later, but as Dr. Helm anticipated, his mentor had no miracle cure. Harriet's second husband—and eight-year-old Albert's beloved father—died four days later, on January 23, 1859.

Before James passed, Harriet had the foresight to speak frankly with him about what she should do if he were to die. "If something were to happen to you, should I continue to live right here?" she asked. He advised her to stay in Byron, adding that she should hire a man to regularly deliver wood and maintain the houses and farms. Ever the equestrian, he also advised her to keep the span of black horses he had carefully trained. "Another thing, Harriet," he added, "bring up your boys to industrious habits. I would much rather Albert, during his vacations in the summer, would go down to my brother's farm and carry water to the hands or do anything rather than tramping around the streets and getting into mischief."

After James passed away, the independent-minded Harriet did not, to say the least, faithfully follow her late husband's dying suggestions. She decided it would be better to sell some of the family's horses, including the pony James had recently bought for Albert; she also canceled his order for a boy's saddle. She stayed in Byron only long enough to sell some of their property—after all she had always disliked the rustic nature of the place and the 644 chawbacons who resided there.

She also was always on guard against the dangers that frontier life posed to her children. Still fresh in her mind was the bitterly cold midwinter day when Spalding arrived home soaking wet, shivering, and alarmingly pale. "Albert, what happened?" she inquired. "Well, Mother," the nine-year-old said through chattering teeth, "I was skating on the river with Charlie Dunning, and I went into an air hole (in the ice). Charlie got off the ice as quickly as he could and ran home, instead of running for help." Realizing that he was on his own and unlikely to survive the frigid lake for long, Spalding had pulled his jackknife from his pocket and chipped handholds in the ice so he could pull himself out of the near-freezing water.[18]

Determined to remove Albert from Byron, Harriet arranged for her treasured older son to board with a sister-in-law's family in Rockford. That would let the boy, who was approaching his 12th birthday, attend one of the new public schools the city had built in the economic boom following the start of train service to Chicago. Spalding's hosts were his uncle Ulysses and aunt Wealthy Ann Warner, who was James's younger sister.

Harriet promised to visit her son every weekend when she brought Mary to her music lessons in Rockford. Despite those visits and the company of his cousins, Spalding recalled these "dark days of utter loneliness" in Rockford with great sadness. In a bit of characteristic hyperbole, he claimed he was "so bashful that I was almost afraid to go out of doors, lest I should meet and be spoken to by someone not a member of my family." It didn't help that Albert, who had been mocked in Byron for being too sophisticated, now saw himself as "an overgrown, unbaked country boy" in bustling, booming Rockford. His new hometown had almost four times as many people as Byron, including a large number of recent Swedish immigrants and such totems of modernity as a railroad station, a farm machinery factory, and two water-powered flour mills, one on each side of the Rock River. "It was my first prolonged absence from home," he wrote years later, "and memories of the homesickness of that period haunt me like a nightmare to this hour."[19]

That sounds like the melodramatic rhetoric Spalding used freely as an adult, but his time in Rockford undoubtedly did forge his character and set the course of his life. Most fundamentally, Rockford was where he was introduced to baseball by local boys, including his cousins Charles and Henry Warner, who had started playing the game before young Spalding arrived. Local lore says Rockford was introduced to the sport by a traveling insurance salesman or a Rockford businessman who saw the game played in New York. In his book, Spalding summarizes his introduction to the sport in just a dozen words: "A returning soldier told me about playing the game in the army."[20]

Intriguingly, when Spalding arrived on his own from Byron, his cousin, Union army sergeant Edward Burson Spalding, happened to be in Rockford recuperating from grievous wounds suffered at the Battle of Shiloh in April 1862. The army had sent him to a new military hospital in Mound City, Illinois, but when Edward's condition declined, his father traveled 400 miles from Rockford, put the 22-year-old on a cot, and brought him home to recuperate over the summer.[21] Edward had permanently lost the use of his left arm, but he nonetheless returned to service and was promoted to first lieutenant. The army eventually recognized his extraordinary gallantry under fire by awarding him a Medal of Honor, the country's highest military decoration.[22] Such a hero could deeply impress a 12-year-old boy, whether discussing battles or baseball.

In a combination baseball history and personal memoir published in 1911, Spalding wrote that "my association with the game of Baseball began at Rockford, in 1865." He may have meant that his association with *organized* baseball started then; Spalding started playing informally soon after he arrived in Rockford in 1862. By the summer of 1865, the sport was popular enough for Rockford to have at least three adult clubs: Sinnissippi, which adopted indigenous peoples' name for the Rock River and represented the city's east side; Mercantile, composed primarily of shop clerks; and Forest City, whose members were tradesmen and businessmen. Spalding and his friend Ross Barnes were too young for those organizations, so they founded a youth team, Pioneer.

Spalding and Barnes had lofty ambitions for the Pioneers; instead of just playing other youth clubs, late in the season, they challenged Mercantile to an exhibition against Pioneer. Members of the adult club initially dismissed the idea but relented when the taunting by Forest City members became more embarrassing than the indignity of playing against children. Worst of all for Mercantile, it lost 26–2.

Hiram Hungerford Waldo, a former teacher, local bookseller, and passionate Forest City supporter, was so impressed by Spalding and Barnes that he decided to find a way to add them to Forest City's roster in 1866, even if they were only 15. Waldo did this by arranging an exhibition game in November 1865 between Forest City and a "picked nine"—that is, an ad hoc collection of exceptionally skilled players with Spalding in the pitcher's box and Ross at second base. The boys' team lost 31–19, but Spalding and Barnes both did well enough to erase doubts about whether their performances against Mercantile were genuine and their potential unlimited.[23]

But, as Waldo soon discovered, Spalding would not be easy to recruit. While the teenager was excited by the idea of playing on Rockford's best club, he was still a schoolboy living at home with a mother committed to having her children receive a superior education—after all, that was why she had uprooted them from Byron. He also worked part-time for a local grocer, fulfilling his father's dying wish that he not be idle because of the family's affluence.

When the 1866 season opened the following April, however, both Spalding and Barnes were on Forest City's roster. Spalding was so eager to join the team that he did something countless children have done since—he played without telling his mother, ducking out of school to do so. That was made easier since Waldo, recently elected president of the club, regularly asked West Rockford High School to excuse Spalding from afternoon classes so that he could pitch; the principal, a baseball fan named James H. Blodgett, was unfailingly accommodating. So, too, was Spalding's employer, Harry Starr. All was set.[24]

Then Harriet found out.

"That disturbed me very much," she recalled with refined understatement four decades later. She immediately arranged to meet Blodgett and put a stop to her beloved oldest child's truancy. As was her way, Harriet got straight to the point: "I don't want Albert to leave school to play ball." Waldo had warned Blodgett that this day would come, and the principal was well prepared to assure the anxious parent that a little exercise in fresh air would not interfere with her son's education. "Now Mrs. Spalding," he said, "I want to tell you that Albert is a studious boy and gets his lessons. His going at two o'clock in the afternoon to play ball once in a while will do no harm." After weighing the educator's assurance, along with Waldo's private counsel and her son's passion for the game, Harriet reluctantly relented.[25]

Waldo, whose only child, a girl, had died when she was four years old, served as the first of several father figures on whom Spalding relied for advice and support when he was a teenager and young adult. His respect for Waldo was evident almost 50 years after the men parted ways, when Spalding wrote in his book that the most difficult questions he faced in his youth were answered by "an appeal to Rockford's Grand Old Man, Hiram H. Waldo, to whom I here pay the homage of man's sincere tribute to man. I held him in honor in the days of my youth. I esteemed him in my early manhood, and now, in my maturer (*sic*) years, I count him as one of the noblest, purest, most unselfish men I have ever known."[26]

With Spalding and Ross in its lineup, Forest City won its first four games in the late spring of 1866. With Waldo as its president, the club hosted a tournament that attracted teams from as far away as Milwaukee, Detroit, and Chicago. Forest City did not win the tournament: The Cream City club from Milwaukee beat their hosts 14–13, Rockford's only loss in its 10-game season. But Forest City and its young pitcher impressed the club that took home the trophy, Excelsior of Chicago.[27]

A year later, when a team of paid players—nominally amateurs who worked as government clerks in Washington, DC—came barnstorming through the West, Excelsior invited Forest City to come to Chicago to play an exhibition game with the visitors.

Chapter 2

A Nationwide Sensation

Intermittent showers drenched Chicago on July 25, 1867, delivering enough rain to temper the heat wave that had been baking the nascent metropolis for several days but not enough to discourage thousands of people from making their way to the new Dexter Park racetrack on the city's South Side. The Union Stock Yard & Transit Co. had recently opened Dexter Park on 80 acres of prairie adjacent to its sprawling, fetid feedlots and slaughterhouses to host livestock shows and trotting races. The company built racehorse stables on the park's western side and a shed for spectators' carriages on the eastern side. In between, it erected a large octagonal structure to house a saloon and betting parlor, and then added a wooden grandstand that could seat as many as 1,500 onlookers.

To tap the growing popularity of the new spectator sport of baseball, the stockyard's managers laid out four bases on the infield of the track.[1] This rudimentary field lacked a backstop, so the ground rules stated that runners could advance only one base if a catcher—playing barehanded and unmasked in those days—couldn't handle a fast or errant pitch.

The tournament's first game, between the Nationals from Washington, DC, and a team of amateurs from rural Illinois, was scheduled to start at 2 p.m., weather permitting. To transport all of the curious viewers—"a fair share of whom were ladies," one newspaper noted—the City Railway Co. began running horse-drawn streetcars to the park from the intersection of State and Lake Streets at 20-minute intervals.[2] People not near the streetcar line took a special locomotive service of the Pittsburgh, Fort Wayne and Chicago Railway, while workingmen drove their wagons.[3] More affluent city folk rode in elegant barouches and landaus over the five miles or so of sporadically paved roads between the center of the city and Dexter Park. They did not know that they were about to witness a contest recently characterized by the official historian of Major League Baseball as the most important baseball game ever played—not to mention the national debut of a phenomenal teenaged pitcher named Albert Goodwill Spalding.[4]

For many Chicagoans, the game was a welcome distraction from the wretched summer heat and the distressing news that radical Reconstruction Acts were meeting stiff resistance in southern states; a Lincoln assassination conspirator was on trial in Maryland; Mexico was in tumult following the execution of Emperor Maximillian; and Kiowa warriors were relentlessly ambushing men trying to build the transcontinental railroad. In Chicago, a boom town where rotting offal from slaughterhouses clogged waterways, cast an unmistakable stench over many neighborhoods, and fouled water supplies, the season's first case of deadly cholera had been reported the previous day—at the Union Stock Yard.[5]

To lighten the crowd's mood and make the day more festive, tournament organizers arranged for a performance by the Great Western Light Guard Band, an accomplished group of local musicians famous for having played at the Chicago memorial service for President Lincoln's funeral train two years earlier.[6] Promoters had attracted spectators by advertising the "Grand Baseball Match" in the *Chicago Daily Tribune* and other local newspapers, hailing the weeks-old Dexter Park as the "Finest Grounds in the West," adding, misleadingly, that it had "seats for 10,000 people." *Space* for 10,000 people was nearer the truth, with much of that number standing in foul ground or sitting in coaches parked in the outfield.[7]

Serious baseball fans—"cranks," in the vernacular of the time—needed no brass bands or promotional humbug to lure them to the ballpark. Amid a post–Civil War boom in baseball's popularity, several thousand of the young city's 250,000 residents made their way to Dexter Park. Estimates of the crowd ranged from 2,500 to 10,000.[8] And the grandstand filled quickly, leaving late-coming spectators to sit on the wet turf or stand in the depths of the outfield.[9] For the most part, they had come to see the visiting team, the celebrated National Baseball Club of Washington, DC, which had already handily won all seven games played so far on its well-publicized promotional tour of what was then the western frontier.

The Nationals had been a middling club when freshly discharged veterans first reconstituted it—winning 10 games and losing five in 1866—but that changed when its supporters, led by a US Treasury official and former Union army colonel named Frank Jones, decided to bolster the team by offering no-show government patronage jobs to talented players willing to relocate to the nation's capital. Jones, an officer in the 31st New York Volunteer Infantry during the Civil War, was particularly helpful in signing players from a renowned club in Brooklyn, where he had lived before the war. He also secured top players from leading clubs in Philadelphia and Rochester, New York.

The Nationals was not the only team to recruit veterans; many who had learned to play baseball while serving in the army brought the game home with them, sparking a mania in cities, towns, and villages throughout Ohio, Kentucky, Indiana, Missouri, and Illinois.

To show off their powerful lineups, clubs took advantage of the nation's rapidly growing railroad network to try to make some money by playing a series of exhibition matches against the best teams in the West. Tours by prominent (and affluent) eastern clubs were not new: The Excelsior squad in Brooklyn, for example, had gained great celebrity by traveling to upstate New York in 1860. Touring stopped during the Civil War, but rapid expansion of railroad networks during the conflict opened broader opportunities when peace returned.

The Nationals' nominal amateurs boarded a Baltimore and Ohio Railroad train in Washington on July 11 bound for Columbus, Ohio, a 400-mile trip at an average speed of less than 30 miles per hour. The travel did not appear to affect the players' performance when they played their first game on July 13 and beat the Capital Baseball Club 90–10. Moving on to Cincinnati, the Nationals outscored the well-regarded local Red Stockings 53–10 and a day later crushed Cincinnati's other club, the Buckeyes, 88–12. Prideful Cincinnati club leaders were so embarrassed by the size of the beating inflicted on the Red Stockings that its officers decided to field the first openly professional team in history in 1869. In Louisville they outscored the city's best team 82–21. Indeed, despite long days on smoky trains and poky paddle steamers, the Nationals' victory margins grew more intimidating the more the club traveled. In Indianapolis, the Easterners beat the Western Club 106–21. Two days later, on a muggy 104-degree afternoon in St. Louis, they pounded the Union Club team 113–26. The next day, despite having journeyed more than a thousand miles and played seven games in the previous 10 days, the eastern team coasted to a 53–26 victory over St. Louis's Empire Club in six innings.[10]

Even in that era, when players went without gloves, fields were often as bumpy as cow pastures, and batters could direct pitchers where they wanted the ball to cross home plate, the scores the Nationals ran up were daunting. The Washington players were scheduled to conclude their tour in Chicago, where they were to play the three best teams in Illinois. Their first victim was to be the Forest City Baseball Club of Rockford, a small agricultural and manufacturing town 85 miles northwest of Chicago.

Forest City, which relied on Spalding to pitch every game, had an unremarkable record that year of three wins and two losses before its exhibition with the Nationals. Spalding worried that the visitors would embarrass Forest City as badly as the Rockford team had humiliated a club from the nearby village of Belvidere, Illinois, by a score of 56–0 early in May.[11] "I knew . . . that every player on the Rockford nine had an idea that their kid pitcher would surely become rattled and go to pieces as soon as the strong batters of the Nationals had opportunity to fall upon his delivery," Spalding recalled years later.[12]

The Nationals players arrived in Chicago at six o'clock in the morning a day before the Forest City game in the comfort of a new Pullman sleeper car operated by the St. Louis, Alton and Chicago Railroad. Out of respect for the "invincible" team from the East, John Gillespie, president of Excelsior, Illinois's recently crowned state champion club, and two other officers went to St. Louis to accompany the Nationals on their 300-mile ride up to Chicago.[13] Other Excelsior members met the Nationals' train at Madison Street Station, where they welcomed the visitors and accompanied them in horse-drawn carriages eight blocks to their lodgings at the city's finest hotel at the time, the six-story Sherman House. The visitors spent the rest of the day resting in the hotel or taking in the sights, from the magnificent Crosby's Opera House to the new Water Tower being built to pump in fresh water from Lake Michigan. That evening, several Nationals players went to McVicker's Theater on Madison Street to see *The Black Crook*, a scandalous musical extravaganza featuring the song "You Naughty, Naughty Men" and a performance by the Parisienne Ballet Troupe—female dancers in skin-colored tights who flitted about the stage singing "The March of the Amazons."

That evening, by contrast, the Forest City players arrived at the Wells Street Station on the eight o'clock Chicago and North Western Railroad train without fanfare and made their way unaccompanied to the five-story Briggs House hotel a block west of the Nationals' distinctly more elegant quarters.[14]

Forest City was captained by its center fielder, Alfred Barker, a store clerk and Union army veteran who was among the club's founders two years earlier and now, at age 28, its oldest player. But Rockford's most valuable player was also its youngest, A. G. Spalding. More than a month shy of his 17th birthday, the callow schoolboy was already nearly six feet tall, and his gangly frame towered over those of most of his older, stockier teammates. His long, narrow, boyishly handsome face and hazel eyes divulged so little emotion that he reminded some of a dour young clergyman. He hid his prominent ears under a thatch of neatly parted chestnut hair. There was not yet a whisker on his face, which, along with his height and citified manners, further distinguished him from the mustachioed, rough-hewn frontiersmen on the Forest City nine, as teams were called then.

Forest City's baggy white flannel uniform, with knickers and long-sleeve jerseys trimmed in blue, partially masked Spalding's age, but there was little to hide his anxiety when he entered the pitcher's box, a six-by-six-foot-square that predated the pitcher's mound. With the playing field surrounded by a crowd that by some accounts equaled the entire population of Rockford, the game commenced at 2 p.m. under a foreboding sky. The Nationals won a coin toss and chose to bat second, gaining the tactical advantage of knowing how many runs they would need to score—or prevent—in the later innings to win.

To Spalding's relief, Forest City scored two runs in the first inning, aided by a dropped fly, a passed ball, and a throwing error by usually unerring Nationals players. His contribution in that half of the inning was to hit a weak groundball and be thrown out at first base. While Spalding was a good hitter, posting a .313 batting average over his career, he was far more valuable in the pitcher's box.

As he prepared to face the first Nationals batter, Spalding was suddenly seized by a bad case of the yips. "I experienced a severe case of stage fright when I found myself in the pitcher's box, facing such renowned players as George Wright, (Frank) Norton, (Harry) Berthrong, (George) Fox, and others of the visiting team. A great lump arose in my throat, and my heart beat so like a trip-hammer that I imagined it could be heard by everyone on the grounds."[15]

As good as he was, Spalding was inexperienced and insecure, and when overcome by anxiety he was prone to pitch wildly. The Forest City catcher George King empathized and would often talk to the young hurler to bolster his confidence, a kindness Spalding treasured his whole life.

At the time, pitchers had to use an underhanded straight arm throw—as fast-pitch softball pitchers do now—and throw the ball where each batter requested. This gave hitters a substantial advantage, allowing even mediocre offenses to routinely run up double-digit scores. Spalding, however, had mastered both a scorching fast pitch and a deceptive slow toss, and he could deliver either with precisely the same arm motion. This baffled many hitters and made it vexingly difficult for them to hit the ball well, if they could hit it at all.[16]

In an unpromising start, Spalding walked the first Nationals batter, the left fielder Ed Parker, and then allowed the opposing pitcher, Will Williams, to hit a long single that brought Parker in to score.[17] Next up was the Nationals' best player, the second baseman Wright. Spalding's trip-hammer heartbeat accelerated at the thought of having to pitch to so celebrated a ballplayer. "I shall never forget my peculiar nervous feeling when I first faced 'Smiling George' in batting position," Spalding wrote in a letter years later, "for the awe in which he and the Nationals were held by all opposing teams was quite enough to set the heart of a young player beating rapidly."[18] In his first at-bat against the teen-aged hurler, however, the renowned Wright could manage only a groundball to Forest City's second baseman, Bob Addy, who threw out Williams at second base.

If such an easy out bolstered Spalding's confidence, it was not for long. The Nationals' next batter, Fox, the third baseman and a recent graduate of Georgetown College, struck a flyball to center field that Barker misplayed, allowing Wright to score and Fox to take second base. The fielding error and resulting run may have been enough for Spalding to "become rattled and go to pieces," as he had feared, but instead the teenager coolly caused the Nationals' right fielder, Seymour Studley, to ground out, and the next batter, first baseman George Fletcher, to harmlessly pop out. At the end of the first inning, Forest City trailed by only one run, 3–2. A light rain began to fall.

Forest City's leadoff batter in the second inning reached base on an error, but the next two batters grounded out to the pitcher and struck out, damping the team's hopes to even the score, much less take the lead. "The Rockford Club had not the slightest thought of vanquishing the Nationals, nor did any of the Chicago boys think so," Berthrong, the Nationals' catcher, wrote in a letter to his father after the game.[19] But then Forest City's shortstop, Roscoe "Ross" Barnes, reached first base on a walk, opening the way for the team's best batters to come to the plate again. With the Nationals' pitcher struggling to grip the rain-slickened ball, the next hitter, Addy, doubled. Catcher George King and first baseman Warren Stearns each singled. Spalding, his adrenaline flowing, smashed a hard double to drive in two runs, and then Barker, Wheeler, and the third baseman, Royal Miller Buckman, each singled. By the time the Rockford right fielder Wallace "Fred" Lightfoot fouled out to make the third out, Forest City had sent 12 batters to the plate and scored eight runs to take a 10–3 lead.

The Nationals came storming back in their half of the second inning, scoring five runs on five hits, aided by a run-scoring balk by the frazzled Spalding—one of five times he was penalized in the game for illegal pitch motions. Still, after forcing the Nationals' center fielder, Ed Smith, to foul out and retire the side, Spalding finished the inning with a 10–8 lead.

Forest City expanded its lead to 15–8 in the third inning, although spectators still believed the Nationals would ultimately prevail. "The vast crowd watched the game with no sort of feeling that the playing of the Forest City Club was going to last; they thought at least the Nationals had not set fairly to work, and that when they did, they would speedily give the Rockford men the go-by," one observer noted.[20]

After five innings, Forest City held onto the lead, 16–11, but "still no one thought of victory for them," a reporter recalled. As the innings ticked by without the Nationals reducing Forest City's lead, sentiment turned and spectators started to "view the game with bated breath and straining gaze, watching with increasing anxiety."[21]

At the end of the sixth inning, with the rain picking up again, the underdogs from Rockford had opened the lead to 24–16. Spalding recalled years later that his teammates' nerves had settled but "none of us even then had the remotest idea that we were destined to win the game over such a famous antagonist."[22] Rockford players feared that thinking of victory, much less talking about it, risked jinxing the game.

The Nationals had no trouble thinking about a Forest City victory, or talking about it. When his team came up to bat in the bottom of the eighth inning, Jones, the National club's president, approached Wright as he prepared to step up to the plate and loudly implored: "Do you know, George, that . . . we are (four) runs behind? You must discard your heavy bat and take a lighter one, for to lose this game would be to make our whole trip a failure."[23]

Whether Jones's exhortation motivated Wright is not clear, but it surely inspired the Rockford players. "For the first time we began to realize that victory was not only possible, but probable," Spalding wrote, "and the playing of our whole team from that time forward was brilliant."[24] Wright, the Nationals' first batter that inning, singled, but third baseman Fox tapped a weak grounder back to Spalding, who wheeled around and threw to second to put out Wright; Addy then threw the ball to Stearns at first to turn a double play. Studley singled, but was promptly caught stealing and tagged out during a frantic rundown between first and second.

Forest City padded its lead in the top half of the ninth inning. Spalding singled to drive in one run and then came around to score on a single by Wheeler two batters later. In all, Forest City scored four runs in the inning and stretched its lead to 29–21. When the Nationals came up for their final at-bats, they could muster only two runs, one of them on a balk by Spalding. Otherwise, he maintained his poise, making three batters hit weak groundballs to the infield. After three-and-a-half hours, the twice-rain-delayed game was over; miraculously, Forest City had won, 29–23. As one newspaper summed it up the next day: "The invincibles were defeated."[25]

Immediately after the final out, hundreds of cheering and shouting spectators flooded onto the field and hoisted the victorious players on their shoulders.[26] The trip back to the Briggs House resembled a parade. As Spalding said, "if you ever saw bantams strut, you would have seen something like it as we went to our hotel that afternoon. We were the talk of the city that night, and Forest City stock was way up."[27] Barker was so proud of Forest City's achievement that he wore his uniform around Chicago for two days after the game.[28]

Newspapers across the country—in New York, Philadelphia, Pittsburgh, Detroit, Cincinnati, Columbus, Louisville, and, of course, in Washington—noted the unexpected defeat of the haughty Nationals by a collection of frontier rustics. The *Louisville Courier* reported that baseball fans in that city were "astonished beyond measure" when the news arrived by telegraph.[29] Other papers were more restrained: "That the National nine did not play as well as was expected is very true and that the Forest City Club surpassed all anticipations, either of their own or of their friends, is equally undeniable."[30]

Chicago sportswriters were even-handed in their coverage of the game in the Friday papers, but the city's boosterish editorial writers couldn't restrain themselves. The *Chicago Times*, for example, smugly opined that "when the Nationals shall have lived among us a few days, imbibed pure water from the clear depths of Lake Michigan, breathed the healthy breezes from the prairies, and taken a few lessons in baseball playing, they will begin to realize how profitable has been their trip to the Northwest."[31]

Nationals players, distressed by their sloppy performance and embarrassed by the loss, sought an immediate rematch, even offering to play Forest City in Rockford. Spalding and his teammates, already basking in the national attention of their surprising victory, demurely declined. "They did not care to mar the honor of winning . . . by risking a signal defeat," the respected sportswriter Henry Chadwick wrote in a dispatch for the *Brooklyn Eagle*.[32]

Denied a rematch, Nationals players tried to explain the loss to themselves, their supporters, and their families. "Our triumphant success in all our previous games gave us too much confidence in our playing abilities," Berthrong wrote to his father after the game, adding, ungraciously, "our second (string) could have beaten the Rockford boys without any trouble, but the fates were against us."[33]

Before Chicagoans had finished reveling in the Forest City victory, they began to turn their attention—and enthusiasm—toward the Nationals' next matchup, on Saturday, against Excelsior. That club had narrowly beaten Forest City twice earlier in the year on the way to being crowned state champions: 45–41 in June in Chicago and 28–25 on the Fourth of July in Rockford,[34] where about 1,600 of Rockford's 10,000 residents had paid 25 cents each to watch the game at Fairgrounds Park.

Excelsior players, having seen Forest City beat the Nationals, were confident they could do so, too. "They thought that the Nationals had been over-rated, and seeing us whip them as we did . . . they felt sure that they themselves could capture them without doubt," Spalding recalled.[35]

City-proud Chicagoans were equally certain, wagering $20,000 on Excelsior (about $450,000 in 2025 dollars).[36] In hotels and saloons across the city, professional gamblers, or speculators, who were following the Nationals on their tour were happy to bet an equal amount on the Nationals. Rules forbidding professional players to bet on their own sport were not enforced until much later, but Spalding, being a minor with no money and orders from his widowed mother to resist vice, abstained from wagering.

Young Albert was fortunate. Nationals players, denied an opportunity to rescue their reputation with a rematch against Forest City, vented their frustration on Excelsior in "one of the most brilliant exhibitions of baseball science ever witnessed."[37] Scoring 21 runs in the third inning alone, the Nationals jumped out to a 33–0 lead on the way to a 49–4 thrashing of the "Champions of the West." Adding to Excelsior's embarrassment, the Nationals whitewashed Chicago's normally high-scoring local heroes—that is, held them scoreless—in six of the nine innings.

The overwhelming win against Excelsior after the striking loss to Forest City sparked a slew of outraged comments and baseless accusations. Chicago newspapers, reflecting the sting felt by civic boosters and the dismay of local gamblers, were immediately suspicious of the Nationals' "stunning" reversal.[38] The *Chicago Daily Tribune* concluded its coverage of the game by stating—with no proof—that the "prevailing sentiment . . . among the greater portion of those who had witnessed the Rockford game" was that the Nationals had "purposely" allowed Forest City to win.[39] Washington papers gleefully repeated the assertion.[40] This view was not limited to Chicago. The *New York Herald* said "the mystery [of Rockford's victory] may be explained by the fact that the Nationals threw off in their game with the Forest City for the purpose of securing bets."[41]

Indignant editorials in Chicago's Sunday newspapers kept the controversy aboil. Ignoring the exceptional pitching by Spalding, the solid defense behind him, and the sloppy condition of the field, editorial writers at the *Tribune* and *Republican* did not appear to even consider that Rockford may have won legitimately. Instead, they claimed that the Easterners had no qualms against rigging games to win bets for the professional gamblers who accompanied them. The *Tribune* characterized the Nationals' tour as "a regular confidence game." For good measure, they accused the Nationals of being a "picked nine"—by which they meant professional players, which was no small insult at a time when true gentlemen played only for the love of the game and its "muscular and social advantages."[42]

"They are professional athletes, while our Excelsiors are but amateurs," *Tribune* editors lamented. "That which is a business of the one is the recreation of the other."[43]

Not all Chicago newspapers—there were about 10 at the time—agreed with the bitter speculation of disappointed boosters and unsuccessful bettors. The *Times* dismissed the rumors as "absurd" before it went on to sarcastically characterize the Excelsiors' loss as a great victory for the team because it proved that its players were the greatest "muffs," or bumblers, in the country.[44] The *Times* added: "Had the pitching of the Excelsiors been as good as that of the Forest City Club, the result [of the Excelsiors' meeting with the Nationals] would have been different."[45]

The Nationals, who were still in town and preparing for a final game the next day, took great umbrage with the press abuse. In the evening, Colonel Jones, the club's president, set out from the Sherman House with his predecessor, a former shortstop and future US senator named Arthur Pue Gorman, to have a word with the city's newspaper editors. First stop was the *Tribune*, whose offices were then located on the same block of Clark Street as the Sherman House.

The *Tribune*, having just settled one libel suit filed by the abolitionist Gerrit Smith, was eager to avoid another. Jones, his long white beard bouncing with each furious phrase, demanded that the newspaper's young editor, Horace White, show him the evidence behind the allegations that his team had thrown the game and bet on it themselves. The editor's response was not recorded, but on Monday morning the *Tribune* published this full and unqualified retraction:[46]

THE NATIONAL BASEBALL CLUB.

In an article which we published yesterday, concerning the match game of the National Base Ball Club, of Washington, and the Excelsiors, of this city, we imputed the gambling operations which were carried on at the Dexter Park, to the gentlemen composing the National Club, and to their connivance. We are satisfied that this was an entire mistake, and that the members of the Club are neither "professional" players nor gamblers, but merely clerks in the departments, and citizens of Washington, of exemplary character, who have taken up the game of baseball for exercise merely, and have brought themselves to a higher state of drill that is customary in the game by longer practice than others. Some of the members of the Club, we find, are our personal acquaintances, for whose characters we are able to vouch.

The game played with the Forest City Club, of Rockford, was fairly won by the latter, and the result is to be attributed undoubtedly to the fatigue of the Nationals, resulting from long travel and constant playing since the 11th of the present month.

That there was a large amount of gambling on the ground is true. Those who bet their money on the Nationals, it appears, were parties who came hither of their own volition from St. Louis, and others who live in Chicago. At all events, we are assured and we believe that they were not members of the National Club nor any friends of theirs. The practice of gambling at baseball matches, we are assured, is condemned by none more severely than by the Nationals, and on the grounds of the Club at Washington any man found betting is, by the rules of the Club, put off the grounds, and if he be a member of the Club, he is liable to expulsion.

A few blocks away, at the *Chicago Republican*'s offices on Washington Street, Jones and Gorman had less success. The *Republican*'s editor, a stubborn Scot named James F. Ballantyne, baldly denied that his paper had impugned any ballplayers. However, he did agree to publish in Monday's issue long letters of protest from Jones and from Chadwick, the *Brooklyn Eagle* correspondent and editor of the *Ball Players' Chronicle*, a short-lived weekly he had founded.

In his letter, Jones angrily decried the "foul aspersions" cast upon the club by the *Republican*'s editorial, and dismissed each of the newspaper's allegations as "false in every particular."[47]

The accusation of professionalism stung almost as much as the claim of throwing the game. Throughout their tour, the Nationals had emphasized that they would not split gate receipts with opponents or accept any other compensation, not even for their travel expenses (though they did accept reduced fares offered by the railroads). Club members, both players and non-players, had pledged to cover all costs of the tour.

To back up the fanciful assertion that his players were all honest amateurs with real day jobs, Jones included in his letter a list of the occupation of each man on his team. Almost all of them were described as clerks in some federal office—mostly in the Treasury Department, where Jones, Gorman, and at least two other Nationals Club leaders just happened to hold management positions. Jones described one player's occupation simply as "clerk, Washington, D. C." None of this, of course, refuted the rumors about do-nothing patronage jobs for promising players. Suspiciously, the team's star, brilliant middle-infielder George Wright, was listed as a "clerk, 238 Pennsylvania Avenue"; Jones neglected to note that this was not the location of a federal agency but the address of a cigar store owned by Richard A. Cronin, an avid Nationals fan.[48]

Chadwick was less strident—almost sorrowful—in his letter to the *Republican*.[49] He noted that he had long crusaded against gambling, characterizing it as "the most potent evil the game has to contend with," and said that "throughout the tour I have yet to see the first action of any member of the club evidencing either any desire to make the contests pecuniarily advantageous to themselves or their club, or in any way to countenance the evil of heavy betting, which you very properly condemn.

"An analysis of the play will show that the victory was fairly won by the Rockford Club," he added.

Jones optimistically concluded, "I trust this statement will be sufficient to induce a retraction of the gross aspersions upon the reputation of [our] club."[50]

It was not. Taking the opportunity to have the last word, Ballantyne used his editorial page to comment on these letters in Monday's paper:

THE BASEBALL CONTEST.

In another column of to-day's Republican will be found a letter from Col. Jones, President of the National Baseball Club of Washington, written in rather an excited style, regarding an editorial which appeared in our Sunday edition. Regardless of the style, however, we publish the letter as it was penned; but it is not, in any sense of the word, a reply to our comments of yesterday, except that it gives us a list of the occupations of the Nationals, showing that they are nearly all engaged in some of the official Departments at Washington, and that they are not "professionals."

There is also a letter from Mr. Chadwick, who is well known in baseball circles, defending the Nationals from the charges made against them in this and other Chicago journals. This letter is quite temperate in its tone, and is better calculated to aid the cause it represents than that of Col. Jones, who has evidently allowed his feelings to get the better of his judgment.

Elsewhere in the paper that day, the Republican added that "the 'outsiders' who accompanied [the Nationals] from Washington readily accepted, and even sought, all offers made against them, and will return with money enough, won from the too hopeful friends of our boys, to pay all the expenses of their trip, and enough will be left over for a 'good spree.'"[51]

The *Times*, which supported the Democratic Party, enjoyed the petulance of its Republican-leaning competitors and took a few lively shots at them, including this: "The cry of fraud raised by the two morning Republican newspapers over the late baseball match, is the basest bawl of all."[52]

Almost forgotten amid all the hand-wringing and tail-twisting were the Forest City players, particularly young Spalding. What had been a glorious victory on Thursday had become, in the eyes of many people, a fraud and a joke by Monday. Once praised as "stunning," the Forest City triumph was demoted to "inglorious" in popular opinion.[53] People assumed the Rockford players accepted the idea "that they won by the consent of their opponents."[54]

Excelsior leaders compounded Spalding's disappointment by publishing their own open letter in the Chicago papers testifying to the integrity of the Washington players—and diminishing Forest City's accomplishment by claiming the Nationals "were not fully rested, and, of course, could not play even their ordinary game" when they faced Forest City. It was cold comfort that the letter writers, Excelsior vice president C. J. Blair and secretary Will Lowe, concluded by saying the Nationals nonetheless "were fairly beaten by the Forest City Club."[55]

That was hardly the end of the public opprobrium over the Forest City win. The rumors rose from the dead like merciless ghosts after the Nationals ended its western tour by thrashing Chicago's second-best club, Atlantic, 78–17 on Monday afternoon. Newspapers, spectators, and bettors took this lopsided score as fresh evidence of chicanery four days earlier. Rumors claimed the Nationals reaped at least $10,000 from gambling on its own games; some gossips hyped the total to $30,000, equivalent to more than $680,000 in 2025.[56]

As painful as it was for Spalding and his teammates, the rumormongering did little to damp the enthusiasm of either team's devoted cranks. When the Nationals arrived back in Washington at 6:50 p.m. on Wednesday, July 31, a brass band and a throng of fans and players from other local teams met them at the station and marched them through the capital to club headquarters on The Avenue between 12th and 13th Streets. The city then threw the team a lavish banquet Friday evening at the elegant Kirkwood House hotel on Pennsylvania Avenue a few blocks east of the White House.

In Rockford, hundreds of townsfolk and a marching band greeted Spalding & Co. at the Fourth Avenue station when their train pulled in. Local folk believed that the team had raised their city's national profile to those of the West's leading metropolises—a signature achievement in an era of unconstrained civic boosterism—and the good folk of Winnebago County wanted to show their appreciation.

The *Rockford Register* dismissed speculation that the Nationals threw their game against Forest City, calling it "base slander" and "an unmitigated falsehood." It added, "all unprejudiced witnesses of the game" had conceded that "the triumph of the Forest City Club was a legitimate one, fairly won by the skill, activity, and endurance of the players."[57]

William Palmer, the proprietor of the Holland House, Rockford's fanciest hotel, hosted a private banquet for the Forest City club, making good on a pledge to fête them in style if they defeated the Nationals. The next evening, a committee of prominent local citizens staged a reception for the team at Brown's Hall, the city's premier entertainment venue. The master of ceremonies, Elijah W. Blaisdell Jr., notable for having been the first newspaper editor to endorse Lincoln for president, compared the courage and pluck of the town's "Victorious Nine" to that of the local men who fought in the Civil War.

"To strangers the result [the win over the Nationals] might appear astounding," he said, "but to men who knew the fiber and the grain of the boys of Winnebago County, who had seen the same material tower up in its stalwart grandeur on the battlefields of the rebellion, these achievements were not so surprising."

A local music teacher, Leonard Bisco Starkweather, took the stage with three other townsfolk to perform "Catch It on the Fly," a song he had composed to celebrate "our gallant boys in white and blue, the glorious 'Forest City.'"[58]

Local dignitaries then presented Spalding with a silver watch and chain for his superb pitching and handed shortstop Ross Barnes a gold pen for his fine performance in the field. Other boosters then rolled out an enormous cake decorated with a white satin banner inscribed "Forest City B. B. Club, Welcome You Who Gained Victory." Smaller streamers carried the name and position of each team member. Dancing followed, lasting well into the night.[59]

"We simply owned the town for months afterward," Spalding recalled decades later, characteristically ignoring the disappointment and embarrassment of the game-fixing allegations and focusing on the glory.[60] When he made the statement, he also had the benefit of knowing that the skill and poise he demonstrated against the Nationals made his name known to the nation's growing ranks of ballplayers and spectators, a valuable asset in his future endeavors in baseball, retailing, manufacturing, and politics. What he may not have realized, even in adulthood, is how speculation about game fixing had reinforced his antipathy toward gambling and taught him an important lesson—one he would use often for the rest of his life—about the ability of the press to shape public opinion.

Chapter 3
An Education

After returning to Rockford from the triumph over the Nationals, Spalding barely had time to settle back into his family's house at 305 South Church Street before he was approached by a man saying he represented the Excelsior club. The man asked the teenager if he would be interested in earning $40 a week as a billing clerk at a wholesale grocery business in Chicago with the understanding he would not be obliged to do actual work at the business so long as he pitched for Excelsior.

He needn't have bothered to tell Spalding that the job would have little to do with commerce. The young pitcher knew why the man made the trek from Chicago. "I wasn't a very good bill clerk, but I was a pretty good pitcher," he conceded years later.[1]

Under-the-table payments like this were becoming a common practice at the time—and a lucrative one for better players. Skilled laborers housed and fed entire families on far less than what some ballplayers were paid for eight months' work. At the time, a grocer in Rockford was paying Spalding $3 a week for a similar job—and not only did the owner expect Spalding to be at his desk every day, he would dock the boy's pay whenever he left to practice or play in a game.

The conflicting job opportunities illustrated Spalding's fantastic good luck to excel at baseball just as the game was metamorphosing from a leisurely pastime run by urban gentlemen seeking exercise into a lucrative entertainment business run by capitalists seeking profit. Railroad networks built or expanded during the Civil War allowed clubs to travel long distances and play the best teams almost anywhere in the country. With regional pride at stake, these tours made games more interesting, attracting more spectators and encouraging the use of incentives (that is, salaries, a share of ticket sales or well-paid no-show jobs) to attract gifted players from other cities and towns and keep home-grown talent from being lured away.

Writing about baseball helped to sell more newspapers—and newspaper coverage helped ballclubs sell more tickets. The *Spirit of the Times*, the *New York Clipper*, and other weekly papers devoted to entertainment added baseball articles and statistics to their coverage of plays, musicals, vaudeville, horse racing, boxing, cricket, race walking (or "pedestrianism," as it was known then), and other events. Newspaper coverage kindled interest in the new sport among a wide slice of society. When the most successful clubs met on the field (or sizeable wagers were at stake), it was not unusual for billiard halls and saloons to offer inning-by-inning updates by telegraph.

As Spalding entered the scene, baseball was on the cusp of living up to the titles that two newspapers bestowed on it in 1856: America's "national game" and "national pastime."[2]

In light of that, Spalding found the Chicago offer tempting, to say the least. There were, however, other considerations. Chief among them was what his mother would think of the idea. "Would she approve of my going to a large city, with its dangers in the busy whirl, and its greater dangers in the temptations that so thickly abound?" Spalding wrote. He was less worried by what his Forest City teammates would say: "I could not afford to rest my business interests on a mere sentiment," he reckoned, though years later, as a team owner, he would expect his players to do exactly that.[3]

Spalding also mulled over the fact that accepting the Chicago offer obviously would violate "at least the spirit" of the National Association of Base Ball Players' rule forbidding its members to pay players.

When he broke the news about Excelsior's offer, his mother and younger sister, Mary, did little to conceal their skepticism about his becoming an itinerant ballplayer. To their minds, a business that pays men to play a boys' game had an uncertain future at best; they urged him to finish his education. Being mature for his age, Albert found high school tiresome, so he and his mother struck a deal: Albert could quit high school a year before earning a diploma if he would enroll at the new Rockford Business College on Main Street when he was not in Chicago playing ball.

She secretly hoped that taking courses in bookkeeping and other office skills at the business college would enable her son to find a well-paying conventional job in Rockford and settle down. Harriet also read a lot into his affection for a local girl, Elizabeth Minott Churchill, even though he was 17 and she was 11. (The Churchill saga did not end in Rockford; in later years, Lizzie, as she was known, will be intimately entangled in Spalding's private life, becoming his lover after he marries another, then bearing his second son—and ultimately his second wife and contested heir to the bulk of his fortune.)

* * *

In any case, Spalding thought the Chicago offer was a superior opportunity to make a living at playing the game he adored without going too far from the family he loved. Baseball, like the entire country, seemed ripe for fundamental change in the postbellum period. Spalding sensed that change meant opportunity; his mother recognized that it also meant risk.

Unable to resolve the matter on their own, mother and son sought the advice of Waldo, the beloved, bewhiskered bookseller and former teacher. Harriet thought he would be an honest broker despite his serving as the Forest City club president and being responsible for recruiting her son and Ross from a junior team.

After Spalding laid out Excelsior's offer, Waldo silently turned it over in his head. He knew that local business owners were preparing to pay some Forest City players surreptitiously, but he also knew that Rockford could never match salaries offered in a big city like Chicago, at the time home to a quarter-million people. "You know, my boy," he finally said, "as a citizen of Rockford, I don't want you to go, and perhaps, as president of the Forest City club, I ought to urge you to stay. But, as a friend to whom you have come for advice, I must say to you, accept the offer and go."[4]

Knowing how disappointed Forest City supporters would be, Waldo smiled and added, "you needn't tell that I advised it."

Waldo's endorsement decided the matter for Spalding and his mother. Other concerns vanished. Spalding, for example, dismissed a widely held assumption that professionalism would debase the game. "I was not able to understand how it could be right to pay an actor, or a singer or an instrumentalist for entertaining the public and wrong to pay a ball player for doing exactly the same thing," he wrote.[5]

Harriet, meanwhile, had to cope with the almost certain disapproval of her family and acquaintances. As she noted, "my relatives and friends were very much opposed to Albert's joining a professional baseball club, thinking it would ruin him. I felt I was doing right in letting him do this, for I knew that Albert never could stand it to be confined in an office."[6]

He accepted the Chicago offer in late September, a little more than two weeks after his 17th birthday and two months after Forest City's triumph over the Nationals. He did not arrive in Chicago in time to pitch for Excelsior when the club defeated a team from Detroit 49–20 on October 5, but a month later he "acquitted himself very creditably" in leading an ad hoc "picked nine" to a 24–13 victory over Excelsior's starters in an exhibition.[7]

Before Spalding could pitch another game, however, his nominal employer, the wholesale grocer, unexpectedly went out of business. Jobless and facing an icy Chicago winter, Spalding decided to stay in Chicago and sell insurance for an uncle until spring and the 1868 baseball season rolled around.. Among his clients, he recalled, was a blacksmith on Lake Street. Unfortunately for both men, two fires began within blocks of each other on the evening of January 28, 1868, and then merged into a $2 million conflagration for which Chicago's horse-drawn, steam-powered fire engines were no match. The *Tribune* said the disaster, which gutted or destroyed commercial buildings on Lake Street and Wabash and Michigan Avenues, was "the heaviest fires on record in this city."[8]

While the Great Chicago Fire three years later would easily surpass the Lake Street Fire in death and destruction, the latter was sufficiently damaging to exhaust the capital of several fire-insurance companies, forcing them to declare insolvency. Spalding's uncle represented many of them, including the insurer that had written the policy Spalding sold to a blacksmith, meaning the workingman would receive a fraction of his claim, if anything. Spalding soon heard about "a large, two-fisted blacksmith" who had lost his business in the inferno and "was looking for a tall, young insurance solicitor." Thus forewarned, the once again unemployed Spalding—having been reminded how tenuous it could be to work for someone else—boarded a train back to Rockford.[9]

The Forest City club had played only twice in Spalding's five-month absence, losing to a nine from Bloomington, Illinois, 67–41 in late September and then beating a team called Star, of Marengo, Illinois, 63–8 in its season-ender on October 4.[10]

Rockford and Forest City enthusiastically welcomed Spalding back, and the club featured his return in a newspaper ad promoting its bright outlook in 1868. "The Forest City . . . intend to spare no pains to eclipse their former triumphs," the club announced in an advertisement in the *Rockford Gazette* on February 27.

"The former pitcher of the club having returned; it is intended to organize a nine that cannot be beaten. It is also intended to give the crack clubs of the East a chance to try their skill and muscle . . . by making an extended tour during the season."[11]

The club did not name the pitcher. There was no need. Everyone in Rockford who cared a whit about baseball knew who Forest City was talking about.

To dissuade Spalding from considering offers to play for clubs in other cities and towns, Rockford business owners offered him jobs that promised a comfortable income without interfering with his ballplaying. He accepted two. One was being a clerk in the office of Alfonso N. Nicholds, a representative of the Charter Oak Life Insurance Company—and, not coincidentally, the secretary of the Forest City club. The other was as a cashier at the *Rockford Register*, edited by one Edward H. Griggs, who also was secretary of the NABBP.

Spalding appears to have been the only Forest City player favored with *two* jobs, but he was not the only one to find accommodating employment in Rockford. Bob Addy nominally worked in a hardware store but spent most of his time playing second base; the teen-aged middle infielder Ross Barnes, Spalding's close friend, was hired as a clerk in the county courthouse; Ernest L. Waxham, the club's primary substitute, worked in club president Hiram Waldo's bookstore.[12]

While he participated in the subterfuge, Spalding wrote years later that he much preferred open professionalism to the "roundabout schemes that were being worked in all large cities to secure good players." Pretending that he traveled from Illinois to Massachusetts to play baseball just for fun "seemed to me to be educating young men in a school of false pretense."[13]

Civic leaders appeared less interested in educating young men than securing the presumed promotional advantages of having a nationally recognized ballclub. After all, Chicago, Cincinnati, and St. Louis were all using local clubs' success on the field to bolster their rival claims to be the unofficial capital of the booming western frontier—or, in moments of overheated enthusiasm, the leading city of the entire North American continent. When Chicago civic leaders set out to assemble a world-beating side for the 1869 season, the *Chicago Tribune* thundered, "It is imperative that Chicago should boast of a baseball club which can not only beat anything in the West, but which shall be able to indicate Chicago's importance as the first city on the continent by bidding defiance to any and all clubs in America."[14]

After Spalding's brief flirtation with Chicago, business leaders in Rockford became more involved in running the Forest City club. They required players to sign contracts that made them employees of a joint-stock company that now owned and controlled the team, not members of a club in which players had a voice. Decisions were to be made by shareholders, led by President J. H. Manny, a wealthy reaper maker and bitter business rival of Cyrus McCormick. The Rockford businessmen's common goal: make the Forest City team successful enough to remind Easterners that Rockford exists and to associate the city with vigor and success.[15]

To properly promote the city, they knew Forest City would have to play the best clubs, wherever they were found. To generate revenue to pay for travel costs—train fares, hotel bills, carriage hires, and meals—the directors moved Forest City's home games from the club's traditional home, a field on North Church Street, where games were free, to the Winnebago County Fairgrounds.

The new site had the advantages of being a short walk or carriage ride from the city center and being fully enclosed by a board fence that would enable the club to charge 25 cents for admission to each game. (For $1 a year, anyone could become a non-playing member of the club and attend home games at no additional cost.) It split the income from ticket sales with visiting teams.

The fairgrounds had its drawbacks, too; for one thing, big trees crowded the foul lines, making it difficult to field flyballs in the vicinity; for another, uneven basepaths ran downhill from second base to third and uphill from there to home.[16]

Spectators did not seem to mind. The visit of a good competitor, especially one of the presumptively arrogant nines from the East, would bring Rockford to a standstill as merchants closed their shops and professional men gave their clerks the day off so they could all go to the ballgame. Hundreds of wagons and carriages would park outside and inside the grounds.[17]

Fred Cone, a Rockford native who later played for the Red Stockings, remembered Rockford residents' reaction to a visit in August 1868 by the defending NABBP champion, the Union club of Morrisania, then a suburb of New York City.

"Banks closed, business men shut up their stores and the judge of the county court gravely informed his lawyer friends that the court had to sit en banc with a number of other estimable judges—of baseball—in a well-known stand out in the remote part of the city given over to the baseball players," said Cone, who played in left field that day.[18]

In the end, roughly 2,500 ticketholders (in a city of 10,000 people) turned out to watch the game, only to be disappointed when the Unions defeated Forest City 23–17.

* * *

Spalding initially had no say in Forest City's management, but he followed its actions closely, learned from its successes and missteps, and was named captain—a position like player-manager today—before turning 20. He figured that enough cash could entice top players to join the roster of a club in a small city on the frontier, and those players in turn could enhance ticket sales. He would soon learn, however, that good players would stay with such a club only if they were paid well *and* were able to play the best competition.

While the NABBP expressly forbade its member clubs to pay their players, the governing body lacked the means and authority to prevent them from doing so or to punish them if they did. Following the successful 1867 tour of the Nationals, whose arrangement of no-show jobs for players was a poorly kept secret, other ambitious clubs, including Forest City, expanded the practice of secretly compensating players.

In April 1868, for example, the Cincinnati Base Ball Club—still stinging from a loss to the Nationals a year earlier, the Ohio club's only defeat all season—elected as president Aaron Champion, an ambitious lawyer who supported professionalism. He hired Harry Wright—the manager of a local cricket club and older brother of the Nationals' superb shortstop George Wright—to clandestinely recruit professionals to play for Cincinnati in 1868. In the brief period before the season began, Wright secured four salaried players; he added a fifth after the season started.[19]

This semiprofessional version of the club, now nicknamed the Red Stockings for its flashy new uniforms, won 36 games and lost seven. It avenged its 1867 loss to the Nationals by outscoring the Washington club 16–10 in a rain-shortened five-inning game on the National Mall in September, but Cincinnati did less well against other top eastern clubs. It lost both games with Athletic—a Philadelphia club that posted the NABBP's best record in 1868, 47 wins and only three defeats—as well as two contests with Atlantic of Brooklyn and one of two with the Union club of Morrisania.

The speed and control of Spalding's pitching led Rockford to 17 wins in 21 games in 1868. It was undefeated in contests against teams from the Northwest—including both games it played against Excelsior, by scores of 20–18 on June 12 and 36–27 in front of a big July 4 holiday crowd in Chicago.

After the second contest, the *Chicago Times* flattered Spalding and scolded Excelsior: "(Spalding) has wonderfully improved in accuracy and precision and to-day he is without doubt the best pitcher in the West. . . . The Excelsiors made a great mistake when they allowed Spalding to return to Rockford."[20]

To right-thinking Rockford residents, Forest City deserved to be crowned as the champions not only of Illinois but of the entire Northwest. Townsfolk raucously showed their pride when the train bringing Forest City players from Chicago arrived at Rockford station at two o'clock in the morning on July 5. About 500 of the town's 10,000 residents met the train, which they illuminated with fireworks. As players disembarked, the city band fell in line behind them and the crowd followed the band, creating a high-spirited parade to Waldo's house, where they serenaded the Forest City club's 39-year-old president.[21]

Outside of Rockford, baseball followers were less impressed by Forest City's wins over Excelsior. They noted that the race to hire professionals led Excelsior to lose many of its top players and then to overspend while trying in vain to replace them; the club was so debilitated by the end of the season that its members voted to disband. Skeptics also noted that Spalding and his teammates fared poorly against top East Coast clubs earlier in the year.

After opening the season by winning its first three games, all against Illinois opponents, Forest City had taken a train to Chicago to play the NABBP's eventual champion, the Athletic club of Philadelphia, on a sweltering June afternoon. A Forest City victory would cement the team's reputation as one of the best in the nation.

Rockford supporters arrived early at the grounds; some disparaged Athletic players as they warmed up while others boasted about Forest City's superior nine—particularly Spalding. The heckling motivated Athletic hitters to quickly pounce on Spalding's pitching and encouraged them to take full advantage of dozens of muffs, or errors, by Forest City's suddenly incompetent fielders. Athletic scored 12 runs in the first inning and 10 more in the second on its way to handing Rockford its worst loss in team history: 94–13. Newspapers said that as many as 2,000 spectators witnessed the bludgeoning.

As the runs piled up—34 in the ninth inning alone—Rockford's exasperated captain, George King, could not figure out how to stop the bleeding. He had moved Spalding from pitcher to outfielder in the fourth inning, returned him to the pitcher's box in the sixth, and swapped him out again an inning later. King even replaced himself as catcher after he allowed 13 passed balls, only to watch his new catcher, starting second baseman Bob Addy, allow 15.[22]

Eight days after the pounding by the Athletics, Forest City lost 31–29 to the Atlantic club of Brooklyn when Spalding gave up 15 runs in the final two innings.[23] Rockford ended 1868 with 13 wins, four losses—and a budget deficit, despite charging admission for home games. Forest City played only about one-third of its games at home because some eastern clubs declined to travel to Rockford, assuming that their share of ticket sales in the small frontier city would not cover the cost of getting there.[24]

Athletic finished the season atop the NABBP standings, winning 47 games and losing seven (or, according to a different source, winning 51 games and losing three).[25] Cincinnati, with half of its roster filled by professionals, posted a record of 36 wins and seven losses.

That some clubs played so many fewer games than others and the number of wins and losses is uncertain testifies to the unsustainably haphazard organization of the player-run National Association and the slapdash record keeping of many clubs. NABBP annual dues were only $10 in 1868, so hundreds of clubs—from big cities to tiny towns—signed up. Each was responsible for arranging its schedule but none was obligated to play a scheduled game if, for example, it lacked funds to travel to where the contest was to be played or its players simply exhausted their enthusiasm for the game at the end of a losing season. That is why the Atlantic club of Brooklyn played 54 games while Cream City of Milwaukee played only five.

Although he was based far from the baseball capitals of Brooklyn, New York, and Philadelphia, Spalding read all he could find about baseball's transition from a recreation to an occupation that could profitably fill the growing leisure time that urbanization and industrialization were creating. He paid especially close attention to Harry and George Wright, superb players who were pioneers in professionalism as well as in the emerging business of making and selling sporting goods.

In addition to delivering news, scores, and statistics, newspapers also taught him something about the business side of baseball. They would have, for example, brought him news of Cincinnati's sensational uniforms, designed by Harry Wright and George B. Ellard, a Cincinnati sporting goods retailer, and sewn by a local tailor, Bertha Bertram. The tight, red knee-high stockings attracted spectators' attention to the players' manly calves—so much so that they caused ladies to blush and led some of the club's own directors to call them "immoral" and "indecent."[26] By contrast, Forest City players that year wore dull gray shirts and pants and light blue caps.[27]

Newspapers also informed Spalding that on December 9, 1868, delegates to the NABBP's annual meeting at Metzerott Hall in Washington, DC, had repealed its rule forbidding teams to pay players. In place of the ban, which its leaders conceded was "a dead letter for years past," the Association created a separate organization for amateur athletes. Three months later, clubs that were already paying players—or thought it necessary to do so—gathered in a dark New York City saloon on a cold and rainy St. Patrick's Day and founded their own rule-making organization, the National Association of *Professional* Base Ball Players.[28]

Cincinnati swiftly announced it would field an entirely professional team in 1869, a move that gave the club first crack at signing the best players. Eventually, 11 other clubs, including Forest City in Rockford, agreed to openly pay at least some of their players.

As the first wholly professional ballclub, the Red Stockings were a sensation. Towns from Maine to California invited them to play local all-star squads. By the end of the season, the Cincinnati ballclub had traveled 12,000 miles to play 57 exhibition and league championship games. It did not lose a single one of them.[29]

Cincinnati's most valuable player, without doubt, was its quick, nimble, hard-hitting shortstop, George Wright. He batted .629 and smashed 49 home runs in just 57 NA championship games during the Red Stockings' perfect season of 1869.

There was one tie, however. In its 40th game of the season, the Cincinnati club hosted the Haymakers of Lansingburgh, New York, now part of the city of Troy. Each club had 17 runs in the top of the sixth inning when Cal McVey, a Red Stockings outfielder, hit a foul tip. The Lansingburgh club president, James McKeon, raced onto the field, insisting it was a third strike and the side was retired. The umpire, James R. Brockway, strenuously disagreed, leading McKeon and the Haymakers' belligerent captain, William Charles "Cherokee" Fisher, to order the team to walk off the field, climb into waiting carriages, and return to the team's hotel. Brockway gave the game to the Red Stockings by default, but the NABBP called the contest a draw.[30]

It turned out that gamblers who had wagered heavily on Lansingburgh—one bettor, John Morrisey, the bareknuckle boxing champion and a member of Congress, allegedly bet more than $17,000 on a Lansingburgh victory—lost their nerve when the score was so close so late in the game. They leaned on McKeon to arrange for a tie, which would void all bets.[31]

The imbroglio was a clear example of gamblers' influence over baseball and of the National Association's reluctance or inability to do anything about it.[32] For Spalding, it no doubt served as a reminder about how allegations of game-fixing had stained Forest City's upset of the Nationals two years earlier.

In 1869, four of the Red Stockings' 65 victories came at the expense of Forest City—the only losses the Rockford club suffered in the 24 games it played that year. Forest City did have the cold comfort of coming within two outs of defeating the Red Stockings, on July 24 in Cincinnati. Rockford was leading by two runs after eight innings, only to lose 15–14 when Spalding gave up three runs in the ninth inning.[33]

Each Red Stockings victory reinforced the conventional wisdom about the promotional value cities could reap by fielding a top-flight ballclub. At a parade welcoming the Cincinnati club home to play a midseason series in 1869, thousands of people filled the sidewalks of Porkopolis, as the city, an important transportation hub for shipping live hogs to eastern cities, was nicknamed then. Men cheered and women waved handkerchiefs as players strode past them.

An older man confided to a stranger standing nearby that he knew nothing of baseball but cheered the team for the glory it was bringing to the city.

"Glory?" the stranger said, hard-pressed to believe the older man's inability to appreciate the greater gift the Red Stockings had bestowed on Cincinnati. "They have advertised the city—advertised us, and helped our business, sir!"[34]

The Red Stockings' perfect season may well have helped local businesses, but it certainly did not do much for the club's bankroll. The Red Stockings' share of gate receipts in 1869 totaled $29,726.26, while salaries, travel, and other costs came to $29,724.87, leaving a profit of $1.39.[35]

Rockford's business leaders were undeterred by Cincinnati's puny profit. The potential to attract even a small share of the extensive newspaper coverage lavished on that city because of the Red Stockings led them to sponsor Forest City on a 7,700-mile, $7,000 tour of eastern cities in 1870. It was, they reckoned, a splendid way to advertise Rockford's railroad service and abundant water power, which already had attracted manufacturers of agricultural machinery, cotton mills, paper mills, planing mills, and woolen mills.[36]

The trip, boosters proudly added, also would be the first in which a western club would challenge the supposedly superior eastern sides, or teams, on their home grounds. To make a proper and lasting impression, club members outfitted players with eye-catching new white flannel uniforms with a hexagonal bib on the chest. The bib was embroidered with the club's initials, "F" and "C," in the same shade of forest green as their belts and new, tight-fitting knee-high stockings.[37]

Before the season got underway, Spalding helped his mother sell the last property she owned outside Byron, a 320-acre farm. In a *Rockford Weekly Register-Gazette* advertisement, Albert said about 150 acres were under cultivation by the current lessee and 80 acres were timberland. A stream of "living water" ran through the property, which he said was "in a good neighborhood and a short distance from a schoolhouse."

Harriet had sold 12 other Byron properties since her husband died eight years earlier, but she could not find a buyer for this farm, which she leased to a local man. Eventually, a Rockford jewelry store owner who saw the ad and said he had always dreamed of being a farmer, offered to buy it from Harriet for $40 an acre—more than 30 times what her late husband James had paid when he bought it from the government. The sum was so high that the buyer, A. F. Hinckley, conditioned his offer on Harriet's willingness to take half of the sale price in cash and half in Rockford properties he owned. Before accepting the offer, Harriet sought Albert's advice. He took Hinckley on a tour of the Byron property, allowing his mother and younger brother to freely inspect the properties Hinckley was offering as partial payment.

As Harriet and Walter discovered, the house was a shambles. The front steps gave way, a cistern didn't work, and one corner of the place seemed to be near collapsing. Walter was not impressed. "I think it is too bad to sell the farm that our father bought from the government, 320 acres, and take in exchange for it cats and dogs," the business-savvy 13-year-old said, using an idiom for unsellable merchandise. "I wouldn't give two cents for that old house."

His mother noted that the property included two undeveloped lots as well as the one with the house, which could always be repaired. After returning from

Byron, Al endorsed the transaction and persuaded his brother to do the same. "Walter, this is the first opportunity Mother has had to sell that farm. It has been advertised for a year, and Mother seems to think it is best to sell it," he said. Demonstrating a natural head for business, Spalding closed the deal by offering "easy" terms on the cash part of the transaction.[38]

* * *

With Spalding pitching practically every inning of every game, Forest City won the first 12 games of its season, including exhibitions with "picked nines" composed of local all-stars, matches with western NABBP members and the first half of its eastern tour. They also won the respect of Easterners who until now had little use for teams in the West. "All the Eastern papers speak in the highest terms of the Forest City Club, both as gentlemen and as ball players," marveled one midwestern correspondent.[39]

Indeed, the *New York Clipper* praised Forest City players for their "gentlemanly deportment and honest style of play" during a three-game series in Washington besmirched by inept officiating and abundant bellyaching by Atlantic players.[40]

One sportswriter admiringly described Spalding's delivery as "peculiar" but effective. "He grasps the ball with both hands, raising them to the level of his head, remaining statue-like for 15 or 20 seconds and then, as he deliberately lowers them, pulls back his right arm, and the ball goes whizzing through the air," he wrote. "His attitude attracts the eye of the batsman, whose aim is thereby nullified, and he falls an easy prey to the catcher or infield."[41]

Forest City's first game in New York, against the Union club of Morrisania in late May 1870, was halted by rain after just three innings and the score tied 4–4. A game against the Eckford club the next day was rained out entirely. By the time the weather let up on Monday, an estimated 5,000 people paid to see the exotic Westerners play their first game of 1870 in New York City—and suffer their first defeat of the year, a 21–13 loss to the Mutuals.[42]

"The Forest Citys, since leaving their western home, have had an uninterrupted march of success, proving victorious in every contest, except yesterday's," a Brooklyn newspaper reported. "With such a record as they possess, it is no wonder they created an excitement among the ball field patrons and a little fear and jealousy among the players who they intended to encounter."[43]

Rockford led most of the game before Mutual batters grew accustomed to Spalding's pitching and tagged the flagging teenager for seven runs in the eighth inning and five more in the ninth (at the time, a coin flip determined the order in which teams batted, and they played nine full innings regardless of the score). The Mutuals' comeback taught Spalding that skillful professional batters can adjust to a pitching style that had flummoxed them earlier in a game.

"The pitcher of the visiting club [Spalding] has a troublesome delivery, made all the more so by a peculiar attitude or pose assumed just before his final swing," a *New York Herald* sportswriter observed. "It is possible the Mutuals lost at first by their admiration of his attitude interfering with their judgement in striking at the ball. This having been overcome, however, they paid Mr. Spalding off by knocking all the grace out of him."[44]

Spalding and his teammates more than held their own for the remainder of their eastern tour, finishing with 13 wins, three losses, and two ties. (Including the games it played against western clubs, Rockford's season record was 28 victories, 11 defeats, and two ties. Since eastern clubs were unwilling to pay for travel to distant Rockford, only about 10 of those games were played at home, foiling club managers' plan to recoup their costs from ticket sales.)

Forest City's success was somewhat overshadowed by news that the Atlantic club in Brooklyn had defeated the Red Stockings in extra innings on June 14, ending the Cincinnati club's two-year winning streak at 81 games. The score was tied 7–7 and there was one out in the 12th inning when Cincinnati's first baseman Charlie Gould knocked down a sharply hit grounder with his bare hand—players did not yet wear gloves. After chasing down the ball, he threw it toward second base to put out a runner, but the ball sailed over the bag and into center field. The Atlantic player continued home to score the winning run.

Baseball fans were still focused on the Red Stockings' shattered invincibility when Forest City played a new Chicago club called the White Stockings two days later. Thousands of spectators trekked to Dexter Park, where "the great mass surged backward and forward like the swells of an enraged sea," according to one account. The gates eventually toppled and spectators raced inside, ticket or no ticket.[45]

The excitement did not last for long. In the first inning, Chicago sent 13 batters to the plate before Rockford could register a single out. Chicago opened a 15–0 lead before Rockford had a chance to bat. Chicago won the game 28–14.[46]

"We swamped them," James Wood, captain and manager of the White Stockings, recalled many years later. "After the fifth inning, we were so far ahead that I gave my boys orders to take it easy."[47]

With the Red Stockings' aura of invincibility shattered, Rockford supporters thought their club had a chance to pin a second defeat on Cincinnati when the clubs met again on July 11, for the third time in less than three weeks. Spalding, who was ill, set down Cincinnati's first three batters in short order and his teammates staked him to a five-run lead in their half of the first inning.

Cincinnati pulled even in the third inning when Forest City's barehanded catcher, Scott Hastings, could not handle a Spalding speed ball and it skittered past him, allowing George Wright, Cincinnati's shortstop, to jog home from third base. By the middle of the ninth, the Red Stockings were ahead by 16–8 and Rockford supporters were drifting away from the fairgrounds. They left too soon.

In his club's last at-bats, Forest City's left fielder Fred Cone reached base on a fielder's error and second baseman Bob Addy followed with a single. Hastings then atoned for his passed ball by doubling in two runs and then scampering home when George Wright tried to return the ball to his pitcher but threw it over his head. Ross Barnes, Rockford's shortstop, promptly ripped a single to left field. Center fielder Joe Simmons reached first when Cincinnati's third baseman muffed a grounder. Tom Foley got on base when a Cincinnati infielder bobbled a double play ball. Outfielder Gat Stires made the Red Stockings pay for that error by shooting a line drive to right field, driving home Simmons and Waterman and moving Foley over to third. Rockford had pulled within two runs with no outs.

"The crowd became wild with excitement," according to one contemporary account. "All crowded in toward the foul line, men and boys shouted, and ladies waved their handkerchiefs. The umpire appealed to the spectators to remain quiet, as nothing could be heard." Perhaps inspired by the cheering, Stires tried to steal second base but was thrown out.[48]

Spalding was up next and drove the first pitch to deep center field to let Foley score and pare Cincinnati's lead to one. Joe Doyle then hammered a hot grounder to shortstop, bringing home Spalding and racing all the way to third when Cincinnati's barehanded first baseman dropped the throw from shortstop, then sailed the ball over the second baseman's head in trying to stop Doyle from taking an extra base. Cone, batting for the second time that inning, hit a soft line drive just out of the first baseman's reach, letting Doyle cross home plate with Rockford's eighth run of the inning, tying the score.

"A nearer approach to pandemonium was never experienced, in this city at least," a sportswriter wrote.[49]

Addy, the next batter, hit a grounder that the third baseman couldn't field cleanly. Cone took the opportunity to advance to third base and, believing the ball to be beyond the fielder's reach, rounded toward home. The ball beat him there, for the second out. The inning ended, with the score tied 16–16, when the next batter, Barnes, hit a soft line drive to the third baseman. The score would have to remain tied because at six o'clock it was too dark to continue. The Red Stockings and Forest City would have to wait for their next scheduled game, in October, to settle matters.

Spalding started and completed that autumnal game in Rockford, which Forest City won 12–5. Spalding gave up only seven hits that day. Winds blowing out toward the outfield caused flyballs to carry, helping Rockford's batters to hit four home runs and Cincinnati's players to hit three. Even Spalding, never known for his power, knocked a line drive over the head of the Red Stockings right fielder Cal McVey ("to the surprise of everyone," the *Chicago Tribune* archly noted) and triumphantly rounded the bases.[50]

In the field, Forest City's most talented players—Spalding, Ross Barnes, and Fred Cone—made spectacular defensive plays. Spalding had never pitched better in his life, preventing Cincinnati from scoring in seven of nine innings.

"The Forest Citys were on their mettle, and the coolness, skill, and precision with which they took care of everything was never surpassed on the ball field," a newspaper enthused. "Their game, both in batting and fielding, has probably never been surpassed. The Reds were fairly outplayed and beaten at every point of the game."[51]

According to historian Marshall D. Wright's meticulous review of records from that sloppily documented era, Forest City finished 1870 with 42 wins, 13 losses and one tie, for a winning percentage of .763. On the part of the season devoted to its image-polishing East Coast tour, the club won 14 games, lost three, and tied two, a winning percentage of .789.[52]

Mutual of New York had the most victories, 68, of NABBP teams in 1870, but because it played more games and had more losses it had only the fourth-best winning percentage, .800. Cincinnati had one fewer win but a markedly higher winning percentage, .917. (For the record, Rockford had the fifth-most victories.) But crowning a champion was not just a matter of wins and winning percentages. Instead, one team challenged another to play a series of games to determine the champion. Neither had to be the best club in the eyes of sportswriters or ticket buyers: Cincinnati, for example, was not invited to compete for the NA pennant in 1869, the year it was undefeated in 57 games.

A greater insult awaited the historic team at the end of the 1870 season. On November 21, two weeks after the Red Stockings' last game of the year, the club's executives made a simple but stunning announcement: Cincinnati would not field a professional side in 1871.

"To employ a nine for the coming season at the enormous salaries now demanded by professional players would plunge our club deeply in debt at the end of the year," according to a statement from the club's executive committee, led by Albert Pearley Cross (A. P. C.) Bonte, a picture-frame manufacturer who succeeded the charismatic Aaron Champion after he resigned in August. "The experience of the past two years has taught us that a nine whose aggregate salaries exceed six or eight thousand dollars cannot, even with the strictest economy, be self-sustaining."[53]

In the perfect season of 1869, Red Stocking players' salaries totaled $9,300, roughly equivalent to $200,000 today. A future Hall of Fame inductee, the shortstop George Wright, was the highest-paid player, earning $1,400; his older brother and team captain, Harry, also in the Hall of Fame, earned $1,200. Evidently, that was too much for team bean counters when admission to a game was 50 cents, equivalent to $12 today.

If the club's announced withdrawal from professional ball was, as some have contended, a bluff designed to reduce players' salary expectations in 1871, it failed. A day or two after the club's announcement, Red Stockings players were scrambling to find positions on other teams. Five of them bolted to the Nationals in Washington: catcher Doug Allison, left fielder Andrew J. Leonard, third baseman Fred Waterman, second baseman Charlie Sweasy, and Asa Brainard, who had learned to pitch from the legendary hurler Jim Creighton when they both played for the Excelsior club in Brooklyn in the early 1860s. The remainder of Cincinnati's lineup—first baseman Charles H. Gould, right fielder Cal McVey, and the Wright brothers—decamped to Massachusetts. A group of Boston business owners, led by a successful 32-year-old net and twine manufacturer named Ivers Whitney Adams, had been secretly talking for some months with the Wrights to bring a professional club to the Hub.

Cincinnati's disintegration made it easier to do so. When his contract with the city's club expired on December 1, 1870, Harry Wright signed a new one with the Bostons and immediately set out to sign talented players to fill roster openings created by the mass transfer of ex–Red Stockings to the free-spending Nationals in Washington.[54]

Wright knew precisely where to start looking for top-flight ballplayers and booked a seat on a westbound train. His destination was Rockford, Illinois.

Chapter 4
Champion

When Harry Wright recruited Spalding to be his pitcher, the 19-year-old already was "acclaimed as one of the finest pitchers in the land," as the baseball historian David Q. Voigt wrote. He also had brains. "He knew how to use his head to fool an opponent," Jack Chapman, an outfielder for the Brooklyn Atlantics, St. Louis Browns, and Louisville Grays, told *Baseball Magazine* in 1910.[1]

In the three seasons since Forest City upset the Nationals, spectators had come to accept professionalism. Rockford, with Spalding in the pitcher's box for nearly every inning, had won 73 games, lost 21, and tied one—a winning percentage of .777. Harry Wright knew that some of the victories came at the expense of untalented amateurs representing small towns in Illinois, Iowa, and Wisconsin, but some wins were against top-tier teams in baseball citadels like New York, Philadelphia, and Brooklyn, an independent city until its merger with New York in 1898.

When the *New York Clipper* selected the best professional players of 1870, it ladled praise on Spalding's pitching and on his character. "He impressed us as a very intelligent and gentlemanly player."[2]

He often did so under trying circumstances. As he quickly learned, men who accept pay to play ball meant they also had to accept severe, sometimes unfair judgement of their performance, and he was not immune. His elaborate pitching stance was a frequent target of ridicule.

After one bruising loss to the White Stockings, for instance, a *Chicago Times* writer mocked Spalding's pitching style—and the team's fielding skills—by recounting one awful inning. It began when Spalding "struck one of his favorite attitudes and handed in a swift one to the striker. [Chicago outfielder Marshall].

King very cheerfully thumped it plumb in the middle, and, while the fielders were busy gathering it in, [King] amused himself by taking second base.

"The Forest City boys gazed at each other in general, and at their attitudinizing pitcher in particular, in blank dismay, and two or three thousand delegates from the Rock River Valley stared in silent amazement at the way the customers in blue and white were taking hold of their 'cannon ball pitcher's' delivery."[3]

Like any team, except perhaps the 1869 Cincinnatis, Forest City was capable of suffering embarrassing losses they would have liked to forget, but the country boys from Rockford, as Easterners disparagingly characterized Spalding and his teammates, certainly had tested the Red Stockings several times during the remarkable perfect season in 1869. In one game, Cincinnati had to score three runs in its last at-bat to beat Rockford 15–14. The *Chicago Tribune* hailed it as "the most exciting and hotly contested game of baseball ever played in this city."[4]

After its unbeaten year, Cincinnati finished the season of 1870 with 67 wins, six losses, and one tie—a remarkable winning percentage of .918, but not good enough to persuade the Cincinnati Baseball Club's new officers to continue fielding a professional nine. When the season ended, they said players' salaries were unsupportable and announced that the club would return to amateur play in 1871. The news turned the professional game upside down. Cincinnati's entire roster was suddenly on the market and clubs up and down the eastern seaboard and as far west as Illinois announced that they would organize openly professional nines within a few weeks.

With many clubs freed to openly pay players, there was little wonder that Harry Wright raced to secure Spalding's services—and those of future batting champion Roscoe (Ross) Barnes, another Rockford native—as soon as Boston Baseball Club president Ivers Adams hired the Wright brothers to build a pennant-winning club in the Hub.

Harry made the arduous train ride to and from Rockford while George filled other open positions in the club's roster; together, they succeeded in assembling an exceptional squad within about a month of the Cincinnati Baseball Club's announcement that it was finished with professionalism. However, a good team—even a winning team—is not necessarily a harmonious one.

There is no evidence Spalding was surprised when Wright turned up in Rockford to offer him $2,500—$500 in cash on the spot—if he would pitch for Boston in 1871. Spalding knew Wright needed a reliable arm because Cincinnati's pitcher Asahel "Asa" Brainard was one of five men from that club who had moved to Washington, DC, to play for the Olympic club. Wright, a virtuous husband and father, would have been disinclined to pursue Brainard anyway because the player was a notorious ladies' man who abandoned his family when he joined the Olympics, even though his wife, Mary, had recently nursed him through a case of smallpox.[5]

What should have surprised Spalding was that a new professional team in Chicago, the White Stockings, had not bothered to contact him before Wright came knocking at his mother's front door. Instead, the Chicago club signed 26-year-old George Zettlein from the Brooklyn Atlantics, owner of a blazing fast pitch who nonetheless would earn the dubious honor of giving up the new league's first home run in May and its first grand slam in September.

Spalding did not publicly comment on the White Stockings' apparent lack of interest in him—or any other Rockford players, save Zettlein, who had agreed to play for the Forest Citys before switching to Chicago—but others did. The *Chicago Tribune* cited the loss of Spalding, Barnes, and Cone when it said the White Stocking officials in charge of assembling a championship-level team of professionals "have succeeded in doing nothing."

"They have, it is true, made several equally expensive and ineffectual trips to the East; have contributed liberally toward the annual dividends of the telegraph companies, and have severally seen three valuable players taken from under their noses and transported to the great Boston nine," the newspaper added. "They had no use for Barnes, Spalding and Cone, whom Harry Wright, the best judge of baseball players in the country, snatched up the instant he had the authority. Boston came to a Chicago suburb for players whom the White Stocking managers, in their superior wisdom, scorned to employ."[6]

Wright may have had the authority to sign men to play for Boston's embryonic ballclub, but the club had no organization to join. The National Association of Baseball Players broke apart at a meeting in November 1870, when amateur ballclubs, a large majority of NABBP members, walked out to express their dissatisfaction with professional clubs using ambiguities in the Association's constitution to control the NA, usually to the detriment of amateurs. Four months later, having received no answer from the professionals, amateur clubs formed their own organization.

Spalding had little sympathy for the old order and expressed no concern about openly embracing professionalism. "The death of the National Association of Baseball Players . . . was expected, natural, and painless," he wrote years later. "The organization had outlived its usefulness; it had fallen into evil ways; it had been in very bad company; and so, when the hour of its dissolution came, no sorrowing friends were there to speak a tearful farewell."[7]

On the evening after the amateurs founded their own organization, men representing 10 professional clubs in eight cities—Boston; Brooklyn; Chicago; Cleveland; New York; Philadelphia; Rockford, Illinois; and Troy, New York—defied an icy rainstorm to convene in Collier's Rooms, a second-floor saloon at 13th Street and Broadway in Manhattan, and found the National Association of Professional Baseball Players—a preposterously unwieldy name that was almost instantly shortened to the National Association, or just the NA.[8]

The date was March 17, St. Patrick's Day. The first games would be played in three weeks.

* * *

Red Stockings players began arriving in Boston shortly after that meeting in Collier's Rooms. Harry Wright instructed the Rockford boys—Spalding, Barnes, and Cone—and four other young players to lodge at a boardinghouse on New Heath Street near Centre Street in a recently annexed part of Boston called the Highlands. Wright rented the house next door so that he could keep his callow charges "under his eye at all hours."[9]

The lodgings were about a mile from where they would play home games, the Union Baseball Ground, built in 1869 and sometimes referred to as the South End Ground. Unseasonably wet, cold weather that month persuaded Wright to keep his players indoors and have them prepare for the coming season by exercising for two or three hours per day in a gymnasium on the fourth floor of the Tremont Building. The gym—80 feet long and 40 feet wide, or about as big as a high school basketball court—was the first such facility in the country when it opened in the 1820s.[10]

Spalding may never have exercised so hard in his privileged life to that point, but he was in good spirits. In late April, before the National Association's 1872 season opened, he penned a letter to the *Rockford Register* to assure friends and family back home that he and the other players from the small city, Barnes and Cone, were thriving.

"We are very comfortably located in the southern part of the city, known as 'Boston Highlands,' in a private boarding house, next door to Harry Wright's;

and as we are all together, so we don't get very lonesome," Spalding wrote. "We are about three miles from the business part of the city, and about one mile from the grounds.

"The grounds are being fitted up at great expense, and when completed will make one of the finest grounds in the country," he continued, showing his natural salesmanship. "We played our opening (exhibition) game on (April) 6 against a strong picked nine, in the presence of about 5,000 people, the largest crowd ever assembled to see a game of ball in Boston."[11] The Red Stockings won, 41–10.

In his letter, Spalding didn't mention an exhibition game the Red Stockings played on March 25 against a team from Harvard University, perhaps because, to even the sides, Boston's battery of Spalding and McVey played for Harvard. Spalding held Boston scoreless through four innings, during which Harvard scored six runs on the way to a 17–10 win over the professionals.

Spalding reminded *Register* readers that the Red Stockings would play in Rockford in mid-July and thanked them for mailing the local paper to him. "We all go for the *Register* just as soon as it comes," he wrote. "We shall be pleased to hear from Rockford friends at any time."[12]

A few days after Spalding reassured the folks back home that all was well, some bored and homesick Boston players painted a different picture. In Washington on a road trip, they met in their hotel to write a letter to Salome Parker, who ran the boardinghouse where most of them stayed when the team was in Boston.

Each player wrote about their first experience as a professional ballplayer on the road. "So far we have been victorious," wrote Charlie Gould, making a joking reference to lopsided exhibition game victories against overmatched amateurs. He then wrote about the season-opening game the next day. "Tomorrow will be the grand conquest of the tour."

Remarkably little else was said in the letter of that game, the 1871 season-opening contest between Olympic and the Boston Red Stockings, the two clubs that had hired most of the players from the defunct Cincinnati team. Instead, the players groused about how the food in Washington did not compare—in quality or quantity—with Mrs. Parker's home-cooked dishes.

"Poor meals! Coming home for big ones," wrote catcher Cal McVey.

"Save some lemon pie for me," chirped backup infielder Samuel Jackson.

Even captain Harry Wright—at age 36 at least a decade older than his teammates—could think of little besides his stomach. "I am just going up stairs to supper and feel awful hungry but do not expect much. Poor meals here. Too hungry to say more."

Substitute outfielder David Birdsall wistfully added, "Oh, how I wish I was home."

Spalding, not known as a wordsmith, echoed that sentiment: "'Would that we were home again.'"

The letter concluded with a nod to Harry and George's mother, Annie, who lived in Harry's house: "All the boys send their kind regards to Mrs. Wright and your family." They signed the letter "The Eleven."[13]

The NA's plan to make its debut in 1871 with a much-anticipated matchup between the Red Stockings and Olympics was scuppered by soaking rain in the capital on Opening Day, May 4. So, instead of making a dramatic debut with a matchup of powerful clubs in a big East Coast city, the NA's first game was in far-off Fort Wayne, Indiana. The Kekionga club (named for the indigenous people's village on which white settlers built the city) beat Cleveland 2–1 in a rain-shortened eight-inning game.[14]

The next day, when Spalding got his opportunity to demonstrate his skills on the big stage—a championship game in the first professional baseball organization—4,000 ticket-holders filled the wood-frame grandstand at the Olympic Grounds while hundreds more improvised viewing spots on nearby fences, trees, and rooftops.[15]

Spectators were treated to an exciting game, if not the skillful exhibition they had anticipated. Boston won the coin toss and sent Washington to bat first. Olympic quickly touched Spalding for six runs and then stretched its lead to 10–1 at the end of the second inning, thanks to the usually resolute Boston shortstop George Wright muffing a flyball.

The Red Stockings took advantage of Olympic miscues to have seven men cross the plate in the third inning and make a game of it. When Boston came to bat in the ninth frame it trailed 15–10, but a five-run lead in a 19th-century game was no safer than a five-run advantage in the home-run-friendly stadia of the 20th century.

Boston's first batter in the ninth inning, Harry Wright, took a base on balls, and first baseman Charley Gould followed with a single. Harry Schafer rocketed a groundball down the first base line for a triple, allowing Wright and Gould to score. This brought the crowd to its feet and Boston to within one run. After Cone fouled out, Spalding entered the batter's box to face Brainard, who was nine years older, five inches shorter, and 20 pounds lighter.

The Boston pitcher cracked a line drive over second base to drive home Schafer and tie the score. George Wright hit a single to move Spalding to second base, greatly improving his odds of scoring. Sure enough, the next batter, Ross Barnes, Spalding's boyhood friend in Rockford and one of the best hitters in the NA, drove a ball deep into center field, giving Al plenty of time to scamper home and register the winning run. As was then the custom, the teams played out the ninth inning and Boston scored again, making the final score Boston 20, Washington 18.[16]

* * *

While the quality of play was exceptional, that inaugural season exposed the National Association's organizational shortcomings. The constitution made each club responsible for arranging its schedule, requiring them to play all eight other clubs five times, including one best-of-three-games series. The constitution neglected to say if clubs had to play all three of the best-of-three-games series if a club won the first two games. Most chose not to play a third game once a series was decided, in part because fewer spectators would pay to watch unnecessary contests and in part to help visiting clubs save on travel costs.

NA clubs in big cities soon learned that their share of anemic ticket sales in smaller localities—Troy, New York, population 46,000; Fort Wayne, Indiana, 18,000; and Rockford, Illinois, 11,000—often would not cover travel costs, so they didn't show up. With authority devolved to the clubs, the National Association was helpless to ban gambling and drinking at games, much less compel members to play every game they were obliged to play so that all clubs could have a chance to capture the championship pennant.

Harry Wright—with his studious protégé Spalding looking over his shoulder—did his best to arrange games while playing for and managing the team. He spent many hours writing letters in longhand to the secretaries of other clubs, proposing dates and locations for games and negotiating how much of the gate receipts the Red Stockings could expect to receive. The Red Stockings' portion ranged from 25 to 60 percent of ticket sales, based on considerations such as the quality of the opponent and the size of the city. Like other club secretaries,

Wright also tried to minimize travel costs by bunching together games against clubs located near one another.

He had no illusions about how professionalism was changing the game. "Baseball is a business now, Nick," Wright wrote to Nick Young, the NA's secretary and manager of the Olympics, "and I am trying to arrange our games to make them successful and make them pay."[17]

It was not always easy to act professionally in the anarchic National Association, as Wright and Spalding discovered. On April 26, 1871, Wright wrote to Young in his capacity as an Association official, to inform him that the Eckford club in Brooklyn and Mutual club of New York proposed to keep all receipts from their home games and said Boston should do the same. Wright rejected the idea out of hand. "We will not play them unless they consent to divide the receipts," pointing out that if one club has already hosted another—and kept all gate receipts—"what is to compel a club to play a return game?" Club managers would know they'd not be paid if they went to the other club's home grounds.[18]

Sharp business practices did not prevent players—then, as now—from having fun.

In June, Spalding, Barnes, and Cone wrote a gag letter to Hiram Waldo, the beloved head of the Rockford club and mentor to Forest City's finest young players over the years. In it, they wrote that famous Americans of the day "send their love to you." The letter had what looked to be the signatures of President Grant, newspaper publisher Horace Greeley, the popular author Brette [*sic*] Harte—and three of Waldo's fellow Rockford residents: Al Spalding, Ross Barnes, and Fred Cone.[19]

* * *

After an awful start, in which Boston lost half of its first 14 games, the Red Stockings slowly gelled as a team and finished with 22 wins and 10 losses.[20] Spalding was Boston's starting pitcher in all 31 games it played, completing 22 of them and winning 19—the most of any pitcher that year. He would, in fact, have the most wins of any NA pitcher for the association's entire five-year existence.

However, he was feted for more than winning games. "Spalding, of the Boston nine, [is] one of the most intelligent players that occupies the position," the *New York Clipper* wrote in its annual summary of the season just ending. "Patient, quiet, unobtrusive, pluck, and possessing the essentials of speed, command of the ball and endurance, and more than ordinary judgment in estimating the powers of his opponents, Spalding ranks A No. 1 in the pitching department."[21]

The end of the Association's first season marked the beginning of a protracted debate over which club was the champion. The NA's constitution, which had been dashed off in the weeks between the Association's founding and its first game, required every club to play each of the eight other members five times, for a total of 40 championship games. But, lured by the opportunity to skip championship games and make money playing against local "picked nines" or to save money by not traveling, NA teams played in only 35 championship games at most (Mutual) and as few as 19 (Kekionga).

Fort Wayne ran out of money and quit the NA in early September, forfeiting its final nine, unplayed games. Those games appear in official records as victories for the opposing teams. Rockford had to forfeit four games in which it played a catcher, Scott Hastings, less than 60 days after he left his previous team, the New Orleans Stars.

NA clubs adopted that 60-day rule to discourage teams from raiding one another's rosters during the season. Washington also had a temporarily ineligible player, George Hall, who jumped from the amateur Atlantic club of New York right after his teammates elected him captain; he was in Olympic's lineup for the first game of the year a few days later. Reflecting the league's inconsistency, the NA did not require Olympic to forfeit any of the 16 games Hall played in (including eight wins), although he was ineligible. Had the NA required Olympic to forfeit those games, Boston could have claimed first place in place of Philadelphia.[22]

Confusing matters further, the Association constitution did not make clear how the champion would be determined. Would it be the team that won the most *series* or the most *games*? What about the club that lost the *fewest* games or *fewest* series? Since teams ended up playing different numbers of games, should the pennant go to the club with the highest winning percentage?

On November 3, three days after the season ended, National Association president James W. Kerns summoned representatives of every member club to a special meeting at the Girard House hotel in Philadelphia to belatedly decide how to determine a champion. The representatives promptly delegated the thankless task to its Championship Committee, led by Harry Wright, with instructions to find a solution by the middle of November.[23]

The answer arrived a month late. In a letter dated December 12, 1871, to Elias Hicks Hayhurst, president of the Athletic club in Philadelphia, the committee stated it had "duly considered the claims and examined the playing records of all clubs . . . and find that the Athletic Baseball Club of Philadelphia presents the best record."

Philadelphia undoubtedly had the Association's best record that year—21 wins and seven losses, for a .750 winning percentage—but the Association knew that at least six weeks earlier. So why the wait?[24]

The White Stockings club, which lost its grounds and all its uniforms and equipment in Chicago's Great Fire in October that year, finished in third position after the Association denied the club's request to count games it had postponed until after November 1 because of the chaos caused by the fire, which killed roughly 300 people, reduced more than 17,000 buildings to ashes, and left approximately 100,000 people homeless.[25]

After witnessing the amount of time and effort his mentor, Harry Wright, invested in running the Red Stockings in a professional manner, Spalding most likely spent much of the two-day train trip back home to Rockford—where he would spend the winter—reflecting on the haphazard, half-witted approach to the business of baseball demonstrated by the rest of the National Association.

* * *

Spalding and most of the other Red Stockings players returned to Boston on March 15 to begin preparing for the 1872 season, starting with an informal meeting at the club's headquarters at 18 Boylston Street. Not coincidentally, that also was the address of Wright & Gould, a retail establishment specializing in tobacco products and baseball goods, George Wright and C. Harvey "Charlie" Gould, proprietors. The ballplayers' entrepreneurship made an impression on their young teammate Spalding, who began visiting other sporting goods stores that were beginning to appear in cities with professional teams.

At the meeting, Harry Wright told his men that they would train in the Tremont Gym for four hours a day, playing practice games outdoors as the weather permitted. He added that the season would start on April 4, a Monday, with an exhibition against a picked nine on the Boston grounds. Beyond that, there were no firm dates.

Wright told the players he was still exchanging letters with other team managers to build a schedule of games that would count toward the NA championship. He said Boston already had received challenges from the Mutual club of New York, the Atlantic in Brooklyn, and the new Baltimore Canaries, so named because of their brilliant yellow stockings.[26]

There would be no challenge from Rockford. The Forest City club that had made Al Spalding (and Ross Barnes and most recently Adrian C. "Cap" Anson) famous in the sport finished the 1871 season in the NA dead last and dead broke. In mid-April, club directors sued stockholders for the balance of their subscriptions.[27]

The championship question in 1872 did not take long to settle. From Opening Day onward, Boston was a locomotive highballing over the 10 other clubs that had put up $10 to join the NA and compete for the championship. Over the winter, the Red Stockings bolstered its roster by adding veteran players from the 1869 Cincinnati machine, catcher Cal McVey and left fielder Andy Leonard. In its first game, Boston smashed the Washington Nationals by a score of 25–3. Twenty-four hours later it defeated the other Washington club, Olympic, 8–1. "Spalding's pitching proved so effective that the Olympics failed totally before the ninth inning, when they made one run," a newspaper reported.[28]

The Red Stockings won 22 of its first 23 games; its only loss in those three months was to Philadelphia, by a score of 10–7, on a blustery and cold late-spring day. Spalding pitched every one of the 48 games that Boston played in 1872, earned a decision in every game but one, and completed the season with 38 wins and an earned-run average of 1.85. He also once again had the best fielding average among pitchers and drove in 47 runs that season, enough to tie for fifth place among all players in the NA.[29]

While Spalding led the defense in frustrating opponents' batters, Boston's enviable offense—led by the club's extraordinary second baseman, Barnes—often seemed able to produce runs on cue. Barnes was the master of fair-foul hits, which were foul balls treated as hits if they touched fair territory first. This rule enabled Barnes to lead the NA in batting average (.423 in 1872), hits, total bases, and slugging average.[30]

By midseason, the Red Stockings had opened a comfortable 5½-game lead in the standings, having just thrashed a club from Middletown, Connecticut, by scores of 16–6 and, on Independence Day, 25–12. To get his players out from under the summer sun, which also kept spectators out of ballparks, Wright, like other managers, treated the boys to a little vacation. He chose Calf Island in Boston Harbor. At the time, accommodations consisted of a few lobstermen's shanties and a jerry-rigged hut made by joining two deckhouses from a wrecked steamship. The players practiced for two hours in the morning and two more in the evening. For the rest of the day, they entertained themselves by fishing, shooting, and swimming.[31]

Upon the team's return from this midseason idyll, it promptly lost two consecutive games for the first time all year. The otherwise undistinguished Haymakers of Troy, New York, struck first, knocking Spalding around for 17 runs—the most scored against the Red Stockings all season. In Boston's next game, the defending champion Athletics shut down the Red Stockings' offense to win 9–1.

Boston also received the unwelcome news that the NA judicial committee decided to increase to nine from five the number of games each team had to play against other teams to compete for the championship in the current season. Adding games to the schedule would give the Athletics and other good teams more opportunities to nibble away at Boston's lead in the standings.[32]

There was a reason for this expansion: six of the 11 clubs that began the season had dropped out of the championship race, withdrawn from the NA, or gone out of business entirely. The Olympics folded in May; the capital's other team, the Nationals, winless in 11 tries, quit in June; Troy, New York, resigned in July; and Middletown, Connecticut, and Cleveland threw in the towel in August. The Eckford club in Brooklyn never formally withdrew but played games only on its home grounds, winning three and losing 26.

Midseason fiddling with the schedule changed nothing. Boston captured the 1872 pennant with 39 wins and eight losses (28 wins and seven losses if one counts only games against clubs that completed the season). Spalding erased any doubt that the Red Stockings would take the pennant when he shut out the Athletics 10–0 on October 5 at the South End Ground in Boston; the game knocked Philadelphia into fourth place, 7½ games behind the Red Stockings in the league standings, and elevated the Baltimore Canaries into second place.[33]

Before the club and its supporters could finish celebrating the championship, the Great Fire of Boston erupted on the evening of November 7. By the time firefighters and ordinary citizens could contain the blaze the next day, it had reduced 65 acres of central Boston to ashes, destroying 776 buildings and causing damage estimated at $73.5 million (more than $1.58 billion in current value).

Players and investors in the baseball club were among the people to lose property, which magnified the impact of the announcement on December 4 that the ballclub had run up large debts in its first two years. The implication was clear: Boston might not have the financial wherewithal to defend its title in 1873.

Accounts of the club's losses varied. It evidently did not archive profit-and-loss statements, and newspapers' estimates varied widely, depending in part on how they treated items like obligations under the lease of its grounds. Estimates ranged from $3,000 to more than $7,000. For example, the *Boston Journal* said the team generated revenue of $18,700 in 1872 but spent more than $22,000. In any case, the *Herald* warned, "the close of the baseball season of 1872 finds the Boston club in a crippled financial position."[34]

Indeed, the Bostons were in such a fix that the club could not pay the players who had just won it a championship. It owed Spalding $800, and the young pitcher said he was in such desperate financial straits he was "forced" to move to New York and accept an old friend's offer to keep the books of the *Daily Graphic*, a weekly paper.

Spalding didn't have to wait long for Boston business leaders to rescue the Red Stockings. On December 11, about 150 supporters of the club met in Brackett's Hall and agreed to abolish the Boston Baseball Association and replace it with the Boston Baseball Club. The Club would buy enough shares in the Association to gain control of the players, grounds, and other Association assets, but none of its debt. Whatever profits the Club made would be sent to the Association to repay its creditors. Fifty-three men agreed on the spot to join the new Club, each paying an initiation fee of $15 and $10 in annual dues. They elected as president Charles H. Porter, an insurance company executive and future mayor of Quincy, Massachusetts.[35]

* * *

Eight teams started the 1873 season and by early July they had been winnowed to four contenders: Baltimore, Boston, and two Philadelphia clubs, the White Stockings and the Athletics. With Spalding wrestling with one of his spring slumps, Boston fell 6½ games behind the White Stockings by July 3, and then lost the first game of an Independence Day doubleheader to the dreadful Resolutes of Elizabeth, New Jersey—that club's second and final victory of the year. The 11–2 defeat shocked Spalding and his teammates back to life; the Red Stockings won the second game by a score of 33–3. Skeptics were still dubious that the team would end the year in glory. When the mediocre Mutuals of

New York thumped the Red Stockings 13–4 in mid-July, the *New York Clipper* declared, "It is very evident that they [Boston] will not be champions this season. Indeed, if they do not show an improvement, in September they will hardly reach a second place in the race."[36]

Philadelphia, still comfortably ahead of Boston in the standings, took its midseason break in the resort of Cape May, New Jersey. Like Boston a year earlier, Philadelphia was sluggish when it returned to the pennant race, dropping five consecutive games. Between the pitching of Spalding, who would lead the NA in 1873 with 41 wins, and the hitting of Barnes, who had a higher batting average (.425) and drove in more runs (66 in 60 games) than any other player that year, the Red Stockings overtook the Whites—winning 13 of the 14 games they played in September—and earned their second consecutive championship.

The Bostons also finally turned a profit, despite a nationwide economic panic over the collapse on September 18 of Jay Cooke and Co., a prominent US merchant bank. It had invested heavily in American railroads and was caught short when European banks, facing their own crises, tried to raise cash by dumping their railroad investments on the market and causing prices to crash. However, at its annual meeting on December 3 in Hampshire Hall, the Boston Baseball Club announced it made $4,245.63 on receipts of $27,832.38.[37]

The Wright brothers and the Rockford boys, Spalding and Barnes, were Boston's highest-paid players, at $1,800 each for an eight-month season. Not bad, since at the time, the average annual pay for working 10 hours a day, six days a week was about $735.[38]

Encouraged by the Red Stockings' performance on the field and at the ticket office, Harry Wright revived an idea he'd hatched during the Cincinnati Red Stockings' unbeaten year in 1869: organizing a tour much more ambitious than any baseball excursion to that point. Wright dreamed of leading a demonstration tour of England to plant the seeds of America's pastime in the land of his birth—it was an idea he had shelved when the Cincinnati Baseball Club quit professional ball and he moved his family to Boston.

Wright felt he couldn't organize the trip himself because his wife was due to deliver the sixth of their seven children in January and he wanted to spend more time with her, so he delegated the chore to Spalding—whose maturity, intelligence, and innate business sense impressed him. Wright already had sent a letter to Athletics president James M. Ferguson, inviting his club to play a series of exhibition games against the Red Stockings in England. "To accomplish this successfully," Wright wrote, "it is necessary that another club should accompany us, and we give your club the preference." Ferguson accepted.[39]

On January 17, 1874, Spalding sailed for Liverpool aboard the Cunard Line steamer *Olympus*. It was the 23-year-old's first trip abroad. His assignment was to secure playing venues, establish relationships with cricket clubs that would host the American tourists, and encourage coverage in the British newspapers. Along with baseball equipment and other necessities, Spalding also carried in his bags fulsome letters of introduction Harry Wright had solicited for him from officers of the St. George's Cricket Club in New York—all of them British expatriates like himself—as well as influential parties in Philadelphia and Boston.

The crossing, the first of many for Spalding, took 12 days. A week after arriving, he had set up base in London and sent the first in a series of naively optimistic letters to Wright and friendly American newspaper reporters, saying that "prominent cricketers were much pleased with the idea and all were sanguine of the success of the enterprise . . . the prospects [are] much better than were anticipated" and that leading sportsmen "have taken matters in hand to make the coming tour a brilliant success."[40]

As time passed, Spalding grew more confident that the tour would be a financial as well as a cultural triumph. The *Boston Post* reported that "letters from Mr. Spalding . . . give promise of the perfect success of the plan. . . . The financial success of the scheme appears to be certain." The *New York Clipper* added: "There is not the slightest doubt of its being a grand pecuniary success." In one letter, Spalding wrote that an exhibition tour featuring aboriginal Australian cricketers in 1868 had grossed £655, or $3,275, implying that white Americans would be an even bigger attraction.[41]

The young American's enthusiasm no doubt was stoked by his introduction to many respected men in English sport, including Charles W. Alcock, secretary of the Surrey County Cricket Club and cricket editor of the *London Sportsman*; John Graham Chambers, a founder of the Amateur Athletic Club; and Robert Allan Fitzgerald, secretary of Marylebone Cricket Club. Two years earlier, Fitzgerald had led such legendary players as W. G. Grace and Lord Harris on a cricket tour of North America. He always appreciated the hospitality Americans had shown him then and was eager to return it.

Midway through his month in England, Spalding persuaded Alcock to promote and organize the American baseball players' tour that summer. The plan was to showcase the skill and athleticism of American athletes by playing a series of baseball games between Boston, the defending National Association champion, and Athletic, the only other side to have won an NA title. For variety, Spalding agreed that, as time permitted, a side of 22 Americans would play 11 Englishmen at cricket.[42]

To pique local interest in America's national game, Spalding also talked Alcock into organizing an exhibition before he returned to Boston—the first baseball game played in England. It was scheduled for February 24 at The Oval, the Surrey club's home ground in the Kennington section of London. Spalding led one side, an ad hoc group of cricketers with only a passing knowledge of baseball, while Alcock headed the other side, which included seven amateur American players in England on other business, including Warren R. Briggs, a former member of the Boston Beacons junior club who was on a two-year architecture fellowship at the Ecole des Beaux-Arts in Paris.

Alcock proved to be a much craftier pitcher than Spalding had expected, and cricket players were much worse fielders than he had anticipated. "As usual, my side got badly whipped," Spalding wrote that evening in a letter to Wright. At the end of six innings, with Alcock's side ahead 17–5, the game was called on account of darkness. Four days later, back in Liverpool, Spalding and Briggs booked cabins on the Cunard Line steamship *Hecla* bound for Boston.[43]

* * *

After an unremarkable crossing, Spalding had ample time in Boston to prepare to lead the Red Stockings' defense of their back-to-back championships. An unseasonable spring snowstorm buried the Northeast and Midwest with snow in late April, forcing the Reds to postpone a season-opening series against the Philadelphia White Stockings and a game against the Hartford Dark Blues. They finally opened their season on May 2, easily topping the Mutuals of New York 12–3, and then reeled off 12 more consecutive victories to open a 6½-game lead over the rest of the field before the month ended.[44]

By July 16, when the Red Stockings and Athletics boarded the new American Line steamship *Ohio* in Philadelphia to begin their promotional tour of England, Boston had a record of 30 wins and eight losses (a winning percentage of .789) and a 4½-game lead over their fellow tourists, the Athletics. Spalding had started every game for Boston up to that point and took a decision in all but one, a 17–16 loss in 10 innings to the resurgent Chicago White Stockings before about 8,000 spectators in the Windy City.[45]

An immense crowd came to Philadelphia's waterfront on July 16 to see the ballplayers off. Police officers kept people off Christian Street Wharf, where *Ohio* was tied up, but the *Philadelphia Inquirer* said, "every available spot was occupied on the surrounding wharves and vessels." Men waved their hats and ladies their handkerchiefs at the 23 ballplayers prepared to sail to Liverpool. Joining the players were 40 investors in the two teams and a gaggle of sportswriters.[46]

As *Ohio*'s crew made ready to weigh anchor, the Boston Baseball Club's president, Nicholas Apollonio, asked his players to join him in the ladies' saloon for a private farewell address. He told them that Porter and Harry Wright must always be obeyed. He also sought to stifle a rumor that gamblers had arranged for the Athletics and Bostons to alternate winning and losing games on the tour. Displaying his measure as a leader of men, Apollonio reminded his players to always play to win.[47]

A gong at eleven o'clock signaled all guests aboard *Ohio* to go ashore. Then two tugboats, *Bruce* and *Commodore Foote*, accompanied *Ohio* as it pulled away from the wharf and down the Delaware River. A flotilla of small craft followed, one of them firing a cannon in salute, temporarily masking the sound of dozens of Champagne bottles popping open. Benjamin K. McClurg's Liberty Coronet Band played continuously on the ocean liner's deck until the ship reached Bombay Hook, where the river empties into Delaware Bay. There, the band, river pilot, and remaining guests transferred to the tugs and returned to Philadelphia.

In contrast to the big and boisterous crowd that saw the ship off, only two people—tourists waiting for a ship to America—were on the dock when *Ohio* arrived in Liverpool on July 27. "They landed quietly, and there was no demonstration in their honor," a newspaper noted the following day. Nevertheless, Harry Wright could not contain his enthusiasm at returning to the land of his birth and decided to transfer to a tug so he could get ashore quicker. As the tug approached land, he leapt onto the dock, but lost his footing and landed bottom-first, to the delight of his companions.[48]

A much bigger pratfall was just around the corner. When the Americans arrived at the Liverpool Cricket Ground on July 30 for their first baseball exhibition, Spalding realized that "the British public [were] thoroughly advised of the forthcoming cricket matches and only slightly informed about the exhibition ball games." Spalding's hand-picked scheduler, Alcock, either did not know enough about the sport to sell it to the public or he believed baseball was so much like the English children's game of rounders that he had little faith his fellow countrymen would take it seriously.[49]

H. S. Kempton, a Boston newspaperman traveling with the teams, was flabbergasted that none of the Liverpudlians he encountered in his travels around the bustling port knew anything about the tour or about the sport it was promoting. "There has been a complete failure to stir up public interest," Kempton wrote in a dispatch to the *Boston Herald*. "The thing has been very poorly advertised. . . . There has been no interest shown in our arrival, and it seems to me very few persons are aware that two American ball clubs are in town."[50]

London newspapers knew that Americans had landed, but showed great confusion about their objective. "It is understood that they will make cricket their specialty," said one paper in the capital, "but at each match they will give practical illustrations of baseball."[51]

The English press warmed up to baseball—and its relatively speedy games compared with never-ending cricket matches—once its sporting correspondents had the opportunity to watch the outstanding athletes Harry Wright had brought over. "Baseball proved to be a most attractive game, and the American players speedily showed themselves splendid athletes," according to a Manchester newspaper. "For something with which to compare baseball we are driven to cricket, and in some respects baseball seems an improvement on our national game. It is very much quicker in its action—two hours are enough to complete the 18 innings, which finish a game. Play never drags: the movements of every player are ceaseless, consequently it is to the spectator much more exciting than cricket." Another conceded that baseball was "more lively and more exciting than cricket."[52]

More exciting than cricket? That was saying something! But before the Yankee baseball promoters got too puffed up on their own publicity, a newspaper in Newcastle Upon Tyne, in the far north of England, deemed the Americans' visit worth no more than one paragraph on an inside page beneath an account of a soccer match between local men and a team of clowns from a passing circus.[53]

Regardless of what the English newspapers printed or declined to print about the Americans, disappointingly few ordinary Britons were interested enough to surrender a shilling to see what the Yanks were up to. Part of the problem was a general disinterest in the American game, and part was distaste for the cricket exhibitions staged for the visitors.

In a gentlemanly gesture, the English sides allowed their guests to put twice the usual number of men on the field when the hosts defended the wicket—that is, when they tried to strike the ball and score runs. Even when a batsman could reach one of the Wright brothers' wicked deliveries, the multitude of defenders gave the unfortunate striker little chance to make a run.

Unsurprisingly, the Americans won six of the seven cricket matches on their tour, tying the seventh when it was cut short by rain. Harry Wright equally disliked the cricket exhibitions because they distracted attention from baseball, the promotion of which was his primary goal, and because his American charges couldn't—or wouldn't—take cricket seriously. "Almost without exception the men hit out heavily at every ball, whether it be straight or crooked, pitched well or badly," a writer for the *Manchester Examiner* observed. "By this process a small average of runs is generally secured, and sometimes a really good ball which would have troubled a scientific batter like Grace is knocked clean out of the grounds. The fielding, as one might have expected, was wonderfully close and good, and with the advantage of eighteen men on the field it was (a) matter of the greatest difficulty to get the ball through the Americans."[54]

Being baseball players, Spalding and his teammates trained to swing at balls in the middle of the strike zone and ignore those out of the zone. Cricketers trained the opposite way. Their priority is to defend the wicket—deflecting balls in the middle of the pitch to prevent them from hitting the stumps and getting the batsman out. They swung more at balls bowled wide of the wicket, and thus unlikely to hit the stumps.

Wright tried to fix the problem, to no avail. Early in one match, he suspended play and jogged out to the pitch to advise Spalding on the proper batting form; when Wright finished, Spalding laughed out loud and continued hacking at every ball bowled his way. No wonder the paying public showed little interest in the tour—it was making a mockery of the national sport. Still, Spalding's graceless batting put him among the top scorers for the Americans and impressed some British cricket writers.[55]

"If Mr. Spalding would deign to polish his style and study the art of offence as well as that of hitting, he might at once take rank with some of our foremost English professionals," the *London Illustrated Sporting and Dramatic News* said.[56]

Amid all the cricket-playing, baseball-demonstrating, and sightseeing, the Athletics and Bostons managed to find time to play 14 games against each other, in Liverpool, Manchester, London, Sheffield, and Dublin. Boston won eight and

Athletic took six. In the end, baseball games to most English and Irish spectators "were objects of curiosity, but not a very intense interest," the *Boston Herald* concluded.[57]

After the last game of their tour, against an All-Ireland team in Dublin, the American ballplayers and their entourage took a train to Queenstown (now called Cobh), to board the American Line steamer *Abbotsford* to Philadelphia. They suffered remarkably rough seas for the first five full days. "Nearly every one of our party was most beautifully seasick," a passenger said. "Many that considered themselves proof against the malady on our voyage over (to Liverpool) had to succumb this time." The storm ended with a "fearful gale" lasting two hours, he added, "and I can tell you we were thoroughly frightened."

Another powerful storm pummeled the iron ship a week later as it approached the United States. "Terrible storm commenced at 4 A.M.," Boston outfielder Andy Leonard recorded in his diary. "Sea running over the deck and into the cabin. Boys sea sick and all hands scared. Storm lasted until 10 o'clock A.M." One passenger, a man returning to Pittsburgh, died during the storm and was buried at sea.[58]

On landing in Philadelphia, the high-stockinged sports ambassadors reverted to sports heroes, as the excitable and enthusiastic hordes that greeted them escorted the players to the elegant Colonnade Hotel for a reception.[59]

Even ardent boosters of the enterprise had to concede that "certainly there has been no money made on the trip," but some asserted that "the receipts proved nearly, if not quite sufficient, to meet the expense of the trip." They did not. By any financial measure, the trip was a failure, grossing $1,679.70 in gate receipts and accumulating $2,308.13 in expenses (each round-trip fare cost $100 in gold). The $647 loss was equivalent in value to $18,000 in 2024. A Brooklyn newspaperman minced no words. "I must say," he wrote, "the baseball players' trip to England proved a total failure, both pecuniary and otherwise."[60]

Harry Wright and his stockholders ignored all criticism, knowing that gate receipts from two farewell exhibition games played in Philadelphia before the tourists left, along with two welcome-home games when they returned, had raised $6,835.56—10 times the nominal loss on the English tour.[61]

The Red Stockings were more concerned about their poor play when they resumed their schedule of championship games. When they left for England in mid-July, the Bostons had a comfortable double-digit lead over the second-place Mutuals of New York. But while the Red Stockings were busying themselves in

Britain trying to sell baseball to cricketers, New York went on a tear, winning 12 of 13 games and pulling within five of Boston. Inconveniently, the Red Stockings dropped five of the first seven games after they returned to the United States. Heading into the final month of the season, Mutual was only one game behind Boston in the standings.

New York would not catch up. Spalding, who started every game, collected 18 wins and a tie in the 23 games Boston played in October. The Red Stockings finished the season 7½ games ahead of the Mutuals, winning their third consecutive championship.

Over the full season, Spalding won 52 games, lost 16, and tied one. (Harry Wright lost two games in relief.) Spalding's .765 winning percentage was 100 points ahead of the Association's next-best pitcher. He also once again had the best fielding percentage among NA pitchers. His offense provided plenty of run support: Boston had the five leading run-scorers in the Association (Spalding was in third place, scoring 80 runs in 71 games) and three of the five players with the most runs batted in (Spalding was fourth, with 54).[62]

Success on the field translated into success at the turnstile, at least for Boston. The Red Stockings grossed $19,005 in 1874 and, not counting the loss on the English tour or the revenue from the exhibitions, the club posted a profit of $813.33—no small feat with the nation's economy still reeling from the Panic of 1873. However, so *much* success—three championships in a four-year-old association, and few ideas about how to prevent Boston from adding a fourth pennant in 1875—was starting to translate into resentment, declining ticket sales, and rising financial losses among other clubs.[63]

"It was becoming monotonous," Spalding recalled in his history of the game. "The effect of such an uninterrupted succession of all-season victories was to destroy interest in the game. 'There's no use going.' 'Boston's sure to win.' . . . Such expressions were heard every day, and gate receipts were small. For myself, I felt that the time was ripe for change."[64]

Competition within the NA had deteriorated so much that cranks could almost hear sportswriters' sighs of despair as they wrote headlines like this, from the *Chicago Tribune* in June 1875:[65]

A Close and Exciting Game Between the
Whites and Bostons Yesterday
But the Boston Club, as Usual,
Gets the Winning Runs.

Chapter 5

A League of His Own

Spalding's concern about the corrosive effect that Boston's domination had on interest in the game did not keep him from pitching even better in his fifth year as a professional. The Red Stockings opened the 1875 season with 26 consecutive wins—10 of them credited to Spalding, who started every game in the pitcher's box. By the time Boston felt the sting of its first defeat of the year—a one-run loss to the St. Louis Brown Stockings on June 5—the NA was more than one-fourth of the way through its six-month season. Boston had built a 5½-game lead over the second-place Dark Blues of Hartford, Connecticut.

Baseball historian Robert Tiemann called Spalding "a master at keeping hitters off balance, either by quick-pitching or by holding the ball while the batter fidgeted. In addition, he was a good batsman, adept at opposite field hitting, and a savvy fielder who helped perfect the dropped-popup double play."[1]

Between uncompetitive teams and games tarnished by gamblers, drunkards, and rowdies, the Association's 1875 season was shaping up to be even worse than the previous year. Fewer and fewer people were willing to pay 50 cents to watch games by themselves, much less bring their families. Thirteen clubs paid the $10 membership fee required to compete for the NA pennant. Six of them—Atlantics of Brooklyn; Centennials of Philadelphia; Elm Citys of New Haven, Connecticut; Nationals of Washington, DC; Red Stockings of St. Louis; and Westerns of Keokuk, Iowa—were so out of their depth that they were out of contention before the end of May. Six others were unable to keep pace with Boston, which looked to be a sure bet to bring home its fourth consecutive Association championship.

Spectators who wanted to bet on the Red Stockings would be hard-pressed to do so on the club's home ground because it was among the few clubs to succeed in controlling vice. As its first president Ivers Adams liked to say, "We have not allowed the sale of intoxicating drinks on our grounds—and that other attendant evil, betting, has been strictly prohibited. These provisions, we believe, have assisted in drawing the better class of our people."[2] This was the management model the abstemious Spalding would use for the rest of his life.

However, the rot throughout the rest of the Association was too obvious to ignore. "The doings of certain slippery ball tossers lately have increased the unreliability of players to a very great extent," the *St. Louis Globe-Democrat* cautioned as the 1875 season approached, "and unless the boys and certain managers 'have a care,' they will run the professional baseball business so far into the ground that it cannot be pulled out."[3]

Spalding believed the National Association was "rotten" with gambling and tolerant of men in the grandstand openly selling shares in betting pools. Players could be seen betting on their own games. "The occasional throwing of games was practiced by some and no punishment meted out to the offenders," Spalding said.[4]

Two games in June 1875 illustrated the pool-sellers' influence: one between Chicago and the Philadelphia Pearls (which returned the White Stockings nickname to Chicago when it rejoined the NA after the Great Fire) and another between the Boston and the Athletics.

In the first game, "a parcel of bunko men, low gamblers, and general disreputables" raised a betting pool that would pay them between $300 and $500 if Philadelphia lost the game, the *Chicago Tribune* reported. They then found "a player occupying a responsible position in the Philadelphias' field" who promised to deliver that outcome. The *Tribune* noted that the crooked player "performed his share of the work to the best of his ability, making all the wild throws possible and muffing everything that came to him."[5]

When a Chicago player got wise to the fix, he demanded to share in the payout. He was rebuffed so he enlisted several teammates to foil the Athletics players' plan by making sure Philadelphia won; it did, 5–4, in 12 innings. Signs of questionable play were abundant: 11 players on the two teams reached base on errors; Chicago pitcher George Zettlein made 11 wild pitches; his battery mate, Scott Hastings, allowed six passed balls. Spectators leaving the grounds were heard to describe the game as "a base swindle on the public," but the NA took no action.[6]

Three days later, about 4,000 spectators came out on a hot and sultry Monday afternoon in Philadelphia to see the NA's best teams, the Athletics and the Red Stockings. The game was tied at 10–10 after nine innings; Boston scored two runs on five singles in the top of the 10th inning and might have brought home more if a spectator in standing room on foul ground had not interfered with a fair ball hit by Ross Barnes. When the spectator threw the ball toward the infield, Barnes stopped running, believing the ball was dead and the play had ended. However, an Athletics player tagged Barnes and the umpire called him out.

In their half of the inning, the Athletics got two men on base, but rang up two outs in doing so. The game was too close to suit the gamblers, who were known to bet $2,000 (about $58,000 in 2024 dollars) or more on games. Their best hope to avoid losing money seemed to be a fast-approaching rain squall; if it arrived in time, it would stop play, resulting in a 10–10 tie and voiding all bets.

The Athletics' next batter languidly strolled in the general direction of home plate, wasting time as the storm approached. The umpire ordered him to step into the batter's box, but the batter hesitated. Suddenly, bettors incited spectators in the grandstand to pour onto the field, easily overwhelming the seven police officers assigned to the game. Play stopped and the rain started. Even after the shower passed, the Athletics declined to resume play, saying the turf was too sodden. The umpire gave up and declared the game a tie.

The headline over the article in the *Boston Globe* the next day decried the "rowdyism" in Philadelphia and stated "the City of Brotherly Love [was] disgraced." The *Philadelphia Times* concurred, calling the rush on the field "a disgraceful ending to the game." It added that a disturbance was not surprising after the poor umpiring in Boston a week prior but noted that Philadelphians would have been wiser to maintain their decorum, "leaving to Boston all the dishonor." A game that *both* clubs tried to throw had plenty of dishonor for everyone involved.[7]

Such widely reported incidents demonstrated to Spalding and others in the professional game how the Association had failed to make any progress in excising gamblers' influence over the sport since a scorching *New York Times* editorial three years earlier had stated that professional baseball was not the national game but merely "an event for the benefit of the betting fraternity." It added that "the professional player, though doubtless occasionally an honest, inoffensive fellow, is usually a worthless, dissipated gladiator; not much above the professional pugilist in morality and respectability." Players "frequently" lose games on purpose, the editorial writer asserted. "It is only necessary for the gambler who has large sums at stake to buy (a player), in order to make certain of winning his bets."[8]

Alcohol was just as widespread and troublesome to owners and many players, including Spalding, who grew up amid Rockford's protracted political battle over prohibition and who, as an adult, abstained from both alcohol and tobacco. He recalled that where liquor was sold, "drunkenness and riot" were "an everyday occurrence, not only among spectators but now and then in the ranks of the players themselves. Many games had fist fights, and almost every team had its 'lushers.'"[9]

The effect of this licentiousness was exactly what he feared: diminished attendance by respectable bourgeoisie. As he noted, "a game . . . whose spectators consist for the most part of gamblers, rowdies, and their natural associates, could not possibly attract honest men or decent women."[10]

The National Association's inability or unwillingness to crack down on gambling, drinking, and rowdy behavior on the field and in the bleachers was as vexing to club presidents as its insouciance toward contract breaking and self-dealing.

Take the case of Davy Force, an infielder for the Baltimore Canaries. He was among 10 veterans that Chicago had wooed away from other Association clubs—seven from the Philadelphia Whites alone—to bring professional ball back to the Windy City as it recovered from the Great Fire. Force was known for "revolving," or jumping from team to team in pursuit of higher pay. To keep him in Chicago for more than one season, the White Stockings' club secretary, William Hulbert, in September 1874 had Force sign a contract committing him to play for Chicago in 1875. Hulbert soon heard that the renewal contract might not be valid because a new NA rule forbade teams to sign players for the next season before the end of the current season. In November, Hulbert again had Force sign a contract for 1875—but backdated the document to September, potentially voiding it. In December, Force signed yet another contract, this one committing him to play for the Athletic club of Philadelphia in 1875.

The question of which team Force would play for in 1875 was put before the Association's Judiciary Committee at the NA's annual meeting in March in Philadelphia, along with a fight over Jack Burdock, an infielder who had signed contracts with both Chicago and Hartford. The committee ruled that Force's pact with Chicago was valid and Murdock's pact with Chicago was not. But that was not the final word, even though the Association's constitution said the committee's decision was not subject to appeal. NA president Charles Spering, who also just happened to be president of the Philadelphia Athletics, criticized the committee's ruling on Force and told the group to reconsider the question on the following day.

The delay allowed newly elected Judiciary Committee members to essentially pack the court. One new member, William Trimble of the new Westerns ball club in Keokuk, Iowa, resigned immediately, saying the travel required of committee members would hurt his saloon-keeping business. Spering shamelessly chose himself to succeed Trimble on the committee, giving Philadelphians—Spering, George Concannon of the Whites, and Elias "Hicks" Hayhurst of the Centennials—a majority on the five-person committee. They promptly decided Force belonged to the Athletics.[11]

Spering won that battle but unwittingly started a war he would soon lose. Hulbert was livid that Spering named himself to the Judiciary Committee so that he could hand Force over to an eastern team. The action affirmed the Chicagoan's conviction that his cherished city was the victim of chicanery by the eastern establishment in Philadelphia and New York.

Hulbert had an unlikely ally in the Red Stockings manager Harry Wright, whose dominating East Coast club was packed with western players. Wright was irate over the Association leadership's habit of ignoring rules that hurt their bottom lines and selectively enforcing rules that afflicted competitors.

"How long will the Association exist if the clubs violate its laws with impunity when they conflict with their special interests?" Wright wrote in a letter to the *New York Clipper*, an entertainment-industry weekly that covered baseball. "What is the use of an Association if the clubs refuse to abide by or be governed by their own constitution, bylaws and code of rules?"[12]

If the eastern clubs unilaterally decided that they did not have to abide by NA rules, Hulbert decided that western teams didn't, either. So, when the Red Stockings traveled to Chicago for three games in the second week in June, Hulbert arranged to discreetly—and, strictly speaking, illicitly—meet Spalding to gauge his interest in returning to Illinois to pitch for the White Stockings.[13]

Hulbert had limited knowledge of the sport, which he had never played, but he knew a lot about raising money and running a business, and that stuck with the ambitious young pitcher, who said he was "greatly impressed by the personality of Mr. Hulbert at our first meeting, in Chicago, early in 1875. He seemed strong, forceful, self-reliant. I admired his businesslike way of considering things."[14]

Hulbert ended his talk by appealing to whatever regional allegiance the pitcher still possessed. "Spalding, you have no business playing in Boston," he said. "You're a Western boy; you belong right here. If you come to Chicago, I will accept the presidency of this club, and we'll give those (Eastern) fellows a fight for their lives."[15]

Spalding was clearly interested but noncommittal. He asked for time to consider the proposal and, in his usual modest manner, let Hulbert know that if he did come he would bring "a team of pennant winners."[16]

Hulbert didn't know one fact unrelated to baseball that meant Spalding might not want to move to Chicago right then: a young schoolteacher who lived in her family's manse in Brockton, Massachusetts, a short train ride south of Boston.

Her name was Sarah Josephine Keith—but she preferred to be called Josie—and Spalding was wooing her. Improbably, the couple had met not in Massachusetts but in Illinois. She had trekked 950 miles to Rockford the previous December for the wedding of her beloved brother, Charles H. Keith, and Emma F. Woodruff, the daughter of a Rockford banker and industrialist.[17]

For the next few weeks, Spalding spent his off hours talking with Josie about their future and studying the White Stockings roster. When Chicago city leaders decided to field a new professional team for the 1874 season to show that the city had recovered from the Great Fire, they did so by signing seven players from the Philadelphia Whites, which finished in second place in 1873. The following year, playing for Chicago, they finished in fifth place with a losing record. When Hulbert approached Spalding in June, Chicago was already 10 games behind the blistering Bostons, in fourth place and falling fast.

Spalding concluded that he would keep only three White Stocking men if he took his talents to Chicago: first baseman John Glenn, outfielder Paul Hines, and shortstop John Peters. He'd have to head east to fill out his roster. He began by recruiting Boston's best players, and when Boston went to Philadelphia for two games with the Athletics in late June, he met with infielder Adrian Anson, who would manage Chicago for many years later in his Hall of Fame career, and Ezra Sutton, a fearless third baseman and solid hitter.

At a White Stockings' board meeting on July 3, 1875, Hulbert read aloud a letter from Spalding. The Boston pitcher wanted to know if Chicago intended to hire a new manager, and then brashly recommended himself for the job. The problem was that Chicago already had a manager, Jimmy Wood, a popular ex–White Stocking infielder who was still recovering from having a badly infected leg amputated. But Chicago boosters ached for a winning club and Spalding's letter arrived as the White Stockings dropped to fifth place, 15 games behind Boston. The board instructed Hulbert to hustle back east to pursue Spalding as a pitcher and persuade him to use his exalted status among his peers to engage any other players that he and Spalding desired.[18]

Hulbert made sure the train he took to Boston arrived in the evening, when someone in the baseball fraternity was less likely to recognize him, and once in town he hurried directly to his hotel, where Spalding awaited him. Hulbert had, as a courtesy, told Red Stockings officials that he would be in Boston and agreed to see them; he wanted to spend as little time in the Hub as necessary, lest a newspaper start speculating as to the real purpose of his visit. Safely in the hotel, Hulbert and Spalding stayed up most of the night in what Hulbert later characterized as "a long and full conference" negotiating Spalding's salary, duties, and authority. Hulbert offered Spalding a salary of $2,000 and 25 percent of Chicago Ball Club's profit in 1876. (A side contract, which Spalding agreed to keep secret, promised the 24-year-old 30 percent of the net profit in 1876.) Spalding also received a $1,000 bonus for persuading the heart of Boston's roster to follow him to Chicago. A team ledger shows that Spalding and Barnes each owned 30 shares in the White Sox; William H. Murray, a grain trader like Hulbert, owned 50 and Hulbert held 22. The club issued 200 shares when it reincorporated after the Great Fire.[19]

Michael Haupert, a baseball historian and professor of economics at the University of Wisconsin–La Crosse, estimates that, in total, Spalding was paid $6,902.86 in 1876, equivalent in value to more than $200,000 in 2024. Thirty years would pass before any other ballplayer earned more money for a single season of work.[20]

Hulbert also agreed to jettison Jimmy Wood as Chicago's manager to make room for Spalding and then added a remarkable clause that "Spalding was to have charge of and conduct in his own person, all the detail business of the (Chicago Baseball) Association." The full board of directors collectively could overrule Spalding, but individual directors could not.[21]

With his own affairs settled, Spalding brought each of the other Boston players he had recruited for Chicago into Hulbert's hotel room to discuss their salary offers and to sign contracts. Barnes, a slugging second baseman whom Spalding had known since they were boys in Rockford, agreed to a $2,000 salary and 25 percent of the Chicago Baseball Association's net profit in '76. Calvin A. McVey, a power-hitting first baseman, also received $2,000 in salary, with a guarantee of two years. James "Deacon" White, a Hall of Fame catcher, accepted $2,400 in salary and the promise of a $100 bonus "provided club proves financial success."[22]

Their work in Boston finished, Hulbert and Spalding boarded a train to Philadelphia to sign Anson and Sutton. The timing of the trip was important because the White Stockings were in Boston for three games, giving Hulbert a credible excuse to be in the Hub if anyone asked. However, if Spalding missed a train and was unexpectedly absent from a game, newspapermen and Red Stocking executives would ask questions that neither Spalding nor Hulbert wanted to answer, for now.

With Hulbert in charge, meetings with the players in Philadelphia were businesslike and quick. Anson agreed to $2,000, with $50 in cash immediately and another $150 when he signed in Chicago. Ezra Sutton also agreed to a $2,000 salary, with $50 paid in cash up front and $350 a month over the winter.[23]

Spalding boarded a train up to Boston to rejoin the Red Stockings while Hulbert, with a fortune in signed contracts secured in his coat pocket, headed back to Chicago to inform his board of the success of his coup. They convened at Dexters Old Store on 22nd Street on the evening of July 16. As soon as Hulbert finished laying out how much in salaries he had promised each player—and informed the directors that he also re-signed rookie shortstop John Peters—the board agreed to everything without a debate.

The next day, the Boston club's treasurer, Frederick E. Long, mailed a letter to Hulbert expressing disappointment at missing an opportunity to meet because of the Chicago executive's "hasty departure" from Boston.[24] In Hulbert's rush to hire away the heart of Boston's roster, he apparently forgot that he had arranged to meet with Boston's leaders.

Had that missed meeting tipped off Boston executives that Hulbert was up to something? The White Stockings thought secrecy was essential to their caper. If news of its raid on Boston's roster was made public before the end of the season in November, Hulbert and Spalding worried that the Association would void the contracts, suspend the players, and kick Chicago out of the NA. However, the secret did not last through the final four months of the season; it was out in less than four days.

On July 20, the *Chicago Tribune* correctly reported that Spalding, McVey, and White had decided to leave Boston and play for the White Stockings next year. The newspaper bragged that "they have formed a nine which ought, in all reason, to carry off the championship of 1876." The same article incorrectly stated the Boston club would dissolve and the Wright brothers would return to Cincinnati to resurrect a professional side there.[25]

Harry Wright did not need a newspaper to learn that Spalding, Barnes, McVey, and White intended to move en masse to Chicago. He first heard about the defections while chatting with one of them over lunch before an exhibition in Taunton, Massachusetts, 30 miles south of Boston. McVey let slip that he was not going to play for Boston in 1876. Wright thought McVey was joking, but soon learned that he was not. After finishing his meal, he walked over to catcher Deacon White to ask if the rumors were true. White then told Wright that McVey was not the only one heading west to Chicago—so were he, Barnes, and Spalding.

Despite the *Tribune*'s article the previous day, Boston club executives were completely taken aback. "To say that Boston managers were surprised at the news of the split in their nine is to give but a slight idea of their feeling," the *Tribune* gloated a few days later. "They were stunned."[26] Hulbert did a little gloating of his own, writing to a brother in San Francisco to gleefully tell him he had signed contracts with Spalding, Barnes, McVey, White, Sutton, and Anson to play for the White Stockings the following year.[27]

Boston newspapers were chary about repeating the *Tribune*'s report on the mass defection, limiting their initial stories to one paragraph. In one, the day after the *Tribune* broke the story, the *Boston Globe* bitterly characterized the departing players as "seceders"—still an epithet with punch a decade after the Civil War ended—and snarkily said Chicago was willing to pay any price for Boston's best players because it "has become tired of running clubs at great expense, only to be beaten by the Bostons."[28]

The Hub's wrath was only beginning to boil. When Spalding arrived at the South End Grounds for a game with the St. Louis Browns in the third week of July, his old friend Barnes walked over to him. "You'll get a chilly reception when you go out on the field today," he said.

"What's the matter now?" Spalding replied.

"Why, don't you know? Haven't you seen the morning papers?"

Spalding hadn't. He had been visiting Josie in suburban Brockton.

"The secret is out," Barnes said, "and there's hell to pay."[29]

Barnes added that a lot of people in Boston thought the news was a joke circulated by him, McVey, and White; the players were happy not to disabuse them of that idea and risk the wrath of team supporters.

Spalding, however, publicly conceded it was all true, saying he figured Boston cranks would assume he organized it all anyway. He then dashed off a telegram to Hulbert: "Everything known and confirmed here."[30]

As Spalding expected, Boston's vociferous assault assumed he was the architect of the plan and thus least likely to change fans' minds, so they heaped the least abuse on him. Barnes, McVey, and White were continually "cajoled, coaxed, offered all kinds of money, and finally browbeaten and insulted," but they refused to capitulate.

Under a similar onslaught of intense intimidation, Anson and Sutton soon regretted agreeing to leave Philadelphia. Sutton said he would remain in Philadelphia, Chicago's contract be damned. Anson wrote a letter to Hulbert pleading to be released from his contract so that he, too, could remain in Philadelphia. He said that his future wife had been born and raised there and did not want him to spend most of the year away from home.

Hulbert was so confident in the White Stockings' all-star lineup that just days after the Chicago club's president George W. Gage died in late September, the blunt grain trader asked Gage's widow to give him the voting proxy for her shares in the club. She agreed to do so, giving Hulbert a majority of shares and allowing him to promptly elect himself president on October 10. As president, he installed Spalding as club secretary. But his confidence in certainty that he could assemble his dream team was fading by the time he showed Spalding Anson's letter. He lamented that Chicago would lose Anson and Sutton, both. Spalding advised him to ignore Anson's letter and refuse to let him out of his contract under any circumstances.

"Oh, what's the use?" Hulbert said, according to Spalding's recollection decades later. "He'll break his contract. We've lost Sutton; we'll lose Anson."

Sutton was a lost cause, Spalding conceded, "but we haven't lost Anson."[31]

Spalding had known Anson since discovering the future Hall of Famer at an 1868 exhibition game in Marshalltown, Iowa, Anson's hometown. Spalding was certain that Anson would never go back on his word. (Anson was less certain of Spalding's principles. Forest City beat Marshalltown 18–3 in that exhibition, and Rockford players said the margin of victory was dishonorably small and requested a reprise on the next day. Rockford won that game by a more satisfying score of 35–5, but Anson said it was because Spalding used a disguised, tightly wound "live" ball for the softer "dead" ball Marshalltown had provided. Live balls were harder, which made them travel farther when hit and were favored by offense-oriented clubs. Dead balls, being softer, did not travel as far or as fast when struck and were preferred by defense-oriented teams.)[32]

Throughout the offseason, Anson repeatedly declared that he would not play for Chicago in 1876; Spalding kept reassuring Hulbert it was a bluff. The following spring, with Opening Day approaching, Anson took a train to Chicago determined to gain his release from Chicago. He offered to pay $1,000 to void his contract; Hulbert was astonished but had the presence of mind to decline. Anson approached Spalding, perhaps hoping for a more sympathetic ear. He said Philadelphia was offering him $2,500 a year—more than he ever thought he would earn.

"I can't afford to lose the money," Anson moaned.

"You can't afford to break your contract," Spalding responded coolly.

Anson turned up the next morning at the White Stockings practice field, wearing well-tailored trousers, a vest, and an expensive double-breasted frock coat. After watching for a few minutes, he picked up a bat and asked Spalding for one of his famous fast pitches.

"What? With those togs on?" the pitcher said. "Take off your hat and coat and get into the game."

Anson paced and thought for a while, then removed his coat and picked up a bat. "Now, Anse, come tomorrow in uniform," Spalding said. Anson did as he was told, and he stayed with the Chicago club for 21 years as player, captain, and manager.[33]

* * *

The Association forbade players under contract to one club to sign up to play for a different club in the following season. Team leaders reckoned that players would not try their hardest for teams they planned to leave. Spalding and his teammates were determined to put the lie to that assumption. "Now, it is just as natural for a ball player to play his best to win as it is for a duck to swim," he wrote. "They don't know any other way to play the game. The 'Big Four' and their associates on the Boston team of 1875 were determined to show the fallacy of the idea that good players ever lose interest in baseball."

The Red Stockings—Spalding in particular—emphatically demonstrated their commitment to continue to do their best for Boston as long as they wore Red Stocking uniforms. They won 71 of the 79 games they played in 1875, for a winning percentage of .899 and a 15-game lead over the second-place Athletics. Along the way they racked up winning streaks of 26, 15, 13, and eight games.

Spalding won an astonishing 54 games that season while losing only five, for an eye-popping winning percentage of .915; his earned-run average for the year was a minuscule 1.59. He also contributed on offense, compiling a .312 batting average and driving in 56 runs.

"As a pitcher—one whose play in the position is marked not only by rare skill but by sound judgment and intelligence—he [Spalding] has had no superior this season," the *New York Clipper* said after the season, echoing the fulsome praise sportswriters and spectators alike heaped on Boston's pitcher after the season ended.[34]

Nonetheless, the White Stockings—individually or as a team—faced the possibility that the National Association could ban them when it convened its annual meeting in March 1876. Whether he would be banned or not, Spalding knew he was leaving Boston, so on his way out west, he paused in Brockton to marry Josie Keith in her family's house on a cold, overcast Friday, November 19. The Rev. Leverett S. Woodworth, pastor of the South Congregational Church of Campello and reportedly a fair ballplayer himself, performed the ceremony.[35]

After spending a couple of days in Brockton, the newlyweds headed out for Spalding's hometown, stopping on the way in New York, Philadelphia, and Cincinnati.[36] They arrived in Rockford on December 1 and were guests in the home of Al's sister Mary and her husband William T. Brown. A week later, the new couple took a train back to Chicago where they would temporarily move in with Hulbert's family. The men had much work to do if they were to devise a strategy for not being blackballed from baseball.[37]

To discourage any more of his prized new ballplayers from reneging on their contracts with Chicago, Hulbert pledged to pay a full years' salary to any player the Association banished for signing with the White Stockings during the 1875 season. He was confident he would never have to make good on that promise.

"Why, they *can't* expel you," he assured Spalding. "They would not dare do it, for in the eyes of the public you six players are stronger than the whole Association." The already shaky NA could not afford to banish its best talent and risk serving up what every schoolboy would recognize as a second-rate entertainment. The men could not explain to themselves or each other why they felt intimidated by an institution as feeble as the Association.

After a pause, Hulbert stood and looked to his collaborator and blurted: "Spalding, I have a new scheme! Let's anticipate those Eastern cusses and organize a new association before the March meeting—then see who will do the expelling." Spalding need not worry about being kicked out of professional ball; Hulbert would build Spalding a league of his own.[38]

Albert and Josie Spalding remained house guests of William and Jennie Hulbert while the two men spent their days drafting a constitution for their new professional organization. "We worked out the new league constitution section by section," Spalding said, "having in mind only one thing—to raise the standard of the game in every possible way, and without much regard to the then existing customs and methods of operating professional clubs. Pool selling and all forms of gambling were prohibited, liquor selling on the grounds was abolished and contract jumping penalized."[39]

The document's fundamental tenet was that their organization would be a league of *clubs*—that is, businesses—and not an association of *players*, like the NA. To stress the difference, Hulbert proposed naming their new organization the National League of Professional Baseball Clubs—an enterprise that is still going 150 years after its birth. Businessmen would own and run the clubs. Players would focus only on playing the game.

In working on the document, Hulbert and Spalding adopted a similar division of labor, with the grain trader taking the lead on business issues while the ballplayer concentrated on rules, scheduling, and other sporting matters. Together, they added language clearly stating that drinking and gambling would not be allowed on the grounds of any League member.[40]

The constitution also proposed raising the application fee to $100 from $10, giving clubs exclusive rights to cities, and requiring League cities to have no fewer than 100,000 people. These changes were intended to weed out small-city clubs that in the past had joined the NA in the hope that home games with big-city teams would boost gate receipts—of which, as the host team, they would receive two-thirds. The scheme made it impossible for visiting teams to cover their expenses much less pay salaries or make a profit.

All these ideas had been proposed in a *Chicago Tribune* article published on October 24, 1875. The author was not identified, but most likely was Lewis Meacham, a *Tribune* staff writer friendly with Hulbert. The article was a useful test balloon, letting the White Stockings president see what other professional organizations thought of his ideas for putting professional baseball on a more businesslike footing. Based on the article's largely favorable reception, Hulbert and Spalding moved forward.[41]

When the men were satisfied with their draft constitution, they sent it to C. Orrick Bishop, a St. Louis lawyer and vice president of that city's Brown Stockings club, to polish the language and make the document as legally bulletproof as he could. Spalding, meanwhile, composed letters to the leaders of three western clubs inviting them to meet at the Louisville Hotel—Kentucky's finest—on December 16. The object: to discuss reforming the professional game. The guest list included Charles A. Fowle, club secretary of the St. Louis Brown Stockings, which finished fourth in the Association in 1875, 26½ games behind Boston; John P. Joyce, club secretary for the Cincinnati Red Stockings of 1869-70, who was reviving professional ball in that city; and Charles E. Chase—ironically, secretary of his family's whiskey distillery, E. H. Chase & Co.—who, aided by Hulbert's counsel, founded the Louisville Grays club.[42]

Hulbert and Spalding invited only Westerners to this initial gathering, thinking they would be more amenable than Easterners to reorganizing the sport by, among other things, giving equal authority to all member clubs. And indeed, the western clubs enthusiastically embraced Spalding and Hulbert's proposal.[43]

Having lived through the debacle of the Association's last season, during which only seven of the 13 clubs had the financial wherewithal to play at least half of their scheduled games, Hulbert decided to limit the number of National League teams to eight—four from the West and four from the East. Boston was an obvious choice, having won four straight NA championships; less obvious was Hartford, Connecticut, which fielded a fine team and finished in second place in 1875 but had only about 40,000 residents, well short of the 75,000 minimum Hulbert and Spalding had put in the League's constitution. Hulbert also invited the Mutuals of Brooklyn and Athletics of Philadelphia; the business benefits of having teams from the most populous metropolitan areas outweighed suspicions that both lineups were in the thrall of gamblers.

On January 23, 1876, Hulbert and Fowle sent a letter to each of the four eastern teams Hulbert was stalking, saying they desired to "confer with you on matters of interest to the game at large, with special reference to the reformation of existing abuses, and the formation of a new association."

The meeting would take place in New York City at noon on Wednesday, February 2, at the Grand Central Hotel on Broadway, an immense, ornate pile in the style of the French Second Empire.[44] Before the gathering, Hulbert met independently with the representatives of each of the four eastern clubs that he and Spalding wanted in their new league: G. W. Thompson of the Athletics, accompanied by two of his club's directors; Nicholas T. Apollonio of Boston, a former bookkeeper, who was joined by Harry Wright; William H. Cammeyer of the Mutuals, the scion of a family-owned shoemaking company; and Morgan G. Bulkeley of Hartford, a banker who would be elected to the US Senate from Connecticut in 1904.

If any notes were taken of the individual meetings, they have long since disappeared. Most likely Hulbert would have wanted to present a recitation of the NA's flaws and then outline his proposed reforms. He also would have wanted to hear objections out of earshot of other representatives so he would have time to form a rebuttal.[45]

Owners were unlikely to object to two features of the Hulbert-Spalding plan: territorial monopolies (one club per city) and a maximum of eight clubs. National League teams would not be expected to undertake expensive travel to remote burgs like Keokuk, Iowa, or Fort Wayne, Indiana, where they could play for a share of gate receipts amounting to only $50 or $60. Spalding had no remorse about the decision to "root out the small fry," despite his long affiliation with the Forest City club of Rockford.

"Unless this was done, at least twenty clubs from different cities are about to apply for admission to contest for the (1876) championship," he told a newspaper reporter. "Clubs that have no earthly chance to win will not be allowed to play."[46]

Harry Wright may have been the only man in New York beside Hulbert and Fowle who grasped how radically different Hulbert's "new association" would be. Wright had been corresponding with Hulbert and Spalding for months on how to fix professional ball's seemingly intractable problems: the lack of competitiveness, abundance of gambling, excessive drinking and brawling, meager to no team profits, and relentless team-shifting by players in search of higher pay.[47]

After some opening remarks about how gambling was threatening the very life of the game, repelling spectators and demoralizing players, Hulbert spoke of the "reprehensible work" of revolving, or inducing players to violate their legal contracts. He said the National Association was either unwilling or unable to extinguish these existential problems and, thus, the NA must make room for a new organization. He then revealed the constitution and bylaws he and Spalding had prepared for just such a new organization; they even had a name for it: "The National League of Professional Baseball Clubs."

On the spot, every team resigned from the National Association of Professional Baseball Players and joined the National League of Professional Baseball Clubs. The date of that meeting in the long-forgotten Grand Central Hotel, February 2, 1876, is accepted as the founding date for the organization, called the National League for short.

Where was Spalding on this momentous day? Arguably, he was as much the father of the League as Hulbert. In a sense, the League was created *for* him and the other seceders, to blackball the NA before it could blackball them. His performance on the field and intelligence off it provided the National League with baseball credibility lacked by Hulbert, who had never played the sport or managed a club.

Spalding, it turns out, was in Illinois, tending to some pressing business: the next stage in his life.

Chapter 6

A Baseball Emporium

Chicago was unusually cold on March 1, 1876, and its residents had to cope with an "exasperating, curse-provoking" early morning deposit of snow. "There was not much of this snow when measured by inches," the *Chicago Tribune* observed, "but a genteel sufficiency when estimated by its results." People planning to go outdoors would do so knowing the temperature was forecast to remain below freezing all day.[1]

It was not an auspicious day to start a business.

Al and Walter Spalding had little choice but to launch their "base ball emporium" on that frigid Wednesday. While he was only 25, Spalding had pitched 2,357 innings in the previous five seasons and instinctively knew that his already aching arm had a limited number of tosses left in it. Also, he could neither pitch nor hit the curved pitches that younger ball-tossers were using to baffle batters throughout the League.

"I knew I was slipping before anybody else did, and that it was time for me to retire," Spalding told his son Keith many years later. He added that his reactions were slowing, which was potentially dangerous since the pitcher's box was only 45 feet from home plate at the time. "When a batter hit a ball in my direction," he told his son, "I noticed that I had to move around to locate it, instead of just sticking out my hand and catching it."[2]

To make the most of Al's celebrity to attract business, the brothers were determined to open their store before the 1876 season, which would turn out to be Al's last in the pitcher's box. That meant they had to locate, lease, stock, and open their store before Al reported for preseason training with the White Stockings on March 15. They hurriedly composed and signed a partnership agreement at their mother's house in Rockford on February 3, the day after club owners meeting in New York had voted to quit the National Association and found a body called the National League. In the Spaldings' partnership pact, each brother pledged $400 in capital; their mother served as witness.

(Many historians have written that the brothers' mother provided $800 to start the business, but between Albert's gigantic contract and his brother's banker-salary savings it seems unlikely they would need to ask their 55-year-old widowed mother for capital. Walter's son Albert, an internationally known violinist and composer, wrote in his autobiography that his father and uncle each invested $400 and his grandmother, Harriet, only witnessed the signing of the partnership agreement. Spalding biographer Arthur Bartlett concurs.)[3]

The brothers composed a handwritten "Articles of Copartnership" that divided the responsibilities for running the company in a way that perfectly suited each brothers' strengths and personalities. Walter, still in his teens but already a bookkeeper at the Winnebago National Bank in Rockford, agreed to "give all of his time and attention to the business" while Al played ball and heaped glory on the Spalding brand name. In offseasons, Albert agreed "to devote so much of his time as may be requisite in advising, overseeing and directing the said business."[4] For years afterward, A. G. Spalding & Bros. offices around the world displayed framed copies of the document, testimony to the company's modest beginnings.

"The brothers complemented each other admirably," Walter's son wrote. "A. G. was resourceful and imaginative. J. W. was sober and balanced. A. G. inspired enthusiasm. J. W. won confidence."[5]

With the partnership pact in their pocket, Al and Walter boarded a train to Chicago, where they settled into temporary accommodation at the Clifton House hotel on Wabash Avenue at Monroe Street. Long-term lodgings would have to wait until the store was up and running.

Back in Rockford, Harriet once again had to fend off doom-mongering relatives and friends who said Walter was reckless to leave a reliable, well-paying position as a bookkeeper at the Winnebago County National Bank to accompany Albert to Chicago and manage a store that sells . . . *baseballs*? "When there was talk of establishing a business in Chicago and it was suggested Walter should leave the bank, all our relatives and friends in Rockford objected most strongly," she wrote later. "The idea of leaving the bank to go into an unknown—to leave a certainty for an uncertainty—was thought most unwise."[6]

The concern was not baseless. The country was in the worst economic depression it had experienced to that time. In September 1873, Jay Cooke & Co. had closed its doors after losing a fortune speculating on railroads. The New York bank, which made its reputation and saved the Union by selling US Treasury bonds to finance the federal government in the Civil War, now could not meet its obligations—including returning its clients' deposits. [7]

Hundreds of other overextended banks toppled as panicked savers tried to withdraw their money. Credit evaporated. Estimates of the total number of businesses that failed in the two years after Cooke & Co. collapsed range from 13,000 to 18,000. Gross national product, then the primary measure of total economic output, fell for an unprecedented 65 consecutive months; at its nadir, GNP was one-third below its pre-panic level. By 1876, the national unemployment rate had spiked to 14 percent.[8]

Undeterred, the Spaldings established their enterprise at 181 Randolph Street, conveniently just around the corner from the Chicago Base Ball Club's office on LaSalle Street, and opened their doors on the first day of March. The Spaldings' storefront was 20 feet wide and 60 feet deep—not very big, but they did not yet need a big space. The business had only three employees: the two partners and an office boy, although their sister, Mary, helped to keep the store's books. "The capital (investment) was small and the beginning necessarily a modest one," the company history noted. Modest indeed. Walter later said sales on the first day totaled $1.50.[9]

Foot traffic into the store soared a few days later, when White Stockings' season tickets went on sale only at the Spaldings' shop and the 23rd Street Grounds. The line of people eager to pay $15 for admission to all 35 scheduled home games snaked out of the store and along Randolph Street because there wasn't enough room for everyone inside the store.[10]

* * *

A. G. Spalding & Bro. was not the first business to sell bats and balls in Chicago, but competitors like Schweitzer & Beer and Vergho, Ruhling & Co. were primarily toy companies and thus unlikely to compete for the professional, semiprofessional, and serious amateur customers the Spaldings had in mind.[11]

Competition from East Coast retailers was another matter. A Canadian outdoorsman named James F. Marsters began selling fishing tackle and other sporting paraphernalia from a Brooklyn storefront in 1857. Long before the

Spaldings' opened their first store, Marsters published a "catalogue of all kinds of fine sporting goods," including baseballs, bats, and uniforms, and accepted mail orders from across the country. Businessmen Andrew Peck and W. Irving Snyder founded Peck & Snyder Base Ball and Sportsman's Emporium in New York City in 1866; they, too, started a catalogue to create a national presence. An even more powerful competitor appeared in 1874, when Alfred J. Reach, the London-born second baseman for the Philadelphia Athletics, founded A. J. Reach & Co. shortly before retiring as a player; it quickly became the nation's biggest sporting goods retailer. Many other small firms or individuals entered the field, often by focusing on some specialty like hand-stitching balls, turning bats, or crafting other individual items.[12]

Spalding's interest in sporting goods as a career was kindled after the impressionable young man from Rockford arrived in Boston to play ball for the Red Stockings. The club's leaders, brothers George and Harry Wright, had separately sold handmade balls and bats to local amateur sides organizing in Massachusetts at the time. George, a future Hall of Fame inductee, teamed up with first baseman Charlie Gould to sell baseball equipment out of Wright's cigar store on Boylston Street. While Wright would not thrive as a retailer until he partnered with businessman Henry A. Ditson five years later, Spalding quickly saw in Wright's business the wealth-creating potential of making and selling sporting goods.[13]

Before the Spaldings moved to Chicago, a mentor in Rockford, possibly Waldo, convinced A. G. of the importance of establishing his name as a brand, a personal guarantee of the unwavering quality of the goods he sold. Putting his name out front also was a way to have customers project his success as an athlete onto the performance of his business.[14]

For A. G., however, it was not enough to let the quality of his products speak for itself. He often claimed that any ball, bat, boxing glove, tennis racquet, golf club, or other merchandise bearing the Spalding name and trademark was of the highest quality possible. Spalding said its tennis racquets, for example, were "made just as well as it is possible to manufacture a tennis racket" and its Official League baseball "cannot be further improved upon." Every year, however, A. G. Spalding & Bro. published a new guide featuring improved versions of goods it had previously claimed to be unimprovable.[15]

On the field, Spalding did let his talent—as a showman and ballplayer—speak for itself. On Opening Day of 1876, he and his teammates took the field in

Louisville, Kentucky, in uniforms by A. G. Spalding & Bro. Their distinctive feature was fez-like brimless caps in different colors for each player. A. G. thought they would help spectators tell one player from another in the era before jerseys were embellished with numbers or names. Sportswriters were divided over the innovation. Some compared the players in caps to "a bevy of horse jockeys" and "a Dutch bed of tulips." Others were supportive. "Much comment was heard on the parti-colored caps but it was generally favorable and the utility of the idea was acknowledged," the *Chicago Tribune* reported, while the Louisville *Courier-Journal* opined that "those individual colors of the Chicagos are just the thing; they should have been adopted long ago."[16]

Spalding made a more substantive impression that day on the field by throwing the National League's first-ever shutout, blanking the Louisville Grays 4 runs to 0. "The credit of the victory belongs to Spalding more than to anyone else, and it is safe to say that better pitching was hardly ever seen," the *Chicago Tribune* reported.[17]

Two days later, in the teams' second game, he shut out Louisville again, this time with additional support from Chicago's potent hitters, who lit up the Grays' error-prone defense for 10 runs.[18]

On May 10, in the White Stockings' first home game as a National League club, Spalding again held the other team scoreless in a 6–0 win. Admittedly, the opponent was a dreadful Cincinnati club, which would end the year 42.5 games behind Chicago in the standings. Still, it was Spalding's third shutout in the White Stockings' first seven games of the season, and he held Cincinnati to three hits despite Chicago's decision to play with a lively ball. Spalding also contributed to his club's offense, launching a double to deep center field and later driving in a run on a deep fly to right.

Spalding reaped more publicity for his business in late May, when the White Stockings traveled to New England for the first game between Boston and Chicago since the "seceders" ripped out the heart of the Red Caps' roster. (Boston had chivalrously returned the Red Stockings nickname to Cincinnati when the Ohio club chose to field a professional nine in the National League.)

The return of the Big Four drew 10,000 to 14,000 spectators to Boston's South End Grounds, according to contemporary estimates; whatever the real number was, the throng was reported to be "the largest that ever attended a baseball match in the world."[19]

It was certainly too many people for the grounds, which could hold at most 5,800 people—and then only by letting hundreds of cranks stand in a roped-off section of the 450-foot-deep center field. When the Boston club exhausted its supply of tickets to the game, men and boys began tearing down the wood-plank fence surrounding the field so they could watch the game.[20]

Spalding and his teammates were unsure what to expect when they arrived about 15 minutes before the advertised 3 o'clock start, but spectators greeted the erstwhile Red Stockings cheerfully, according to one witness. Another said the Boston supporters "wildly cheered" when the Chicagos appeared on the field.

The handful of Boston police officers assigned to keep order could not clear the hundreds of seatless spectators roaming the field when the Chicago players tried to warm up, but reinforcements arrived and herded stragglers off the park. The crowd was generally jolly; when an overloaded plank in the bleachers snapped and rudely dumped dozens of people on their rear ends, "there was an uproarious shout of merriment."[21]

In the end, it almost didn't matter to the spectators that Chicago won by a score of 5–1. "Last Year's Bostons Defeat This Year's Bostons," shrugged one newspaper headline.[22] Nor were Red Cap fans particularly worried about wild pitching by the new ball-tosser Joe Borden. "He was probably nervous—and naturally enough," the *Boston Globe* generously speculated. "He had to pitch against the best pitcher in the United States."[23]

Newspaper editors were pleased to see so many fellow Americans pay 50 cents to watch a ballgame when parts of the economy were still trying to recover from the recession. "The fact that a base-ball match can call out 10,000 paying spectators in these hard times is one of the distinct triumphs of American civilization," the *Boston Evening Transcript* crowed.[24]

It also was a good sign for A. G. Spalding & Bro. because clubs in the new league needed gate receipts to pay for new uniforms and other equipment. Al secured orders for those goods by using his connection with Hulbert—soon to be elected the National League's president—to open doors and his charm to close sales. It certainly helped that A. G. was the winningest pitcher of the 1870s and still going strong.

Spalding would go on to win 47 League games in 1876, the sixth time in his six years as a professional that he had the most wins of any pitcher. In his big-league career, he won 204 games and lost 53, for a winning percentage of

.794. His career earned-run average, 2.13, ties him with Giants legend Christy Mathewson for eighth place all-time among major-league pitchers.[25]

The White Stockings, as widely anticipated before the season, handily won the first National League pennant behind Spalding's pitching, Ross Barnes's .429 batting average, and Deacon White's league-leading 60 RBIs in 66 games. Chicago finished six games ahead of the Hartford, Connecticut, Dark Blues and St. Louis Brown Stockings. Boston, without its Big Four, took fourth place, 15 games behind Chicago.[26]

* * *

At first, A. G. Spalding & Bro. carried mostly baseball paraphernalia. Since it owned no factory, the company filled its store's ornate cherry cabinets with goods that established manufacturers made to Al's exacting specifications.[27] One standing requirement was the prominent display of the family name and the company trademark on every item for sale.[28]

The budding business had to do some work in-house, as Walter, with the help of his mother and sister, scrambled to fill a flood of mail orders. "I recall an order for shirts that the Indianapolis club sent in," Harriet recalled years later. "Walter had the knit shirts all right, but the great difficulty was to get the name 'INDIANAPOLIS' put across the front of each shirt. He could find someone who would cut the letters out of red broadcloth but no one to sew them on. . . . I said, 'Bring them down and I will sew on the letters.'"

There were 11 shirts to letter, and when she got to the last one it was almost dark outside. She took the last shirt to Al's wife, Josie, who was sick in bed, and asked her how it looked. "She said, 'Oh, Mother, you have got the Ns wrong side up!'" Harriet remembered. "Fortunately, they were only basted [loosely stitched in preparation for sewing]."

The Spaldings soon expanded the "Western base ball emporium's" stock with equipment for many other sports, including cricket, croquet, and archery, as well as fishing tackle and firearms.

A Spalding company history says the Chicago shop's sales in its first year totaled about $11,000, roughly equal in purchasing power to $320,000 today, and made a profit of approximately $1,100. Meanwhile, the White Stockings paid A. G. his promised $3,000 salary and $1,000 bonus for persuading other Boston players to follow him to Chicago. If A. G. was perturbed by the store's modest profit in its first year, he showed no sign of it, and for good reason: He and Walter saw opportunities aplenty.[29]

"Owing to our close connection with the game at that time, and our knowledge of the sport, we had very little trouble in rapidly commanding a pre-eminent position," Walter wrote in an article reflecting on A. G. Spalding & Bros.' 20th anniversary. "Our main object being to produce an article that could not be duplicated or subjected to any kind of criticism. We believed then, as we believe now, that the articles and different products of our own factory bearing the trademark 'Spalding,' which is a guarantee, are the best advertisements we can have."[30]

In its inaugural season, the National League required home clubs to supply game balls. They had to weigh between 5 and 5¼ ounces, measure between 9 and 9¼ inches in circumference, and contain a rubber core that weighed no more than one ounce, was wound in woolen yarn, and covered in leather. Those standards may sound precise, but they gave most teams ample opportunity to gain an advantage. Clubs were left to decide on their own how much *less* than one ounce the rubber core in their ball could weigh and how tightly or loosely the yarn could be wound—factors that made the difference between "live" and "dead" balls. Teams that relied on their defenses naturally provided softer dead balls, while those with strong offenses supplied springier live balls.

At the National League's winter meeting at the Kennard House hotel in Cleveland, the White Stockings reported a profit of $37,000 and an 8.5 percent jump in attendance as Chicago cranks finally had a pennant-winner to support.[31] That was good news for A. G., who owned 30 shares of stock in the club. Even better, team owners ended the practice of permitting home clubs to choose game balls and decided to permit only one kind of ball in 1877, a moderately lively one made by Louis H. Mahn in Boston. Its patented design combined a double leather cover sewn with a novel herringbone stitch to make the ball exceptionally rugged, which was welcome since one ball was expected to last an entire game.[32]

Players and cranks alike called it the Mahn ball, but it was in fact owned by A. G. Spalding & Bro. Al had learned of the design while he was living and playing in Boston. Days before marrying Josie and leaving Boston in 1875, he discreetly acquired the patent from Mahn and arranged for the Mahn Sporting Goods Co. to continue manufacturing the balls under its own name—for the time being. The agreement with Mahn is mentioned in the Spalding brothers' partnership agreement, which states that "all profits arising out of a certain agreement made Nov. 17, 1875, between L. H. Mahn of Boston and the said party of the first part shall be considered property of the firm."[33]

The Spaldings kept their ownership of Mahn secret because the Boston ballmaker's reputation was one reason the League did not accept a competing offer from J. D. Shibe & Co. of Philadelphia. While A. G. and Walter believed it was unwise to say outright that they effectively owned Mahn's company, they knew there was value in being affiliated with his firm. So, in an advertisement in the *New York Clipper* in June 1876, the Spalding company said that its "New League Ball" was "manufactured under letters of patent of L. H. Mahn."

Choosing a new ball for 1877 came alarmingly close to being irrelevant because delegates at the Cleveland meeting expelled clubs representing the two biggest cities at the time, New York and Philadelphia, for failing to play out their schedules. Both clubs had declined to travel west once they gave up on winning the pennant race. This denied the western clubs a chance to make money on tickets and concessions. The New York club, the Mutuals, said travel costs would exceed any revenue it was likely to earn. The Athletic club said it was essentially insolvent because so many potential spectators skipped ballgames in favor of spending their time and money at the Centennial Exhibition in Philadelphia.[34]

Regardless, their decisions clearly violated Article XII of the League Constitution, which stated in part that "if any club shall, *of its own fault* [emphasis in original], fail to finish its series with every other club, its games shall not be counted at the close of the season, and such club shall not be eligible to enter the championship lists the ensuing season." Hulbert felt he had to demonstrate that he was willing to risk the loss of income from the most populous cities—and possibly the collapse of the entire circuit—to show that the League, unlike the National Association, would strictly enforce rules regardless of the consequences.

To help League clubs earn more from gate receipts, Hulbert moved the Dark Blues of Hartford (population roughly 40,000), to Brooklyn (population 500,000). Whether that alone would be enough to bolster the League's business outlook for a six-city circuit was an open question as the 1877 season began. Team owners soon had the answer. All six clubs lost money that season. St. Louis lost the most, $8,000; Chicago, with its large salaries, finished $6,000 in the red; the Hartfords of Brooklyn, as the itinerant Connecticut ball club was called, lost $2,500; and Louisville was in the hole for $2,000.[35] Even the Boston Red Stockings, who took back the pennant, lost $2,230.85.[36]

Cincinnati Reds owner Si Keck walked away from his club in mid-June, declining to put more money into a losing proposition.[37] A *New York Clipper* contributor from Ohio wrote "eight or ten of our wealthy citizens" had agreed to put up $10,000 to carry the club through to the end of the season, and then be accepted into the League at the winter meeting.[38]

When the NL board of directors met at the Kennard House in Cleveland on December 4, 1877, the first order of business was to vote Cincinnati out of the League for failure to pay its annual dues. It then erased Cincinnati from the record and issued new standings stripped of every game involving Cincinnati. Boston won the championship with or without counting the Cincinnati games and was awarded the pennant. Louisville, Hartford, and St. Louis all finished ahead of the defending champion, Chicago, which had Spalding in the pitcher's box for only 11 innings in four games. Otherwise, he shifted positions around the infield, served as team captain, and built the sporting goods business with his brother. It was a heavy workload, even for a 27-year-old.[39]

"For integrity of character and general ability and intelligence in the business of running a baseball team, Mr. Spalding is the equal of the best. . . ," a *New York Clipper* writer opined. "But this season he had too many irons in the fire, and in his attempt to Captain the nine, to run the general business of the club, and at the same time manage his own baseball business and store, he undertook more than any one man could properly attend to, and the result was a measurable failure."[40]

* * *

Obscuring their true relationship with Mahn worked out well for the Spaldings because some clubs complained in the first month of the 1877 season that the "Mahn balls" they received from National League Secretary Nick Young "were too soft, and, after a little use, grew flabby on the outside, so that one could be picked up by the slack like a kitten by the scruff of its neck or a small boy by the slack of his breeches." Club executives meeting at the Hotel Bates in Indianapolis in May told Young to "instruct Mr. Mahn to make a harder and livelier ball."[41]

Mahn's new ball was harder, but no more satisfactory. Clubs complained that the new version, partially wound with dense cotton thread instead of all woolen yarn, was too hard—as hard as "a billiard ball covered with thin and tightly stretched horsehide." Players were afraid to catch one. The League ordered Mahn to produce a third version, which lasted out the season.[42]

Starting with the next season, in 1878, the League sourced its game balls from A. G. Spalding & Bro. The company remained the exclusive supplier of balls to the National League for the next century. A. G. created the opportunity by promising to not only make a ball acceptable to all (learning from Mahn's mistakes) but to pay clubs a dollar for every dozen balls they used. The cost of obtaining the League's imprimatur was more than offset by the added sales generated by telling millions of amateurs and schoolchildren that they, too, could play with the ball professionals used.

While they were securing the privilege to make the League's official ball, the Spaldings also hoped to get the job of publishing the annual manual the League used to circulate its meeting minutes, rule changes, team stats, and constitutional amendments. Its contents were as soporific as its formal title, *Constitution and Playing Rules of the National League of Professional Base Ball Clubs*. Informally, it was called the League book.

Owners thought so little of the book that they delegated the choice of a publisher to Young. In mid-February 1876, when Young awarded the job of publishing the first League book to the Philadelphia sporting goods outlet Reach & Johnston—run by the recently retired Athletics infielder Alfred J. Reach—the Spalding brothers were in Chicago, scrambling to open their store.[43]

When the next National League Annual Meeting convened on December 5, 1877, again at the Kennard House hotel in Cleveland, the League book had a new publisher: A. G. Spalding & Bro. The language League leaders employed in delegating the selection of the publisher also had changed. In the 1876 book, which documented the February meeting at which the National League was founded, the owners stated "that the publication of the Association books, *for the benefit of the Association*, [emphasis added] be left in the hands of the Secretary." When the Spaldings were awarded the job, the owners' directive meeting was simply: "On motion, It was *Resolved*, That the publication of the 'Official Book' be left in the hands of the Secretary." No mention of benefiting anyone or anything.[44]

It is possible, of course, that the first quotation was just a sloppy copy of a similar idea expressed by the defunct National Association. The League was hurried in preparing for its inaugural season and is known to have borrowed language from the Association's constitution.

On January 24, 1877, the second edition of the League book went on sale alongside an annual publication entitled *Spalding's Official Base Ball Guide*, edited by A. G. Spalding and Lewis E. Meacham, sports editor of the *Chicago Tribune*. (Spalding was nothing if not loyal to the men chosen to edit his guide. While Meacham died soon after finishing the first *Guide*, his successor, Chadwick, was editor for 25 years, until he died in 1908, and John B. Foster, a former sportswriter for the *New York World-Telegram*, held the job for 21 years, until he retired in 1939. The guide ceased publication in 1941.)

Spalding's guide had the entire contents of the League book—updated playing rules, noted amendments to the league constitution, and summaries of actions taken at the winter meeting in Cleveland in December. It added page after page of statistics on how well or poorly each League team and every player batted, fielded, ran, and threw in 1877. It also had articles by leading sportswriters who recapped the season just ended and handicapped the season to come, gave instructions on how to play positions, and compiled statistics on other circuits seeking to compete with National League clubs.

Other publishers offered similar annuals—the first of which, *Beadle's Dime Base-Ball Player*, which debuted in 1860, followed by *DeWitt's Base-Ball Guide* in 1868. But Spalding was the only publisher who, by unilaterally stretching the terms of his contract with the League, could give readers the impression that his privately owned guide was an official National League publication. It quickly came to dominate the field, giving the Spaldings the ideal marketing channel they wanted.[45]

A. G.'s ambition in this area was so transparent that even his mentor, Hulbert, mocked it in a letter to the secretary of the St. Louis club; when he mentioned the League book, he added, "beg pardon, 'Spalding's Advertiser'." As that jibe suggests, the remarkable thing about Spalding's management of the League book and his private guide was not just the volume of advertising, it was the fact that a large majority of ads were for Spalding's merchandise.

By 1879, when Spalding casually mentioned in the preface of the guide that he was unilaterally combining the League book with his publication—a maneuver he acknowledges "makes the possession of a copy (of *Spalding's Base Ball Guide*) by every player not only desirable but even imperative"—A. G. Spalding & Bros. (the abbreviation of "brother" was made plural in 1878 when the Spaldings' brother-in-law William T. Brown joined the firm) accounted for almost three-fourths of all advertising. Only one other sporting-goods company appeared in the publication: Wright & Ditson of Boston, which had a single page.[46]

The first League book, published by Reach & Johnston in 1876, had 40 pages; A. G. Spalding & Co. republished it in 1881 with a letter naming Spalding's company as publisher and 10 additional pages of advertising—seven for its own merchandise.[47] Each year's guide was longer and more laden with ads, most of them for Spalding balls, Spalding bats, Spalding uniforms, Spalding hats, Spalding shoes, and more with each new edition: gym equipment, boxing gloves, archery apparatus, footballs, basketballs and on and on. Spalding's urge to sell was not limited to advertising; the *Guide*'s question-and-answer columns gave him opportunities to pitch softball questions to himself. A few examples:

Q: Does the League adopt a regular bat, same as they do a ball?

A: No, the players select that, and they have universally adopted the Spalding trade-marked bat.

Q: Why does the League adopt a special ball for all their games, and what one has been selected for 1880?

A: To insure uniformity and guard against fraud. The "Spalding League Ball" was again adopted as the official ball of the League.[48]

Spalding aggressively sought to discourage potential competitors with a warning in the first pages of its guide. "We have paid the National Professional League liberally for the *exclusive* privilege of publishing the official Book of the League, containing the Constitution, Playing Rules, etc., and have gone to great expense and labor in securing and tabulating the batting and fielding averages of nearly every professional ball player in America.

"We hereby warn all parties that the Book is copyrighted, and the . . . publication of any extracts from it, in book form, will be followed by a prosecution to the fullest extent of the law."[49]

When the 1883 edition of the *Spalding Guide* landed on his desk, Abraham Gilbert Mills—who was elected League president after Hulbert died—was sickened to see that it called itself an official League publication.

The assertion appeared in a Publishers' Notice brimming with Gilded Age bombast: "'Spalding's Base Ball Guide' is now the highest recognized authority on the game of Base Ball, and is the only Guide published that has any sale or circulation. *It is the official publication of the National League* [emphasis added] and the Northwestern League, and also the official book of the American and Western College Associations."[50]

As an aside, the Publishers' Note said Spalding also printed the "League Book," which it did not grace with the adjective "official" even though it was the NL's formal channel for distributing new rules and constitutional changes to its clubs.

Mills then discovered that Spalding's publication also included the following attestation:

> *WASHINGTON, D.C., March 7, 1883.*
>
> *By the authority vested in me, I do hereby certify that Messrs. A. G. Spalding & Bros., of Chicago, Ill., have been granted the* EXCLUSIVE *[emphasis in the original] right to publish the Official Book for 1883.*
>
> *N. E. YOUNG,*
>
> *Secretary National League of Professional Base Ball Clubs.*

With no context, Young's declaration that Spalding had exclusive rights to publish the "Official Book" undoubtedly led many readers to erroneously conclude that the publication they held in their hands *was* the "Official *League* Book." Nothing in the *Guide* sought to make clear that Young's certification applied only to the *actual* League book, not Spalding's advertising-laden simulacrum.

On April 10, 1883—exactly one year after Hulbert died—Mills wrote an indignant letter to Spalding to remind the ambitious young entrepreneur that while he called his company's collection of statistics and analysis "Spalding's *Official* Base Ball Guide," it was not an official publication of the League, and that Young's declaration should not appear in the *Guide* because it applied to "an altogether different publication"—that is, the actual League book.[51]

Mills added that misrepresenting the *Guide* as a League publication was compounded by the errors—or intentional lies—it contained. He cited a footnote that Spalding added to Rule 13, which established the size, weight, and construction of the ball. The footnote stated: "The 'Spalding League Ball,' having been adopted as the official ball of the National League for 1883, must be used in all match games played under League rules."

That was "an unmitigated falsehood" and "certainly untrue," Mills indignantly wrote to Spalding. The rule applied only to games between League clubs competing for the League championship, Mills said. In exhibition games against independent teams, clubs were free to use any ball they wished to play with, regardless of whether they played under League rules.

The League president added that it was outrageous for Spalding to call his guide a League publication because it included schedules and statistics for organizations unaffiliated with the National League, including the American College Base Ball Association, and organizations directly in competition with the League, notably the American Association of Base Ball Clubs.

Spalding replied promptly and politely, but Mills thought the Chicagoan had—unintentionally or otherwise—misunderstood his complaint. "You know very well that I have no objection to the publication of your Guide," the League president shot back. "On the contrary, I heartily approve of it, and would be very glad indeed if such a publication should find a very large circulation and prove profitable to you.

"What I objected to specifically, and still do object to, are certain false statements contained in the book, for which there is no possible excuse."

Mills then repeated his objection to Spalding claiming that his *Guide* was an official National League document. "Your Guide is not the official publication of the League, and you have no right or authority for stating that it is," Mills wrote, showing his exasperation.

Separately, Mills told Young that "while I have the kindliest personal feelings toward Spalding," his inclusion of brazen falsehoods in both the Guide and League book "indicates a disposition to use the League in any way he pleases to aid his money-getting schemes."

Mills archly added that Young appeared to be shirking his responsibility to oversee production of the League book and block publications purporting to be the League book. "It is quite apparent to me . . . that while Spalding is supposed to publish this book under your direction, he has never submitted a proof to you for your inspection," Mills wrote to Young. "Had he done so, the official book of the League would surely not contain the schedule of the American Association, and the North-western League, nor sundry other matter that certainly is not League business."

Mills began reading past issues of *Spalding's Guide* to see how long it had been mischaracterizing its relationship with the League. He began with the first guide, which had the long-winded but precise title *Spalding's Official Base-Ball Guide, added to which is a complete reprint of the League book*. In 1880, the title became *Spalding's Base Ball Guide and Official League Book*, which erased the line between the truly official publication and a private one. The next year's issue went further, claiming in its preface that major changes adopted by the League over the winter "will be found in no other form excepting that in which it is herewith presented, as the Guide is, by special contract with the league, made the sole medium of publication of the proceedings of that body."[52]

In another scorching letter, Mills angrily dismissed that assertion as a "blatant falsehood" and reminded Spalding that all League proceedings also appeared in the League book, which Spalding's firm was handsomely paid to print. Mills turned aside Spalding's invitation to meet in person to resolve the matter. "For my part," Mills wrote, "I much prefer that what is said on this subject between you and me be in writing, so that the record may be available for future reference should occasion require."[53]

Spalding realized it was time for him to retreat on this issue, but he did not concede defeat. His Publisher's Notice in the 1884 *Guide* did not claim that the guide was an "official publication of the National League." Readers seeking an unabridged and updated version of the League constitution were advised to look in the League book; the guide offered only an abbreviated version. In explaining the change, Spalding did not mention Mills's demand that the guide stop masquerading as the League book. Instead, he cited his publication's success:

"The 'Guide' has attained such a size—160 pages—as to preclude the possibility of publishing in the same issue the League Constitution in full, and other interesting League matters. We are therefore compelled, in addition, to publish the 'Official League Book,' which contains only official League matter as furnished by Secretary Young, including the League Constitution in full."[54]

Spalding nonetheless continued to call his company's annual publication *Spalding's Base Ball Guide and Official League Book* in 1884 and for at least a decade more, successfully outlasting Mills's tenure at the League.

Chapter 7

The Big Mogul

The National League's second season, in 1877, was a disaster on many levels. Every club lost a packet by playing in the shrunken circuit. Hulbert showed no sign he was in any hurry to revive attendance by replacing clubs in New York and Philadelphia. Near the end of the season, Louisville's Grays suspiciously lost nine consecutive games in August, turning a 3½-game lead in the standings into a 5½-game deficit in two weeks and igniting a scandal over hippodroming, or game-fixing. Almost unnoticed, the defending champion Chicagos meekly ended the year nearer in the standings to cellar-dwelling Cincinnati than pennant-winning Boston.[1]

At the end of the 1877 season, Spalding, aged 27, announced that he was retiring as a player. Ten months later, however, he did participate in one final championship game for Chicago, playing at second base in a game against Boston. Spalding had two hits, but committed five errors in a 5–2 loss. Sportswriters were kind in their accounts of his performance: "A. G. Spalding played second base, and, as might have been anticipated, did not play the position as well as he might have done," said one. Another said only "his playing was not remarkable."[2]

(The same cannot be said about his professional career overall. Comparing statistics across eras is hardly a conclusive way to judge players but can help put the workload of 19th-century pitchers in some perspective. In six years as a professional pitcher, Spalding averaged 54 starts and 46 complete games per season; the top major league pitchers in 2024 started 33 and completed 2. And despite the shorter seasons in Spalding's day, he pitched in an average of 480 innings and faced more than 2,100 batters every season, compared with 208 innings pitched and 361 batters faced by leading hurlers in 2024.)[3]

Spalding remained the White Stockings' secretary after he retired as a player but devoted most of his attention to his small business, for which he and his brother Walter had big plans.

Their first significant step in that direction was gaining control of the Wilkins Bros. factory in Hastings, Michigan, Spalding's primary supplier of archery equipment, baseball bats, croquet mallets and balls, fishing tackle, and Indian clubs. James and Walter Wilkins founded the plant in 1876 in a former cultivator works. It was by far Hastings' biggest employer, with 135 of the town's 2,000 residents on the payroll. However, the business was struggling, and William Wilkins decided in the summer of 1878 to sell his interest in the firm to his brother. James, short of both capital and goodwill with Hastings' only bank, offered to sell a half-ownership in the factory to its biggest customer, A. G. Spalding & Bros.

When the Spalding brothers made the long trek from Chicago to Hastings to inspect their potential acquisition, they were unimpressed by both the plant and its proprietor. The Chicagoans did, in the end, agree to buy the half-interest on offer, using $10,000 that their brother-in-law, William Thayer Brown, had paid for an equal share in the Spaldings' sporting goods business.[4]

While the three new investors were comfortable with investing a significant amount in the factory, none volunteered to manage the acquisition, which would require relocating to Hastings deep in Michigan's heavily forested Lower Peninsula and nearly 200 miles from Chicago. Their solution was to share the most powerful executive positions—Al was made president, Walter vice president, and Brown secretary-treasurer—and manage the factory remotely. Wilkins, the superintendent, would be their man on the ground, sending daily written reports on raw materials, production, and inventory. The factory made a lot of products—turning a thousand cords of wood into bats and shipping 33,000 croquet sets in 1879—but not any profit. Left on his own with a greatly reduced ownership stake in the factory, Wilkins borrowed and spent money with alarming alacrity.[5]

"It soon became necessary for someone to go there and look after the business, and it was decided that I should go to Hastings," Brown said later. "I went there to stay 60 or 90 days, and I stayed for five years." His wife, Mary, and mother-in-law, Harriet, soon joined him in Michigan. In Brown's second year there, it was clear that Wilkins had to go. "Mr. Wilkins and I did not agree as to the best methods of handling the business," Brown, a master of understatement, recalled. "I was more conservative than he was."[6]

After two years of intracompany battles, during which Wilkins took unauthorized salary advances to pay for a divorce, Spalding returned to Hastings for a showdown. The first step was to persuade Andrew J. Bowne, president of the Hastings National Bank, to lend A. G. Spalding & Bros. enough to either buy out Wilkins or get the factory back on its feet. Spalding didn't have enough to do both.

At their meeting, Bowne listened attentively to the presentation and then got to the money question.

"Mr. Brown, how much money do you estimate it will take to see you through if you buy out Mr. Wilkins?" the banker asked.

Without so much as a sidelong glance at Spalding, Brown replied, "I thought it would take $50,000." Spalding's knees buckled when he heard that figure—roughly equivalent to $1.6 million in 2023—but he had the presence of mind to say nothing. Bowne paced for a bit and thought for a while, and then turned to the two young men, still in their twenties.

"Well, boys," he said, "you buy him out and I will see you through."[7]

Spalding did buy out Wilkins and renamed the factory The Spalding Manufacturing Co. Thus, A. G. Spalding & Bros. became the first sporting goods dealer to produce many of the goods it was selling, giving the company more control over quality, costs, price points, and profit margins.[8]

A. G. Spalding & Bros.' decision to integrate its manufacturing, wholesaling, and retailing operations produced results that ached to be noticed—and were.

"Mr. Al Spalding may be said to be the king of clubs," *Northwestern Lumberman*, a trade paper, proclaimed. "The concern of which he is the moving spirit not only leads in the sporting line but manufactures more ball bats than any other establishment in the business." The Hastings factory alone churned out approximately 500,000 bats per year. It not only made more bats but more *kinds* of bats: 22 styles and sizes priced from 10 cents for a child size to $1.50 for a professional model, available in the batsman's choice of ash, basswood, or cherry.[9]

In February 1881, five years after opening for business, A. G. Spalding & Bros. had outgrown its Randolph Street shop and leased a bigger space in the Andrews Building at 108 Madison Street between Clark and Dearborn Streets. The stone-faced brick building, which was erected in 1873 and demolished in 1908, had four floors above ground and a roomy basement, but no elevator. The elaborate cherry wood cabinetry of the retail shop was on the ground floor, with the tailoring and shipping departments in the rear behind a mirrored wall that made the shop appear to be twice as big as it was. Offices and the booming wholesale and mail order businesses took the second floor, inventory was on the third, and the top floor was where athletic and outdoor clothes were sewn. Gymnastics equipment and bicycles shared the basement.[10]

The company's rapid growth increased its need for capital, and Brown found it at the Hastings National Bank in Michigan. Brown, who had begun his career at a Rockford bank, said the Spalding company's debts to the Hastings bank exceeded $112,000 at one point; Bowne syndicated the debt with other banks to reduce his institution's exposure to the risk that the Spalding company might go bust, but he never asked Spalding or anyone else at the company for a nickel's worth of collateral. It was lucky for Spalding that he didn't ask for collateral, Brown added, because "there was a few years there when it was a question of whether we were going to pull the thing out or not." Hard work, he added, enabled the partners to steer the company through and "very materially" reduce its debt before Brown returned to Chicago.[11]

Spalding was tested again a year later, when a forest fire swept into Hastings on a hot day in an unusually dry August, overwhelming efforts to control or extinguish it. The fire consumed a wagon-making business, an opera house under construction, and a hotel, but the Spalding Manufacturing Company bore the greatest financial loss; its factory, worth an estimated $18,000, was reduced to ashes. Spalding received news of the fire while vacationing with Josie and their eight-year-old son Keith on Fire Island near New York City. He quickly set out for Michigan to personally assess the damage and wasted no time in filing an insurance claim and used the settlement to pay off the debt on the Hastings plant and build a new plant in Englewood, a neighborhood on Chicago's South Side. Eventually, A. G. Spalding & Bros. would own 10 factories and employ 3,600 people.[12]

Even after leaving Michigan, the three partners maintained their relationship with Bowne and eventually had an opportunity to return his faith in them. An economic slump in 1893 was accompanied by a sharp decline in government gold reserves, which guaranteed the value of the dollar. Concern that companies might default on their loans, combined with fear that paper money could lose value triggered an economic panic that shuttered 15,000 businesses, including 600 banks. A. G. Spalding & Bros. lent Bowne $20,000 of scarce cash to help the banker survive the crisis. Bowne died in June 1896 before he could completely repay the unsecured loan, but he had arranged for his estate to settle the debt.[13]

* * *

Having started the process of vertically integrating his company—that is, buying his suppliers and distributors to have more control over the cost and supply of raw materials, retail prices and, thus, profits—Spalding turned to increasing his company's share of the sporting goods market. He began by recruiting independent retailers across the country to become "depots," or exclusive retailers, in their city or region. In exchange for exclusivity, they had to agree to carry the entire line of Spalding's athletic goods "at all times."

A. G. Spalding & Bros. invested very little in establishing retail outlets that it owned. In the spring of 1884, it opened a branch office at 47 Murray Street in New York City. It was primarily an effort to improve service to college teams and other mail-order customers in the East—a fulfillment center, in modern parlance—but it also gave the midwestern firm a beachhead in the country's largest market. The latest edition of the *Spalding Guide* had sold out its 50,000-copy print run and a second edition was ordered. As his mentor William A. Hulbert archly noted years earlier, the *Guide* was as much a catalog for Spalding's sporting goods business as it was a record book for organized ball, so sales of the *Guide*, which cost 10 cents, could be used to forecast demand for the sporting goods advertised within.[14]

The branch house proved to be a good investment when a fire roared through the A. G. Spalding & Bros.' flagship store and company headquarters in Chicago on a Sunday morning in late October 1884. Six engine companies and two hook-and-ladder trucks were dispatched to the scene, but six more engines and a third hook-and-ladder were summoned soon after firefighters arrived and assessed the extent of the blaze. Even with all that equipment, the fire burned for two hours, consuming everything inside, an inventory that members of the firm estimated to be worth $80,000.[15]

Years later, Spalding told a *New York Times* writer that he was never intimidated by fires, financial troubles, obstreperous players, or other potentially existential threats to the business he had spent years building from scratch. Running a multimillion-dollar business was nothing compared with pitching a close game in a pennant race.

"I never struck anything in business that did not seem a simple matter when compared to complications I have faced on the baseball field," he told the interviewer. "A young man playing baseball gets into the habit of quick thinking in (the) most adverse circumstances and under the most merciless criticism in the world—the criticism from the bleachers. If that doesn't train him, nothing can. Baseball in youth has the effect, in later years, of making him think and act a little quicker than the other fellow."[16]

Once the fire was extinguished, Spalding signed a lease for a new store a block away at 164 Madison Street and telegraphed his biggest suppliers instructing them to duplicate his company's recent orders. He could not, however, duplicate valuable lists of customers' names, addresses, order histories, and billing records kept in the Chicago headquarters. Luckily, some of that information was safely stored in the New York office.[17]

Undaunted by the fire, Spalding redoubled his plans to expand beyond Chicago, starting with a fully outfitted retail store at 241 Broadway in New York City and expanding the firm's wholesale business by leasing the basement and subbasement a few doors away, at 233 Broadway. Walter moved his family to New York so he could launch and manage the enterprise. Along with Al, he also diligently signed up more depots.

By 1889, the Spaldings had 35 domestic depots and seven more in Australia, Canada, Hawaii, and New Zealand. Twenty-one other businesses, unwilling or unable to carry the entire line of Spalding-branded merchandise, agreed to become "local agencies" for the brothers' empire. It wasn't enough.

That same year, Spalding bought the retail business of his biggest competitor, A. J. Reach & Co. of Philadelphia, for $15,000, significantly expanding his company's share of the retail market for sporting goods. The acquisition was a surprise to many because the Reach company, founded and run by former Philadelphia Athletics player Alfred J. Reach, was larger than the Spalding company. Less well known was that Spalding had, for some time, filled its customers' big orders with balls, gloves, and other equipment stamped with the Spalding & Bros. trademark but manufactured by A. J. Reach & Co.[18]

The Reach Company lacked the capital to buy the raw materials and pay workers to fill a large order from the National League for Spalding's Official League Balls. But Reach did have a partner, Ben Shibe, who had found a way to maximize the number of leather cover pieces that could be cut from each irregular piece of horsehide and developed a way to pre-punch holes in the cover pieces to make the hand-sewing of balls quicker and more consistent. They were very valuable suppliers.[19]

To find a way to resolve their lack of capital problem, Spalding met with Brown, his brother-in-law, partner, and manufacturing wizard, and Julian W. Curtiss, the company's secretary, at the elegant Lafayette Hotel in Philadelphia to work up a solution. After several days of talks with Reach, they decided the Philadelphian could raise working capital for his factories by selling his retail operations to . . . A. G. Spalding & Bros.[20]

The reasons for the sale may have puzzled ordinary citizens who bothered to think about it, but the effect on the nascent industry seemed obvious. "A. J. Reach Sells Out: A. G. Spalding Now Has a Monopoly in the Retail Sporting Goods Line," was the headline on one newspaper's account of the agreement.[21] Others concurred. "With one bold stroke Spalding Brothers has absorbed their great rival, the A. J. Reach Company, lock, stock and barrel, and made themselves supreme in America, and, in fact, the chief sporting goods house of the world," said one.[22] Another explained why: "The firm already has establishments in New York, Chicago, San Francisco, Melbourne, and London and branches in many of the smaller cities in the United States and Canada."[23]

Perhaps because Congress was poised to enact antitrust legislation to try to rein in monopolies and trusts that were "rationalizing" markets by reducing or eliminating competition, Spalding stopped short of buying A. J. Reach & Co. outright (that would have to wait until 1934) and kept the Reach trademark on products acquired in the transaction to maintain the appearance of a competitive industry. He did the same when A. G. Spalding & Bros. bought 9,997 of 9,999 shares of the Wright & Ditson Company of Boston early in 1892, after Henry Ditson, who handled the business end of the partnership, died of heart disease a few months earlier. The venerable New York firm Peck & Snyder also lived on only as a trademark after Spalding acquired the partnership early in 1894—and with it, "the largest and most complete athletic goods store in the world."[24]

Once each acquisition was done, responsibility for smoothly integrating the businesses into A. G. Spalding & Bros. largely fell to Walter. Al turned to other business interests, including the White Stockings, land speculation in Illinois and New Mexico, and an investment to disassemble Libby Prison, a notorious Confederate prisoner-of-war camp in Richmond, Virginia, ship every brick more than 600 miles to Chicago, and reassemble it as a tourist attraction.

Acquired companies remained separate entities in the eyes of the state of Illinois, where Spalding's company had incorporated. Keeping track of all of them was bothersome and time consuming. When New Jersey enacted its General Corporation Act of 1888, permitting corporations to own other corporations, A. G. Spalding & Bros. reincorporated in the Garden State in 1892 and put all its companies in a holding company; investors who owned shares in any of the individual businesses swapped their stock in those companies for shares in the holding company.[25]

Such was Spalding's reputation by this time that when a Pittsburgh newspaper reported on the corporate shuffle, it concluded the brief article by guessing at Spalding's motive: "The presumable object of the (holding) company is to control the sporting goods trade of the country."[26]

Each of the acquisitions had its own logic. Buying Wright & Ditson, a prodigious publisher of annual sports guides, enabled Spalding to shut down publications on sports already covered by *Spalding Guides*. Wright & Ditson also led the fields of tennis and golf equipment, markets where Spalding was weak. Reach was a fierce competitor in baseball equipment. Victor Sporting Goods helped to make Spalding the leading provider of gear for the fast-growing sport of college football. Together, they comprised a kind of all-star team of sporting goods firms—and Spalding owned them all. No wonder the *Sporting Life*, a weekly widely read by baseball executives, players, and fans, referred to him as The Big Mogul.[27]

* * *

Spalding's appetite to dominate his industry and influence the sporting world may have led him to do more than buy up competitors and cut out the jobbers, or middlemen, who sold Spalding equipment to retailers. His company was widely suspected of inducing the Amateur Athletic Union, the powerful national governing body for amateur sports, to recognize only those records set by athletes using Spalding gear. He certainly had a close relationship with AAU secretary James E. Sullivan, who was chairman of the AAU Records Committee—and, starting in 1892, concurrently president of the Spalding-owned American Sports Publishing Company.

Not surprisingly, Spalding's firm was chosen to publish the official AAU handbook as well as the official rule books for every sport AAU oversaw—essentially every sport then being played by organized amateurs.

Holding both jobs simultaneously put Spalding's man in a position of unchecked power, which he did not wield wisely or fairly. In 1902, for example, Arthur Duffey of Georgetown University ran the 100-yard dash in 9.6 seconds. No one had ever run the event that fast, and no one would run it any faster for over a quarter century. The AAU expunged his achievement from its record book years later when a magazine asserted that some athletes, including Duffey, had once accepted expense reimbursements that exceeded AAU maximums. The real reason? According to Charley Paddock, gold medal sprinter at the 1920 Olympics, the AAU had retroactively erased Duffey's record because he had stopped wearing track shoes made by Spalding and had his shoes custom made.[28]

Duffey sued the AAU, seeking to have a court compel the association to return his achievements to the record books. He lost in court.[29]

At a track and field meet in Philadelphia in 1905, John C. Garrels of the University of Michigan threw the discus 135 feet ½ inch, far exceeding the world record. However, the AAU refused to accept Garrels's throw as a record, saying the discus he used—and which field judges had approved—did not conform to AAU rules. The discus Garrels used wasn't made by Spalding. Sullivan issued the decision.[30]

At a meet in Chicago a few weeks later, Garrels threw the discus 140 feet 2⅜ inches—more than 11 feet beyond the world record.[31] Sullivan was not at the meet, but he ordered that Garrels's discus be sent to him from Chicago for inspection, and the Spalding man again said the non-Spalding discus did not conform to AAU rules.[32]

Spalding's Official Athletic Almanac for 1905, which Sullivan edited, carried an ad for Spalding's Olympic Discus, which it described as "an exact reproduction of the discus used in the Olympic Games at Athens." Presumably, that discus met the AAU's standards because the *Official Athletic Almanac for 1904* said: "The Spalding Official Discus should always be on the grounds." ("This retails for $5.00," the rule book helpfully added.) Elsewhere, the almanac described the disc used in the Athens Games as being "surrounded by iron," while AAU rules specified a rim made of steel, not iron. A small point? Yes, but Sullivan used a similar cavil to disqualify Garrels; the Michigan man used a discus that differed from the AAU rule only in the kind of metal in its rim: aluminum instead of iron or steel. The weights and all other measurements were identical.[33]

The rule book also said, "Any competitor may use his private discus if it conforms to the rule, in which case other contestants shall be allowed to use it if they wish," but critics of the governing body scoffed at that clause. An article in the monthly magazine the *World To-Day* observed that "the rules of the A.A.U. describe the Spalding discus so minutely that in order to use a discus made in accordance with the A.A.U. rules it is necessary to infringe upon the patent held by Spalding."[34]

The article's author, Charles J. P. Lucas, a doctor and amateur athlete in Cambridge, Massachusetts, characterized A. G. Spalding & Bros. as "a decided detriment to amateur sport" in the United States because of its extraordinary influence over the Amateur Athletic Union. "Take the A.A.U. rule book," Lucas wrote. "Glance through its pages and what do you find? The Spalding discus is the official discus; the Spalding basketball is the official ball of the A.A.U.; the Spalding football is the official ball for intercollegiate contests."

Such a de facto monopoly, he asserted, practically required amateur athletes to use Spalding gear if they wanted their achievements to be recognized and did not want to risk being suspended for a rules infraction and required to prove their innocence if they wanted to be reinstated.[35]

Lucas said the regulatory body's bias for Spalding was particularly galling because Sullivan, in addition to being a top official of the A.A.U., was simultaneously president of the American Sports Publishing Company, a profitable Spalding-owned business that published the rules and playing advice for dozens of sports—and thus provided A. G. Spalding & Bros. with a reliably effective medium for advertising its goods.

Lucas added that Sullivan, in his role as chief of the Department of Physical Culture at the Louisiana Purchase Exhibition and Summer Olympic Games in St. Louis in 1904, was responsible for banning the display of sporting goods not made by Spalding.

On another occasion, Sullivan was alleged to have abused his considerable authority to enforce amateurism in collegiate sports by revoking the amateur status of University of Chicago football star Walter Eckersall after he led the Maroons to a national championship. Sullivan accused Eckersall of having accepted expense money while playing in a summer baseball league—sponsored by Spalding. Eckersall's friends and teammates said Sullivan's true motive for punishing the quarterback was that he had declined to wear Spalding brand football boots.

Like many other sporting goods dealers in the late 1880s, Spalding was caught flat-footed by the introduction of "safety bicycles," an English innovation that used equal-sized wheels instead of the mismatched wheels found on the difficult-to-mount and dangerous-to-ride high-wheelers that had been introduced two decades earlier.

Spalding entered the safety bicycle market in 1890 by asking the Lamb Knitting Machine Company in Chicopee Falls, Massachusetts, to produce a moderately priced model called the Credenda. Lamb usually made rifles and eggbeaters as well as knitting machines, but it retooled under the guidance of Albert H. Overman to manufacture bicycles. Overman had founded the Overman Wheel Company in Chicopee Falls in 1882 (wheel being a synonym for safety bicycle). He agreed to help Spalding find a manufacturer for Credendas because he was assured they would be sold exclusively in Spalding's retail stores and catalog and would not compete with Overman's highly regarded Victor cycle. Overman also agreed to make Spalding, a fellow Illinoisan, a "special agent" for distribution and sales of Victor cycles in nine states.[36]

Victors were exceptional—and expensive. Overman would accept no less than $125, which, adjusted for inflation, was about as costly then as certain Italian racing bikes today. Unsurprisingly, sales were weaker than expected, particularly after another deep recession hit the United States in 1893, but Overman continued to make and ship bicycles. Spalding's storage depots were soon full of Overman's overpriced machines.[37]

Spalding asked Overman to take back unsold bicycles before the next year's models arrived and refund $54,000 that A. G. Spalding & Bros. had paid up front for the inventory. Overman refused to do any such thing, saying their contract obligated Spalding to accept 40 percent or 60 percent (sources vary) of Overman's output regardless of the economy and denying that his company had a duty to buy back bikes the sporting goods mogul could not sell.[38]

Three years to the day after contracting with the Lamb Knitting Machine Company to make his bicycles, Spalding bought the company and its plant. He said the production of ice skates and gym equipment would be consolidated in the Chicopee factory, which would still make Credenda bicycles—and, in a direct challenge to Overman's Victor—would start making models that cost as much as $125. The unidentified Spalding official who made the announcement cheekily added: "It is understood that this arrangement will not interfere with the connection of A. G. Spalding & Bros. with the Overman Wheel Company as general agents for the sale of the Victor wheel."[39]

In fact, it did interfere with Spalding's relationship with Overman. It ended it.

Overman Wheel expressed its displeasure with Spalding's decision to enter its high-end bicycle market by invading the general athletic-goods business with an expanded line of Victor Sporting Goods, including baseballs, bats, boxing gloves, footballs, tennis balls, and tennis racquets.

Spalding, tacitly acknowledging that his firm's relationship with Overman was dead, dumped A. G. Spalding & Bros.' entire inventory of Victor bikes on the market for $85 each. That was almost one-third below Overman's regular price. Next, Spalding wrote to every Victor bicycle dealer and offered to sell them Credendas at deep discounts.[40]

The Overman Wheel Company sued A. G. Spalding & Bros. in the US Circuit Court of Massachusetts on April 2, 1894, for breach of contract. Overman, which sought $100,000 in damages, said its contract with Spalding forbade the sporting goods maker from selling Overman's Victor model at a discount and from making a high-quality bicycle that would compete with the Victor.[41] The Spalding company countersued Overman Wheel Company, accusing the manufacturer of supplying it with defective bicycles, which Spalding workers were obligated to repair, and overcharging it for advertising.[42]

Overman Wheel Co. filed for bankruptcy in 1897, after a glut of cheap bicycles in the market forced it to lower prices, starving it of the cash it needed to meet payroll and pay its bills. Victor Sporting Goods was left on its own until Wright & Ditson acquired it in 1918.[43]

A. G. Spalding & Bros. bought the merged entity in 1929.

Chapter 8
League Leader

William Hulbert woke up on Easter Monday in April 1882 feeling remarkably well. Congestive heart disease had confined him to his home on 40th Street in Chicago for six months and had nearly killed him over the winter, but for the last three weeks the barrel-chested businessman had rallied. Over the weekend he felt well enough to ask his doctor if a driver could take him in a carriage to the White Stockings' practice on that Monday so he could look in on the men and see how they were shaping up. The team had run away with the League pennant in 1881 and its first game of the new season, on May 1 in Buffalo, New York, was approaching.

Hulbert's physician initially approved of the excursion but changed his mind when the day arrived. The temperature that morning was near freezing and falling, a fresh breeze was blowing out of the northeast, and light snow was falling. It was all too taxing for a man in Hulbert's condition. He would have to spend another day at home, in bed. Shortly before five o'clock in the afternoon, Hulbert called out to his wife Jennie and asked her to summon a doctor immediately. The excruciating chest pains and shortness of breath had returned without warning. Before the doctor arrived, William Ambrose Hulbert was dead, aged 49.[1]

The National League was as prepared as it could be to recover from the loss of its founder. At its annual meeting at the Tremont House hotel in Chicago six months earlier, Hulbert said he would serve out his term as the League's president but not seek another. Club owners agreed that in the event Hulbert could not complete his current term, A. H. Soden of Boston would step in as its president until the newly elected Abraham G. Mills could take office, in December 1882.[2]

The White Stockings had made no such arrangements. With Hulbert gone, anxious Chicago players and stockholders turned to Spalding, his lieutenant, for reassurance. Using his natural leadership skills and the authority of being club secretary, he met with players and investors two days after Hulbert's death to assure them he would keep the club on a steady course until its board met later in the month to choose Hulbert's successor. At that meeting, the board unanimously elected Spalding as president of the club and John A. Brown as secretary.

The board also agreed to buy Hulbert's stock in the club, paying his widow face value — $2,000—even though the organization had asked investors to pay in only 40 percent of the nominal price of their shares.[3]

Soon after 31-year-old Al Spalding ascended to the presidency of the Chicago Base Ball Club, a plaque with the phrase "Everything Is Possible to Him Who Dares" appeared on his desk. The maxim, cribbed from a novel, *The Seamy Side*, that was serialized in a monthly literary magazine, captured the risk-taking, swashbuckling, pugnacious image he wanted to project.[4]

He barely had time to place the plaque on his desk before his businesses started to consume his days. Among his first tasks as president of the Chicago Ball Club was to strike a deal to allow Western Union to build and operate a telegraph office on the White Stockings' grounds in exchange for $200 worth of telegraph service annually. It was a good deal for the club, whose travels required frequent communication by telegraph, but it was perhaps a better deal for the gamblers Spalding despised: They and their customers would not need to come to Lakefront Park to conduct their business because details of every game would be transmitted by telegraph almost in real time to pool halls and saloons throughout Chicago.

* * *

The previous October, as Hulbert was being confined to his home to rest, a group of businessmen who were eager to enter the baseball business but unable to join the League met in Pittsburgh to discuss starting their own major league. Less than a month later, they announced the birth of the American Association, which would place teams in Baltimore, Cincinnati, Louisville, Philadelphia, Pittsburgh, and St. Louis. Opening Day would be May 1, 1882. The question for Spalding was: How should he and the rest of the League treat this upstart circuit?

The AA did not encroach on any of the League's self-declared exclusive markets and did not overpay for players while filling its rosters. Indeed, it shared the National League's interest in having only one team per city and in not raiding other teams' rosters and setting off bidding wars for players. These common interests enabled the major leagues and high-minor Northwestern League to draft and sign an agreement spelling out what was and wasn't permitted. Territorial exclusivity was sacrosanct, for example, and contracts with players were to be honored by all.[5]

However, conflicts remained. The American Association still intended to schedule Sunday games where local laws allowed them to do so; it would not bend on its plan to sell beer on its grounds and would consider hiring players the National League blackballed for rowdiness, insubordination, drunkenness, or other infractions. This threatened to roll back some of the fragile progress Hulbert and Spalding had achieved in improving the public's perception of professional ball—work that was far from over. The *New York Times*, which normally paid scant attention to sports, had recently taken time to editorialize that the so-called national pastime "was, in the beginning, a sport unworthy of men, and is now, in its fully developed state, unworthy of gentlemen."[6]

Boozing, betting, and brawling were still common enough to dissuade many refined prospects—college graduates in particular—from even considering a baseball career. Amos Alonzo Stagg, the venerated Ivy League athlete and later multi-sport coach, said that when he was preparing to enroll at Yale he received extravagant salary offers to play professional baseball in Detroit, New York, and Indianapolis. He chose Yale. Years later, he explained his decision by saying that professional ballplayers in the 1880s "were a hard-bitten lot, about whom grouped hangers-on, men and women, who were worse." He added: "There was a bar in every ball park, and the whole tone of the game was smelly."[7]

Spalding set out to improve the game's image by treating players and patrons alike as if they were royalty. When playing out of town, the White Stockings stayed in the finest hotels willing to accept ballplayers and traveled to and from ballparks not in one-horse buses but in a fleet of fine barouches pulled by white horses covered in black blankets embroidered with "Chicago. Champions." In Chicago, Spalding made Lakefront Park into a model of the kind of facility that would naturally attract the better classes to baseball. Back-to-back pennants attracted consistently big crowds—more than 130,000 paid to see 45 home games in 1882—which enabled Spalding to invest about $10,000 in expanding the park to accommodate 10,000 spectators: 2,000 in the grandstand, 6,000 on bleachers, and 2,000 more in standing room. He eliminated the spaces where pool sellers and other gamblers once met to conduct their noxious business.[8]

Atop the grandstand, Spalding added 18 private compartments, precursors of today's luxury boxes. He furnished them with upholstered armchairs and cloaked them in heavy drapes to protect boxholders from wind, dust, and prying eyes. Spalding had his own box outfitted with a telephone, one of only about 3,500 phones in the entire city of 600,000 people, and a brass gong with which he expressed his feelings about the progress of the game.[9]

He also instructed Anson to make the players act like gentlemen. "The men may complain to the umpires, but I don't want to hear any swearing from where I am sitting in the stands," he told his captain. "We want to make the place respectable for the ladies." For spectators' convenience, each game at the renovated grounds was staffed with six ushers, six refreshment boys, three cushion renters, and eight musicians. *Harper's Weekly* declared Lakefront Park "indisputably the finest in the world in respect of seating accommodations and conveniences."[10]

To protect that investment and minimize any negative fallout from the Association's loose rules about playing on Sundays and selling alcohol, Hulbert advised Spalding to avoid mentioning the so-called Beer and Whiskey League when speaking in public. He also told his protégé to rebuff AA requests to play exhibition games with any NL team. Spalding followed the advice, and to put the differences between the leagues in even sharper relief, he redoubled his campaigns against drinking, gambling, and rowdyism.

It wasn't easy, or successful. Whenever he raised the topics of liquor, late nights, or loose women, players groaned. "What are you running here? A Sunday School or a base ball club?" the bibulous, base-stealing catcher Michael "King" Kelly asked at one such meeting. Spalding told the players that he routinely received letters from "prominent citizens and patrons of the game"—that is, the higher-class people Spalding ached to fill his beautiful ballpark—complaining about ballplayers' after-hours "drunkenness and debauchery;" the men dismissed such tales as being either exaggerated or cut from whole cloth.[11]

Since Spalding didn't frequent saloons or pool halls, he couldn't definitively rebut players' claims with his own firsthand accounts of their misconduct, so he engaged a Pinkerton detective to snoop for him. The detective's inch-thick report detailed the nightly travails of seven of the 15 players through a roster of saloons and taverns up and down Clark Street. When Spalding confronted players with the report, Kelly challenged its accuracy. "In that place where the detective reports me as taking a lemonade at 3 a.m. he's off," Kelly said. "It was straight whiskey; I never drank a lemonade at that hour in my life."[12]

Spalding levied $25 fines on each of the seven players named in the report.[13]

Later in the season, when the team was preparing to board a train to Detroit, Kelly and his drinking partner, the pitcher Jim McCormick, thought they spotted the Pinkerton agent in the station. Kelly walked up to the unsuspecting gentleman and "after denouncing him in most violent terms as a Pinkerton detective, hauled off and smote him with all his might," said Spalding. McCormick then approached the man from behind and "kicked the poor fellow's pants clear up on his shoulders." Then Kelly and McCormick raced to the track and jumped onto the platform of the rear car.[14]

Spalding often recounted tales of players' antics in the field, including the time Kelly pretended to catch a long flyball for the third out in the dusky final inning of a close game, causing the opposing team to strand three runners and handing Chicago a narrow victory. But the club president, whose manner the *New York Times* once described as being that of a Church of England bishop, never saw anything amusing in well-paid ballplayers slacking off or playing while intoxicated.[15]

In 1884, for example, the White Stockings lost 14 of their first 20 games and were already 11 games out of first place before playing their first game in Chicago. To be fair, Chicago did play all of those first 20 games on the road in only 27 days interspersed with eight long, slow, bumpy, sooty train rides. Spalding, however, was less interested in the losing streak than newspaper articles about Anson losing control of some debauched veterans. He didn't question the articles' accuracy because Anson had written to him during the road trip, naming the players who were drunk during games; Spalding summarily fined each man $50.[16]

By return letter, Spalding told Anson it was "mortifying" to run a ballclub that was "notorious throughout the country" for being "the most dissipated nine on the road."

"I am thoroughly disgusted with the miserable exhibition we have made on this trip so far, and, while we may have so far lost our skill that we cannot regain the position we once held in the baseball world, yet there is one thing that we can do, and that is to make our players understand that they must tend to business and give an equivalent for the high salaries they receive," Spalding added. "I also want you to report to me any indifference or carelessness in play that may be shown by any of the players, and if I become convinced that any of the players, for any reason, are not playing up to their highest standard, and doing the very best in their power to win games, I will make the fine for this offense double what it will be for dissipation.

"I am tired of apologizing for the shortcomings of some of our men, and trying to explain away their many misbehaviors that are reported to me," he concluded. "So, from now out, anyone who violates any of our regulations will have a chance to estimate its cost in dollars and cents."[17]

Tighter discipline paid dividends. Chicago won 60 percent of the games remaining in the season, climbing out of seventh place in the eight-team league to finish in fifth place. It went on to win pennants in 1885 and 1886, the club's third and fourth championship titles in six years. Spalding's investments in assembling the NL's best team and building the best grounds was paying off handsomely: The White Stockings posted a profit of $62,000 in the regular season of 1886, second only to Boston, which earned $65,000.[18]

After the regular season, Chicago, the National League champion, and the St. Louis Browns, winner of the American Association title, agreed to play a series of games to determine which club deserved to be called world champion. (The same two clubs had done the same after capturing their respective league pennants in 1885; Providence and New York pioneered the playoff idea in 1884.)

Before the 1886 playoff, Spalding, the fervent gambling foe, suggested to the St. Louis club's owner, a brewery owner named Chris Von de Ahe, that they make the series more interesting by having each team bet its half of the gate receipts; Von der Ahe, a spirited German immigrant who resented the National League's sanctimonious opposition to beer sales at ballgames, took up the bet. The series began in Chicago, where the White Stockings won two of three games. In the only one McCormick was sober enough to pitch, he allowed 13 hits and six earned runs.

St. Louis won the first two games at Sportsman's Park and came from behind to tie the next game in the eighth inning. The score was still tied 3–3 in the bottom of the 10th, with the Brown Stockings' center fielder Curt Welch on third base and catcher Doc Bushong at bat. Clarkson fired in a pitch that Kelly could not quite handle. As the ball skittered to the backstop, Welch tore home with the winning run.[19]

St. Louis captured the series for the second year in a row and cost Spalding gate receipts of $13,920.10—roughly equivalent to half a million dollars in 2024—in his bet with Von der Ahe. The Chicagoan was so furious he refused to pay train fare home for players who had lost their cash betting on themselves.[20]

One month after the series ended, Spalding began dismantling the Chicago club by selling the contracts of five of its starting players. Outfielders Abner Dalrymple and George Gore went first, to Pittsburgh and New York, respectively. Spalding next summoned Kelly to his office. He was going to require all Chicago players to sign a temperance pledge and was sure Kelly would refuse. A nasty public spat would follow.

"Mike, how would you like to play in Boston?"

Dumbstruck, Kelly could manage only a weak response: "What's the matter with Chicago? I like it here."

"Mike, you'll like it in Boston. I know because I played there once. Those Irish fans will really adopt you." Since Spalding had no intention of sharing any of the cash Boston was paying for Kelly's contract, the player remained silent. Spalding closed the sale when he told Kelly Boston could pay him $5,000 a year—twice as much as Chicago paid him in 1886.

"Well, if that's the way it is, that's the way it is," Kelly replied. "And if there is money in it for me, it's all right." With that, he picked up his hat and left Spalding's office.[21]

Chicago shocked the sporting community when it announced that Kelly would join the Boston club after it had agreed to buy the future Hall of Fame member's contract from the White Stocking for the then-astonishing sum of $10,000. In addition to paying Chicago for the right to Kelly's services, Boston also paid Kelly an annual salary of $5,000. McCormick's contract was auctioned off in April, with the Pittsburgh Allegheny club taking home the prize, reportedly by agreeing to pay $2,000 to Chicago and $2,800 a year to the player.[22] Still, McCormick, who ran a saloon in Paterson, New Jersey, in the offseason, did not go quietly; he defamed Spalding and Anson every chance he got once his trade was announced. Spalding gave back as good as he got. "He drank about as much as all the rest of them put together," he said. "He lost all his effectiveness before the season was half over and was a useless 'back number' the latter part of the race. Then he said it was rheumatism that bothered him. Rheumatism! Bah!"[23]

Spalding paused his clearance sale of players during the 1887 season, which concluded with Chicago falling to third place. He resumed peddling players in January 1888, dispatching Billy Sunday, the teetotaling, base-stealing center fielder, to Pittsburgh. The Chicago club's president ended his spree with another blockbuster: letting the Boston club have the pitcher John Clarkson, another future Hall of Fame resident, for another $10,000 check.[24]

Why would the president of a pennant-winning powerhouse dismember his roster in such short order? Was it the lousy play that caused him to lose the bet with Von der Ahe, whom Spalding considered socially inferior? Was it that players' misconduct distracted him from his business, which was growing rapidly in the 1880s?

At the time, Spalding said he was embarrassed by the boorish behavior of several players and exasperated by the truculence of a few, principally Kelly and McCormick. "Last year the Chicago management was sharply criticized because of the dissipation of some players. The criticism was deserved," he said. "I talked with the players at fault as kindly as I knew how. The policy of conciliation failed. Then I fined the men guilty of dissipation $25 each. It did no good in the cases of Kelly and McCormick."

When taking money *out* of the players' pay envelopes failed to persuade the men to reform, Spalding offered to put more money *into* their pay envelopes to achieve the same goal. McCormick was offered a $350 bonus and Kelly an extra $200 if they would abstain from consuming "malt or spiritous liquors" for a season. This, too, failed. Spalding decided they had to go.[25]

In his memoir published more than 20 years later, Spalding expressed a much different reason for selling off his team's best players. It was not that they were so *bad*, it was because they were so *good*. "The players were so capable that they were expected to win every game. It did seem almost impossible for them to lose. . . . Experience has shown that keeping the same players together for too long a time is prejudicial to the interests of the game. I had learned that lesson in my notice of the effect of the four years of successive championship victories gained by the Boston team, and felt that the time had come for a change in personnel of the Chicago nine."[26]

Whatever his motive, Spalding declared his idea a success. "The action [selling off five of his starting players] already procured good results," Spalding added, "as our men this year do not drink and they take pride in keeping up the reputation of the club."[27]

The action may have boosted Chicago's reputation off the field but certainly not its reputation on the field. Before the action, Chicago had won six of the

National League's first 11 championships; after Spalding cleaned house it would not win another pennant for two decades.

* * *

Spalding had better luck in dealing with many players' noisome habit of bullying and bickering with official scorers—at least he stopped the practice in Chicago. Scorers decide matters such as whether a batter reaches base on a hit or an error and whether a toss that scoots past home plate is the pitcher's fault (a wild pitch) or the catcher's mistake (a passed ball). Such decisions can, over the course of a season or career, have a significant influence on earned-run averages, batting averages, and other statistics used to negotiate salaries.

Spalding stopped players from harassing the scorer by giving the job to a woman who had been attending White Stockings' home games regularly for years and learned to keep a flawless written record of each game—tallying every pitch, putout, walk, hit, run, and error. Her name was Eliza Green Williams, and she caught Spalding's attention by self-assuredly sitting in seats intended for players' family members. They were on a first-name basis for some time when Spalding asked her if she would consider being Chicago's official scorer. Players in the 1880s were unlikely to think a woman would hold such an important position, and if they did find out they would not be so ungentlemanly as to browbeat her the way they did many men. She took the job.

Williams and Spalding agreed to keep her hiring a secret—she to avoid the players' whining about her scoring decisions and he to avoid ridicule for trusting a woman in what had always been a man's job. "Manager Anson never knew who was official scorer for the club, nor did any of the players, newspapers, or the public," Eliza's son, Charles G. Williams, said when major-league owners proposed keeping scorers' names secret to protect them from players' influence. In her day, Williams concealed her identity by signing box scores with her maiden name, E. G. Green, and having her son mail them to the League office. She held the job from 1882, the year Spalding became president of the White Stockings, until he sold his interest in the club a decade later.[28]

While Spalding would outfox players to resolve some problems, he just outwaited them to settle others.

During the dog days of summer one year, Spalding was working in his office over the store on Madison Street when an acquaintance entered unannounced and eager to share gossip about the White Stockings, who were halfway through a long road trick back east.

"Well," the visitor said, "either the newspaper correspondents or the Chicago players are managing to raise a devil of a rumpus down East."

"I should say you are pretty right in that calculation," replied Al, "with chances 100 to 1 in favor of the correspondents."

"Yon don't think the team is going to pieces then?"

"I don't look as though I entertained any such belief, do I?" the mogul replied with a broad grin.

"Do you believe there has been any trouble between Anson and Pfeffer?"

"Oh, possibly Anson has slapped a fine onto Mr. Pfeffer's neck, and if he has done so the chances are that the big fellow is in the right. Anson is not the man to fine a player merely for the fun of fining him, and Pfeffer knows it, and I know it also, and am therefore surprised that Pfeffer above all others should have been fined."

The postman entered Spalding's office and deposited the morning's mail on the club president's desk. A letter from Pfeffer was in the pile. It contained few details but plenty of venom, suggesting the player was still white hot when he penned it. Spalding laughed as he drafted the following telegraphic response:

"Fred Pfeffer, Willard Hotel, Washington, D.C.—Letter received. The matter will be investigated and if any injustice has been done you it shall be righted. Do not air your affairs through the newspapers, but play ball and win the pennant. A. G. SPALDING."

As Spalding finished composing the missive, a friend burst into the office, breathless and agitated. "Have you read the papers?" the friend gasped. "Have you seen the reports that the club is going to pieces down East?"

"Yes," Spalding said with a smile. "I've read 'em all."

"You have read about Anson and Pfeffer having a row and Pfeffer swearing he would not play another game with the team? That the balance of the boys are going to stand by Pfeffer, etc.?"

"Yep. I've gone through the whole business."

"Well, great God, you look as though you enjoyed the news!" the visitor blurted out, exasperated at Spalding's calm demeanor.

"My dear, dear man, when you have been in the business as long as I have—if you ever get there—you will not let such a little thing as your team going to pieces (in the newspapers, I mean) bother you one particle. Now, if it will make you feel any easier, I will tell you that the team is not going to pieces; that Mr. Pfeffer will play ball just the same this afternoon as he has always done; that there is no dissension in our ranks; and lastly, that you may look for the pennant of 1887 to wave over the West Side grounds next fall, or see Chicago in second place after giving the winners the hardest fight on record."[29]

In 1883, as the season wound down with Chicago trailing the league-leading Boston club by four games, three White Stockings players—pitcher Larry Corcoran, catcher Frank Sylvester "Silver" Flint, and center fielder George "Piano Legs" Gore—agreed among themselves to refuse to sign contracts for 1884 unless Spalding met their salary demands. Corcoran set his price at $4,500, Flint at $3,500, and Gore at $2,500. Spalding paid them no attention and went about signing the rest of the team, including future Hall of Fame inductees Cap Anson, John Clarkson, and "King" Kelly, all at modest salary increases.

Days and then weeks ticked by without Spalding asking to negotiate with the three holdouts or even suggesting that he would ever come to the bargaining table. The players were contractually bound to the White Stockings, and the National League, American Association, and Northwestern League had agreed before the 1883 season, in what came to be known as the National Agreement, to raise to 11 the number of players each team could "reserve." To reserve a player was to forbid him to negotiate with any club but the one for which he was currently contracted to play. When introduced in 1879 to stop the top five players on each club from "revolving," or changing teams, the clause proved to be such an excellent tool for limiting player salaries—it effectively outlawed competition for their services—that club owners repeatedly raised the number of players they could reserve.[30]

Flint was the first to fold in the face of Spalding's apparent indifference. He came to the team president with a dubious tale about being approached by the club in St. Louis, coincidentally his wife's hometown. After a brief talk, Spalding generously agreed to pay him $2,500 to catch for half of the next season.[31]

Gore was more difficult to corral. He had gone up against Spalding before, and won. In 1878, Gore batted .324 playing for the New Bedford Whalers of the International League, a top-tier minor circuit. Spalding offered the 24-year-old outfielder $1,200 to move to the White Stockings. That was about four times what New Bedford was paying him, but Gore turned Spalding down and held out for $2,500. They eventually settled on $1,900.[32]

This time, Spalding had the advantage of the reserve clause—Gore would have to play for Chicago or not play at all, at least not in a major league. Gore also had committed to coach a professional team in New Orleans over the winter and had to move there soon.[33] The center fielder finally capitulated and settled for $2,000.

Corcoran took a different tack, declaring early in the new year that he would play in the new Union Association, a competitor to the National League and American Association that was not bound by the reserve clause. Spalding couldn't stand losing a valued player like Corcoran to some Johnny-come-lately team owner—particularly one in a new association that threatened his monopoly in Chicago. He dispatched Cap Anson, his field manager, to locate Corcoran and persuade him to stay with the White Stockings.[34]

Soon enough, Spalding received the telegram he wished for:

"I signed Corcoran this afternoon. Send the $400.00 advance money to me. I will write full particulars. A. C. Anson."

Spalding was so delighted that he dashed off a letter to share the news with NL president A. G. Mills: "Whoop-la!" his letter began. "Corcoran has signed and the back of the Union Association is broken . . . ."

The Corcoran news was correct, but Spalding's wishful thinking about the UA was not—yet. He had been predicting the Union Association's collapse since scuttlebutt began to circulate in late August 1883 about a group of businessmen preparing to launch a third professional baseball circuit. The men, from Baltimore, Chicago, New York, Philadelphia, Pittsburgh, Richmond, St. Louis, and Washington, first met on November 12, 1883, at the Monongahela House hotel in Pittsburgh. Interest in the clearly lucrative baseball business was so high that men who were unable to attend the meeting—representing Brooklyn, Hartford, Milwaukee, and Indianapolis—sent telegrams asking to be considered for membership.[35]

Spalding early on had grasped that for this new Union Association to be financially viable, it would have to situate its clubs in cities that already hosted National League or American Association teams. This would kill the territorial exclusivity that was the foundation of peace between the established major leagues and was just starting to help all teams in those circuits see a bump in attendance and profits.[36]

On top of that, the Union Association committed itself "to ignore the 'eleven men' rule now in vogue in the League and the American Association."

In other words, it would disregard the established leagues' reserve clause, which effectively made players property of their teams and kept player salaries below what they would fetch in an open market.[37]

By the time Union Association officials gathered at Earle's Hotel in New York City at the end of September to decide which eight of 15 clubs that had asked to join the circuit would be accepted, the League was ready to fight. On the day news of the Union Association meeting appeared in newspapers, so, too, did articles about a rhetorical broadside printed in the Chicago *American Sports*, a Spalding-owned paper.

The unsigned editorial characterized the Union Association's commitment to reject the reserve clause as a "club-wrecking policy" and said that the men behind the UA were determined to "go into the 'cut-throat' business helter-skelter." It then shifted into an ad hominem attack of the sort Spalding had used in the past and would employ again in the future to demean and demoralize a series of competing baseball organizations.[38]

"If this program [the Union Association] were backed up by men of means, responsibility, and respectability, the League and Association clubs might well feel alarmed at an outlook so injurious to their own prospects and so detrimental to the interests of baseball generally," the commentary asserted.[39] "But we search the list of officers and directors in vain for the name of one person of means or responsibility, or whose business and social standing is such as to inspire confidence either among ball-players or ball-patrons."[40]

Spalding belittled a cofounder of a minor league called the International League, L. C. Waite of St. Louis, as an "ambitious demagogue." He dismissed Waite's accusations against Spalding as unproven and unprovable, and then said why he had not shared his proposal with the IA's creator: "I sent the paper to officers of three or four clubs whom I believed to be intelligent, clear-headed, experienced men working not for personal notoriety but for the material interest of the clubs, and capable of passing impartial judgment upon the merits of the plan.

"Consequently," he added sarcastically, "I did not send it to Mr. Waite."[41]

Despite Spalding's public doubts about the "means" and "social standing" of the men behind it, the Union Association caused some League clubs no small amount of grief in its only year of operation. Player salaries soared as teams from all three professional leagues bid for the better players. The average salary for St. Louis Browns players rose to $3,000 in 1884, although the club dropped to fourth place in the standings from second place a year earlier. Before the 1884 season, the Chicago Union club poached pitcher Hugh Dailey from the National League's Cleveland Blues and said it would pay Emil Gross of NL's Philadelphia Phillies to be his catcher. A. G. Mills asked Spalding to talk with Gross and persuade him to stay in Philadelphia. "You must know Gross quite well," he wrote to Spalding, "and I do think you would be doing a service to the Philadelphia club, to your own club, and to the common cause if you can induce Gross to keep his word with Philadelphia."[42]

Spalding did not induce Gross to stay in Philadelphia, nor could he prevent the heart of Cleveland's roster—pitcher Jim McCormick, infielder Jack Glasscock, and catcher Charles "Fatty" Briody—from jumping to the Cincinnati Outlaw Reds of the Union League in August (although he did help to dissuade the Blues' president, C. H. Bulkeley, from disbanding the team midseason after the players had bolted).

In the end, it did not matter. Most UA teams were unable to simultaneously compete financially with both established National League clubs and the richest owner in their own circuit, Henry V. Lucas.[43]

The scion of a wealthy property-owning family in St. Louis, Lucas had spent lavishly to build a dominant team and succeeded spectacularly—perhaps too spectacularly. His St. Louis Maroons won all 20 games they played in the UA's first month and cinched the championship with five weeks remaining in the season. Such competitive imbalance gave fans little reason to pay 25 cents to watch Union games; weaker UA clubs quickly crashed for lack of revenue. Three of the eight teams that started the Union Association's season were not around to finish it, nor was one of the four hastily arranged mid-season replacements. Only two clubs sent delegates to a UA meeting in January 1885; they voted to disband the circuit. Lucas, his club—and his fortune—were warmly welcomed when he asked to join the National League.[44]

After the smoke cleared, Spalding had managed to keep Chicago all to himself—just as the city's booming population was surpassing those of Philadelphia and Brooklyn.

Rockford Forest City club at the peak of its glory, in 1867 or 1868, around the time it beat the Washington Nationals. Teen-aged Spalding sits to the right of club president Hiram Waldo.

Spalding led the Boston Red Stockings to four pennants in five years in the early 1870s.

The interior of the A.G. Spalding & Bro. store on Randolph Street in Chicago. Offices and manufacturing were on the upper floors. CHICAGOLOGY.COM

Portraits of the 1877 Chicago White Stockings, defending champions of the new National League. Clockwise from the top are: Ross Barnes, John Peters, Cap Anson, George Bradley, Charlie Waitt, Paul Hines, Cal McVey, John Glenn, and Al Spalding in the center.

Spalding in his early 30s, when he was aggressively building his sporting goods empire. SPALDING'S OFFICIAL BASE BALL GUIDE FOR 1882

Spalding and his first wife, Josie, bought this house in the Kenwood section of Chicago in 1882 and lived there for almost two decades. HANNA HOLBORN GRAY SPECIAL COLLECTIONS RESEARCH CENTER, UNIVERSITY OF CHICAGO LIBRARY

Harper's magazine called Chicago's Lakefront Park "indisputably the finest in the world" in an 1883 article. The White Stockings had to move a year later because the ball ground was illegally built on federal property. W. P. SNYDER, HARPER'S

Tour organizers outraged Roman authorities by offering 1,000 pounds sterling to let them play a baseball game in the Colosseum. CHICAGOLOGY

Plans to play a ballgame in the shadow of the Sphinx were stopped by the difficulty in running on sand and spectators' penchant for snatching groundballs. Players settled for climbing the sculpture. CHICAGOLOGY

Spalding bought this summer "cottage" near the shore in Rumson, N.J., in 1893 for $104,000, the equivalent of $3.7 million in 2024. MONMOUTH COUNTY HISTORICAL ASSOCIATION

Spalding and his second wife, Elizabeth, moved into this octagonal house in the Theosophical Society community near San Diego in 1901. He died there in 1915. SAN DIEGO HISTORICAL SOCIETY

A.G. Spalding in 1910, when he unsuccessfully campaigned to be the Republican nominee for a US Senate seat representing California. BAIN COLLECTION / LIBRARY OF CONGRESS

Chapter 9

Color Line Blind

While there is ample evidence of Spalding's conviction—as a businessman, if not a moralizer—to eradicate gambling, drinking, fighting, and other ills plaguing professional ball in the 1880s, there is none to suggest that he actively opposed or even questioned the establishment of a color line. Indeed, he employed one of the most intractable supporters of segregating the sport: Adrian Anson, who managed Chicago's National League club while Spalding was the club's president and an intimate advisor to two League presidents.

Anson's status as the best-known League player of the era and the manager of a successful team amplified his calls to ban Black players from the sport and gave license to lesser-known athletes to first shun Black teammates and then join the call to segregate baseball.

Granted, Spalding was a callow teenager when segregation became explicit at an NABBP convention in December 1867. The men at that gathering in Philadelphia adopted a resolution that said, "no club composed of persons of color, or having in its membership persons of color, shall be admitted into the National Association."[1]

Like most NAPBBP strictures, segregation was lackadaisically enforced. At least 60 African-American men played in minor leagues—mostly on all-Black ballclubs—in the late 1800s, as Spalding rose in stature and power. But even after Hulbert's death and Spalding's elevation to president of the Chicago club, he appeared to tolerate segregation so long as it didn't get in the way of business.

In the summer of 1883, Chicago squeezed into its schedule an exhibition game in Toledo, Ohio, with the local member of the highly regarded Northwestern League, the Blue Stockings. The hot, muggy Friday was supposed to be an off day between National League championship series in Detroit and Buffalo, but Spalding, like other club owners, coveted fat gate receipts from exhibitions played in smaller but baseball-mad cities like Toledo.

Losing a rest day didn't sweeten Anson's mood, and after the train carrying the White Stockings chuffed into Union Station in Toledo, Anson took a stroll around town, loudly announcing to total strangers that he would not allow his team to take the field if the Blue Stockings played their starting catcher, an African American named Moses Fleetwood "Fleet" Walker from Steubenville, Ohio. In fact, the Toledo manager, Charlie Morton, had planned to give Walker a day off to rest his hands from the pounding they took by catching without a glove, but when he learned about Anson's bigoted bluster the 28-year-old Toledo manager added Walker back to the lineup and had him play in the outfield.[2]

When Walker began warming up with his teammates, Anson loudly insisted that he not be permitted to play. Morton ignored him, so Anson started to usher his players off the field. A newspaper reported that the Toledo manager marched over to "the beefy bluffer" and said "he could play his team or go, just as he blank [*sic*] pleased." But, Morton reminded Anson, if he forfeited the game, he would also forfeit Chicago's take from ticket sales. Anson grudgingly backed down. "We'll play this here game," Anson muttered angrily, "but won't play never no more with the [racial epithet] in." The defending National League champion Chicago edged past Toledo by a score of 7–6 in 10 innings.[3]

The undiluted ugliness Anson displayed in Toledo was familiar to Black ballplayers in the 1870s and '80s, as Reconstruction was disassembled and Jim Crow grew. A few months before the Toledo game, for example, the executive committee of the Northwestern League, convened at Boody House hotel in Toledo to consider "a motion . . . by the representative from the Peoria, Illinois, club that no colored player be allowed in the league." The motion was intended to expel Walker and forbid his younger brother Weldy from joining a team. After a bitter argument, the motion was withdrawn.[4]

Two years earlier, when Walker played for the Cleveland White Stockings, his team went to Louisville, Kentucky, to face the local Eclipse ballclub. A private policeman, egged on by Eclipse team members, forbade Walker to step onto the field. The private cop tried to forcibly eject the Oberlin College graduate from the grounds but stopped when spectators complained that he was giving the bum's rush to a talented catcher. Walker was permitted to watch the game but forbidden to participate in it.[5]

Chicago returned to Toledo in 1884 for another exhibition with the Blue Stockings, now a member of the major-league American Association. The game gave Spalding another opportunity to muzzle Anson on racial matters, but he chose instead to ask Toledo to punish Walker for being Black. Three months before the game, John A. C. Brown, a lieutenant of Spalding's and secretary-treasurer of the White Stockings, wrote to Morton to assure him "the management of the Chicago Ball Club have no personal feeling about the matter"—of having Black and white men play together—but "the players do most decisively object, and to preserve harmony in the club it is necessary that I have your assurance in writing that [Walker] will not play any position in your nine July 25th."

Morton evidently had already written to Brown about the Chicago club's demand that Walker sit out the game, but he was not as unequivocal as Brown desired. "I have no doubt such is your meaning," Brown wrote, "only your letter does not express in full [*sic*]. I have no desire to replay the occurrence of last season and must have your guarantee to that effort."[6]

It is inconceivable that Brown would have demanded Walker's exclusion without Spalding's knowledge, approval—and perhaps input. As the game day approached, Brown did talk with Spalding about Anson's intention not to play if Walker did. Spalding wrote directly to Anson to "strongly urge" him to take to the field in one game because not to do so could tarnish Cap's reputation and elicit further criticism of Chicago's behavior. "Your leaving the club at Toledo will only add another argument for the 'croakers,'" Spalding added, using contemporary slang for complainers.

He also noted the financial risk in not playing. "You should understand full well how difficult it is to get a game without your presence," Spalding wrote. Curiously, Spalding didn't advocate on behalf of Black players even if only to increase the number of talented players and put downward pressure on players' salaries. Perhaps Spalding feared that integrated teams would drive away the upper-class spectators he was trying to attract.

Walker did not play against Chicago on the warm, overcast Friday when the White Stockings came to town; a white player from Youngstown, Ohio, James "Deacon" McGuire, was behind the plate for Toledo. The club released Walker on September 29, 1884. He was the last Black major leaguer until Jackie Robinson took the field for the Brooklyn Dodgers 63 years later.

Black players continued to play professionally in high minor leagues several more years. Their number peaked in 1887, when rosters included George Stovey, considered the best African-American pitcher of the 19th century; Frank Grant, a second baseman who may have been the best Black player at any position in the 19th century; second baseman Bud Fowler; pitcher Robert Higgins; and Fleet Walker.

Opportunities for Black players faded as more newspapers reported on griping by some unidentified white teammates. "A number of colored players are now in the International League, and to put it mildly their presence is distasteful to the other players," the *Toronto World* reported.[7] The *Sporting News* lamented, "How far will this mania for engaging colored players go?"[8]

In the middle of the season, team owners in the International League, a high-minor circuit that may have benefited the most from signing talented Black players who had been denied the opportunity to play on major-league teams, voted to forbid its clubs to sign new contracts with Black players.[9] The ballot came hours before the International League club in Newark, New Jersey, was scheduled to start Stovey in an exhibition against Spalding's White Stockings. A white player, Mickey Hughes, started as pitcher in place of Stovey, who was released at the end of the season.

Chapter 10

Are Players Chattels?

Before the Union Association crashed the party, National League and American Association clubs took full advantage of their regional monopolies in 1883 and raked in revenue from people who were willing to pay for a distraction from the latest recession, which would, at its worst, shrink the economy by a third. Baseball seemed to be immune to the economic contagion.

"The professional baseball season of 1883 was, beyond question, the most successful one known in the history of that class of the fraternity," Spalding crowed in his guide for 1884. "Not only was it marked by a financial success beyond precedent; but, in the operations of the several championship campaigns on the field, the work done was of a character decidedly superior to that of previous years."[1]

Club owners were feeling so flush that they amended the National Agreement to set a minimum salary of $1,000 for players (while also raising to 11 from five the number of players each team could reserve).

A year later, however, the arrival of the Union Association and the persistence of the recession reversed the fortunes of the National League and American Association. "Only a minority of the clubs of the two leading associations of the year had a surplus of funds in their treasuries at the end of the season," according to Spalding's 1885 guide.[2]

Presidents of NL and AA clubs blamed players' salaries for the losses posted by most teams in 1884, forgetting to mention who had agreed to pay the salaries. They appointed a conference committee to meet in Saratoga, New York, in August 1885 to explore ideas to rein in players' pay, routinely the largest expense for professional teams. They also wanted to find a face-saving way to repatriate players who had jumped to the Union Association and, under the terms of the

National Agreement, ought to be blacklisted. Spalding was among three club presidents nominated to represent the National League; the American Association sent three presidents of its own. The plan: work out solutions to those knotty issues, which would be put to a vote by the two organizations' full memberships at their respective winter meetings in November.[3]

Spalding entered the talks with experience both as a club executive well able to resist players' salary demands and as a former player familiar with ways to squeeze as much money as possible out of club executives. (One can't help but wonder if the middle-aged Spalding ever reflected on the astonishing $6,000 the young Spalding was paid in his first season playing for Chicago.) In any case, Spalding certainly knew the challenges the committee faced.

"The most difficult problem the League has had to solve . . . has been that of how to control and regulate the salaries of players," he wrote in his 1884 *Spalding Guide*. "The club rivalry for the possession of the best players each season, has been, from the very outset, an obstacle to an equitable arrangement of the salary question; and this has led to an increase of club expenses of this kind until the subject became one involving the future existence of even the most wealthy of the League clubs.

"Within the past year or two," he added, "this salary question has passed beyond the bounds of a reasonable remuneration for professional service on the ballfields to the region of exorbitant demands, which, if complied with, would eventually bankrupt the strongest company in the professional arena."

He then resurrected the argument that ballplayers should be grateful for whatever their clubs wanted to pay them because it would be more than the $10 they could earn for a week of 10- to 15-hour shifts as, say, a streetcar driver, a brakeman, a porter, or an assistant at some ordinary trade.[4]

Players had heard this canard often enough, from Spalding and others, and responded.

"It may be, and undoubtedly will be, claimed by some that these men who make now from $2,000 to $3,000 and $3,500 in seven months playing ball could hardly make as much in seven years at anything else that they could do," a correspondent identified as "Veteran" wrote in an open letter to one paper. "This may be true, but it is a child's argument and it is high time it was so recognized. . . .

"If anyone was to say that an opera singer, an actor, an acrobat, a minstrel or any other showman would not be paid a large salary because he could not earn one-tenth as much at anything else, he would be held up as the laughingstock of the community. He [any other showman] is paid for his special qualifications and ability to make money for his employer. I claim the ball player is paid in the same way—and he should be—[because] he and his comrades are worth to the management just what their services produce.

"Every good player is a drawing card of more or less attracting power and the aggregate drawing power of a team is largely due to its individual attractiveness."[5]

* * *

At the August meeting in Saratoga, Spalding and the other conference committee members drafted several options for the two major circuits to consider at their respective winter meetings scheduled for November. In fact, the League and Association took up the salary question at a special meeting, closed to the public, beginning Thursday, October 15, at the elegant Fifth Avenue Hotel in New York City. The club presidents' reception of the committee's work is not known, but discussions dragged on through most of the day, then resumed the next morning and continued well into the wintry Friday night. As midnight approached, the League and Association issued their salary-saving ideas in an amended National Agreement. Among other things, the new Agreement increased the number of players a team could reserve, forbade clubs to give players advances on their salaries, and, with no advance warning, capped players' salaries at $2,000 per season.[6]

Not surprisingly, players took the news—particularly the salary cap—badly. "The time has arrived when the players must take some action in the matter," said a member of the New York club. "Since the organization of the League and American Association, the legislation has been solely in the interests of the clubs. The players have been ignored at every meeting, and restrictions one after another have been laid upon them until now they can stand it no longer."

Club owners had disconnected pay from performance, the player said. "A club can engage a player, reduce his salary to $1,000, and compel him to play for that sum, although he may have a standing offer of five times that amount elsewhere," the unidentified player said. "He cannot accept the high salary simply because he is reserved. Should he do so, paying no heed to his reservation, he will be on the same footing with a man who has [fixed] a game and, of course, he would not be eligible to play in either of the associations thereafter."[7]

Players weren't alone in criticizing the salary cap. Several baseball writers did, too: "There cannot be any reason adduced why any player should receive less than he is worth," the *New York Clipper* correspondent in Boston wrote. "While all will admit that no player is worth $4,200, most of us will be forced to admit that there are plenty of players who have a market value of over $2,000." He added that the clubs' decision, made in secret, appeared to him to be "dictatorial and selfish."[8]

Less than a week after the NL and AA announced the terms of the new National Agreement, John Montgomery Ward, Tim J. Keefe, and seven other players on the New York Giants founded the Brotherhood of Professional Baseball Players, although news of the decision was slow to filter out. A union in all but name, the Brotherhood was created to represent players' interests in the development of professional ball. Ward, a practicing lawyer in the offseason, was elected president.[9]

The salary cap certainly was a factor in the organization's founding. At least five of its first members—Ward, Keefe, Jim O'Rourke, William "Buck" Ewing, and Roger Connor—earned more than $2,000 in 1885. (Arguably, they were worth every cent of their salaries: All five are now in the Hall of Fame.)[10]

The Brotherhood was meant to fight not just for salaries but also for players to be treated with dignity. Take just one example: Spalding was just settling in as captain of the White Stockings when Cal McVey, one of the players to have risked his career by leaving Boston for Chicago a few months earlier, sent Spalding a telegram saying he could not meet the team in St. Louis because his three-year-old daughter, Lulu Marie, was dying in a Chicago hospital. The child passed away on a Monday and was buried the next day; Spalding told McVey to come to the ballpark on Wednesday, ready to play.[11]

Players also were looked on as disposable assets. During the five-year peak of Larry Corcoran's pitching career, he won at least 30 games in four seasons and pitched three no-hitters. In his rookie year with Chicago, he shared pitching duties with Fred Goldsmith but still racked up 536⅓ innings in 63 appearances, winning 43 games, losing 14, striking out a league-leading 268 batters, and posting a 1.95 earned run average.

When Goldsmith began to break down in 1884, Spalding told Corcoran to pick up the slack but denied him a raise. The 24-year-old appeared in 60 games, throwing 516⅔ innings and, not surprisingly, developing a sore pitching arm. When Corcoran told Spalding that he was physically unable to pitch in 1885, Chicago promptly dropped him. Corcoran said Spalding cut him loose to avoid paying his salary for the remainder of the year. In an interview, Spalding dismissed the 5'3" Corcoran as a "little sniveler."[12]

Spalding's behavior was not especially egregious compared with his peers. Clubs routinely mistreated even their best players when it suited them. One team fined a pitcher $100 for attending his own wedding in another city on a day he was not scheduled to pitch. Another blackballed Charley Jones, the first professional player to hit two home runs in the same inning, when he refused to play until the team gave him $378 in back pay. One club suspended "Curry" Foley, the first professional batter to hit for the cycle, because he asked for time off to deal with his rheumatism; the team, convinced he was malingering, kept him on its reserved list but refused to play him—or *pay* him—for three years.[13]

By the summer of 1887, 90 League players had joined the Brotherhood—more than three-fourths of the 117 men who would play in at least 20 games that season. (It did not include any American Association players, who were organizing their own version of the Brotherhood.) Ward and Keefe, the Brotherhood's leaders, thought their members were ready to approach the League to discuss the issues most important to them. To find out what those were, the Brotherhood arranged to meet at Earle's Hotel in New York City at the end of August to map their strategy.[14]

In addition to removing the salary cap, Brotherhood members wanted to rewrite the contract between players and the League to clearly state the salary to be paid for the seven-month season and include explicit language on how the reserve clause would work. Neither were in contracts then in use. Surprisingly, the players favored retaining the reserve clause, with a few changes to be negotiated with the League.

They condemned the practice of selling players' contracts, which had become a lucrative side business for some clubs, and said that all player releases should be unconditional—that is, if a team struck a player from its roster, it would lose the right to reserve him; another club would be free to sign the player without having to compensate his former team. Likewise, if a club collapsed, it could not sell the rights to its players; each man would be free to join a new club without having to buy his contract from the defunct club.

The players also shared the League's concern about alcohol. To discourage drinking, Brotherhood members recommended a series of stepped-up fines: $25 for a first offense in a season, $50 for a second, and $100 for a third. A fourth offense would result in suspension and, if warranted, blacklisting.[15]

Ward, the Brooklyn Superbas' manager Ned Hanlon, and the Washington Nationals' manager Arthur Irwin were named to a committee to negotiate with the League, and Ward asked President Young to arrange a meeting with the appropriate League representatives "at as early a date as possible, in order that everything may be fully settled before the time arrives for the signing of contracts for 1888." Ward had already sent a letter to Young in mid-August, before the Brotherhood meeting in New York, to alert him that League players would soon ask to meet League officials with the aim of working up a mutually acceptable new contract.

As the Brotherhood's positions leaked into the newspapers, sportswriters scratched around for indications of how club owners would react. Spalding, a former player who was present at the League's birth and was its de facto leader, was a natural person to invite. But just as he had learned to use the press to steer public opinion his way if he had something to sell or promote, he also had learned how to bottle up information he wanted to keep to himself, at least for the time being. A *Sporting Life* correspondent learned this firsthand when he buttonholed Spalding on a Chicago street that summer.

"What do you think of the result of the ball players' meeting of yesterday?" the writer asked.

"Nothing," Spalding replied curtly.

"They took up the question of contracts and suggested certain changes they seem to think advisable."

"Yes?"

"Did you not read the report of the meeting in this morning's papers?" the shocked sportswriter asked.

"Yes."

"Well, then, tell me what you think of it."

"The time for the discussion of contracts has not come yet. I'd rather not."

"Do you feel kindly disposed toward the Brotherhood?"

"What difference would that make?" Spalding asked.

"Possibly none at all; possibly a good deal. What I mean is, do you think the objects of the organization are worthy ones?"

"Do you know what those objects are?" the magnate parried.

"Yes, I think I do."

"Ah? You are well posted then?"

"Why, they are the general good of ball players, are they not? A kind of benefit organization?"

"Are they?"

"Are they not?" asked the reporter, set back on his heels.

"Why, yes; I guess that is right."

"Are the relations between the clubs and the Brotherhood going to be amicable?"

"Perhaps. I hope so."

"Would you, together with the other League club presidents, consent to meet a committee from the Brotherhood to talk over the contract and other questions?"

"My boy," said Al after a moment's silence, "why discuss Christmas presents during the ice cream season? Let's go to lunch."[16]

* * *

Young had no intention of meeting representatives of the Brotherhood to discuss contracts or anything else, despite his initial, optimistic reply to Ward's overture. After that, the League executive "informally" shared Ward's letter with NL leaders at a meeting at the Coleman House hotel in Asbury Park, New Jersey, on August 15. He later said that based on the magnates' reactions, "I felt fully justified in writing to Mr. Ward (on) August 20 that I had no doubt the League would cheerfully meet a committee of its players to consider the question of a new form of players' contract." Spalding was at the meeting and may well have reacted positively to Ward's letter, but Young didn't say whom he had spoken with.[17]

In any case, when Ward next wrote to Young two weeks later to formally ask for a meeting between the Brotherhood and the League "at as early a date as possible" so that a new contract could be ready for the 1888 season, the National League president anxiously retracted his statement that league magnates would "cheerfully" meet with players. After walking back any suggestion that a new contract could be ready for the next season "in the absence of a regularly scheduled league meeting," Young wrote, not very convincingly, that he had only "unofficially" replied to Ward. "I had no authority to recognize any communication from the Brotherhood," he said. He advised Ward to approach the NL board directly to arrange a meeting.[18]

Ward was dumbfounded. "We wrote to you expecting *you* to present the proposed meeting to the full League body," he wrote back to Young. In other words, part of Young's job remit was scheduling meetings like the one the Brotherhood was requesting.

Perhaps the magnates wanted to appear tough on a union when labor organizations generally appeared to be gaining members and power. A big one, the Knights of Labor, was poised to strike four big western railroads controlled by the notorious stock manipulator Jay Gould. Perhaps National League board members just hoped that if they ignored the Brotherhood it would go away.[19]

Despite its antipathy toward the labor group, the NL did decide to incorporate the reserve clause in players' contracts, rather than continue to make an oblique reference to the National Agreement, where the clause was buried. League leaders balked at adding salary figures to contracts because they paid many players more than permitted under a "limitation rule" the League and American Association had adopted to slow the growth of players' pay.[20]

Young challenged Ward's bona fides, saying the NL had not formally recognized him as a Brotherhood member—and, in fact, the league, not the Brotherhood, had paid all his expenses when he traveled to Chicago for a meeting of the Joint Committee on Rules in November. "This would scarcely have been done had you been an accredited representative of the Brotherhood," the National League president asserted.[21]

Mustering his lawyerly skills, Ward said the National League had paid for his travel because it had invited him to the meeting. He added that the committee initially said he could attend as a player but not as a representative of the Brotherhood because most NL clubs did not recognize the labor organization. John B. Day, owner of the New York Giants, for which the future Hall of Fame member Ward played shortstop, tried to persuade the committee to accept Ward as a Brotherhood delegate, but they would not budge. At least not until they received a telegram from Spalding supporting Day and tipping the scales in Ward's favor.[22]

"Do the magnates of the League really think they can crush this movement by simply refusing to notice it? If so, they make a most grievous mistake," Ward wrote in his last letter of the autumn.[23]

"If its demands had been shown to be unreasonable they would have been notified accordingly," he concluded. "But having been refused a conference, or even a recognition by the magnates of the League, the issue is forced upon us, and since we cannot go forward with you, we will be obliged to go alone."[24]

During the exchange of open letters between Young and Ward, *Lippincott's* magazine published a 4,800-word jeremiad entitled "Is the Base-Ball Player a Chattel?" in its August 1887 number. The author? Brotherhood cofounder John Montgomery Ward, and as the title suggests it is a full-throated criticism of how the National League had twisted the once-useful reserve clause into "a mere pretense for the practice of wrong."

The clause empowered NL members to "reserve" five players from their 1879 rosters—that is, they could pick five players who would be forbidden to take their talents to another team willing to pay more money. No such power was granted or even discussed when players signed their 1879 contracts; it was applied retroactively to the players that teams wanted to reserve in 1880. That original sin should render the rule invalid, he said, but the perfidy persisted.

To justify this extraordinary measure and distract public attention from the real causes making it necessary, the clubs tried to shift the blame to the players. They declared that players were demanding extortionate salaries, and that the rule was needed as a protection against these. They attempted to conceal entirely that the real trouble lay in the extravagant and unbusinesslike methods of certain managers and in the lack of good faith among the clubs themselves. According to them, the player who accepted a proffered increase of salary was a disorganizer and a dangerous character, from whom protection was necessary, while the club official who offered it was but a poor weak instrument in his hands. Was it really wrong for the player to accept a larger salary when offered?[25]

It became so when League leaders, starting with Hulbert and Spalding, were able to persuade competing circuits—the American Association and Northwestern League, among others—to adopt the reserve clause or risk having National League clubs raid their rosters.

"The effect of this," Ward wrote, "was that a player reserved was forced to sign with the club reserving him or quit playing ball altogether."

A player could try to escape by sitting out a season or joining a semiprofessional team out west or down south, but if he wanted to play topflight professional baseball again, he'd have to surrender to the team holding his contract. Ward's description of the reserve rule's impact may have been overwrought, but it accurately conveyed the Brotherhood's anger: "Like a fugitive-slave law, the reserve-rule denies him a harbor or a livelihood, and carries him back, bound and shackled, to the club from which he attempted to escape."

* * *

For all of Ward's histrionics, he still had not persuaded Young or the magnates who controlled him to recognize the Brotherhood as a legitimate players' representative. That would change in November 1887.

A League meeting at the Fifth Avenue Hotel on November 19 began routinely shortly before noon, and club representatives quickly disposed of issues like whether visiting teams should receive a percentage of gate receipts or a flat fee and whether to pay an umpire for games he missed after being injured on the job. Attention then turned to relations with the players and their Brotherhood. Its representatives, Ward, Hanlon, and Dan Brouthers, were staying at the less-ostentatious Barrett House hotel, awaiting an invitation to the magnates' meeting.

It did not begin well. When the players' delegation arrived, Ward and John Rogers, owner of the Philadelphia franchise, quickly started trading rhetorical jabs about why the players insisted on having the league recognize the Brotherhood as representing players before the player would present their ideas for a new contract. Indeed, the players' representatives declined to take their seats until the League accepted that the Brotherhood, through Ward, Brouthers, and Hanlon, could bargain on behalf of its members.

During a pause in the discussion, Spalding finally broke the impasse. "I am inclined to think we should recognize the Brotherhood," he said. "I move that a committee of three be appointed by the chair to confer with the Brotherhood with regard to a contract, and to report such changes as they can agree upon." Spalding's motion passed unanimously, a measure of the respect other club presidents had for him.

Young immediately put him on the League committee, along with Day and Rogers. The Brotherhood formed its own committees and the two met in conference. By half-past three that afternoon a new contract was ready to present to players and magnates; it was ratified with minor alterations.[26]

The Brotherhood's lawyer drew up the new agreement, which was clearly more equitable than the previous one. Managers would no longer have the discretion to fine players for some trivial offenses or suspend them indefinitely, for example, and clubs no longer could reserve players and pay them less than the amount on their contracts. Clubs would no longer deduct 50 cents a day from player's pay packets to cover part of the travel costs when the club was playing at an opponent's grounds.[27]

Arthur H. Soden, the parsimonious president of the Boston club and father of the reserve clause, said he thought the new contract was "fairly equitable . . . in fact, as much so as you can make it between a responsible party and an irresponsible one."

He was visibly irritated that the League had yielded to the Brotherhood, giving the organization credibility and the players courage—and he did not hesitate to identify who, in his opinion, was to blame. "The main thing they were after was to be recognized," Soden said after the meeting ended. "They gained that point, but we never ought to have allowed it. And we never *would* have had to recognize them if the Westerners had kept their mouths shut and let Rogers alone."[28]

Chapter 11

The World Tour

While still a young man in the 1880s, Spalding was successful beyond the wildest imaginings of his boyhood in a remote patch of the Illinois frontier. Between his stints in Boston and Chicago, he won five championships in seven years as a professional; as a club executive in Chicago, his organization won five of the League's first 12 pennants.

He was not a religious man, but he was a leader among the legions who proselytized professional baseball from its inception, preaching about its physical, mental, and moral benefits while at the same time proving himself to be the best pitcher of the first generation of players for hire. He also had taken others' idea of selling handmade baseballs and bats to amateur, collegiate, and semi-professional players and used it as a foundation on which he built what had become the largest sporting goods manufacturer and retailer in the world. In the spirit of the era, when monopolies and trusts acquired competitors to control entire industries, A. G. Spalding & Bros. came to dominate sporting goods in the same way: buying out its rivals.

The company opened two lavishly appointed flagship stores, in Chicago in 1876 and in New York nine years later. Ballplayers often spent time in the shops when playing games in either city, their presence giving the heavily trafficked businesses a priceless patina of authenticity and glamour. Spalding also had opened 29 privately owned "depots of supplies" across the United States (and one in Canada) to handle regional wholesale and retail sales "on equally as favorable terms as if ordered direct from our Chicago and New York houses," the company promised.[1]

Al was president of the Spalding Manufacturing Company, which ran the factories that purportedly made every product bearing a Spalding trademark. He was leveraging the popularity of his annual *Base Ball Guide* to create what would be a considerable publishing house, the American Sports Publishing Company. That business would quickly boast of a backlist of hundreds of titles on physical activities from archery to weightlifting. A handwritten note from him could persuade eminent athletes and coaches to agree to write for his company: Ty Cobb on playing outfield, Johnny Evers on turning double plays, Walter Camp on winning at football, James Naismith on how to play basketball, which he invented, and three-time US national men's singles champion Oliver Campbell discoursing on lawn tennis.

Spalding was 37, rich, renowned, and respected.

He was also unfulfilled.

Despite his occasional efforts to persuade the rest of the world to embrace baseball as he had, it remained a game played almost exclusively by Americans for Americans. His attempt to seed the sport in Great Britain, the land of his forebears and seat of the greatest empire on Earth, failed to bear fruit. Rather than risk another costly disappointment across the Atlantic, Spalding in 1888 chose to pursue opportunity across the Pacific, in the British colonies of Australia and New Zealand.

He was older, more experienced, and mature when planning and executing this new adventure, and thus aware of its increased cost. Not only were New Zealand and Australia much farther from the United States than England, the cities he had to visit—Melbourne, Sydney, and Adelaide—were much farther from one another than were the English cities visited on the 1874 tour. That meant spending more time and money on travel expenses and reducing the number of days available for playing exhibitions (and selling tickets)—even if Australians and New Zealanders proved to be more interested in baseball than their British cousins.[2]

Ever eager to get his business's name in the papers, Spalding announced his imperial endeavor in his office over the sales floor of the Madison Street store in Chicago, squeezing a bundle of newspapermen in the modest space—jockeying for position to be sure they could see Spalding and hear him read the overseas cablegram in his hand. When he felt the time was right, Spalding said the cablegram arrived that day from Sydney, Australia, and had cost him $15—equivalent to more than $500 in 2024. It contained only three words: "Sport. Chicago. Kenwood."[3]

Puzzled reporters looked warily at one another to make sure their competitors did not know what it meant. Spalding explained: It was a cipher from a trusted business agent in Australia and each word represented a phrase agreed on before he left for Sydney almost two months earlier. (Kenwood was the neighborhood in Chicago where Spalding lived with his wife and son.) The words meant, "Arrangements complete. Grounds engaged. Prospect extremely favorable. I have announced that you are coming."[4]

"This cablegram means that arrangements are now being made in Sydney for my trip to Australia at the close of the coming baseball season," he added. "It is an enterprise which I have been thinking of for five years. Three months ago, I decided to put it into execution." He did so by hiring Leigh S. Lynch, the longtime business manager of the Union Square Theater in New York, at a salary of $300 a month, to travel to Australia, a country with which he was already familiar, and gauge local interest in paying to watch a traveling band of foreigners play a sport that few Australians or New Zealanders had ever seen.[5]

Spalding was undeterred by doubters who questioned the colonists' familiarity with baseball—Australians played their first game of baseball in 1857; the next one 31 years later, as the Spalding tour steamed across the Pacific. He had heard the opposite was true, and chose to believe that.

"After considerable correspondence and many interviews with persons who had been in Australia, I decided to make the venture," the intrepid capitalist said. He reckoned that the tour he had in mind would set him back at least $25,000, so he deposited $30,000—equivalent to more than $1 million in 2024—in a special bank account to show that he was good for the expected expenses.

Publicly, Spalding avoided discussing potential profits and losses, preferring instead to let people believe he was shrewd enough to make money on the excursion regardless of the obstacles it faced. After Spalding announced the tour in Chicago, his representative in Minneapolis, Fred Leland, returned to the Twin Cities to promise that the "Australian tour," as it had come to be known, would sell out exhibition games in St. Paul and Minneapolis as the tourists traveled by train to a rendezvous in San Francisco with a steamship bound for the antipodes.

The exhibitions in Australia and New Zealand would be just as fruitful, he declared. "It is a great country for sports," Leland said of Australia, a place he may never have seen, "and very anxious to see Americans play their great national game. . . . Al Spalding knows what he is about, and wouldn't go into this unless he saw money ahead."[6]

Spalding was in it for the money, but not the pittance likely to be made from selling tickets to exhibition games. That was a common misapprehension among skeptics of his proposed tour.

"Spalding's American baseball team leave Chicago for Australia about the middle of October. We do not think that the venture is likely to be a success financially; in fact, it is hard to see how a big deficit can be avoided," the *Sydney Mail* opined. "The game is utterly unknown here, and a baseball club started by our own Americans last season is now filling a nameless grave.

"If the game were made familiar to the public beforehand, so that they might understand what they were looking at, there would be some chance of paying hotel bills; but the Australians all through are as unacquainted with the mysteries of baseball as the Chinese with those of cricket."[7]

Spalding concurred that financing the tour with ticket sales was bound to fail, which was why he had no intention of trying to do so. "In my judgement," he said, "such a trip would prove a losing venture to any man who undertook the journey with any expectation of making money out of the gate receipts of his games. In undertaking such a trip, I do so more for the purpose of extending my sporting goods business to that quarter of the globe and creating a market for goods there, rather than with any idea of realizing any profit from the work of the teams I take with me."[8]

At most, gate receipts in Australia and New Zealand would only partially offset the expense of the tour; receipts from a series of exhibition games in the United States would cover a larger share of the travel costs of all 40 or so members of the group—two teams of 14 players each, club officials, newspaper reporters, and the wives of several players. Spalding said he would cover the remaining deficit, which he expected to be $5,000, out of his own pocket, as a cost of expanding his sporting goods empire beyond the United States. "I shall be perfectly willing—for my judgment tells me that I can easily afford it—to spend a few thousand dollars to the end of establishing branch offices in Sydney and Melbourne, and that is principally what takes me there," he said.[9]

Any financial anxiety Spalding may have harbored over the tour's cost undoubtedly was eased by the knowledge that he was, at the same time, negotiating to sell the contract of John Clarkson, a future member of the Hall of Fame. Boston soon agreed to pay Spalding $10,000 to acquire the talented but temperamental pitcher.

* * *

After initially promising to take only the top players—the "flower of baseball-dom," in the words of one booster—Spalding chose his own Chicago club to be one of the teams to make the journey to the South Pacific; the other side would be a picked nine representing the best of the rest of the League. Choosing Chicago seemed like a good idea in mid-June, when the club was four games ahead of Detroit in the standings and appeared to be pulling away. It didn't. Chicago had an awful July and finished the season nine games behind the New York Giants. Embarrassingly for Spalding, Anson petulantly forfeited Chicago's last game of the season, in Philadelphia, just a week before players on the Australia tour were scheduled to report to Chicago for a series of sendoff ceremonies.[10]

Finding the players that Spalding wanted on the tour proved to be more difficult than he anticipated. Members of his Chicago squad signed up quickly, and since they played for him, Spalding was reasonably sure of their character. The other side, a picked nine named "All-America," was more challenging. Spalding said he did not want to openly ask for volunteers because to do so "would be certain to result in a deluge of applications from undesirable players in the fraternity."[11]

"It was absolutely essential that all who did go should be men of clean habits and attractive personality, men who would reflect credit upon the country and the game," he said, although evidently he was willing to compromise on those lofty ideals to produce a better game. The ill-tempered and stubbornly racist Cap Anson would continue to play for and manage the Chicago club, for example, and the hard-drinking but crowd-pleasing King Kelly was invited to join the All-America side.

Kelly initially accepted Spalding's invitation but later reneged so he could help his brother open a business in New York City. Other All-America players dropped out as the date for sailing drew closer, citing illness or other reason they could not honor contracts they had signed. "Happily, however, capable men were available," Spalding said, "and the corps lost nothing in playing capacity by reason of the action of those who dropped out."

About a week before players were scheduled to gather in Chicago to begin the tour, they received a letter from Spalding suggesting what and how they should pack for the sea journey ahead. To begin, he cautioned them that passengers' trunks would be stored down in the ship's hold, and thus not accessible more than once a week.

"I would advise the purchase of a small steamer trunk (cost about $4)," he advised. "This can be slipped under your bunk, and so used daily." A large portmanteau or satchel could hold changes of linen for the 26 days at sea, as laundry could not be done on board, he added.

He helpfully recommended where in San Francisco his traveling companions could buy "essential" goods like flannel pajamas (Eggleston's on Market Street for $5 a suit) and steamer chairs (Sullivan's at Hayward and Market Streets). To change money, he endorsed Sutro & Co. on Montgomery Street; British sovereigns—gold £1 coins—sold for $4.84 each; they were accepted on board the ship and in the colonies.

Spalding also advised that it was customary to tip one's bedroom steward and table steward but unwise to do so until the end of the trip. The ship had an excellent barber who charged 25 cents for a shave and sold brushes, caps, combs, perfumed soap, toilet water, and underwear at "reasonable" prices.[12]

Thus enlightened about life at sea, the players and other members of the tour party converged on Chicago, where the 9,200-mile journey was to begin. The departure was feted with a parade through Chicago's business district on a bitterly cold and windy Saturday. The First Cavalry Band led the parade but not for long. The crowd surged onto the parade route, separating the band from the players seated in fancy carriages, each pulled by four horses with brightly polished tack and feather plumes atop their heads.

The players wore eye-catching new uniforms "as fine as silk" that Spalding designed and had made. Chicago players wore gray flannel shirts and breeches with black trim and stockings. All-Americas had white flannel trimmed in blue that matched their stockings. All-America jerseys had the players' League teams embroidered on their chests. Many players tied red, white, and blue silk sashes around their waists.[13]

Even without its band, the parade arrived at its destination, the West Side Park at Congress and Loomis Streets, where John Clarkson and Jim McCormick once pitched for pennants—until their contracts were sold to other teams. For this exhibition, however, Chicago added a celebrated starter, the very man who sent Clarkson and McCormick packing: Spalding.

Aged 38, the once-feared pitcher, a little thicker around the waist than the willowy wunderkind of two decades ago, had agreed the previous day to pitch a few innings after "your old friends and admirers in Chicago" delivered a petition asking him to do so. It had almost 400 signatures, many belonging to prominent men on the Board of Trade and social clubs. The White Stockings' usual starter, John Tener, made way for his boss.[14]

Spalding still delivered the ball as he did a decade earlier, when a sore arm led him to retire after having pitched to more than 12,000 batters in 2,886⅓ innings over seven seasons. To players in 1888, his straight-arm delivery looked comically old fashioned but proved as difficult to hit as his pitching in Boston.

"The 'know-alls' predicted that A. G.'s delivery would be pounded everywhere, but nothing of the kind was done," a *Tribune* writer said after the game. The All-America team did score four runs in the first inning, but none was earned because the defense committed four errors in the unseasonable cold. Spalding struck out three batters and did not allow another run over the next three innings. At that point, as planned, he was relieved by Tener, a 6'4" Irishman who would go on to be elected governor of Pennsylvania in 1910. The crowd loudly cheered Spalding each time he came to bat, and in the first inning he drove the ball over the center fielder's head but stopped at first base, visibly winded, and settled for a single.[15]

The game, which began at half-past two, took an hour and 50 minutes to play—an unusually long time in that era. Chicago outscored All-America 11–6. With the 1,500 spectators still applauding long after the final out, the players had to dash to the clubhouse to change into travel attire. They then hopped into the fancy barouche carriages waiting in front of the ground and were whisked to Union Station, where they would board a special Chicago, Burlington, and Quincy Railroad train scheduled to depart at half-past five.[16]

The train, which consisted of two Pullman sleeping cars, one of them the new luxurious Galesburg model, as well as an extravagant Pullman Cosmopolitan dining car and a baggage car—all draped in white linen banners announcing "Spalding's Australian Baseball Tour"—departed 25 minutes late. If anyone was unhappy with the delay, they hid it well.

After dining on oysters, boiled salmon in Hollandaise sauce, prairie chicken, and English plum pudding with brandy sauce, Spalding's guests began playfully teasing one another about their performance in the season just ended and speculating about what lay ahead. "Everybody is in the best of health and spirits," Jimmy Ryan, a power-hitting Chicago outfielder, wrote in his diary, "and sounds of revelry were heard into the 'wee' small hours of the morning."[17]

The Burlington Line would transport the ballplayers as far as Denver, stopping en route to play exhibition games in St. Paul and Minneapolis, Minnesota;

Cedar Rapids and Des Moines, Iowa; Omaha and Hastings, Nebraska; and Denver.

The traveling party added an unexpected guest in Omaha, a Black teenager who had been the White Stockings' mascot until he quit to join a troupe of traveling performers. Clarence Duval told the ballplayers that his theatrical companions had abandoned him in Omaha, and he asked to resume his position with the club, which included a spectacular display of baton twirling as he led the team onto the field before every game. Duval was, like other mascots of the era, expected to bring luck to the club. An exceptional dancer, he also entertained his fellow tourists on the sea voyages to come.

Sadly, the tour members lost their beloved Pullman cars in Denver. The Pullmans' standard-gauge wheelsets—the wheel and axle assemblies—were too wide to operate on the narrow-gauge tracks of the Denver & Rio Grande Railroad on the western slope of the Rocky Mountains.

After two games in Denver, the teams put on exhibitions in Colorado Springs and Salt Lake City and Ogden, Utah, where they transferred to the Central Pacific for the rest of the trip to the Pacific Coast. Newspaper estimates of the number of spectators at some games suggest that the 24 contests played from Chicago to San Francisco could have drawn a total of perhaps 70,000 ticket buyers, at 25 or 50 cents a head.[18]

* * *

The Central Pacific Railroad delivered Spalding and his followers to San Francisco—the last few miles by ferry from Oakland—at three o'clock in the afternoon of November 3, two weeks after leaving Chicago. To keep players virtuously engaged in the infamously bawdy seaport while waiting to sail to Hawaii, Spalding scheduled exhibition games. West Coast followers of the game were not impressed, to say the least, by the first game, in which Chicago committed 10 errors while losing to the All-Americas 14–4.

Newspapers fulsomely expressed the city's disappointment on behalf of their readers. "Everyone present went there with the expectation of seeing the greatest game of ball ever played here," the *San Francisco Chronicle* said, "and almost everyone left the grounds at the close disappointed and disgusted at seeing one of the poorest."[19]

Two days later, the touring professionals committed 11 errors while losing to a local cellar-dweller, the Pioneer club. This invited more pointed opprobrium from the press. "Perhaps they may be able to play ball, but no one, not even their most intimate friends, will accuse them of having attempted to do so since their advent in this city," the *San Francisco Examiner* stated. "Spalding should send them back East, or else insist on their playing ball. He should never attempt to introduce baseball in a foreign land with the All-Americas."[20]

Tired of taking a beating in the papers, the All-Americas gave one to the Stockton club, thumping the recently crowned California League champion by a score of 16–1.[21]

* * *

The RMS *Alameda*, the Oceanic Steamship Company vessel that would transport the teams and their entourage to Australia, initially was scheduled to depart San Francisco on November 7 "or immediately on arrival English mails," which Oceanic was handsomely paid to deliver to the South Pacific colonies.[22]

Torrential rain in California delayed the mails for more than a week. Spalding used the time to schedule other exhibition games—nine in all—and plan a banquet in the swank Baldwin Hotel to express his gratitude to San Francisco's press corps and the California League for their hospitality during the tour's extended stay in the Golden State.

In best Gilded Age fashion, the menu was extravagant in form and content. Menus made to resemble baseballs listed themed dishes, such as "Oysters on the Home Run," "Petit Pâté à la Spalding," "Stewed Terrapin à la Ward," and "Frisco Turkey à la Foul." Each course was paired with a Californian wine. The banquet was served in the hotel ballroom, lavishly decorated with candy-covered bats, baseballs, and other game gear.

When it was finally time to sail, several thousand San Franciscans crowded the Oceanic Steamship Company's dock to see off the touring players. Spalding parked himself at the gangplank, shaking hands and counting heads to make sure no one in his party was left behind. As the ship began inching away from the dock, Spalding called for three cheers for the San Francisco press and three more for Californian baseball players. Excited baseball enthusiasts on the dock happily complied and cheered nonstop as *Alameda* muscled its way toward the Golden Gate and the open ocean beyond.[23]

* * *

When the ship was two days out of port, the National League owners gathered at the Fifth Avenue Hotel in New York City to consider rule changes and other business; it was the only League meeting Al Spalding did not attend in the 15 years he owned a stake in the Chicago club. Walter attended in his older brother's place and voted his proxy.

On the final day of the meeting—four days after *Alameda* had sailed for Hawaii with the Brotherhood's leader John Ward safely incommunicado (wireless telegraphy was still a decade in the future)—the National League moguls adopted a stepped salary cap advocated by John T. Brush, the unapologetically parsimonious president of a new club in Indianapolis.

Brush, a department store owner, had purchased the club to promote his business but soon learned that clubs in small cities could not sell enough tickets to outbid big-city clubs for the best players. Indianapolis, for example, had roughly 100,000 residents in 1888 while New York City, Philadelphia, and Chicago all had populations exceeding one million. New York's baseball team drew more than 300,000 *spectators* that year.[24]

Brush's plan, which contained elements of payroll-limiting ideas that Spalding had previously shopped around, authorized the League's secretary to individually assess every player after the last game of the regular season and sort them into one of five classes based on a list of qualities, some of which were comfortably quantifiable, such as batting, fielding, and baserunning, while others were distressingly subjective, such as teamwork and personal conduct "both on and off the field, at all times."

Top-ranked Class A players would be paid $2,500 annually; Class B players would receive $2,250; Class C, $2,000; Class D, $1,750; and Class E, not more than $1,500. To try to close the so-called Kelly loophole, each of these salary steps would include regular pay and all bonuses, rewards, gifts, emoluments, "and every other form of compensation expressly or implicitly promised him for his services as a player." The league felt that such precise legalistic language was necessary because a year earlier, Boston paid Kelly $2,000 in salary, which was the highest amount acceptable to the League; yet Kelly took home $5,000 in total pay, the lowest amount acceptable to the player. Boston accomplished this by separately doling out $3,000 for the use of Kelly's image to advertise games.[25]

Ballplayers—at least those not steaming across the Pacific Ocean hundreds of miles from land—were outraged by the classification system, which they contended punished them for owners' inability to restrain their spending. They grumbled that clubs would selectively evade classification just as they had evaded previous efforts to cut salaries—at least when pursuing players they desired. "This rule was the subject of incessant complaint by the players, and caused intense and constantly growing irritation among them," the *Sporting Life*'s editor warned.[26]

Talk of a players' strike began to circulate, and not only among players. The *New York Times* presciently noted that "from present appearances a war between managers and players is imminent." A "reliable source" said the Brotherhood was trying to contact Ward during a 12-hour stopover in Honolulu and urge him to return to New York at once. If true, the effort was in vain because the independent Kingdom of Hawaii did not yet have a cable connection.[27]

After the League meeting adjourned, a clutch of club owners lingered in the city for several days, trying to deliver deals conceived during the conference. The most surprising development came from the Giants' owners, who announced they would sell John Ward's contract to the Nationals for a record $12,000. That would mean a nice profit for Brush and his fellow investors in the club and an easy way to remove the troublesome Brotherhood leader from the publicity pulpit of New York City. Brush said he turned down higher offers for Ward's services because when he cabled Ward to ask if his release could be sold, the player replied, "Only to Washington."[28]

There were many reasons to doubt that claim. To start, Washington finished dead last in the standings in 1888 and was expected to repeat the feat in 1889. The New Yorks, meanwhile, had captured the National League pennant that year and went on to defeat the St. Louis Browns of the Association in six games out of 10 to become world champions, a feat they were poised to repeat in 1889. Also, Ward also had recently wed Helen Dauvray, a beautiful and successful actress who displayed no interest in giving up New York's vibrant theater scene for Washington's. (Months later, when Ward returned to the United States, he put the lie to the claim that he had approved a deal with Washington and said he would not play for the Nationals unless he got most of the $12,000 transfer fee.)[29]

* * *

Alameda took a week to traverse the 2,400 miles of ocean between San Francisco and Honolulu, arriving on the morning of November 25, a day behind schedule. As planned, The Royal Hawaiian Band and several hundred expatriate Americans, including the US minister to Hawaii, George W. Merrill, welcomed the players as they disembarked. After a breakfast of the Hawaiian staple poi, or mashed taro root, the teams marched in formation to the Royal Palace for an audience with King Kalākaua. Only one event had been stricken from the day's agenda: baseball.

Spalding had scheduled a game between Chicago and All-America on their scheduled day of arrival, a Saturday, but by arriving a day late the game would have required the teams to play on Sunday. Spalding sanctioned baseball on the Sabbath only as long as it was allowed by local laws. After looking into the matter, he concluded that "the missionaries who were looking after the moral welfare of the natives had closed the door against Sunday entertainments good and tight."[30]

American expatriates and others assured Spalding that the authorities were unlikely to interfere with such a popular event. They added that they'd raised $1,000 to supplement revenue from ticket sales.

Spalding was unswayed. "There was only one thing to do," the Victorian magnate decided. "We obeyed the letter and spirit of the law, called the game off, and left a lot of disgruntled Americans and disappointed kanakas, to say nothing of the much-coveted shekels."[31]

Seventeen hours after arriving in Honolulu, the Spalding entourage was at sea again, on a two-week, 3,900-mile leg to Auckland, in the English colony of New Zealand. After only one day at sea, Anson lamented to the most senior player in the entourage, George Wright, that all the players did was eat and sleep, and risked being embarrassing when they faced fitter athletes in New Zealand and Australia.

"See here, George, this kind of life will never do for American ballplayers upon a missionary tour," Anson said. "We shall be as stiff as old women and as fat as aldermen by the time we reach Australia, if we don't take exercise of some kind. Can't we arrange to have a little cricket practice?"[32]

Wright approached the ship's captain, Henry Morse, to ask what could be done to let the players break a sweat. The next day, half a dozen members of the ship's crew installed an open-ended canvas tunnel on the promenade of the port-side quarter-deck. The canvas kept cricket balls from sailing overboard when struck by a batsman. Wright scrounged 50 feet of cocoa matting to lay on the smooth oak deck planking to simulate bowling on turf. Players instantly took to the jerry-rigged practice pitch, with many playing for two or three hours each day.[33]

Meanwhile, Spalding was eager to get back on the original schedule and offered to give Captain Morse a £100 bonus and to pay for excess coal consumed if *Alameda* would recoup the day it fell behind schedule while waiting to depart San Francisco. However, the five-year-old iron-hulled steamship could not make up the lost day, although it did consume enough fuel in the effort that *Alameda* had to take a second day to recoal while tied up in Auckland. Thus, the tourists had to play their only exhibition game in New Zealand—their first game in a month and the first one abroad—on December 10, a Monday, which limited attendance to about 1,000. Chicago won, scoring 22 runs to the All-Americas' 13.[34]

As the tour prepared to move on to Australia, Spalding announced that it would not, as originally planned, revisit New Zealand on its return to San Francisco. It would, instead, continue sailing to the west, stopping in South Asia, the Middle East, and Europe en route to New York. The Spalding stunt had become a world tour.[35]

It is not certain when Spalding developed a longing to do this. If, as some historians suspect, the Chicago magnate timed the trip to isolate Brotherhood leader John Ward while League owners unilaterally adopted the salary-classification plan, Spalding may have opted to sail around the world to use exotic ports of call to distract the players in his charge and reduce the chances that they might stew about salary caps and devise ways to force owners to retreat. Of course, Spalding may have simply wanted to try to recover from his failure to establish baseball in Britain during his 1874 excursion or may have thought that steaming completely around the world was a better story for the newspapers.

Advocates of the adventure abounded. Many, notably Harry C. Palmer, baseball editor of the *Sporting Life*, stretched the truth nearly to the breaking point in trying to excuse the disinterest British sportsmen showed for baseball in 1874. "The English tour," he wrote, referring to the series of baseball games and cricket matches Spalding had organized there 15 years earlier, "was in reality but a mutually agreed upon and experimental trip, undertaken with very vague ideas as to what the result would be, artistically or financially. At the time, Albert Spalding was the young, popular, hard-working pitcher of the Boston Red Stockings, with little more than his energy, ambition, and love of the game to draw on for the success of the trip."[36]

This time, Spalding was no longer a callow, well-meaning but inexperienced player; he was a cunning and successful business magnate, the acknowledged head of the National League, and a man with firm goals for this excursion. To help achieve those goals, he hired S. Sanford Perry, European agent of the Chicago, Burlington and Quincy railroad and leader of an amateur baseball team in Liverpool, to assess the feasibility and potential financial returns on a new series of baseball exhibitions in Britain.[37]

Leigh Lynch arranged for a reassuringly enthusiastic welcome for the tourists when they arrived in Sydney on December 14. As *Alameda* steamed past the headlands defining Sydney harbor, Spalding's entourage saw several substantial vessels steaming toward them at high speed. "Nearer and nearer they drew until we could hear the bands of music with which each steamer was provided," Palmer recalled. One by one they slowed down and dropped alongside newly arrived vessel, "until the *Alameda* had become the center of a puffing, cheering, banner-bedecked escort."[38]

The contrast with the failed 1874 tour of England must have impressed Spalding. He had been considering a redemption tour of Britain at least since the delay in San Francisco, when a letter from Alcock, advance man of the 1874 tour, had miraculously found its way to Spalding. Alcock had heard of the Australian adventure and wrote to urge Spalding to encourage him to add England to his itinerary. Britons' attitudes had changed, he wrote.

Perry, the railroad agent in Liverpool, was also optimistic, and the players ardently endorsed going home via Europe. Spalding was convinced that was the right thing to do. He had his secretary look for a westbound passenger ship with enough cabins to accommodate the 30 or so remaining members of his entourage. The secretary found one in the SS *Salier*, a German Imperial mail steamship that could take the group as far as Suez.[39]

Lynch had drawn up an ambitious schedule for the Australian segment, 13 games in four cities over 20 days. A healthy crowd of 4,000 spectators turned up for the first of three games played in Sydney. The Chicago and All-America teams then played three in Melbourne, three in Adelaide, and one in the gold-mining town of Ballarat before finishing with three more in Melbourne.

The contests did not inspire Australians to throw down their cricket bats, as Spalding hoped they would, but many did come to appreciate the occult charms of baseball upon hearing that the Chicago club had posted a net profit of £12,000, or more than $55,000, in 1888.[40]

The final baseball game between the American sides was part of an outdoor sports festival that included a three-inning ballgame between Chicago and the

Melbourne baseball club, which American expatriates had founded a year earlier; an Australian rules football match between local clubs, Carlton and Port Melbourne; a ballgame between Chicago and All-America; and an exhibition of long-distance throwing, which New York Giants pitcher Ed Crane won with a toss of 128 yards 10.5 inches. Event organizers estimated that 17,000 spectators spent at least part of the day at the grounds.[41]

* * *

By the time the Spalding World Tour left its next port of call, Colombo, in what was then called Ceylon, the players and guests had traveled together for three months, most of that time at sea. Books had been read and reread; card games played ad nauseum. Athletes, being naturally competitive, enjoy a good prank, and Spalding's players were no different. When a US consul in Colombo had advised that an abundance of communicable diseases and poorly coordinated train and ship timetables made it unwise to tour India, the players realized that meant two more weeks at sea. It was time for a laugh.

On the night after leaving Colombo, a group of ballplayers, sportswriters, and two Australian big-game hunters on their way to Africa drank through half a case of Monopole Champagne.

Shortly after midnight one night, a deafening cannon report shook the ship, rousing tipsy passengers from fitful sleep. Within seconds, passengers heard someone cry, "Pirates! Pirates! My God, boys, the Chinese pirates are upon us!"

A second ear-splitting report rattled the 3,000-ton vessel. Befuddled ballplayers tumbled out of their berths. Treasurer John Tener grabbed his bags of gold and hid in his stateroom closet. Ed Crane forgot to collect his valuables but did rescue a pet monkey. Anson stuffed his wife's jewels into his mouth, told her to hide under her bunk, and then armed himself with a bat. Ned Hanlon wore his hat and held a pair of trousers in one hand and a valise in the other.

"Confusion and panic reigned supreme," Palmer said. "Whether the ship was sinking, was on fire, or had really been attacked, we did not know, but in our dazed condition we were quite willing to believe that something terrible had happened."

Until, that is, they noticed Philadelphia's Jim Fogarty, the best defensive outfielder of his generation, roaring with laughter.

Passengers soon learned that *Salier* had just fired a salute in honor of the 30th birthday of German emperor Wilhelm II, and that Lynch and Fogarty had improvised the pirate raid. "It was fully a week before some of the boys would consent to smile when the affair was mentioned," Palmer added.[42]

* * *

The radical change of itinerary after Australia proved much more difficult than anticipated. In Egypt, for example, Spalding scheduled a game in the shadow of the Sphinx and hired camels to transport some players to the site, donkeys to transport others, and carriages for the wives, sportswriters, and other party members. The motley convoy was scheduled to leave the Hotel d'Orient at ten o'clock in the morning of February 9, but Spalding had not anticipated that hundreds of unsolicited translators, guides, donkey wranglers, souvenir peddlers, and fruit vendors also would descend on the tourists once their plans circulated through Cairo. After a brief reign of chaos in the square in front of the hotel, Cairene police arrived to extricate the Americans.[43]

The game began immediately after lunch on a diamond drawn in the sand near the pyramid of Cheops. Spectators numbered in the hundreds; most were Bedouin nomads unlikely to ever see another game. "Every time a fly was hit the natives would run their horses out into the field to see how it was caught," Ward wrote in a dispatch to a New York newspaper. "It may be said, however, that very few fly balls were caught, owing to the excessively difficult locomotion." The Sahara's sand made running, fielding, and hitting maddeningly difficult—and sliding downright dangerous. "Some players ploughed up the sand to such an extent that they were all but buried," Ward wrote.[44]

Without a doubt, the game, won by the All-Americas by a score of 9–6, provided the tour with unforgettable images of American players sitting or standing on the Sphinx and playing a game using a pyramid as a backstop. But to those who were there, like John Ward, "the game was full of errors and perspiration."

Ward and the other players finally learned of the classification plan and salary caps more than two months after the League adopted them when the *Stettin*, the steamship that carried them across a stormy Mediterranean, docked at Brindisi, Italy, on February 15.[45] There, they received mail for the first time in weeks. Newspapers gave sketchy details; Ward used his lawyerly reasoning skills to fill in the blanks. He was eager to return home and marshal Brotherhood members to oppose classification, and quit the tour when it reached England, and returned alone, departing Queenstown, Ireland, on March 14.[46]

His ship tied up at Hoboken, New Jersey, on the morning of March 23, and Ward disembarked in high style, wearing a silk hat, dark blue Prince Albert coat and vest, light checked wide trousers, patent leather gaiters, and light brown kid gloves. On the dock, he told waiting reporters that he had not yet studied the new system in detail, but was "utterly opposed" to what he knew of it. He said he had discussed the matter with Spalding while on the tour, and said, "He thinks, with me, that it is a very dangerous experiment, and I think he will do his best to oppose it when he has the chance. When he first heard about it, he expressed himself to me very strongly against it."

Spalding had missed the players' initial reaction to the classification plan because he left the tour in Brindisi and took a train directly to Naples, where his wife and son waited to reunite with him.

Back in Europe, the sudden decision to add a Continental leg to the excursion and play another 17 games in 35 days had Perry, Lynch, and Spalding racing to secure venues and have advertising translated, printed, and posted before each game. That occasionally resulted in embarrassing missteps. When Perry could not find an available venue for a game in Naples, for example, he "astonished the savants and archaeologists" by proposing to play baseball games in the excavated Colosseum at Pompeii. "This offer was indignantly refused," a newspaper noted.[47]

Undaunted, Spalding had Perry go to Rome and asked the authorities there the same question about their bigger, more famous Colosseum. Spalding was willing to pay £1,000 for the privilege. Again, government officials, scandalized by such a sacrilege, forcefully declined. (Neapolitans had to settle for a local cricket ground; Romans watched in the Villa Borghese, a public park.)[48]

Plans to play in Vienna and Berlin were scratched due to cold and snow. A game in Genoa, Italy, was canceled.[49]

The game in Paris should have been among the best of the tour. The sky was clear, the temperature warm, the location just across the River Seine from the new Eiffel Tower, which was within weeks of opening to the public. The game was well played by both teams, despite a small ground and sandy infield. In the top of the second inning, Chicago shortstop Ed Williamson took first base on a walk and decided to steal second. As he approached the bag and began to slide, he hit an obstacle in the basepath and "tore all the flesh off the knee cap of my left leg," he wrote to a friend. Williamson's wife, who had accompanied him on the tour, took him to a hospital in Paris, where doctors closed the wound with stitches and told him he would be able to resume playing in a few days. When the team boarded ferries to England that evening, Williamson was with them.[50]

"I was advised to remain in Paris, but, stubborn as a mule, I refused, and left with the boys for London, crossing the channel," he recalled in another letter. "Oh, God! what a night I put in. Not only did my knee cause me excruciating pain, but I suffered greatly from sea sickness."[51]

A powerful storm raged when the crew weighed anchor and as soon as the ship left the harbor it "plunged and pitched, tossed and shivered, while the wind whistled through the rigging, threatening to carry the ropes and spars with it," Jimmy Ryan wrote in his diary. "The scene below deck was undiscribable [*sic*] and as all the hatches were batten [*sic*] down tight, the smell was horrible. Men, women, and children were huddled together in the first cabin, some singing, some joking, but the greater majority, praying. Then, aside from these, was another party, who were so awfully seasick that they couldn't do either, if they wanted to."

In his weakened state, Williamson tumbled around his cabin like a ball in a bingo drum. "In moving, I tore one of the stitches from my knee," he later wrote. "Immediately upon my arrival here [England] I called in another physician and learned the wound had not been thoroughly cleaned." The damaged joint had become infected and when doctors reopened it to clean it out, they found his condition to be worse than expected.[52]

Williamson was instructed to recuperate in bed for a month. That meant he not only missed the 13 games the tourists played across England, Ireland, and Scotland in 15 days, he also missed sailing home with his teammates on the White Star liner *Adriatic* on March 28.[53]

Worse, Williamson was left hanging about whether Spalding would help with the medical and rehabilitation bills. "I think he probably intends to do the right thing with me, but I have heard nothing definite from him up to date," Williamson said after Spalding left for New York.

Anson was no more reassuring. "When Anson saw me, he said he wanted me to get ready to go to work in three weeks," Williamson recalled. "I told him I wasn't anxious to start in, and didn't think I would be able to. He replied that I must obey the orders of the club and get ready for business."[54]

Spalding did pay for two-thirds of the cost of Williamson's hospital stay in London but, despite a promise that "the season will not be lost to you, play or no play," he did not offer Williamson a contract before the season began or pay him a salary until he returned to the field in mid-August. By June, Williamson's teammate Tom Burns said the shortstop was so short of funds that friends organized a benefit game between amateur Chicago City League sides. The event raised about $1,000, of which Williamson received $800.[55]

People knew the genial player as a key member of Chicago's "stonewall infield" who hit 27 home runs in 1884, the major-league record until Babe Ruth hit 29 in one season 35 years later. Many were mystified by stories asserting Williamson's employer stood by as the player exhausted his savings and had to rely on the charity of friends. "The universal question is: Why doesn't Spalding assist the man?" a *Detroit Free-Press* editorial inquired. "He was injured while playing for the Chicago club and it would be no more than humane for [Spalding] to come to the rescue."[56]

Spalding and his brother Walter denied that the club had cut off Williamson but did not say what they had done on his behalf.[57]

* * *

The ballgames played in Great Britain, games Williamson had to miss while he was recuperating in a London hospital, comprised the most successful part of the tour by far. Perry and Alcock had scheduled the American teams to play 13 games over 14 days in 11 cities throughout the British Isles, from London to Glasgow to Dublin. The first game, held on a cold and drizzly Tuesday at the Oval cricket ground in the Kennington district of south London, attracted a particularly noble spectator: Albert, the Prince of Wales and future King Edward VII. After receiving three cheers and a tiger from players, the prince invited Spalding to accompany him and his brother-in-law, Prince Christian of Schleswig-Holstein, in watching the game from the Royal Box. Spalding giddily accepted.

As the game progressed, the prince became increasingly interested in some of the arcane aspects of baseball, peppering Spalding with questions—"What is that for?" "Why is he doing that?"—and then nodding when he came to understand another nuance of the game. Spalding answered as best he could while standing between and behind the seated royals, as protocol required. But the Prince of Wales's short stature and stiff neck quickly overtaxed the middle-aged, 6'2" Spalding's ability to repeatedly bend down and speak directly into his royal highness's ear to be heard.

When the Prince of Wales reflexively slapped Spalding's leg in his enthusiasm for one extraordinary play, Spalding took it as license to pull up a chair and sit between and behind the royals and place his hand on their shoulders. When the game was over and Spalding was preparing to leave the Oval, the American consul, Robert Newton Crane, "laughed immoderately" at the sporting goods magnate for breaching court etiquette.

Spalding was unapologetic. "I see nothing in it to cause me to blush," he said. "If I violated the code of court etiquette, I must plead that I was not at court but at an American ball game. If I sat in the presence of Royalty, it is certain that Royalty sat in mine. If I tapped the future King of Great Britain on the shoulder, it was nothing more offensive than a game of tag, for he had first slapped me on the leg."

The Prince of Wales did not appear to take offense at Spalding's chumminess. When a newspaperman asked the royal for his opinion of the new sport, the prince diplomatically answered: "I consider base ball an excellent game; but cricket a better one."[58]

The game at Kennington Oval was the first in a physically draining schedule. But the players—and their leader, Spalding—were buoyed by the number of English, Scottish, and Irish people who came to baseball exhibitions to see what the fuss in the newspapers was about. Detailed records of gate receipts have yet to turn up, but journalists who watched and wrote about the games often estimated the attendance at each one—2,000 in Glasgow, 7,000 in Liverpool, 12,000 in Blackpool, 22,000 combined at three games played in London.

Taking the figures at face value suggests the aggregate attendance for games played in Britain easily exceeded 50,000. Even if skeptics discount those contemporary estimates by half, attendance far outstripped that of Spalding's 1874 tour of the land of his ancestors. He must have been gratified—and deservedly so—when he and his entourage boarded the steamship *Adriatic* in Queenstown on March 28 to return to America.

Although Spalding had, no doubt insincerely, asked that there be no elaborate events to welcome the tour members home, a crowd of perhaps 200 friends and celebrities packed the upper deck of the *Laura M. Starin*, a sidewheel steamer early on the morning of April 6 to be sure they would be among the first to shake the hands that had spread the national pastime around the globe.

Adriatic was spotted off Fire Island at 1:50 a.m. and was routinely quarantined until health inspectors could complete their business. After waiting five hours, the captain of the *Starin* pulled his vessel up next to *Adriatic*, and some tourists—including Spalding—began climbing between ships so they could slap the backs of old pals and shake hands of baseball enthusiasts they didn't remember meeting in the past.

The noise was deafening. "Every steamboat of any kind, large and small, whistled and tooted until people were compelled to place their fingers in their ears," recalled one person who was there. A valiant brass band struggled to be heard over the whistles and cheering, but its musicians themselves could barely hear their instruments.[59]

Spalding and his party finally went ashore on West 21st Street at five o'clock and climbed into waiting carriages to go to the Fifth Avenue Hotel, where they would stay until they played an exhibition in the city Monday. They would play nine more ballgames as they worked their way back to Chicago, where the excursion began six months earlier.[60]

New York gave the players a sample of what awaited them in the last stretch of the tour. After Monday's game, they changed into evening wear before being transported to Delmonico's, at the time the country's finest restaurant, as guests of honor at what one newspaper promised to be "the grandest banquet known in the annals of the game." The event drew 300 men—ladies were sequestered with an orchestra in a balcony overlooking the dining room. Attendees spanned politics, finance, publishing, theater, and sports, and included Mark Twain; Theodore Roosevelt, president of the police commission and future president of the United States; Spalding's brother Walter; and the presidents and leading members of the New York Athletic Club and Manhattan Athletic Club.[61]

Praise for Spalding by speaker after speaker was as lavish as the souvenirs, an illustrated book about the tour bound in red, white, and blue ribbon, and a menu divided into nine innings and illustrated with scenes of places the ballplayers visited on the tour.

The New York banquet itself was so extravagant that it ran up a deficit even when drawing 300 guests, each paying $10 (roughly equivalent to $344 in purchasing power in 2024). Former National League president A. G. Mills, who was chairman of the banquet committee, wrote to the Spalding brothers to obtain permission to print additional copies of the menu from that evening and sell them for a dollar apiece as souvenirs to help cover the debt.

Chapter 12

Breaking Point

Spalding's around-the-world tour ended as it began, with parades and feasts and speeches in his boisterous adopted hometown, already known as the Windy City because of its boosters' relentless self-promotion. He and his entourage could not have been welcomed back to Chicago more grandly if each of them had been one of the royal personages they had recently introduced to America's pastime. Throngs of jubilant Chicagoans crowded into the Dearborn Street Station to greet the tourists when their train from Cincinnati slowly eased into the Romanesque Revival edifice on the afternoon of April 19. Cheers and huzzahs echoed off the arched iron-and-glass roof of the train shed, almost drowning out a brass band when it struck up the hymn "Home Again (From a Foreign Shore)" as Spalding regally alighted from the car.

The players, in the "jolliest spirits," formed up behind their leader to walk to the Polk Street exit, where a line of 65 carriages awaited the travelers and the local dignitaries on the welcoming committee. An excess of exuberant fans blocked the way, squeezing in to pat the players on the back or shake their hands. The crush of admirers trapped some players on the platform for several anxious minutes until a phalanx of police officers arrived and helped them push through the well-wishers and climb into one of the 11 carriages reserved for them. Spalding was in the lead vehicle, of course, accompanied by Anson and Lynch, the tour's advance man. In nodding to the crowd, Spalding, still in his late 30s, presented as the monarch of the metropolis.

The entourage was relieved as well as exhilarated when the carriages finally began to move slowly down Polk Street, but, astoundingly, the throng of spectators seemed to grow. Multitudes lined every street along the parade's circuitous two-mile route to the Palmer House hotel. The line of march began with the

25-piece First Regimental Band, followed by a detachment of Zouave soldiers in their braided jackets, baggy trousers, and tasseled fezzes. Scattered among the carriages were dozens of local athletes in full uniform: ballplayers from six amateur and industrial clubs in the city, track and field competitors, rowers, and mounted cyclists. Scottish pipers played. A. G. Spalding & Bros. employees spontaneously joined the procession, exalting in their status as hirelings of the Great Man.

Cannon reports from a nine-gun salute echoed off the skyscrapers rising from the ashes of the Great Fire—the Home Insurance Building, the Rookery, and the two newest: the Rand McNally Building and the 13-story Tacoma Building. The spectacle conveniently passed in front of Spalding's flagship store, and then proceeded a block down State Street to the Palmer House.

At the grand hotel, business travelers found the corridors and parlors filled with more than 200 friends, many of them prominent business leaders, and no fewer than 30 elected officials. Chicago's current mayor, Dewitt C. Cregier, was there, as was a celebrated former mayor, Carter H. Harrison, who also owned and edited the *Chicago Times*. Spalding pinballed through the ornate fluted columns rising out of the patterned marble floor of the hotel's expansive lobby, seeking out social friends and business associates. There he found, among others, John R. Walsh, a banker and part owner of the White Stockings who would later serve time in the Leavenworth federal prison for a fraud that toppled his Chicago National Bank and two others; Frederick Ullman, a powerful lawyer who would soon help Spalding break baseball's first union; and Lucious Fischer, a local paper-bag magnate who invested alongside Spalding in two ill-fated businesses.

When Spalding and his players navigated to the Palmer House's elegant Dining Hall for a formal banquet, they found the room festooned with flowers in baskets, garlands, wreaths, and banks. Affixed to the head table was a large model of a baseball park rendered in candy, with 18 miniature players in position. On each side of that was a floral design of two crossed bats and a baseball. Waiters in cutaway coats and white ties stood at attention on the highly buffed marble floor as the guests found their seats. On the tables were 16-piece settings of Haviland bone china trimmed in 24-karat gold, which the hotel owner's wife, Bertha Palmer, had personally acquired in Paris.

When Spalding was invited to address the crowd, he kept his remarks unusually brief, perhaps because by then it was well past eleven o'clock. He spoke far more about the joy of returning home than he did the adventure of visiting so many exotic ports of call on his 182-day, 30,000-mile, $50,000 excursion. "I want to tell you that although there may be some great and good places in the corners of this earth, I think that Chicago is the sweetest, dearest place on this globe," he said. The room erupted with thunderous applause.

The universal good will would not last for long.

While players were courteous and respectful throughout the welcome-home hullaballoo, they were privately furious about the classification system. They believed it enabled owners to grade men like so much livestock, take a larger share of each team's income, and punish players with even less recourse than they had before. Owners liked it because grades determined pay, making it easier to cut expenses.

Players were perhaps angriest with Spalding, not only because he was the most influential team owner and had floated a similar grading system years ago, but because they suspected him of having tricked Ward, Fred Pfeffer, and other Brotherhood leaders to join him on the round-the-world promotional cruise, essentially sequestering them while the other owners adopted the changes and gave players three weeks to sign new contracts or be forever banned from the game.

Players also were incensed by the treatment of two popular veterans, shortstop Jack Rowe and third baseman Deacon White, whom owners had threatened to ruin professionally and financially for refusing to move to new clubs that had purchased their contracts.

With Opening Day of the 1889 season less than a week away, players talked about whether to strike or demand to negotiate with the owners. Ward, who had graduated from Columbia Law School four years earlier, used his lawyerly powers of persuasion to induce Brotherhood members to honor their contracts and play while he arranged to negotiate with Spalding; Rowe and White, however, still refused to report to their new teams.

The battle over those players began in October 1888, when Frederick Kimball Stearns, the owner of the Detroit Wolverines, decided to close his money-losing team and get out of baseball, even though it had won the National League pennant just a year earlier. To recoup his investment, Stearns sold all his players' contracts to other teams. The rights to Rowe went to the Pittsburgh Alleghenys and White to the Boston Beaneaters. But the men asserted that Detroit's contractual rights to their services had expired along with the team and they would not report to their new clubs. Instead, they said that they would play for the Buffalo Bisons, a minor-league club in which they had recently invested.

Their nominal new employers said they would hold the men to their contracts, even though the agreements were with a team that no longer existed. "He'll play in Pittsburgh or he'll get off the earth," Stearns angrily said of Rowe.[1] Spalding and other League officials warned the players that if either of them suited up for their own team in Buffalo, owners would forever blacklist the men and their club. White and Rowe shot back that as far as they were concerned, their obligation to Detroit ended when the Wolverines' owners dissolved the team—and, after consulting a lawyer, they added that they looked forward to testing this theory in court.[2]

Toward the end of June, however, White and Rowe were compelled to reconsider their position in light of the Bisons' poor performances on the field, where they lost twice as often as they won, and at the gate, where ticket sales did not cover salaries, travel, and other expenses. The men were running out of cash and knew that to actually earn some money, they needed to go back to their old teams.

White went to Pittsburgh in early July to seek a truce with the Alleghenys. In the meeting, White, then 42 years old, said he was well past his prime, his sight was deteriorating, and his rheumatism worsening, but the Alleghenys' president, William A. Nimick, still refused to release him. White then offered to join the team if Nimick would let Rowe play for Buffalo; the owner refused. Instead, Nimick offered to pay both men bonuses of $1,250 as well as salaries of $500 a month if they would join his team for the second half of the season.[3] The bonuses cinched the deal, symbolically giving the players a share of the bounty Detroit received when it sold their contracts. Capturing the frustration and resentment of players ensnared by the reserve clause, with their services bought and sold at team owners' sole discretion, White famously quipped: "No man is going to sell my carcass unless I get half."[4]

Thanks to Ward's diplomacy, the 1889 season opened as scheduled, with two American Association games on April 17 and the first two National League games a week later. Spalding's Chicago squad traveled to Pittsburgh for its first game, which was delayed by a thunderstorm and eventually played on a soggy ballfield sprinkled with sawdust in a losing effort to firm up the muddy basepaths. Pittsburgh clubbed 12 hits in the game and won, 8–5.[5] It was a bad start to a bad year for Spalding and his White Stockings.

Fans grumbled about Spalding having sold Chicago's best players, among them Clarkson and Kelly—but they still paid to watch games: The club set a franchise attendance record of 217,070 in 1887, despite finishing in third place, six-and-a-half games behind Detroit. It broke that record a year later, drawing 228,906 paying spectators while finishing nine games behind the pennant-winning New York Giants.[6]

Some of the growth in attendance was a natural result of Chicago's booming population, which doubled in the 1880s to more than one million people as the city became the main portal through which grain and livestock from the Great Plains were shipped to the big cities in the East. Immigrants were drawn to Chicago to work in new factories—the Pullman Palace Car Company, for example, opened its massive railroad-car works in 1881—and in the emerging meatpacking industry, which was made possible when the introduction of refrigerated boxcars ended the need to transport live cattle to the East Coast. But the spike in ticket sales had another effect: Spalding realized that truculent, impudent, and expensive star players were not essential to achieving financial success in baseball.

Players took another lesson from the transactions. The reserve clause not only suppressed wages, it turned players into property that could be bought and sold without having any say in the matter or sharing in the proceeds. Simmering disaffection over arbitrary discipline came to a boil in June 1889, when Mordecai H. Davidson, owner of the American Association's Louisville Colonels, which at the time had won eight games and lost 40, fined second baseman Dan Shannon for making errors and catcher Paul Cook for what he said was bad baserunning.

Their teammates came to the men's defense and threatened not to play in the next game unless Davidson rescinded the fines. Rather than back down, Davidson raised the stakes and said he would levy a $100 fine on any team member who refused to play and another $25 each if they lost. Six players refused to play in the next two games and Davidson fined them $1,200, tacking on another $500 for using bad language and refusing to slide. Other American Association owners, concerned that the players threatened to join the Brotherhood, bought the club from Davidson in July and reimbursed most of the fines. The incident showed the players the power of supporting one another when dealing with owners and managers.

At the end of May, Ward wrote to Spalding demanding the National League honor its earlier pledge to bar teams from cutting players' salaries when reserving them—that is, when forbidding them to move to or even negotiate with another team. The League had indeed agreed to stop the practice when it met with players' representatives at its annual meeting the previous November, but it had not followed through. Spalding told Ward that the National League could not change the standard contract unless the other parties to the National Agreement agreed to do the same; the other major league at the time, the American Association, had refused to do so, he said.

Sensing that the growing number of player complaints meant labor troubles ahead, National League president Nicholas E. Young created a committee of three owners—Spalding, John Day of New York, and John I. Rogers of Philadelphia—to address the Brotherhood's grievances. Young called it the "Brotherhood Committee" but Spalding preferred to call it the National League's "war committee." He certainly was combative, openly diminishing the players' complaints and scoffing at suggestions that internal turmoil might encourage outside investors to once again challenge the National League–American Association duopoly, as Henry Van Noye Lucas, the St. Louis real-estate heir, had tried and failed to do with the Union Association five years earlier.[7]

Spalding appeared to seek labor peace by suggesting to Ward that they meet to discuss players' concerns face-to-face when the Giants came to Chicago in June for three games with the White Stockings. Ward accepted the invitation and on June 24 the men met at Spalding's store on Madison Street where they talked for two hours about the classification plan, salary caps, and one particular grievance: a $250 salary cut forced on Elmer Ellsworth "Sy" Sutcliffe when Detroit sold the catcher's contract to Cleveland in the offseason. As the meeting ended, Spalding told Ward he didn't think any of the issues were urgent enough to require immediate action but promised to consult with the other committee members and respond soon.

On July 2, Spalding wrote to Ward at the Pittsburgh hotel where his team stayed during a series with the Alleghenys and informed the Brotherhood leader that the full committee had, not surprisingly, agreed with him that it was "inadvisable" to consider any player complaints before the league's regular annual meeting in November. "We fail to discover any necessity for immediate action in the points you raise," Spalding concluded.[8] He did not write—though he and Ward both surely knew—that November was after the season ended and players returned to their offseason homes, costing the Brotherhood the leverage of threatening to strike.

Ward did not reply.

The players were in no mood for Spalding's high-handedness. In their eyes, classification and salary caps were only the latest in a litany of disrespectful conduct by owners in both the National League and the American Association.

As soon as the Giants were back in New York, Ward had Brotherhood leaders convene at the Fifth Avenue Hotel. The date—July 14, 1889—was coincidentally the centennial of the storming of the Bastille and the start of the French Revolution. The players' objective was revolutionary in its own way: to explore the feasibility of creating a professional league of the players, by the players, and for the players. Ward instructed Brotherhood members at the meeting to identify wealthy baseball fans in each city they visited and ask if they would be interested in entering the baseball business, informing them the National League was coming off its two most profitable years in history. These potential backers must be willing and able to provide large amounts of capital quickly to finance a rival to the National League and, crucially, they must share control and profits with the players.[9]

The new organization, which the players code-named the United Business Association, would not have a reserve clause or establish arbitrary salary bands, as the National League had done. Players would earn at least as much as they did in 1888, before the National League introduced its classification system and salary cap, and in addition to their salaries would share in team profits exceeding $10,000.[10] Multi-year contracts would assure investors that their most precious assets, the players, could not walk out the door at any moment, and would offer players a modicum of job security without shackling them to one team forever. Voting blocs of players and the capitalists backing them would democratically administer the new league and each team in it.[11]

As Brotherhood members mapped out their revolution, Spalding aggravated players by proposing to extend salary caps and player classification to minor-league teams. He proposed limiting player salaries in the top-tier minor leagues at $200 a month for a seven-month season, with player salaries in lower-tier clubs capped at $150, $100, and $60 a month. Every minor-league player would be bound to play only for the team holding his contract, with one exception—any team in the National League or American Association could hire away any minor leaguer in exchange for a $1,500 "bonus," payable to the player's team. In a sop to players, Spalding said that team owners could, if they wished, give one-fourth of each bonus to the man whose talent was being sold.[12]

Spalding made his proposal to stiffen the spines of minor-league owners who worried too much about fans' complaining that big-league teams cherry-picked top minor-league players, sometimes during a close pennant race. "It is very evident," Spalding wrote to National League president Nick Young, "that the minor leagues require some governing power to force them to . . . release a player upon receipt of a fair bonus, while now they hesitate about doing it on account of adverse criticism."[13]

The Brotherhood's response was swift and unequivocal. Spalding's proposal "would be fiercely opposed by all the professional baseball players in the country," said Timothy J. Keefe, the Brotherhood's secretary and a star pitcher for New York.[14] A "prominent" but anonymous player attacked Spalding personally in the *New York Times*: "This man Spalding is for himself all the time, and he cares little or nothing for the players. . . . The scheme to pay part of the bonus on sales to players is a good one, but it will hardly effect [*sic*] Mr. Spalding, as he is about done selling now that he has pocketed the cash in the Kelly, Clarkson, and Gore deals."[15]

Spalding was not the only owner to realize that the reserve clause not only could help small-market teams compete with wealthier clubs; it also tamped down players' salaries by eliminating competition for their services. National League pay averaged about $2,000 in 1877, before owners introduced the reserve rule, but only $1,500 five years later.[16]

While Spalding dismissed rumors that someone was signing up players for a new organization to rival or crush the National League, Brotherhood members and sympathetic capitalists were hustling to recruit NL veterans and lease ballpark sites with the aim of playing a full season of major-league ball in 1890. Inevitably, as the men talked with more people, their activity drew the attention of baseball writers.[17] On September 11, the *Sporting Life* published a page-one article outlining the Brotherhood plan.[18] The paper incorrectly characterized the new league as a trust but accurately identified Albert L. Johnson, a streetcar magnate, as a prime mover along with Ward, and named six of the eight cities where the new enterprise sought to site franchises.

A longer, more detailed account appeared 11 days later on the front page of the *Chicago Tribune* and was picked up by newspapers across the country. "A Great Ball Trust" read the top of a multi-deck headline, followed by "The Brotherhood Has Organized a New League." The *Tribune* repeated *Sporting Life*'s error in describing the new league, but it referred to the operation by its code name, "United Business Association," and contained enough detail—target cities, organizational structure, profit sharing, and participating capitalists—to give it undeniable verisimilitude. The new league "contemplates the taking of the baseball business out of the hands that have nursed and fostered it into health and prosperity and the placing of it into new ones, the owners of which guarantee to divide the profits with their players," the article read.[19]

After the *Sporting Life* article, Spalding and other National League leaders had been able to convince themselves that the Brotherhood was behind the rumor of a new league—that it was simply a ploy to gain leverage in future negotiations about whether to repeal classification and salary caps. The *Tribune*'s more-detailed article was harder to shrug off. "I was not prepared for such a ponderous plot as that outlined in the *Tribune*," Spalding admitted, adding that he was confident the plan would sputter out before the new league could play its first game.[20] National League president Nick Young laughed off the news as "the annual baseball scare," but added that it would be discussed at the annual meeting in November.[21]

Spalding did not want to wait until the league's annual meeting in mid-November to extinguish this fire. He wrote to Ward on September 27, saying the league was ready to meet to address their concerns. Ward received Spalding's new offer a full week before the season was over and replied by telling him the league had missed its chance to talk. The Brotherhood committee that was to meet with the league in June was dissolved when the league rejected the idea.[22]

Tension between owners and players did not bother the ticket-buying public. More than 1.35 million paying customers passed through National League turnstiles in 1889, 6 percent more than the previous year and close to the 1.4 million record set in 1887. The League champion New York Giants were an exception—their ticket sales fell by one-third in 1889 because New York City had turned the team out of the original Polo Grounds shortly before the season to extend the street grid. The Giants had to host "home" games in three different ballparks in two states. Overall, the AA drew 1.27 million spectators, 27 percent more than in 1888.[23]

Robust attendance figures like these bolstered the Brotherhood's assertion that owners had been disingenuously poor-mouthing when they adopted the classification system and salary cap.

As the 1889 season began to wind down and loose-lipped players filled in the outline of the Brotherhood's ostensibly "secret" plan, Spalding invited Chris von der Ahe, owner of the American Association's successful St. Louis Browns club, to come to Chicago to discuss the older leagues' plan to beat the players. In a parlor of the Palmer House, Spalding convinced Von der Ahe that the Brotherhood's cooperative model of team ownership posed as great a threat to him and his fellow Association capitalists as to those in the National League. Von der Ahe readily agreed, and before he left the hotel he told waiting newspapermen that the Association would fully ally itself with the National League.

"It is a question of capital against labor, and capital must stick by capital," he said, adding that he was not speaking officially for the Browns much less the other owners. Absent-mindedly twirling his watch charm around his finger, he added in his nearly impenetrable Prussian accent: "If Johnny Ward had been a member of the St. Louis baseball team, the Brotherhood would never have been formed. I would have kicked him out the moment he began to get the big head and make trouble."[24]

Von der Ahe touched off a whirlwind of speculation when he concluded: "The final upshot of this struggle between the proprietors of the clubs and the players will be the formation by the former of a single baseball league for the entire United States. . . . Not exactly a trust—though some would be sure to call it that—but one league. That's what this squabble will bring us to."[25]

Spalding, as was his way, was much less forthcoming than his guileless guest. He said the White Stockings had no plans to consolidate the two established leagues and he had not proposed any such thing to Von der Ahe. When a sportswriter asked if the Browns owner had raised the topic, Spalding gave a nebulous reply: "Yes, in a general way, but the idea is not a new one. It has been talked of for several years to my knowledge." Throughout the interview, Spalding spoke a lot but said very little. He raised the idea of taking legal action against men who play for the new league while simultaneously seeming to dismiss the idea. "Our lawyers have assured us that we can enjoin our reserved players," he said at one point, "but I am by no means certain that we shall apply for an injunction. . . . I don't say we will enjoin them, and I don't say that we will not."[26]

Spalding engaged in this sort of rhetorical legerdemain to keep his options open, keep his enemies off balance, and sully the reputation of the Players' League without damaging the reputations of its players. He would need those men to repopulate the National League after he found a way to bury the Brotherhood.

When the 1889 season ended, scores of National League players, including a large majority of Spalding's White Stockings, broke with custom and refused to sign contracts to play for their teams in 1890. Spalding publicly shrugged off the contract boycott, saying he was confident that players would change their minds as tempers cooled. Privately, however, some NL owners were frantically shopping for minor-league, industrial-league, and even amateur-league players to take the field the next spring if veterans declined to do so. In early October, the Boston Red Stockings had inquired about acquiring every player on the roster of the Omaha Omahogs, a team on its way to winning the Western Association pennant.[27] The Boston men lost interest after finding out that at least five of the Omahogs would not jump to the Players' League.

Still, NL owners had reason to be concerned because players were not begging to return to the National League, as Spalding often predicted they would, and their new league was efficiently leasing grounds and erecting grandstands. In an interview on the front page of New York's *Evening World* as the 1889 season concluded, Al Johnson, the PL's business leader, said the Brotherhood was most likely ready to introduce its own league the following spring and warned that the new league would probably kill the reserve rule, player classifications, salary caps, and the sale of players' contracts—and that the players and their financial supporters, including himself, would share profits.[28]

* * *

Masses of businessmen, players, reporters, and cranks filled the marble and mahogany lobby of the Fifth Avenue Hotel in New York on November 4, hoping to witness history. The Brotherhood of Professional Ball Players convened what it said was a routine three-day meeting, but people knew that if Johnson was right about players starting a new league in 1890, they would need to announce it soon—perhaps that very day.

Brotherhood president John Ward gaveled the meeting to order at noon, and seven hours later he and the rest of the governing board emerged from their hotel parlor with a document to explain its intentions and preemptively defend the Brotherhood from the owners' anticipated attacks.

"It is no longer a secret that the players of the league have determined to play next season under different management," the statement began, and then went on to explain why players felt the radical step was necessary. "There was a time when the league stood for integrity and fair dealings. Today it stands for dollars and cents. Once it looked to the elevation of the game and an honest exhibition of the sport. Today its eyes are upon the turnstile. Men have come into the business with no other motive than to exploit it for every dollar in sight.

"Players have been bought and sold and exchanged as if they were sheep instead of American citizens," the Brotherhood statement added. "Even the disabandonment [*sic*] and retirement of a club did not free the players from the octopus clutch, for they were then peddled around to the highest bidder."[29]

Ward said the circuit would shed the code name "United Business Association" in favor of the "Players' National League" and was in the process of securing ballpark sites and filing papers to incorporate each franchise. He promised more details before the end of the year.

In the days after the Brotherhood of Professional Baseball Players declared its members' independence, Spalding and his fellow National League owners stayed uncharacteristically quiet.

Some National League owners wishfully thought the Brotherhood's actions were a bluff because the Players' League seemed unprepared to start play in 1890. When the players delivered their November bombshell, Opening Day was only five months away and the insurrectionists had yet to build any ballparks, sign any players, or hire any umpires. National League owners tried to convince themselves that the Brotherhood league was no more than a bargaining chip that players intended to trade for repealing the reserve clause or player-classification system.

Spalding did not think the players were bluffing, although he was careful to appear unconcerned in public. When a reporter asked him in late October what the National League planned to do about the Brotherhood, Spalding shrugged. "What is there to do?" he said. "All that any one knows of the Brotherhood's intentions has been learned from the newspapers. There is nothing of a sufficiently authentic or definite nature to warrant action upon our part."[30]

Privately, he was less sanguine. On his way to New York two days after that interview but before Johnson's interview was published and the Brotherhood met, Spalding stopped in Pittsburgh to meet with Al Pratt, manager of his store there and a former player with the local American Association club, the Alleghenys. Spalding told Pratt he was sure the Brotherhood's plan for a new league was a "go," and he did not expect them to seek concessions at the NL's annual meeting in two weeks. The time for concessions had passed. He said he was already scouting replacement players from the minor leagues.[31]

In New York, Spalding at first kept a low profile at the Fifth Avenue Hotel, which usually served as his New York City base, because the Brotherhood planned to use the same venue for its meeting. That meant the hotel's lobby, corridors, drawing rooms, dining rooms, and reading rooms would be crowded with people he would rather not see just yet. He also did not want to risk being publicly heckled by Brotherhood members, as other League figures had been, nor was he eager for reporters to buttonhole him in search of an incautious remark. When the Brotherhood met, he took a quick trip down to Philadelphia to oversee A. G. Spalding & Bros.' acquisition of the retail business of A. J. Reach & Co., its closest rival in the sporting goods industry.

He returned to New York when the hubbub over the players' statement had quieted down. Radiating his customary calm and confidence, he stopped in the Fifth Avenue Hotel's Corinthian-columned portico to tell waiting reporters and fans what he had said many times in the past six weeks and would repeat many times in the future: The league always treated its players fairly, so the Brotherhood rebellion had no foundation. He expected most if not all of his veterans to re-sign with the team before the spring; those who chose not to come back could easily be replaced. "There are plenty of first-class men in the minor leagues," he said.[32]

Spalding did not mention that National League owners had pledged $250,000 to defeat the Brotherhood and that he had already released Cap Anson and other trusted aides to run down veteran players at their favorite offseason haunts—family homes, hunting cabins, fishing holes, saloons, farms, anywhere they could be located—and browbeat, bribe, or beg them to sign National League contracts before a Players' League representative could find them. Nor did Spalding reveal that he had hired men to comb the South, Midwest, and West for the best minor-league, semiprofessional, or even amateur players they could find and sign.

The scramble to find and sign players had comical moments. The Philadelphia outfielder Ed Andrews tracked down a potential Players' League recruit to his house in Erie, Pennsylvania, only to learn that his quarry was out hunting. Andrews gamely waded across a sizeable marsh to find the player and succeeded in signing him. By the time they started home, the tide had come in and the marsh water was much deeper than Andrews wanted to navigate. The newly signed, 23-year-old, 140-pound player generously offered to carry the 30-year-old, 160-pound Brotherhood man piggy-back across the marsh.

On another trip, Andrews knew that a sought-after catcher, Andy Sommers, was at home in Cleveland but not answering his doorbell. After hopping a fence, Andrews found the catcher in his backyard, but Sommers refused to sign a Players' League contract even after pledging that he would. The player's immigrant father was happy to explain. "It vas all your own misdakes in vading so long to send Andy a gondract," the father said. "Andy would not haf signed mit Glassgock yisderday ef you had gom here furst." Andrews had been beaten out by Jack Glasscock, a player rounding up players for the National League.

National League owners on November 11 assembled for their annual meeting in the Fifth Avenue Hotel, where the heavy mahogany doors of Parlor F frustrated potential eavesdroppers loitering in the corridor. Spalding, in his role as leader of the war committee, wasted little time in recommending that the League make a strategic retreat by discarding the classification system, ditching salary caps, and releasing players from the reserve clause if their team went out of business or quit the League. He suggested that the league pay Sutcliffe the trifling $250 difference between his Detroit and Cleveland salaries. His fellow owners endorsed his ideas.

Doing so would cost league owners little but would let Spalding credibly claim the high ground when speaking publicly. "The League has up to the present time given the Brotherhood everything they have asked for," he said after the meeting, "and if, after this action, the players are determined to make an effort to jump the League and join a rival organization, they must prepare themselves to take the consequences."[33] To make clear what that meant, the owners convened a "law committee" to study legal options to enforce players' contracts.

Spalding did not invite representatives of the American Association to join in any of these actions, even though it was meeting at the same time in the same hotel and, as a signatory to the National Agreement, it had as much to lose if the players prevailed. But the AA was riven by a nasty personal feud between the owners of its leading clubs, St. Louis and Brooklyn, and was incapable of electing a president, even after taking 40 ballots over two full days. The impasse persuaded Brooklyn and another financially strong club, Cleveland, to quit the association and request shelter in the National League. Spalding recognized that adding the clubs would fortify the NL for its war with the players while at the same time gravely wounding the American Association. Getting rid of the AA and the Players' League would enable the National League to monopolize major-league baseball. However, adding the Association franchises to the

National League would require more travel and allow for fewer open dates to play money-spinning exhibition games. NL owners voted to welcome the Association refugees from Brooklyn and Cleveland—but not St. Louis, which Spalding blackballed because its owner, a brewer, insisted on selling beer at his ballpark—and postpone talks about schedules and costs.

Before the meeting concluded on November 21, the National League issued a 1,660-word rebuttal to the Brotherhood's argument in favor of starting its own league. The NL document, written by Spalding, Day, and Rogers, was a mélange of self-pity, half-truths, invective, and bombast. It began by asserting that back in 1876 the National League had rescued professional baseball from a "slough of corruption and disgrace." Because its predecessor, the National Association of Professional Baseball Players, was "controlled and dominated" by players, it was riddled with "contract-breaking, dissipation, and dishonesty."

The NL then pivoted to defend the reserve rule. The owners' statement asserted that players' salaries had "more than trebled" under the reserve rule, so "the use of such terms as 'bondage,' 'slavery,' 'sold like sheep,' etc. becomes meaningless and abused." For good measure, the League heaped inflammatory adjectives on the Brotherhood, calling it "evasive," "contradictory," "mendacious," and an "oath-bound secret organization of strikers." It dismissed the Players' League as merely "the efforts of certain overpaid players to again control [baseball] for their own aggrandizement but to its ultimate dishonor and disintegration."[34]

Brotherhood leader Fred Pfeffer, the White Stockings' erstwhile second baseman, heard Spalding's voice in the owners' broadside and aimed his written reply directly at his former boss without using his name. "I must say, those self-glorified magnates throw bouquets at themselves in great style," Pfeffer said with a smile. He added that it was "a well-known fact" that the chairman of the committee behind the League's broadside was president of a franchise that paid dividends of 20 percent annually in each of the preceding five years, doubling investors' money over that time. He said that degree of profitability should be the standard by which to measure the fairness of the salary caps owners imposed on players.[35]

Pfeffer warned owners to be careful when they claimed exceptional business sense. "None of the Brotherhood players that I know of have ever been connected with a 'Freight Bureau scheme'," he said, again not naming his target.[36] But everyone knew that Spalding was among the prominent Chicago businessmen who had invested in a recent fraud by that name.[37]

Despite National League owners' bluster—orchestrated by Spalding—that few players would risk jumping to the Players' League, it became clearer each day that players were most eager to bolt. By December, Players' League rosters were brimming with the names of men who only few months earlier had played in the National League, including 11 of the 14 members of Spalding's 1889 White Stockings team. Even Spalding's coveted groundskeeper, Billy Houston, quit to work for the local Players' League club.[38] Only Anson, infielder Tom Burns, and pitcher Bill Hutchison stuck with Spalding.[39]

New York was in worse shape. All but two of its players had jumped to the Players' League and owner John Day was having trouble signing replacements good enough to compete for fans with the two major-league teams in nearby Brooklyn. Spalding floated the idea of having Day buy the best players on the Indianapolis club, a financially weak organization that the league intended to close anyway. The Hoosiers had finished next-to-last that season but had a respectable roster that included the "Indiana Thunderbolt," Amos Rusie, a flame-throwing right-handed pitcher who was still in his teens but on his way to the Hall of Fame.[40]

As time grew short and options ran low that winter of 1889-1890, National League owners moved the legal option back to the front burner. Spalding's personal lawyer in Chicago, Frederick Ullman, and the white-shoe Wall Street firm Evarts, Choate, and Beaman assured NL leaders that the reserve clause in their contracts was enforceable and that courts would order players back to their National League teams. Several executives, Spalding among them, had been dubious about suing players, fearing the consequences if a judge invalidated the contracts. But Day, chairman of the league's legal committee, adamantly advocated action, convinced that a decisive legal strike would swiftly bring the players to their knees.

In public, at least, Spalding was on board, if only because he had no better idea at this point and he was simultaneously establishing a professional baseball league in England and negotiating to buy A. J. Reach of Philadelphia. "When the men signed our contract last year, it was under the agreement that we had the right to reserve them for this year," he said. "I have notified every one of the players that they must come to the front and sign for the next year. I'll fix them if they don't, for my attorney assures me not one of them will be able to play ball in Chicago when I serve the injunction, and you can bet your bottom dollar I will preserve my rights."[41]

The players were unconvinced. When the Brotherhood's leader, John Ward, heard that he was to be the first player to be sued, he smiled. "The sooner the better;" he said. "We are ready to meet them in any court."

Two days before Christmas 1889, the Giants' corporate parent, the Metropolitan Exhibition Co., petitioned the New York Supreme Court for an injunction to require Ward to play for its team. In Philadelphia, the NL franchise took its sinker-ball pitcher Charlie Buffinton and barrel-chested second baseman Bill Hallman to court in the City of Brotherly Love with the same goal.

The case against Ward was heard first.

As Spalding had feared, it did not go well for the League.

Justice Morgan J. O'Brien of the New York Supreme Court denied the plea for a temporary injunction on January 28, 1890. His reasoning: The National League's contract was unenforceable because it was so blatantly unfair—players were effectively bound to their team for life on vague or nonexistent terms, while teams could fire players for any reason or no reason with 10 days' notice. He added that an injunction was not necessary because the team had time to try the case in civil court before the 1890 season would begin. Day did just that, only to hear Justice Abraham R. Lawrence rule in Ward's favor on March 31; Justice Lawrence's decision echoed Justice O'Brien's view that the National League's contract was unenforceable.[42]

NL owners had no better luck in Pennsylvania. Philadelphia County Court judge M. Russell Thayer reached the same conclusion on March 15, 1890, and dismissed the Athletics' suits against Hallman and Buffinton.[43]

With the National League having struck out in court, Spalding pivoted to what he believed to be a more accommodating institution: the newspapers. He used NL executives to spread gossip about Players' League stars bickering among themselves, squabbling with their financial backers, or secretly agreeing to return to the National League. Players were exasperated by the relentless flood of falsehoods. "The League men will resort to almost anything to do us up," said Pittsburgh outfielder Ned Hanlon. The latest calumny from "these Chicago fellows" was that the pitcher Hank O'Day had signed a League contract. "Why I won't be surprised at anything the League people say any more," Hanlon said.[44]

The lies did not inhibit Players' League supporters from leasing ball grounds and erecting wooden bleachers and grandstands. The PL Chicago franchise tried a shortcut by offering $21,000 for a three-year lease of the park Spalding had been renting for $1,000 annually. Distracted by the Brotherhood War, Spalding hadn't noticed that his lease had expired, and had to pay $7,000 a year to wrest it away from the Players' League.[45]

Publicly, Spalding sought out interviews to personally denounce Brotherhood leaders as "conspirators," "rebels," "hot-headed anarchists," and "revolutionists," denigrate their league as a "dangerous experiment;" and deride their financial backers as "long-chance capitalists."[46] Such inflammatory language reflected the sometimes bloody battle then underway across the country between capital and labor. In Chicago and elsewhere, police and state militia members had beaten or shot striking railroad workers, quarry men, streetcar operators, and other working people who rebelled against pay cuts and 12-hour work days. Nationwide, the number of strikes—involving people in mines, factories, railroads, garment mills, farms, and docks—rose from 2,639 in the first half of the 1880s to 7,029 in the second half.[47] Just two years earlier, a judge in Illinois had sentenced seven "anarchists" to hang for the bombing in Haymarket Square, about a mile from Spalding's store.

National labor leaders, including Samuel L. Gompers, president of the American Federation of Labor, and the senior-most members of the powerful Brotherhood of Carpenters and Joiners of America, publicly backed the Players' League, adding that their members were ready to lend moral and financial support "to see the players succeed in freeing themselves from League slavery." (The support was not bilateral: when a citywide carpenters' strike in Chicago threatened to prevent the completion of the city's Players' League park before the season began, the team's financial backers hired non-union men to finish the job.)

While Spalding relentlessly bashed the Brotherhood, he took a softer and friendlier (if less sincere) line with rank-and-file players, praising their intelligence and expressing his confidence that "they will all come round in due time and ask for the privilege" of returning to their League teams.[48] However, a *Pittsburgh Dispatch* columnist noted that Spalding and other NL executives hired men to scour the country and sign young players "by the gross" as quickly as they could.

"If all of the old players are really safely signed," he asked, "why are legions of youngsters being secured?" He answered his own rhetorical question with the understatement of the year: "It really seems to me that there is considerable bluffing all round."[49]

Chapter 13

Brotherhood War

On Opening Day of the 1890 season, a sunny, unseasonably chilly Saturday, waves of cheers and waving handkerchiefs hailed the reigning National League champion New York Giants as they marched in formation into their new 14,000-seat ballpark in the far northern reaches of Manhattan, at 155th Street and Eighth Avenue, to take on an undistinguished team from Philadelphia, the Phillies.[1]

An hour earlier, in another brand new ballpark situated just 10 feet away, across an alleyway, a different club named the New York Giants, this one affiliated with the Players' League, had marched onto its playing field behind the 69th Regiment Band to meet a different undistinguished team from Philadelphia, the Athletics.

The number of runs each team scored that afternoon were of far less interest to the teams' owners and players than the number of spectators they attracted. This was the first day of head-to-head scheduling between the National League, starting its 15th season, and its breakaway rival starting its first.

It was quickly obvious which New York Giants had won the day: 12,013 people paid to see the Players' League team lose 12–11, while only 4,644 witnessed the National League Giants get shut out 4–0.[2]

New York was no fluke. The new Players' League teams attracted larger crowds in every city where the National League had, at Spalding's urging, scheduled its Opening Day games on the same day as Players' League games to starve the upstart circuit of spectators. The results, it is safe to say, were not what Spalding expected. In Boston, 8,334 spectators braved 49-degree weather to make their way to the Players' League opener at the new Congress Street Grounds near Boston Harbor, while a National League game at the South End Grounds, about two-and-a-half miles away, drew fewer than half as many people. Almost 9,000 paying customers trekked to Exposition Park in Allegheny City, Pennsylvania, to see the local Players' League team, the Burghers, lose to the Chicago Pirates, while only about 1,500 watched the local National League team defeat the Cleveland Spiders in Recreation Park across the river in Pittsburgh.[3]

At this early stage of professional baseball's development, it appears that "cranks," as devoted spectators were then called, were more attached to individual players' talents and personas than they were to abstractions like teams and leagues. The National League had sold baseball as a form of entertainment on a par with theater and music, so owners should not have been so surprised when their customers followed the most talented and popular entertainers to the Players' League. Cranks were voting with their feet, and the National League was losing in every city.

Spalding, perhaps sensing trouble, helped his franchise avoid the embarrassment of playing before a small Opening Day crowd by making sure its season began in Cincinnati, where there was no Players' League club. The Chicagoans—which sportswriters recently re-nicknamed the Colts because its roster had so many inexperienced players, including an outfielder that team leader "Cap" Anson had found in the Chicago City League—defeated the Reds 5–4 before a respectable crowd. (The number of spectators was 6,311, roughly 6,500 or "nearly 10,000," depending on the paper one read.)[4] Whatever the actual tally, it was cold comfort for other National League owners. For them, Opening Day was a debacle as unsettling—and ominous—as the Union army's defeat at the First Battle of Bull Run, a Civil War memory still fresh to many. Hubris and underestimation of a foe had again led to a loss and made clear that they might well lose a war they had told themselves would be easy to win.

In the days immediately after Opening Day, attendance at ballgames began a natural decline as the excitement and ballyhoo of a new season faded, but National League owners were not prepared for how fast and far it would fall for their clubs. In an extreme example, a mere 80 fans turned up on April 23 to see the Alleghenys outscore Cleveland 20–12.[5] Three days later, Spalding and the Alleghenys' president, William A. Nimick, revealed that the National League's club in Pittsburgh, by far the smallest city with two professional ballclubs, would move its next series, against Chicago, to the Windy City.[6]

The announcement, made just three days before the four-game series was to start, produced a whirlwind of speculation that the National League had come to realize the folly of matching the Players' League schedule and would rearrange its entire calendar to avoid conflicts. Spalding denied that the National League was even considering any such thing. By this point, he spoke authoritatively for the league, having leveraged his chairmanship of the NL's war committee to act as the organization's de facto leader. The considerable wealth he reaped from his sporting goods company, along with the skillful way in which his brother Walter and brother-in-law William T. Brown managed the business in his absence, allowed him to focus on the Brotherhood War.

He did not confirm the Alleghenys' story that they needed time to make "some improvements" to Recreation Park, but he did say that he accommodated Pittsburgh's request because doing so would enable him to avoid a 25-game homestand in September by moving three of those contests to Pittsburgh. "I assented for that reason only," Spalding said.[7] Conveniently, the Chicago Pirates of the Players' League would be in Cleveland on the very days Spalding agreed to host the Alleghenys, allowing his club to avoid what the avid monopolist saw as bothersome competition when his team played its first home games.

Moving the games to Chicago gave a modest boost to Pittsburgh's dreadful finances. Only 381 people had passed through its turnstiles for its game with Cincinnati in Pittsburgh on April 28, suggesting the club, as home team, netted about $114 as its 60 percent share of gate receipts. The next day, in Chicago, it played before 2,365 fans; as the visiting team, its 40 percent share of the gate would have been about $473. The gain evidently was enough to persuade Pittsburgh to expand the practice.[8] By year's end, the woeful Alleghenys would play 29 of its 68 "home" games on the road.[9]

Lacking the deep pockets of other National League investors—notably Spalding, the sporting goods millionaire—Pittsburgh's Nimick, owner of a modest publishing company, could not survive for long on such meager revenue, as soon became apparent. After his club finished its series in Chicago, it traveled to Cleveland for four games. When the team arrived, Nimick was greeted by news that the owner of his home ballpark had filed a court claim for $3,000 in unpaid rent. If that sum was not paid in full by Saturday, the sheriff would seize and sell the club's assets, including its grandstands, at public auction.[10] Nimick said he had merely forgotten to make the payment, an excuse that even his vice president, J. Palmer O'Neil, scoffed at.[11] Adding to the concern, Paul Hines, a Pittsburgh outfielder and first baseman, said Allegheny players had not been paid for the second half of April; the club vigorously denied the assertion and Nimick fired him the next day.[12]

On hearing about the court claim, Spalding took a train to New York to meet Nimick and learn firsthand the scale of his financial trouble. Spalding invited some other National League club executives, including presidents John Day of New York and Charlie Byrne of Brooklyn as well as David Hanley, secretary of Cleveland. When sportswriters buttonholed Spalding after the meeting, his determination not to display any weakness to the Players' League led him to deny the meeting had occurred. So did Nimick. Later in the day, however, Byrne mentioned having attended the gathering and Spalding had to change his story. "The recent conference of National League magnates was not a meeting in the regular sense," he coolly equivocated in his authoritative public-speaking voice, "but four representatives of league clubs got together and talked over the situation." If anyone asked him the difference between a business meeting and a meeting to discuss business, his reply was not recorded.

None of the participants revealed what they had discussed. Outsiders speculated the league was about to move the Pittsburgh club to Indianapolis, a city with fewer than half as many residents as Pittsburgh at the time. A more likely topic was how to coax Pittsburgh stockholders to put up additional capital to keep the team going—a move that would likely topple Nimick, who showed no sign of having any capital to invest. Sure enough, Nimick resigned as president of the Alleghenys the next day, May 9, putting O'Neil in charge.

The promotion was a dubious achievement for the former insurance company executive: Pittsburgh's attendance would remain minuscule all season long, as the club compiled one of the worst records in the history of the sport: 23 wins and 113 losses. Pittsburgh never did host Chicago in September, to make up for the games moved to the Windy City in May; the teams agreed in June to play all three of the contests in Chicago, as originally scheduled.

On his way back from New York, Spalding took the opportunity to assure baseball fans that the National League's troubles were receding. "The Pittsburgh club will finish the season—at least, so I am assured by its directors and stockholders," he said. Another weak club, Cleveland, would do the same, he added. "As for New York," he offered, unbidden, "it is in as solid financial condition as Chicago."[13]

Newspapers sensed the public's interest in the leagues' competition at the turnstile and quickly added attendance figures to their coverage of games. Just as quickly, Spalding encouraged National League teams to inflate their numbers. At least one team didn't even bother to count its patrons. Instead, it waited to see the number of spectators announced by the Brotherhood club across town and then claimed to have had a larger crowd. In this war, as in others, the first casualty was truth.

At times, the lying was comically flagrant. In his book written two decades after the Brotherhood War, Spalding recalled when a reporter approached him and Jonathan Brown, the Chicago club's secretary, after a particularly lightly attended contest in the Windy City's West Side Grounds.

"What's the attendance?" the writer asked.

"Twenty-four eighteen," Brown replied without hesitation.

Spalding knew that was a lie but waited until the journalist walked away before he asked, "Brown, how do you reconcile your conscience to such a statement?"

"Don't you see?" his lieutenant replied. "There were twenty-four [spectators] on one side and eighteen on the other. If he reports twenty-four *hundred* and eighteen, that's a matter for his conscience, not mine."[14]

Reporters quickly cottoned on to the magnitude of deception, and some said they would count spectators by themselves. "As the average daily attendance, leaving Sunday out, is about 300, the task is not a hard one," one sportswriter tartly noted.[15]

That did not stop Spalding and other National League club executives from hyping their attendance figures while disparaging both the number and quality of Players' League fans. O'Neil, the Pittsburgh team executive, once asserted without offering any proof that almost half of the 8,400 people who attended one Players' League game across town were admitted for free, and as a result consisted of lower-class spectators. "There were servant girls with aprons over their heads! There were women with babies in their arm! There were workmen in blouses!" O'Neil said with obvious distaste. "We did not have as many people at the League grounds as they did at the Brotherhood, but those we did have there, so to speak, were there in dress suits. It is just such a crowd as we want." In exasperation he concluded, "The only object of the Brotherhood people seemed to be to get a crowd at the grounds," as if that was not the point of professional baseball.[16]

Immediately after Opening Day, his Pittsburgh club having played only one game, O'Neil boarded a train to Chicago to meet with Spalding and seek advice on avoiding the tsunami of red ink he saw on the horizon. Harry Palmer, the

Sporting Life correspondent, editor of the new Spalding-backed monthly *Sporting Review*, and former *Chicago Tribune* sportswriter, stopped by Spalding's office in the middle of the conference, ending it. O'Neil made some blandishment about installing opera seating—that is, individual seats rather than bleachers—and otherwise improving his ballpark to better compete with the Players' League. He then raced back to Pittsburgh. Spalding told Palmer, whom he had known for almost two decades, that he had little to say about Opening Day crowds other than that he was satisfied with the attendance at Cincinnati and was not worried that his team would play to empty benches at home or away at any time during the season.[17]

Predicting that the grandstands would never literally be empty was an empty boast. Spalding's fellow executives, notably Col. John I. Rogers, firebrand president of the Phillies, did not need attendance to drop to zero to worry about losing their fortunes. "None of the National League clubs expected to make any money this season," he said, "but we were not prepared, and we are surprised, at the great falling off in the attendance."[18]

Playing baseball before minuscule audiences—even if composed of dandies in the higher socioeconomic strata—sapped National League players' morale. Before the Giants took the field for their third game of the season, president John Day felt the need to give a pep talk in which he told his players not to worry about the number of people in the stands and just focus on playing their best ball. "If you do that," he promised them, "the public will soon appreciate it and empty benches will give way to large attendance."[19] The defending champions took the field and promptly gave up four runs in the first inning, eventually losing 7–3 to Philadelphia, which had finished 20 games behind New York in 1889. On a bittersweet note, fewer than 500 spectators showed up to witness their defeat.

National League owners and sympathetic sportswriters predicted again and again that NL attendance would recover when the novelty of the Players' League faded. In fact, National League attendance steadily declined. On May 9, only 451 people saw a game in New York between the Giants and the Boston Beaneaters; three days later, the turnstiles tallied 687.[20] That was about one-fifth the 3,200 fans the Giants drew on an average day a year earlier.[21] With salaries, travel expenses, and other costs rising as revenue from ticket sales was plummeting, National League owners quickly grasped the scale of the disaster they faced.

Losing courage as fast as they were losing money, they asked Spalding to pursue "a new and more economical policy," whatever that might be.[22]

Rather than remain on the defensive and exchanging lies about attendance, Spalding redoubled the National League's effort to breach the Brotherhood's unity and drive wedges between the players and their financial backers as well as among the players themselves. "The League, having been robbed of nearly all its men, was perfectly willing to engage in any act that would sow discord in the ranks of the Brotherhood," he recalled years later.[23]

On May 6, Spalding gave an uncharacteristically pessimistic prophecy about how the Brotherhood War would kill baseball. "People no longer ask who will win the pennant, but rather who will win the fight [between the National League and Players' League]," he said. "It is not the score or the base-hit column that is first looked for in the newspapers, but the number who attend this or that game. . . . It is clear to me that under the present regime the real interest in baseball will soon die out. I regret to say it, but I am convinced that this is the case."[24] His unvarnished gloom may have been sincere, but it also may have been meant to warn the Players' League financial backers that the payday they anticipated might never come.

Players' League leaders and their allies lined up to heap scorn on Spalding's eulogy for the national pastime.

"Inasmuch as Spalding has made every cent he has in the world out of baseball, and established his reputation by deserting Boston some years ago in precisely the same manner that the players deserted the League, his talk seems a little out of place," a writer for the *Detroit Journal* commented.[25]

"The senseless talk about the public losing interest in baseball is hardly worth denying," said Frank H. Brunell, the Players' League secretary. "There is no danger that the old master's dog-in-the-manger idea of baseball will be swallowed by the public."[26] Brunell, a former *Chicago Tribune* sports editor who would go on to found the *Daily Racing Form*, said Spalding was spreading falsehoods and offered to refute the Chicagoan's claim that the Players' League had inflated the attendance at a recent game in Philadelphia. The official count was 17,000, but Spalding said the real number was nearer 7,000. Brunell said he had in his possession a receipt showing "nearly $4,000" in ticket sales for the game. At 25 cents each, that suggests the turnout was much closer to Brunell's figure than to Spalding's.[27]

A few days later, the *Boston Globe* characterized Spalding's lament about the decline in baseball's popularity as "a precious bit of humbug." Using its own attendance data for the first 58 National League games in 1889 and 1890 (and the 55 Players' League games played over the same period in 1890), the paper said 45 percent *more*—not *fewer*—people had passed through big-league turnstiles in the season thus far. National League owners could be forgiven for thinking otherwise because the number of people who came to *their* games had indeed plunged, by almost half.[28] Average attendance at Boston and Pittsburgh home games had declined by 75 percent; Spalding's club was close behind, losing almost two-thirds of its average daily attendance.[29] The new league was decisively winning over the old league's legions of cranks.

Brotherhood leader John Ward noted the overall figures in his predictably lawyerly retort to Spalding. "There was nothing to justify" the Chicago president's despair, he wrote, because, despite unfavorable weather, people were still coming to watch games. Patronage was just divided among more teams, to the detriment of National League clubs because so many well-known players had left them. "There was no decrease," Ward said. "The League itself was suffering only from its own folly."[30]

On arriving in New York to address the Pittsburgh club's financial crisis, Spalding conferred with representatives of League clubs in Brooklyn, Cleveland, New York, and the Steel City. The *Globe* said the Alleghenys averaged barely more than 400 fans at its home games, although others thought that figure was too generous by half. Even with 400 paying customers, the club would net only about $120 a game, not nearly enough to cover salaries, travel costs, ballpark expenses, and administrative outlays. It later emerged that Pittsburgh was on its way to lose $60,000 that year.[31] One rumor was that the Alleghenys were up for sale. Another was that the League wanted to move the team to Indianapolis or Baltimore.

National League representatives said nothing publicly after concluding their two-day meeting other than to deny having met. One thing is certain: It produced an honest, if overdue, reckoning by Spalding. "One league or the other must go to the wall, as they cannot go on as they are now doing, each cutting the other's throat," he told a bundle of reporters waiting outside the meeting room. "The public is being overdosed with baseball, or rather, with the fight for patronage between the two leagues. The Brotherhood clubs should draw far better than they do, for they contain many of the men who were most popular with the crowds in days gone by. On the part of the National League, I freely confess we are not drawing satisfactory crowds. As the situation stands there is no money in it for anybody. The opposing leagues are waging a war of extermination. It cannot last. One or the other must give way."[32]

The long train ride home gave Spalding time to reflect, and when he stepped off the Pullman car in Chicago he clearly, if unrealistically, declared that the National League was prepared to do whatever was necessary to beat the players. "There will be no compromise," he said. "It matters not to the National League whether it plays to empty [bleachers] or not." He said players and management were locked in a savage dogfight, "and the side with the most bull dog blood in it will win."[33]

Spalding's combative loquaciousness was becoming so out of character that people began to comment on it. "The war has changed Al Spalding greatly," said one. "He has done more talking in the last eight months than he had previously done in eight years." Players had come to consider him "the best single-handed talker in the National League."[34]

At the same time he was waving a rhetorical cudgel at Players' League financiers, Spalding offered an olive branch to the players. "It is not the players we are after in this fight, it is the backers of the clubs," he said. "I'm convinced the players have been misled in this thing, and we are not after them. In fact, we feel very kindly toward them, but we want to make their backers suffer."[35]

This was greeted with no small amount of sarcasm. "A. G. Spalding says the National League holds no animosity towards the Brotherhood players," one columnist wrote. "Why, of course not. The magnates love the players, and all the cast-iron laws of old and the classification rule were simply harmless, little experiments indulged in more as a joke than anything else."[36]

Without singling out Spalding, Ward criticized National League owners for using inflammatory, apocalyptic rhetoric that was a bigger threat to the future of professional baseball than the Players' League ever could be. "I honestly believe that, rather than see the Players' League succeed, the old league would prefer to see the national game dead, and would itself gladly inflict the blows," he said.[37]

Spalding aimed his next barrage directly at the Players' League, claiming it was so short of cash that it could not survive if bad weather curtailed ticket sales on Decoration Day, as Memorial Day was then called. If the sun shone on that day, he added, the Players' League would surely "explode like a firecracker" before it could reach the Fourth of July, which typically drew the largest crowds of the year.[38]

Other National League team executives followed Spalding's lead, serving up the same cocktail of vitriol and wishful thinking. "The Brotherhood will not last the season through," said Charlie Byrne, a real estate man who had founded the Brooklyn club along with George J. Taylor, editor of the *New York Herald*, and—despite Spalding's unvarnished contempt for gamblers—two casino owners, Ferdinand Abell and Byrne's brother-in-law, Joseph Doyle. "I know from a personal talk with two Brotherhood players that there is trouble in their camp," Byrne added. "They said things were not what had been represented to them. Why, the Brotherhood is practically dead now."[39]

As Byrne must have known, the National League was worse off. Its franchises in Cleveland and Philadelphia as well as Pittsburgh had suffered such big financial losses that their owners were rumored to be ready to fold their cards.[40] Even Day, owner of the league champion Giants, confided to his friend William "Buck" Ewing, a former New York catcher who had jumped to the Players' League, that he would be happy to sell his team and wash his hands of baseball.[41] "Both the leading organizations are losing money hand over fist," a baseball executive moaned. "Taken as a whole, I should say the attendance at Brotherhood games has been 20 percent larger than that of the National League, but even this has not paid expenses."[42]

Despite his having acknowledged the unsustainable losses that each league inflicted on the other, Spalding reflexively dismissed such "defeatist" ideas and fell back on manly martial metaphors. "As yet, only the opening guns have been fired," he said. "The slaughter is yet to come—and the League is prepared for slaughter."[43]

It was not, however, prepared for insolvency. In mid-July, when Day beckoned his peers to an urgent meeting in Brooklyn and informed them that he was broke and unable to pay to keep the Giants on the field, the news hit Spalding and the rest like a wild pitch to the solar plexus. Rumors of disastrous losses at teams in all three major leagues had been circulating almost since Opening Day. Ticket sales during the conflict never came close to paying for the train fares, hotel bills, and other costs of playing ball in far-off cities 60 times a year while renting and running a home ballpark, and paying players' salaries. National League owners had discounted talk of trouble in New York because Day had a comfortable income from other business interests. By the time he sought help from his fellow owners, those businesses were teetering and the usually affable Day was on the edge of despair. Until they heard it directly from him, National League owners did not believe that the club, which had earned a profit of $45,000 a year earlier, was on its knees and close to ruin.[44]

Allowing the franchise to fail—or, worse, allowing Day to make good on a threat to sell out to the Players' League—was unthinkable. The collapse of its club in the country's largest city not only would humiliate the league, it also would devalue the remaining franchises, spook the ticket-buying public, panic creditors, and, perhaps most galling to the prideful Spalding, bolster the Brotherhood. It could be the final out for the National League.

Without hesitation, Spalding offered Day $25,000 in cash in exchange for stock in the Giants; Arthur H. Soden, a successful roofing contractor and president of the Boston Beaneaters, did the same. John T. Brush, who owned a department store in Indianapolis, agreed to take Giants stock in lieu of the $25,000 Day owed him for the players he acquired from Brush's Indianapolis Hoosiers before the season opened. Abell, the casino owner, and Reach, then president of the Phillies, each put up $6,250 for one-fourth the amount of stock the other men received.[45]

Day kept some stock in the Giants' holding company, but his fortune was gone, his spirit was broken, and he would die, destitute and almost forgotten, in 1925. "John B. Day, who was once a millionaire, is now a pauper, for all the money he made in former years has been lost this season," a person who was described as a "baseball official in a position to speak authoritatively" said at the time.[46]

The cash injection kept the National League's flagship franchise in business to the end of the season, but there were no bailouts for American Association clubs in distress. The Brooklyn Gladiators—after losing 14 games in a row—disbanded in August in Syracuse; the Association replaced Brooklyn in the schedule with the Baltimore Orioles, which had quit the Association before the season began.[47] A month later, the Philadelphia Athletics' owners, Henry Clay Pennypacker, William Whitaker, and Bill Sharsig, released every player, filled the roster with little-known, low-cost substitutes, and limped through to the end of the season.[48] They explained that they had lost $17,000 since April—equivalent to about half a million dollars now—and wished to lose no more.

Spalding had not disclosed his trip to Brooklyn to salvage the Giants, but because he patronized only a few high-end Manhattan hotels and usually visited his retail store near City Hall Park when he was in New York, people recognized him and his visit soon became widely known. When asked what brought him east, he could have said he wanted to see his Colts play the Bridegrooms in Brooklyn. Instead, he told inquisitors that he had come to the city on business unrelated to baseball. He denied any desire to buy control of the Giants, saying the club was in fine fettle under Day.

"Some of Mr. Day's friends have persuaded him to increase the capital stock of the New York Club to $100,000 and give them an opportunity to become associated with him in the enterprise," Spalding said, as if a sudden injection of so much capital (equivalent to $3.5 million in 2024) was routine. "This confidence in the ultimate success of the National League in its fight with the Brotherhood and the value of a League franchise in New York is substantially shown by their eagerness to take all the stock they could get."[49] Spalding's off-the-cuff characterization of the Giants'—and the National League's—doleful situation was breathtakingly untruthful.

Chicagoans, who knew him best, were having none of it. "It has been an open secret for two years that he has wanted to obtain control of the New York National League club, and he may now realize his wish if he wants to," the *Chicago Tribune* stated in an unsigned article. The writer went on to acknowledge the National League's tenuous future and said, "Spalding is too shrewd a business man to take hold of a venture unless he feels confident of ultimate success."[50] Spalding had, indeed, often spoken of his desire to own a ballclub in New York, but this was hardly the time to make such an investment. It would be enough to invest $25,000 to make sure the Giants could play out the remainder of the season, attract more spectators in the stands, and limp along financially.

After returning to Chicago, Spalding summoned Day to meet with him in Rockford, where he thought they could confer privately about the Giants' future. Day's unexplained passage through Chicago and Spalding's sudden impulse to visit his hometown did not go unnoticed. When Spalding was back in the Windy City, he strained reporters' credulity by insisting he and Day had not gone to Rockford intending to meet but had serendipitously bumped into each other at the train station, where they had a short, friendly chat.[51]

It is not clear if Spalding was any more forthcoming with National League president Nick Young, nominally the organization's highest authority. When Young was asked if there was any foundation for reports that Spalding had acquired Day's interest in the Giants, he slapped his desk in anger and heatedly replied: "None whatever. New York is just as solid as Boston or Chicago, and I am in a position to know that Mr. Day has no intention of selling out to Mr. Spalding or anybody else."[52]

Displaying media savvy acquired as a ballplayer, team manager, franchise owner, and businessman, Spalding concocted a story to distract the public from the mysterious meeting of moguls in New York, his chance encounter with Day in Rockford, and the news that his brother, Walter, was now signing the New York club's checks. It also would give Players' League financial backers something new to worry about. A cooperative or naïve reporter in Minneapolis, citing "baseball magnates who are in A. G. Spalding's confidence," revealed a heretofore secret plan to merge the National League, American Association, and minor-league Western Association into a "big baseball combination."

This super-league, according to the article, would consist of two divisions of eight teams each. At the end of the year, the division winners would face off in a "world's championship series." The writer, who was not identified in a *Brooklyn Eagle* reprint of his article, opined that Spalding's idea would "make it very uncomfortable for the Brotherhood" and—somehow—increase the number of "first-class players" in the merged operation.[53]

None of that was true, but it did capture the public's attention and give Spalding a window to renew efforts to mortally wound the Players' League by secretly wooing stars back to the National League. He engaged two loyal lieutenants, "Cap" Anson and John Day, to personally approach the rival league's marquee players and discreetly offer them big bonuses to switch circuits.[54] Spalding's wish list included future Hall of Fame members Roger Connor, William "Buck" Ewing, and Mike "King" Kelly as well as a hard-hitting infielder, Danny Richardson, and the former Chicago pitcher Mark Baldwin.[55] Some players were approached more than once or by more than one National League emissary.

Spalding personally solicited his old nemesis Kelly when the Boston Reds traveled west for a series with the Chicago Pirates. He opened the negotiation by putting a check for $10,000 (equivalent to $350,000 in 2024) in front of the Boston slugger. Next to it he laid a three-year contract with Kelly's old team, the Beaneaters. Spalding said he was authorized to let the player fill in whatever salary he wanted.

The usually garrulous catcher was speechless. After running a meaty, calloused hand through his thick, jet-black hair, he asked for some time to think.

Spalding suggested he take a stroll in the warm summer air and return with a decision in 90 minutes.

At the appointed time, Kelly returned and gave his answer: "I've decided not to accept."

"What?" Spalding exclaimed. "You don't want the $10,000?"

"Aw, I want the 10,000 bad enough," Kelly explained, "but I've thought the matter all over, and I can't go back on the boys."[56]

The personal integrity of this player, who had so often been depicted by Spalding as an untrustworthy carouser and wastrel, was in stark contrast to the Chicago president's.

The ostensibly secret recruitment campaign, wholly unsuccessful, was soon public knowledge and fodder for newspaper writers' outrage and mockery. "The astonishing part of the story was that the elephantine Anson should have been selected as the agent for such a peculiarly delicate job," observed one reporter.[57] Another concluded that since "Anson is not a thoughtful man," his "clumsy missionary work" must have been the brainchild of the National League's "ruling clique," led by Spalding, and "shows how desperately driven these warriors must be."[58]

Rather than acknowledge his failure or his critics, Spalding went back on the attack. He released a document that claimed to prove that the Players' League club in Chicago, the Pirates, routinely inflated its attendance figures, and by how much. He collected the figures by hiring men to loiter outside the Pirates' ballpark and use mechanical hand-held counting devices to tally the number of spectators passing through the gates at each game from July 21 through August 2. The Pirates said 39,159 people attended those 12 games; Spalding's detectives said they counted 20,032—and, they asserted, more than one-third of them used complimentary passes or discounted ladies' tickets.[59]

Spalding said he was compelled to commission the count because "the tactics of the Chicago Brotherhood base-ball managers have disgusted me more than ever with the [baseball] business," and he felt it was imperative "to expose and show them up in their proper light to the public."[60] Nick Young said that Spalding also paid for attendance counts at Players' League ballparks in Cleveland and Pittsburgh.[61]

Brotherhood leaders and many newspapers were skeptical of Spalding's private head counts, as everyone involved in them had a motive to undercount Players' League patrons. They also found his self-righteous tone to be comical, considering that the National League had been artlessly inflating its attendance figures almost from Opening Day.

Prompted by a reporter, Spalding conceded that his club and the rest of the National League also padded their attendance reports. "Yes, yes, I don't deny that I did, and I never made any pretense to deny it," he inaccurately shot back with uncharacteristic anger. "The whole thing is a farce anyway. We—the League—readily admit that we're in the soup and losing money hand over fist. They, on the contrary, claim to be making money—and I don't propose to sit by and see them do it. When they say they are making money they tell us an untruth, and they know it."[62]

George Munson, business manager of the Chicago PL team, ignored the allegation his league had padded its attendance and focused on Spalding's intemperate admission that his club also had done so. The National League has used "every possible means . . . to hoodwink the public," Munson said. "Spalding tells the truth in part when he admits that the number of people who attended games at his park have been grossly exaggerated. . . . Publication of his exaggerated attendance day in and day out has become the laughingstock of the city."[63]

Spalding tried to regain control of the narrative by claiming the Players' League had inflated attendance first. "We had to do it," he said. "It wouldn't do for us to say we had 700 people and the Brotherhood come out with 3,000, when they didn't really have more than we did. We had to put our figures somewhere near theirs, or else appear ridiculous."[64] He had not foreseen that the NL could appear just as ridiculous if the extent and magnitude of the attendance artifice became known, as it did.

The question at this point was not whether either side was lying, but which side was lying more effectively—and more discreetly. The National League was losing in both areas. "Public confidence receives a severe shock when a League magnate actually admits that he has been giving the newspapers a false count, thus deceiving both public and newspapers for a very trifling supposed advantage," *Sporting Life* wrote. "Yet that is precisely what Mr. A. G. Spalding has been imprudent enough to do."[65]

The rebel league's secretary, Frank H. Brunell, turned the tables on Spalding by hiring men to count the number of fans at a game in Chicago. Brunell said his men counted 840 spectators; the Chicago club's official count was 3,625, but the visiting team was paid only for 611 ticket-buyers.[66] Tacitly acknowledging that his figures were as open to bias as were Spalding's sums, Brunell publicly called on Spalding to join him in asking the Associated Press to review both leagues' books to see which was telling taller tales.

Spalding did not reply. Instead, he boarded a train for Boston, where he met Day on August 8 to make another attempt to pry "King" Kelly from the Players' League. The catcher replied to their written invitation with a short note saying that he had no time to waste and suggesting that the magnates "confer among themselves in a warmer climate"—that is, go to hell.[67] Ward was not surprised to learn of the poaching excursion. "No doubt Spalding would give up a large sum of money to injure the new league," the Brotherhood leader said, "but he is not as powerful as he thinks himself, even with the money he has made out of the base-ball business."[68]

Moving on to New York, Spalding hosted a luncheon with Day, Byrne, and Reach. "A jollier party of League magnates I never saw together," the sportswriter Henry Chadwick commented. The *Brooklyn Eagle* said, "no one would have supposed from the gayety of the magnates that they were respectively presidents of the four losing clubs of the National League."[69] The fancy feast was likely meant to impress the select few invited reporters as much as the magnate guests, who were not beacons of hope in such tough times.

From his earliest days in both sporting goods and baseball management, Spalding learned the value of courting the popular press; it didn't matter to him if the papers were criticizing his White Stockings or praising them as long as the articles stoked public interest and filled the grandstand and bleachers with paying customers. In the Brotherhood War, the business stakes were higher so his media strategy was more aggressive and ultimately more damning.

Before the season began, he dispatched the Chicago club's secretary, Jim Hart, to go to New York and recruit writers to relocate to Chicago and, as Hart put it, "boom the League for all they are worth." He guaranteed one well-known sportswriter a salary far in excess of what the *Chicago Tribune* paid, with Spalding personally making up the difference. That scheme crashed when the *Tribune*'s managing editor, Robert W. Patterson, got wind of it.[70]

Around the same time, Harry Palmer hurriedly incorporated a company to publish a new newspaper, the *Chicago Sporting Review*, starting on May 1. The monthly sold poorly, according to *Newsdealer*, a trade publication.[71] No matter. Palmer's primary task appeared to be serving as a conduit for Spalding to anonymously disseminate falsehoods about the imminent collapse of the Players' League or to test-run compromise proposals that could not be traced back to him.[72]

In New York, Spalding bought the *New York Sporting Times* and installed another acquaintance, the acid-penned former *Cincinnati Enquirer* sportswriter Oliver Hazard Perry "O. P." Caylor, as editor. After Spalding bought the weekly, he moved it into the building that housed his New York retail outlet until he shut the paper down in 1891, once its usefulness in the Brotherhood War had passed.

After the magnates' lunch concluded, but with the future of his club and his league still appearing to hang in the balance, Spalding boarded SS *Servia*, a fast and luxurious Cunard Line steamer bound for Liverpool. Some people thought he was going to England to try to salvage the four-team National League of Great Britain he had helped to start earlier in the year; the circuit was in danger of breaking up over a disagreement about the number of American players allowed on each club. Others speculated that Spalding was fed up with the Brotherhood War or was running away from a possible financial crash.[73] He said he was taking a working vacation.

The war committee chairman was not even halfway across the Atlantic Ocean when an embarrassing new development rocked the National League club in Pittsburgh: The Meridian National Bank of Indianapolis on August 13 sued Nimick personally to recover a $2,406.39 debt. He had borrowed from the bank earlier in the year when the league taxed each club so it could pay Indianapolis owner John T. Brush to suspend his franchise and make its players available to New York.[74] Not long after the bank filed its suit, which revived gossip that Nimick was in financial peril, A. G. Spalding & Bros.' representative in Pittsburgh, A. G. Pratt, apparently on his own volition, initiated a separate lawsuit, seeking to recoup $700 owed for uniforms and equipment he delivered to the Pittsburgh club before the season began.[75] A Pittsburgh hotel said the club owed it $500 for boarding its players, and a local newspaper said the Alleghenys hadn't paid for its advertising for two years.[76]

While the American Association was nominally a neutral third party in the war between the Brotherhood and the National League, it was not immune to the effects of more major-league competition, especially in Brooklyn, Chicago, and Philadelphia, where one or both of the other leagues also had franchises. Revenue per team had declined—how much was hard to say, as managing partners often did not share financial information even with their investors—but losses were big enough to compel some teams to steal from their players. When the Association's club in Syracuse released a young pitcher named Mike Morrison on August 2, he asked the team's owner and manager, George K. Frazer, for the $124 in salary he was owed since his last payday. Frazer said he had suspended Morrison without pay—and without informing him—after he made five wild pitches, walked two men, and hit a batter with a pitch during a game two weeks earlier. This was the first that Morrison had heard of the unpaid suspension, and he objected. Frazer fined him $50 and then handed the pitcher $13, saying that was all he was due.[77]

With Spalding out of the country for so long, discipline among National League owners slowly waned. Several openly advocated a truce or some kind of compromise with the Players' League—a heresy their war committee chairman would never countenance. A breach came in late September, when Cincinnati's team president Aaron Stern announced that he and his partner, club treasurer Harry Sterne, were negotiating to sell the franchise to the Players' League.[78] The sale was completed four days before Spalding was scheduled to arrive back in New York.

"The strange part of the whole affair is the inactivity of the League magnates," a newspaperman noted early in the month-long negotiations. "So far as known they have made little or no effort to block the deal. At this particular time the Cincinnati club is an important factor in the parent organization. The League may survive its loss, but it will be badly crippled."[79] Indeed, other observers said letting Cincinnati go to the Players' League would likely persuade Brooklyn to follow suit, and the loss of revenue from those popular clubs would convince both Pittsburgh and Cleveland to disband, leaving only four teams in the National League.[80]

NL magnates seemed unwilling or unable to act without their leader, Spalding, to issue orders. "With President Spalding in Europe, the other League magnates maintain a discreet silence," one careful observer of major-league ball noted just about the time Al Johnson asked Stern and Sterne to name their price for the Reds.[81] Before Spalding sailed out of New York harbor, his brother Walter suggested devising a code for sensitive baseball-related transatlantic cables they might need to exchange while A. G. was away. "He said he shouldn't need any code; that he had left money enough in Chicago to run his club through the season; that the only message he wanted to receive was the one word: 'busted'," Walter recalled. "If he got that, he said he should understand that the Players' League had gone to the wall."[82] Evidently A. G. hadn't considered the opposite scenario.

When Spalding returned to the United States on Wednesday, October 8, reporters were waiting for him at Pier 43 in Manhattan as he disembarked from the Inman Lines' elegantly appointed fast steamship *City of New York*. They peppered him with questions about Cincinnati's defection and asked if he would put aside his personal enmity for the "anarchist" leaders of the Brotherhood and negotiate directly with the Players' League to end hostilities.

Unlike the pugnacious team owner of eight weeks earlier, the fully rested Spalding who stepped off the luxury liner was a model of diplomacy. "I am in favor of a conference with anybody on anything," he said. "I know the gentlemen behind the Brotherhood are businessmen, and I should like to have a sensible business talk with any of them. This baseball war has gone far enough. It is not interesting to the public, and a change must be brought about."[83]

He wasted no time in trying to bring about a change. After settling into his room at the Hoffman House hotel on Broadway between 24th and 25th Streets, Spalding met informally with John Day, who already was trying to broker an amalgamation of his New York Giants with the Players' League club with the same name, and Allen W. Thurman, president of the American Association and owner of its franchise in Columbus, Ohio. He said the capitalists financing the Players' League were amenable to discussing a settlement among the major leagues rather than extend the war into 1891. Would the National League be interested in talking?[84]

When the National League owners convened at noon the next day in Parlor F of the Fifth Avenue Hotel, Thurman repeated what he had told Spalding the previous evening. At least one National League owner, Arthur Soden of Boston, forcefully opposed negotiations, preferring to make good on the League's rhetoric about fighting to the death. Other owners wanted peace on as favorable terms as they could get. They voted to talk.

National League president Nick Young asked three other American Association club owners—Chris von der Ahe of St. Louis, and William Barnie and Harry Von der Horst of Baltimore—to come in from the corridor, where they had been left to pace, smoke cigars, and gossip. John Ward popped into the corridor outside the meeting room to check on the status of the talks. Association and Players' League owners greeted him warmly, shaking his hand and patting him on the back.

Newspaper reporters asked him for his views on the peace talks. "I am for peace first, last and all the time, and stand prepared to do all in my power to bring about that result," he said. "It is evident to everybody that war is a losing game. . . . Thousands of dollars have been thrown away and it is about time we cried halt."[85] Ward then walked back early-season declarations by several Brotherhood members that they would forever refuse to take the field with players who had sided with the League. "This talk of refusing to play with Glasscock, Denny, Clarkson, or any of the deserters from our ranks is all bosh," he said. "Of course it is a bitter pill, but for the sake of peace and harmony we will swallow it."[86] He would not be as forgiving once peace actually arrived.

Spalding later told a friend that he felt unprepared for such a meeting so soon after spending six days crossing the Atlantic, but his confidence grew as talks proceeded. "When I entered that first conference and saw all those elegant-looking gentlemen, each clad in evening dress, while I had on the tweed suit I wore while crossing the Atlantic Ocean, I said to myself, 'These gentlemen intend to frighten us,'" he recalled. "But after having talked with them for thirty minutes I made up my mind I would drive a coach-and-four through the Players' League within six weeks."[87]

Inside Parlor F, Thurman, who was already being hailed as the "White-Winged Angel of Peace" for getting all parties to the negotiating table, spoke first. He said it was obvious to him and others that a compromise was needed to avoid catastrophe for all parties, and then offered his recommendation to start a conversation. Thurman called for two leagues of eight clubs each, with all other organizations—Rochester, Syracuse, and Toledo, which had just been admitted to his American Association to keep the AA viable—relegated to a minor league. Each major-league team would enjoy a geographic monopoly except for baseball-mad Boston and Chicago, which could support two teams each. He also recommended dissolving the American Association.[88]

Thurman added that he had already spoken with Players' League owners, and they were amenable to a settlement along the lines he had just laid out. Three men representing the rebel league were at that moment at the St. James Hotel, just two blocks away, waiting for an invitation to negotiate, he said. In the end, National League and American Association leaders chose to reconvene in two weeks' time to give themselves adequate time to discuss Thurman's plan with their peers.

When leaders of the National League, Players' League, and American Association returned to New York on October 22, they quickly ran into a roadblock: The Players' League had doubled the size of its delegation to six, including three

Brotherhood leaders—Ward, Ed Hanlon of Pittsburgh, and Arthur Irwin of Boston—despite Spalding's stipulation that the National League would never negotiate with "terrorists" who ran "an oath-bound secret society" like the Brotherhood. Thurman declined to call the meeting to order. Johnson said his delegation should have six members because the men representing the National League and American Association, which were parties to the National Agreement, would act as one. Thurman called for a vote by the nine men who had been present at the previous meeting. Predictably, the idea failed, six votes to three. Johnson then withdrew from the meeting entirely, and the talks appeared to be dead before they had even begun.[89]

As the magnates filed out of the parlor, Johnson said to Spalding: "When will we see you again?" Spalding replied: "I'll be up in my room tomorrow evening. Come up and talk matters over." The next day, Johnson, accompanied by E. B. Talcott and Wendell Goodwin of the PL's Brooklyn club, crossed 23rd Street to call on Spalding in his room at the Hoffman House, where they could speak privately and informally. The gathering included Charlie Byrne of the National League's Brooklyn franchise and Jim Hart, business manager of Spalding's ballclub. Over the next 90 minutes, the men discussed what might be done to assist both league's failing franchises in Cleveland and why the National League would never negotiate with Brotherhood leaders, even if they owned stock in their teams. Then, to Spalding's astonishment, the Players' League men voluntarily disclosed the magnitude of their teams' losses for the season, made clear they had "lost about all the money they cared to sink into baseball," and were eager to stop their losses as quickly as possible.[90]

Spalding instantly grasped that the opposing side's well-meaning candor gave him a tremendous advantage in negotiations. Just two weeks earlier, he had gone hat in hand to the Players' League offering to merge the leagues as equals, but Frank H. Brunell, secretary-treasurer of the Players' League, curtly rejected the idea.[91] Now the National League leader knew he did not need to settle for merging with the rebels. If he could keep the scale of the National League's financial losses a mystery and convince the Players' League money men that he was willing to continue prosecuting the war, he could defeat the Brotherhood. Its weak point was its financial backers; if he could bluff a few big franchises to run up a white flag, the Players' League would collapse and most likely take the Brotherhood with it.

"I knew that they were on their last legs, and I was equally aware that we had troubles of our own," Spalding later wrote. "We had been playing two games all through—baseball and bluff. At this stage I put up the strongest play at the latter game I had ever presented. I informed the bearers of the truce that 'unconditional surrender' was the only possible solution of the vexed problem. To my surprise, the terms were greedily accepted. I had supposed that they would at least ask for *something*."[92]

The PL backers believed time for negotiation was running out. In the important New York market, Talcott, managing partner of the Players' League Giants, already was in private talks with John Day of the National League Giants about merging their clubs and deciding what to do with their adjoining ballparks. Meanwhile, Spalding boarded a train to Chicago with John Addison, owner of the Players' League club in the Windy City, and he used the 25-hour trip to discuss their baseball investments.[93] Spalding made a back-of-the-envelope estimate of the value of the Chicago Players' League club that—after deducting the cost of a new ballpark—was half what Addison expected. When he protested, Spalding advised him to act soon because the New York clubs were about to merge. Once that happened, he said, the Players' League would be finished.[94]

Not long after returning to Chicago, Addison and other Players' League club leaders received a letter from the secretary of the league's New York franchise saying his team was nearing an agreement to merge with the National League club in that city. The news was particularly alarming because the league president, E. A. McAlpin, was an investor in the New York franchise, and the author of the letter, Frank B. Robinson, also was an investor—and McAlpin's son-in-law. The league's captain appeared to have climbed into a lifeboat and then suggested that others also should consider abandoning ship. The Boston Reds renewed their commitment to continue fighting but Brooklyn disclosed that it, too, was in talks with its National League rival.[95]

Ward put on a brave public face, but his assertion that consolidation rumors were false was unconvincing. "All this talk about consolidation is a myth," he claimed. "It is being given out to deceive the public. There has been no consolidation in general." In a sign of the chaos resulting from secret meetings and poor communications, he amended his remarks: "The New York clubs, however, have undoubtedly come together."[96]

Some leaders of the revolt were openly disdainful of their financial supporters' effort to broker a fair deal with Spalding and his peers. "It doesn't pay to fool with a buzz saw and the capitalists in this city ought to know this," Tim Keefe, the PL Giants pitcher, said. "The National League is very shrewd. The various club presidents sit back in their chairs and certain Players' League backers run all over the country to see them about a compromise. Why, the Players' League had the old organization 'killed' three weeks ago. Now everything has changed."[97]

Rather than wait for their scheduled annual meeting on November 11, the Players' League convened an emergency private meeting in New York on November 1. Addison talked about the "raw deal" Spalding had offered him. The idea of merging their clubs evaporated when Spalding insisted that Addison and his fellow investors in the Chicago Pirates reimburse him the $5,000 he had paid in a bidding war with the PL club for use of the West Side Grounds. He also expected them to pay all the interest on the loans to build a new ballpark. When Addison refused those terms, Spalding offered to buy his team for $15,000; the directors of the Players' League club heatedly rejected that offer, too, saying they had invested $35,000 in the Pirates' ballpark a year earlier.[98] The meeting ended in another stalemate with no announcement about whether the team executives would take action.

Scuttlebutt about additional defections was unending. In addition to New York and Brooklyn, consolidation in Pittsburgh seemed inevitable, with the resulting team playing in the National League, and Spalding appeared certain to wear down Addison in Chicago. Only Boston, Cincinnati, and Philadelphia appeared to be committed to the Players' League. To clear up matters, Charles A. Prince, president of the Boston Reds, called another Players' League meeting in Philadelphia on November 6. If he hoped it would produce some good news or at least clarity, he was disappointed. Neither Ward, the Brotherhood leader, nor Johnson, the streetcar baron who toiled so hard to create the league, bothered to attend. Addison dialed in by phone.

If something was learned or decided, participants did not share it with reporters camped outside the hotel parlor where the magnates met. They did learn that Talcott had sent the conferees a telegram updating them on negotiations in New York: "We could make a satisfactory arrangement here. Hope other clubs can do same. Would like to see something definite done within thirty days."[99]

While Players' League magnates felt a noose tightening around their necks, Spalding, for the first time in a long time, resumed a normal routine. Having turned 40 while abroad, his priorities were changing. He spent more time with his wife Josie and their son Keith, who had turned 13 in October. He caught up on his sporting goods business, focusing on the Philadelphia retail outlet he had recently bought from A. J. Reach and hiring his wife's younger half-brothers, Horace and Elijah Keith, as managers. He also made time to attend the American Horse Show in Chicago, where he saw his black gelding Bert Bashan win a blue ribbon and a $100 prize in the road wagon category.[100]

The annual meeting of the Players' League, on November 11 at the Monongahela House hotel in Pittsburgh, generated no news beyond the widely anticipated resignations of the New York and Pittsburgh clubs.[101] By contrast, the National League's meeting, at the Fifth Avenue Hotel in New York, opened with stunning news: King Kelly strolled into the lobby with Arthur H. Soden and William H. Conant, two of the three largest shareholders in the National League club in Boston, and announced that he had forsaken the Brotherhood and the Players' League and would play for the Beaneaters in 1891.

A circle of friends gathered around him and he showed them a $500 stock certificate for his old Players' League team and said he had another one just like it. "That was hard-earned money," he said wistfully, and then folded the worthless souvenir and tucked it in a jacket pocket. "I refused $15,000 to leave the Brotherhood," he said, referring to one of the inducements a National League suitor had offered, "and I've stood by them faithfully. Now, it looks as if it were every man for himself. Hereafter I'm going to look out for Mikey."[102]

Indeed, others—owners and players alike—did the same. A telegram from McAlpin said Addison was willing to sell the Players' League club in Chicago for $25,000, although Spalding, the natural buyer, declined at that price. Meanwhile, Spalding received telegrams from former White Stockings outfielder Jimmy Ryan and infielder Ed Williamson asking to return to his team. Pittsburgh offered Ward $10,000 a year to play for the consolidated and recapitalized club there. Others in the National League were not as forgiving; NL leaders said they would accept any Brotherhood members at the negotiating table—except Ward.[103] The same day, 350 miles west, in Pittsburgh, the Players' League closed its formal meeting by choosing its negotiating team: Johnson, Prince, and Ward.[104]

Some Players' League financial backers conferred informally on a train to New York. Publicly, they proclaimed they would press ahead with a six-team league (with franchises in Boston, Brooklyn, Chicago, Cincinnati, Philadelphia, and Washington). Privately, they had abandoned the idea and agreed only to send one more letter to Young requesting another round of discussions, although they knew there was nothing left to discuss. On arriving at Jersey City to take a ferry to Manhattan, the Players' League owners received the dispiriting news that Addison, leader of the league's Chicago franchise, had just that day capitulated to Spalding and agreed to sell his club.

Over at the Fifth Avenue Hotel, National League owners enjoyed glasses of wine and expensive cigars while reveling in the Brotherhood's defeat and congratulating themselves for their magnanimity to the Players' League capitalists. They also jokingly celebrated the Pittsburgh Alleghenys' extraordinary year by presenting President O'Neil with a blue silk pennant with 113 white stars—one for each loss in its 136-game season. O'Neil accepted the gift, which was Spalding's idea, and good-naturedly said he would hang it next to the championship pennant of 1891, drawing a hearty laugh from the other magnates.[105]

J. Earl Wagner, a 28-year-old meat wholesaler and a co-owner of the Players' League club in Philadelphia, was enraged by the disrespect Spalding and the other National League owners demonstrated for Players' League leaders. "I know of no better way of illustrating their methods than to say they would take a man into a room, turn off the [lights] and then sandbag him," he said, using a contemporary term for knocking a man unconscious in order to rob him. "They want everything in sight and still talk about magnanimity."[106]

As the year wound down, National League and American Association leaders sought to make peace among recent antagonists and prepare the game for the 1891 season, which was only four months away. They chose Spalding and Thurman for the job, and gave them considerable latitude to get it done. This meant weeding out weak teams in the Association and replacing them with clubs that were stronger both financially and competitively. They recommended dropping Brooklyn, Rochester, Syracuse, and Toledo from the Association and adding Boston, Cincinnati, Milwaukee, and Washington. They also made peace with the Wagner brothers in Philadelphia, backers of the Players' League team in that city who had been so bitterly and publicly critical of the National League. Thurman and Spalding assured them that they would control the revived Athletics franchise in the American Association, which took over the club after it went bust in September.[107]

During his prolonged stay in New York to hurriedly rebuild the two surviving major leagues and respectfully bury the third, Spalding also sought to repair his relationship with players. He asked Tim Murnane, a former player who became a respected sportswriter for the *Boston Globe*, to arrange a meeting with Ward, the Brotherhood leader. The two met on December 13 at the grand new Manhattan Athletic Club on Madison Avenue at 45th Street, where they cordially reminisced over lunch about the world tour, the league war, and how to restore major-league ball to its prior health. It was the first time the two men had spoken since Ward left the world tour early and returned home to try to sink the classification plan and salary cap that owners had adopted in his absence. "You gave us a hard battle," Spalding said.[108]

He still faced a hard battle with Addison over buying the Players' League club. Even after settling on a valuation—$25,000, Addison's original asking price—Spalding insisted that Addison and his partners make good on back pay they owed their players. Having once worn a uniform and been stiffed by a team, he was resolute that ballclubs must always pay their players what they are owed. He also was resolute that he should avoid buying "a flock of law suits" filed by players owed money by Addison.[109] A lawyer for the players said they would accept 90 percent of the roughly $6,000 in back pay and settle for half the face value of their stock in the team. When Addison accepted the terms, Spalding gave him two checks for the $25,000 price of the PL Chicago franchise. One was for $6,435.67, which was exactly what the team owed to its players; writing a separate check for that precise amount was Spalding's way of assuring they would receive what they were owed. The other check, for the remaining $18,564.33, was for Addison to distribute among the team's investors.[110]

The next day, Fred Pfeffer, an outspoken Brotherhood leader and member of the Players' League club in Chicago, visited Spalding in his office above the Madison Street sporting goods store and extended his hand. Spalding shook it vigorously and invited the wayward player to sit down. The two quickly fell into amiable conversation. Pfeffer said the revolt had been a failure and a mistake but had only good intentions. As he prepared to leave, Pfeffer said he wanted to play ball again and would go anywhere to do so, although he hoped to play on Spalding's Chicago team again. Spalding said he would be in touch and sent the player on his way.[111] When Chicago released its roster for the 1891 season, Pfeffer would again be the club's starting second baseman.

The final act of the Brotherhood War took place in New York on January 16, 1891, when the National League and American Association met separately at the Fifth Avenue Hotel to adopt a new National Agreement. Among other things, it required men who had jumped to the Players' League to return to their pre-war teams, thus avoiding a bidding war for talent. The assembled magnates also agreed to shuffle Association and Players' League teams, but only after owners of the National League club in Boston put up stiff resistance to having a cross-town competitor and secured assurances that the second club would not have "Boston" in its name and would not undercut the incumbent team on the price of admission.

Ward, Johnson, Brunell, and other die-hard Players' League members were meeting at the St. James Hotel two blocks north of the more elegant Fifth Avenue Hotel. When they received the news that the Players' League clubs in Philadelphia and Boston had formally moved to the American Association, they voted somberly and unanimously to dissolve their organization. The group then retired to Nick Engel's Home Plate bar on 27th Street to hold a wake for their dreams.

Thanks to Spalding's bluffing, cunning, intransigence, and a bit of luck in coaxing his opponents to unwittingly show their cards at a crucial moment, the Players' League—the circuit with better players and more fans—was dead. The era of monopoly baseball, which exists to this day, was born.

Chapter 14

Private Passions

At the National League's darkest hours during the Brotherhood War, Spalding, the League's field marshal, suddenly announced that he would sail to Europe in the middle of the 1890 season for an unspecified length of time to handle some undisclosed matters. His fellow owners and the press did not publicly pry into why he chose to go to England at such a critical time, but they could be forgiven for wondering: What could be more important to Spalding than a life-and-death struggle over the future of professional baseball?

No one noted publicly that his wife, Josie, had sailed to England in June with their son Keith, then aged 12, and a maid. She was still there six weeks later, when Spalding's longtime lover, Elizabeth Churchill Mayer, booked passage to England on the Cunard Line ship *Etruria* for herself and her son George, also 12. Lizzie, as she was known, was an aspiring singer who had recently separated from her husband of 15 years, George J. E. Mayer, and was going to London and Paris to take voice lessons.[1]

The idea of his wife and his mistress in England at the same time evidently weighed on Spalding when he knew he should have been focused solely on the existential threat the Brotherhood posed to the League. While Britain at the time was home to 37 million people, making it unlikely the two women would cross paths, Spalding appreciated that the American expatriate community enjoyed nothing more than gossiping about one another. He wanted to avoid an unmediated (and potentially unpleasant) meeting between Josie and Lizzy, even if he thought his wife might already have suspected his philandering. He chose to go to England.

It was too late for Spalding to cancel a lunch meeting of magnates that he organized for August 8, 1890. Calling off a gathering of the League's top strategists just days before it was scheduled could suggest that he or his guests—John Day of the New York club, Charles Byrne of Brooklyn, and Al Reach of Philadelphia—had no wily strategies to pitch to one another. So, he booked a stateroom on a steamship, Cunard's SS *Servia*, that was scheduled to leave for Liverpool on the day after the lunch. He told his peers and the public that his working vacation would not interfere with negotiations because the League's position was clear and immutable.[2]

"You can say for me that the League will positively not listen to any propositions of compromise which does not in the start name an unconditional surrender," he said. "A compromise which in the very least would recognize any of the brotherhood revolutionists would do more harm to the game—harm from which it could never recover."[3]

Spalding arrived in England on August 17 for what would turn out to be a three-and-a-half-month stay. It's not known if the two women in Spalding's life ever met up. But some details of the trip are known: Lizzie took classes with William Shakespeare, a teacher at the Royal Academy of Music, and visited Helena Petrovna Blavatsky, a founder of Theosophy, a mystical belief system that encourages the comparative study of religion, philosophy, and science and emphasizes a universal brotherhood of humanity. Lizzie already was close to the leader of the Theosophical Society in America, Katherine Tingley, and gave vocal lessons at the society's elementary schools in New York City.[4]

On September 27, Josie and Keith checked in to the Regent Hotel in Leamington Spa, a resort town in the English Midlands about 95 miles north of London. The hotel's register records the arrival of a party consisting of mother, son, and servant, but makes no mention of Spalding, who presumably remained in London. Lizzie stayed in the capital as well, and subsequent events suggest that she and Spalding enjoyed a tryst.

Spalding and his family were booked to return to New York on the *City of New York*, a swift, luxurious Inman Line steamship departing Liverpool on October 1. A late addition to the passenger list was Elizabeth Churchill Mayer. She had arranged to sail on the White Star Line's equally fast *Teutonic*, but at the 11th hour changed her mind and opted for the Inman ship, which departed one hour after *Teutonic*. The change meant Lizzie spent the crossing to New York—all five days, 21 hours, and 19 minutes of it—on the same ship as her lover and his wife. Both parties had private cabins, and the baseball historian John Thorn speculated that Spalding's son and Lizzie's son played together.[5]

After arriving in New York, Lizzie boarded a train back home to Indiana, where she settled into rented rooms at 50 West Washington Street and resumed teaching at the Fort Wayne Conservatory of Music.[6]

A little more than a month later, she abruptly resigned from the conservatory after realizing she was carrying Spalding's baby. She told her puzzled employer and acquaintances that she wanted to return to Europe for more voice training. Along the way, her younger, unwed sister, Sarah Churchill, joined her and accompanied Lizzie to England, to help her with the newborn and her adolescent son.

Lizzie and Sadie found their way to Brighton, a popular seaside resort south of London, where they rented No. 12 Bloomsbury Place, a terraced house not far from the water, and hired a servant: all expenses presumably paid by Spalding. In a United Kingdom census taken April 5, Lizzie described herself, falsely, as a widow "living on her own means." Two months later, on June 14, 1891, she gave birth to Spalding's second son and entered him in the national registry of births as simply "Male Brown."

* * *

The lovers met as children in Rockford, and some historians have said they talked about marriage before he left to join the Red Stockings. He was 20 years old at that juncture and Lizzie was but 14—both well below the median ages for first marriages at the time.[7]

Spalding met Josie when she came to Rockford from Massachusetts for the wedding of her brother Charles in December 1874. Charles Briggs, the son of a local industrialist, escorted Josie to the ceremony, but Spalding's sociable sister, Mary Lorette, was likely to have found a clever way to introduce her famous sibling to Josie. In any case, the 23-year-old teacher stayed in Rockford for two months.

Lizzie, meanwhile, married George J. E. Mayer, a businessman from Fort Wayne, Indiana in January 1875, but it seems to have been an unhappy union.[8]

Before they met, he'd lost his modest inheritance investing in a professional baseball club, Kekionga of Fort Wayne. He filled the roster with touring players who were stranded in Indiana when their financial backers went bust. Kekionga fared no better, staggering through 19 games—losing 12—before exhausting its treasury and going out of business.[9]

Mayer then opened a jewelry store, but it went bust; Lizzie later stepped up for her feckless husband and sued the sheriff to retrieve some of the inventory seized on behalf of creditors but not claimed. Mayer opened a store in Oshkosh, Wisconsin, only to have it fail in a matter of months. An "automatic coffin" invention of his, strangely, did not prove as profitable as he anticipated.

He then tried his hand at the hospitality business, taking a job at the Mayer House hotel, formerly owned by his father; it burned down. When the Mayer House's latest owner, Charles H. Nix, offered Mayer a position managing the Pishcotaqua Park House hotel on the north shore of Lake Geneva, Wisconsin, Lizzie chose not to accompany her husband.[10]

As one historian put it, Lizzie may have begun to suspect she had chosen the wrong ballplayer when she married Mayer.[11]

Separated from her husband and responsible for her son, George Jr., Lizzie accepted an offer to manage the voice culture program at the Fort Wayne Conservatory of Music. First she decided to spend the summer of 1888 in Chicago. The *Fort Wayne News and Sentinel*, which was run by her uncle, William Page, generously reported that Lizzie would stay in "her" Chicago home—although it was most unlikely she could afford to buy property in Chicago considering her modest means.[12]

More likely, Lizzie and her son were guests of her high school friend Mary Spalding. Conveniently, Mary's house was a short walk from Albert's manse on the south side of the city, creating an opportunity for Lizzie to rekindle a romance with her childhood beau.[13]

* * *

In August 1892, more than a year after giving birth to Spalding's younger son, Lizzie decided the infant was healthy and strong enough to cross the Atlantic, which he did with Lizzie, her older son, and her sister. On arriving in New York, Lizzie took the boy directly to Chicago and, as planned, delivered him to Mary and Will Brown. They changed his name to Spalding Brown and raised him as their own.

With the sensational double axe murders of Lizzie Borden's father and stepmother dominating newspaper front pages in 1892, Lizzie, now aged 35, dropped her girlish nickname and reclaimed her given name, Elizabeth.[14] She also persuaded her son George to stop using the first name he shared with his absent father and start using Durand, the family name of her grandmother. Mother and son settled in New York, where she gave private voice lessons.

In his mid-40s, Spalding was financially comfortable enough to buy a 75-acre estate in the beach community of Seabright, New Jersey. Spalding and his wife began spending their summers at the "cottage," which was actually a large, shingle-style mansion covered with turrets, gables, porches, and porte cochères. Their son would join them whenever his boarding school, the Hill Preparatory School in Pottstown, Pennsylvania, was not in session. After leaving Hill, Keith would spend a year on a cultural tour of Europe—his uncle Walter leased a villa in Florence—and then enroll at Yale.

Business matters slowly consumed more and more of Spalding's time, attention, and energy as he, Walter, and Will consolidated their company's factories in Massachusetts and entered new businesses with which they were unfamiliar.

How much time Spalding and Elizabeth spent together in this period is unknown, but she was as busy as he was. Her responsibilities at the Theosophical Society grew beyond teaching and performing to include administrative work related to an expanding list of Lotus Circles, or elementary schools, and, later, Tingley's goal of founding a Theosophical community at Point Loma in San Diego. In 1897, Elizabeth moved to the community, which had come to be known as Lomaland. She later was named director of the Isis Conservatory of Music at Point Loma.[15]

Josie began spending more time in Europe, often in Keith's company. In the spring of 1899, after enjoying a mild winter in Florence, mother and son were returning home on the American Line's *Paris* when the fast steamship ran aground off the rugged Cornish coast of England at about 1:30 in the morning of May 21.[16]

Despite the hour and a steady rainfall, all 386 passengers and 372 crew members swiftly and safely evacuated the stricken vessel. Many survivors, including Josie, had vivid tales to tell. "I was well forward and felt the shock," she recalled, describing how the ship's impact with the ocean floor woke her in her first-class cabin. "When I aroused my colored maid, she insisted upon staying in bed, exclaiming: 'If we must drown, let us drown in bed.' It was with some difficulty that I persuaded her to go on deck, even when rescue was assured."[17]

* * *

Summer at the shore was particularly pleasant in the month after Josie's maritime misadventure. Memories of the record-high temperatures of the previous summer were forgotten amid the pleasantly warm, sunny days of 1899. On the day after Independence Day, with her husband in the city for important business meetings, Josie treated herself to a long ride on one of the bicycles her husband manufactured, coasting down the wide roads between the Navesink and Shrewsbury Rivers, and leisurely pedaling past the meticulously maintained and landscaped "cottages."

She cut short her idyll when she felt a sharp pain in her abdomen. She immediately turned for home, even though each push on the pedals made the pain worse. Once inside, she vomited violently. With the help of her maid, Josie took to her bed. The nausea and pain were no better the following day, nor the day after that. On Saturday, July 8, two physicians whom Spalding summoned from New York City arrived at the house on Rumson Road to care for Josie. They removed her appendix, but she died that night. She was 48 years old.[18]

Less than a year after burying his first wife, Spalding made Elizabeth Churchill Mayer his second. The ceremony took place at the Theosophy property in Point Loma, on June 23, 1900. His passport application from this period said he had hazel eyes, a small mouth, a florid complexion, and oval face.

The couple broke the news to families and friends with a single telegram to the new Mrs. Spalding's sister, Fanny Moffat, in Rockford. The newlyweds expected her to share the surprise with all interested parties. There is no record of Fanny or anyone else informing George J. E. Mayer who, despite his wife's frequent claim to be a widow, was still very much alive when Spalding and his longtime lover exchanged vows. He died on April 29, 1902, in St. Louis, aged 54.[19]

After returning to the United States from a working honeymoon in Paris, Albert and his new wife petitioned the Orphans Court of Monmouth County, New Jersey, to let them adopt their own son, telling the court that his parents were dead. The court approved the adoption and, for a while, the boy's parents called him Spalding Brown Spalding. They eventually dropped that unwieldy moniker and started to call him Albert Goodwill Spalding Jr. But Walter had already named his son, a violin prodigy who made his solo debut in Paris at age seven, Albert Spalding, so, to avoid confusion, family members referred to the new son as "Goodwill."[20]

The Spaldings also arranged to settle permanently in the Theosophy community at Point Loma. Waiting for them was an elaborate white stucco octagon house designed by Tingley herself. It had an amethyst dome, hand-carved mosaics, hand-painted frescoes, and an external spiral staircase. Spalding paid $10,000 (about $360,000 today) for the house. While he lived in Lomaland for the rest of his life, Spalding always said he was not a practicing Theosophist. He did, however, serve on the Society's board and eventually told the *Chicago Tribune* that he sympathized with the organization's work but wasn't "so ardent a Theosophist as Mrs. Spalding."[21]

The Spalding house in California still stands, on what is now the campus of Point Loma Nazarene University. It has been repurposed as the university's administration building and is named Mieras Hall.

Chapter 15

Bicycle Boom and Bust

Spalding's enthusiasm for running a baseball club was waning by the mid-1880s. His perfunctory decisions to sell the core of Chicago's pennant-winning team—Kelly, Clarkson, Dalrymple, McCormick, and Sunday—left more than a few followers of the game wondering if piling up money had become more important to him than winning championships.

While he certainly never objected to piling up money, at least when it was to benefit the Spalding empire, he quit club management because he had unquestionably succeeded at it. Maintaining a dynasty is not as stimulating as building one. His future as president of the Chicago club must have appeared to be an obstacle course filled with the same old obstacles: truculent players, obdurate owners, and demanding fans.

He said the world tour should have provided him a clean exit from baseball club management if only the Brotherhood's revolt had not drawn him back into the business. With the Brotherhood crisis behind him, Spalding took on his next challenge: bicycles. Public demand for bicycles was helping to define the Gay Nineties, a decade remembered for technical innovations from gaslights to primitive automobiles and cultural icons like Teddy Roosevelt and the Gibson girl.

The selection again demonstrated Spalding's business luck, savvy, and, ultimately, his questionable ethics.

As early as 1880, A. G. Spalding & Bros. had tentatively begun selling "ordinary" bicycles—also called high-wheelers or penny farthings because their front wheel was four or five feet in diameter and their rear wheel was about one-third as big. The machines were lightning fast but difficult for beginners to mount and tended to launch riders over the handlebars during sudden stops. Not surprisingly then, the market for them was limited.

In the middle of that decade, a British company, Starley & Sutton Co., introduced a radically new bicycle design that seated the rider on a steel-tube frame between equally sized wheels. Cyclists powered the machine, called the Rover, via pedals connected by a chain to a sprocket on the rear wheel. It was easy to mount, easy to ride, and abolished the risk that an emergency stop would catapult the rider into the street. People called it the "safety bike." The market for this kind of bicycle seemed unlimited. Safeties were speedy compared with walking, modern in an era embracing mechanization, and cheaper and easier to maintain than a horse.[1]

A month after Rovers appeared in British shops, the Overman Wheel Company of Boston began importing them to the United States. Sales of the marvelous machines were so brisk that Albert H. Overman leased factory space in Chicopee Falls, Massachusetts, to make safeties in America.[2]

Early in 1890, between his world tour and the players war, Spalding visited the Overman factory in a successful effort to strike a deal making A. G. Spalding & Bros. the exclusive western dealer for Overman's Victor brand bicycle, priced at $135 to $140. The two companies also agreed to engage the Lamb Knitting Machine Co., also in Chicopee Falls, to produce a less-expensive bicycle that Spalding could sell to people unable or unwilling to pay for a Victor; this new machine, priced at $90, would have a different brand name, Credenda, to maintain Victor's exclusive image.[3]

Spalding's capital, charm, and clout apparently impressed Overman because before the sporting-goods magnate left Chicopee Falls, Overman Wheel had elected him vice president.[4]

His luck could not have been better; the bicycle craze was building—and only 27 domestic companies manufactured bicycles, parts, or accessories. The historian Norman L. Dunham estimated that America made roughly 40,000 bicycles in 1890.[5] Eight years later, census data says the stable of manufacturers had grown to 312 and that they churned out 30 times as many bicycles—1.2 million.[6]

Barriers to entering the industry were low—Lamb, the knitting machine maker, switched almost overnight to manufacturing bicycles. At the same time, demand had so outpaced supply that prices were high—$140 (roughly $4,800 in 2024, adjusted for inflation) for a "top grade" bicycle—while production and selling costs were relatively low.[7] With profits high and climbing, the industry attracted a flock of new companies.

The only trouble was that many of them were undercapitalized.

Of the 1.2 million bicycles produced annually at the end of the decade, more than half—653,000, according to the *Cycle Age*—were made by just 19 companies. The rest came from hundreds of underfinanced shops popping up across the country.[8] And this led to trouble for the rest of the industry, including Spalding.

"They went into it expecting to make up their machines and sell them and get their money back in two or three months. They found that this could not be done," George Pope of the Pope Manufacturing Company testified before the federal Industrial Commission on Trusts and Industrial Combinations in 1901. The commission was gathering information on the explosive growth of trusts and other business arrangements to "rationalize" markets—that is, restricting competition to raise prices and improve profits. Pope's company, founded by his cousin Albert Augustus Pope, was among the largest, most innovative bicycle makers in the 1880s and '90s.[9]

"They were pressed for money," he said of the newcomers to the bicycle business, "and they or their competitors were compelled to throw their machines on the market and get cash out of them, even if they got no profit." They had to sell to raise cash for making the next year's model. In a market crowded with new manufacturers, quick sales usually meant deeply discounted sales, which drove down prices for other producers.

To try to avoid cutting prices, losing market share, or filling warehouses with unsold merchandise, Spalding first offered to sell Victor and Credenda bicycles on the installment plan: a small deposit ($5 in cash) and 12 monthly installments that worked out to 39 cents a day for a Victor ($147.35 overall) or 26 cents a day for a Credenda ($99.99). He still lost many middle- and low-price buyers to mass market retailers like Sears, Roebuck & Co., which sold its Vicuna model for $15.95, plus shipping. Vicunas might not have been as well made or as finely finished as a Victor, but many buyers didn't care.

"Competition was of the cut-throat order," Pope stated.[10] Not every American bicycle company was in the red, he added, and the industry overall "had been very profitable up to 1895." However, cost cutting across the industry was so severe and persistent that "it was feared that even the strongest could make no profit."[11]

Back in October 1893, when the bicycle fad was taking off, Walter Spalding bought the Lamb Knitting Machine Company, renamed it the Lamb Manufacturing Company, and installed his older brother as president. The Lamb factory continued to make mid-range Credenda bicycles for sale by A. G. Spalding & Bros., but no longer with Overman as a middleman. Owning the factory also allowed Spalding to make a high-grade model, The Spalding, comparable to Overman's Victor machine but costing only $125.

To promote the new cycle amid an economic slump and severe supply-and-demand imbalance, the next year the company hired a team of top professional bicyclists to ride the new Spalding model in races across the country. The initial year was a success for The Spalding Team, ending with their sponsor being elected president of the National Board of Trade of Cycling Manufacturers. The following autumn, however, a rider on another team accused two of Spalding's best riders, Fred J. Titus and L. D. Cabanne, of conspiring to fix races at an event in St. Louis in August.[12]

The men forcefully denied the allegation, for which they were summarily banned for life. Spalding criticized the race authority, the League of American Wheelmen, for imposing such a harsh penalty and not letting the riders testify in their own defense. The affair was a profound embarrassment for Spalding, who took little solace when the L.A.W. reinstated the Spalding riders—and their accuser—at its next national assembly.[13]

Before publicly announcing the sale of the Spalding bicycle, the brothers demanded that Overman take back a thousand Victor bicycles that didn't sell and refund the money they had paid up front for them. Overman refused to take back any wheel at any price, saying the contract that gave the Spaldings the exclusive right to sell Victors in nine western states also required them to buy 60 percent of the Overman factory's output.[14]

Spalding, as was his wont, ignored the contract. To get rid of his unsold Victors, he cut their price to $85—a move certain to infuriate Overman, who insisted on sticking to list prices—and advertised the deep discount in Chicago, Philadelphia, and New York—noting that the bicycles were "the same as those that have been sold at $150.00."[15]

Still furious at Overman for insisting on sticking to the agreed terms, Spalding used his ubiquitous advertising to sell the deeply discounted Overman machines "as is," implying they were defective and his company could not be held accountable for mechanical trouble with the overstock he was trying to unload. "These are new and sold on the reputation and under the guarantee of the manufacturers," read one ad, "but we are in no way responsible for them after they leave our store."[16]

Overman Wheel opened a Chicago office to assume control of sales in the states that were once Spalding's exclusive turf. For good measure, Overman sued A. G. Spalding & Bros. for breach of contract, seeking $100,000 in damages. Spalding's company responded by countersuing Overman for $160,000.[17]

Rather than duke it out with the Spaldings in court, Overman chose to battle them in the marketplace. He expanded his Chicopee Falls factory and in the summer of 1894 began selling Victor brand sporting goods, including baseballs, bats, footballs, tennis racquets, and uniforms. He was determined to undermine the most profitable part of Spalding's empire.[18]

Overman, however, could not dislodge A. G. Spalding & Bros. as the manufacturer of the official ball of the National League, the unofficial supplier of track and field equipment to the Amateur Athletic Association, and the preferred supplier of gear to professional and amateur leagues in many other sports. By the end of 1897, Overman lacked enough cash to make a loan payment and had to have his creditors reorganize its debts. The company split off Victor Sporting Goods as a standalone business and reorganized the bicycle business as an automobile maker in 1901. One fewer competitor and one more victory for Spalding.[19]

* * *

Overman was not the only bicycle magnate up against a wall in 1897. The previous two years had been very profitable for big manufacturers, but they were running out of customers. The bicycle craze that in some ways defined the 1890s was losing steam. Most people who wanted a machine and could afford to buy one already owned a bicycle and were less susceptible to sales pitches about the improvements in each year's new models. Yet the industry couldn't help itself: Factories and workshops continued to make wheels for which there were no buyers.

When cycling magnates elected Spalding to the National Board of Trade of Cycle Manufacturers in 1895, he assured the public that the organization "is in no sense a combination, trust, or monopoly." It was a tacit acknowledgement that cartels are bad for the public. But he said that as the bicycle boom was near its peak.[20]

By 1898, it was becoming clear that a bust was imminent, if not already begun. Even voluminous advertising, usually a reliable tool to recharge sales, had no effect. Advertising historian Frank Presbrey said that by 1898 bicycle firms were 12 of the top 50 advertisers in America. The bicycle industry bought more advertising than the sporting goods, hotels, and tobacco industries.[21]

Despite such a massive effort, end-of-the-year bicycle inventories rose and profits fell year after year. Net earnings in 1897 were $3,708,867—less than half the $7,763,460 of 1896.[22]

The Spalding company's decision in 1898 to sell the entire inventory of its prized Philadelphia store to Gimbels indicated the bicycle slump was causing liquidity problems for Spalding that made it concede defeat in its battle with the revolutionary retailers known as department stores.[23] The brothers also stopped selling to "jobbers," middlemen who bought in bulk from manufacturers and sold at a markup to retailers. Eliminating these intermediaries would give the company more control over retail prices of its goods.[24]

Despite his public statements opposing the era's embrace of monopolies and trusts, Spalding began listening to advisers telling him that rationalizing the bicycle market by eliminating competition might be the only way to avoid an industry crash. In March 1898 Spalding, advised by the white-shoe law firm Alexander & Green, began calling on bicycle factory owners around the country and collecting options to buy their properties in cash and in full in the near future.

He soon had options on more than a hundred factories, according to the *Commercial and Financial Chronicle*, but the project was nonetheless a botch from the very start.[25] The options gathered in March were to expire on April 30, giving Spalding and his advisers at Alexander & Green an impossibly brief period to have property assessors and financial auditors make fair estimates of the market value of more than a hundred businesses. Spalding asked his peers to extend their options to June 1 and all agreed to do so—except for R. L. Coleman, combative owner of the country's biggest bicycle manufacturer, the Western Wheel Works in Chicago. Through his lawyer, Frederick Stimson, Coleman said Spalding already had reneged on a promise to invite only the largest bicycle makers into the trust; now he was reneging on his promise to exercise the options by April 30.

"Mr. Spalding had gathered so many people, including parts makers and others not included in the original proposition, as to make the whole scheme absurd and render it impossible to raise the money to carry out the original cash proposition," Stimson said.[26]

In mid-May, Spalding instructed the cooperating factory owners to be in New York City the following Monday and gather at the Waldorf-Astoria hotel, where Spalding used a suite on the 13th floor as his office. The telegram also told the men to be prepared to transfer their property to the trust, which had been incorporated only days earlier in New Jersey as the American Bicycle Company.

Despite the telegram's promising language, the A.B.C. was not prepared to disburse the millions of dollars in cash factory owners expected. The inchoate trust didn't have that much cash. Investors were skeptical of the trust's ability to control the market well enough to dictate production levels and prices, so they stayed away from its debentures. When the sellers answered Spalding's call and came to New York, all he could say was that he would appreciate their extending the expiration date of their options again, to August 1.[27]

Factory sellers were furious. Trust executives had publicly denied the trust would request another extension up to the moment Spalding issued a letter asking for precisely that. The negotiations and paperwork needed to acquire all the companies that would comprise the trust (all 58, 48, or 44 companies—the count kept changing) was an "enormous amount of work," Spalding explained to the disappointed factory owners. "It is an utter absolute, physical impossibility to audit, appraise, compile, and properly consider the necessary figures in connection with the different plants on which I hold options within the short space of time given in some of the options." he wrote. "Therefore, I would respectfully request that if you still desire to dispose of your bicycle business for cash that you make an extension of time on your option. . . ."[28]

Businessmen whom Spalding had bidden to New York only to be kept waiting two to six days for an audience were unmoved. "Why, I have neglected my business and paid a big hotel bill for a week, and so far I've got no nearer the throne room than the elevator door," one factory owner lamented.[29]

When Spalding finally got around to buying factories, in June, his initial insistence on all-cash deals was all but forgotten; outside investors were too chary about the trust's future to put money into A.B.C. Instead, Spalding offered factory owners a choice of cash or A.B.C. bonds for 30 percent of their property's appraised value; A.B.C. preferred stock for 30 percent; and A.B.C. common stock for 50 percent.[30] The total included a 10 percent bonus to compensate for the fact that this new offer was riskier than cash.[31]

"A great majority of the people approached were so dazzled by the prospect of unloading their plants at the expense of a syndicate of good-natured, unsuspecting capitalists that it seemed to them that all they need do was to follow that good advice, 'Ask and ye shall receive,' with perfect assurance of attaining the desired result," a contributor to the trade magazine the *Cycle Age* observed incredulously as the buying began.[32]

The dealmaking stopped abruptly early in July, when Spalding was summoned to his summer home where his wife of 24 years, Josie, was dying of appendicitis.

* * *

We do not know precisely what Spalding paid for the factories he collected because, as president of the A.B.C., he had arranged to buy every property himself and then sell them to the trust—at a profit, of course—in one transaction. "The amount Mr. Spalding paid for each plant was a private matter between him and the former owners, and was not known to the owners of the other plants," said Pope, who became vice president of the trust when Spalding was overwhelmingly elected president. "I believe, however, that the method and terms of payment were similar in all cases," Pope added.[33]

When A.B.C. incorporated in May 1899 it authorized the issuance of $80 million in debt and equity—enough, founders thought, to buy all the factories they wanted and still have plenty of operating capital to get the trust off the ground. They soon halved that sum on the advice of their underwriters, who found investors were skeptical of the proposal. Spalding, who was referred to as "the promoter" in legal documents, had to reel in as many sellers as he could with $10 million of debenture bonds, $10 million of preferred stock, and $20 million of common stock. He was motivated to be as frugal as possible because, Pope said, "when the promoter had turned over to the sellers of the property so much of the preferred and common stock as was required by his bargains with them, the remainder was left in his hands as profit."[34]

Appraisers and accountants said the 48 target companies Spalding acquired had a fair market value of about $20 million, including physical plant, patents, receivables (cash owed to them), and profit earned between late 1898, when the appraisals were made, and the close of 1899, when ownership was transferred. Using the incomplete information available, historians estimate Spalding's gross profit may have been between $1.6 million and $11.3 million. Dewing however, assumed that after paying lawyers' fees and bankers' commissions, "there remained only a small profit."[35]

* * *

The American Bicycle Company formally commenced operations on September 1, but it was difficult to tell at many of its factories. Spalding and the other magnates who created the trust were so busy with legal and financial matters that they had little time to plan how to integrate its disparate parts into an efficient whole.

Spalding did not share his plan, if he had one, before he resigned as president of the A.B.C. at a special meeting of the trust's board of directors in January 1900, just after the opening of the bicycle industry's annual show at Madison Square Garden. He was 49 years old and said he was eager to retire.[36]

"It was a great relief to Spalding, whose physician had told him that he was on the verge of nervous prostration and that it would be necessary to go away for several months," Theodore F. Merseles, third vice president of the A.B.C., said when asked at the show why his boss had stepped down just four months after launching the trust. "Spalding has been under a terrible strain for nearly a year. First, with the organization of the company; next, the death of his wife; and, finally, the details of starting the business."[37]

A.B.C.'s precarious financial position—a lack of working capital and an irreversible decline in sales—was widely known for months, but investors still expected to receive a semiannual interest payment when they turned up at the offices of Baring, Magoun & Co., the trust's fiscal agents, on September 2, 1902. Instead, they received a statement from R. L. Coleman, Spalding's successor, that began, "Interest on this company's debenture bonds, due this day, will not be paid at this time." It did not say when the interest would be paid or even if it ever would be paid. A temporary receiver would take control of the company and work with its creditors to try to fix its finances.[38]

Remarkably, Spalding walked away from the collapse unscathed. He profited from acquiring the companies that comprised the trust and avoided losing money by including the former Lamb Manufacturing facility in the package of properties he sold to the trust. "Apparently, A. G. Spalding organized the trust, made a considerable profit, and promptly left the firm," sports historians Lawrence K. Fielding and Lori K. Miller wrote in their analysis of the A.B.C. "He had little interest in reviving the bicycle industry. His actions reveal a man intent on personal financial gain."[39]

The trust did emerge from receivership, only to stumble along, losing money, before closing for good in 1903. A. A. Pope bought its assets and tried his luck in the automobile business.[40]

CHAPTER 16

Trust Buster

SPALDING CERTAINLY DESERVED TO STEP BACK FROM HIS CAREER. IT HAD BEEN 33 years since Rockford's victory over the Washington Nationals vaulted him into the world of professional baseball and 24 years since he and Walter founded the modest baseball emporium that had grown into the nation's dominant sporting goods house.

So, he handed off the sporting goods business to Walter, who was more than ready to move into the president's office, and began spending more time at the new Midlothian Golf Club near Chicago. But retire? Spalding was not really the retiring type.

Three months after resigning from the American Bicycle Company and announcing his retirement, Spalding was back in harness, agreeing to serve as the director of athletics for the United States Commission to the Paris Exposition. The event, the first world's fair of the 20th century, incorporated the second modern Olympic Games, and Spalding's job was to watch over the American athletes who would sail to France to compete. The US commissioner-general to the Paris Exposition, Ferdinand W. Peck of Chicago, tapped his old acquaintance Spalding because he thought the magnate had the gravitas and negotiating skill required to resolve a conflict between the Amateur Athletic Union and the Intercollegiate Association over which organization would oversee the American team.[1]

After accepting the job, Spalding made a quick trip to France in the second half of May to represent the United States at an organizing meeting for athletics. Ever resourceful, he took the opportunity to pick up an Olympics program in French, have it translated into English, and ordered 5,000 copies to attract American athletes unfamiliar with the modern Olympic movement. He also instructed US athletes on how European rules differ from American rules.

While not a regular churchgoer himself, Spalding lobbied the French organizers for assurances that US athletes would not be scheduled to compete on Sundays. Whether due to poor translation or a cultural misunderstanding, Americans were scheduled to compete on some Sundays; they chose to sit out instead.[2]

Spalding returned to Paris early in July, this time accompanied by his new wife Elizabeth and James E. Sullivan, who was both secretary of the A.A.U. and president of the Spalding-owned American Sports Publishing Company. Spalding had engaged him to serve as deputy director of athletics, tasked with day-to-day management of the US athletes while Spalding concentrated on an elaborate A. G. Spalding & Bros. display at the world's fair. As an athletic event, the Paris Games were a disappointment, run by French bureaucrats who treated them as a sideshow to the Universal Exposition. There was neither an opening nor closing ceremony, the rituals that define the Olympics as a unique athletic and cultural phenomenon, and competitions were spread out over the five-month-long exposition. Many athletes said they were not aware at the time that they were even competing in the Olympics.[3]

As a promotional opportunity for A. G. Spalding & Bros., the Paris Games were a smashing success. The company won a grand prize for the "finest and most complete line of athletic goods" exhibited at the Exposition.[4]

His work in Paris would have been a fine farewell to public life, but the League was again in crisis and Spalding was reeled back in to save it. This time the primary problem was not a competitive new major league, though one was rapidly gathering momentum. The bigger issue—the existential threat—was internal, a schism among NL owners over whether professional baseball should allow syndicates or reorganize as a trust. Owners opposed to such ideas were counting on Spalding to intervene—this time in opposition to a trust. "Spalding was the League Moses in 1890 when he saved the old League from utter destruction," J. B. Billings, director of the Boston club, said, "and can do more for the game than any other man."[5]

The crisis was precipitated by Andrew Freedman, a real estate tycoon and business partner of the Tammany Hall political boss Richard Croker. A judge in 1893 had appointed Freedman to be the receiver of the deeply indebted Manhattan Athletic Club. His duties included managing Manhattan Field, then the home of the Giants, until he stabilized the athletic club's finances. He was not an enthusiast of the sport but he quickly became an enthusiast of its profit potential.

On January 17, 1895, the team announced that Freedman had acquired 51 percent of the ballclub's stock for $65,000, or a little more than half its face value. Sellers included Spalding, his brother Walter, and Cap Anson, who together held shares with a face value of $26,000. They, like several other big shareholders, had received the stock in exchange for cash they injected into the club to keep it afloat during the Brotherhood War.[6]

At first, the other owners welcomed Freedman. Spalding, whose brother had sat on the Giants' board of directors since the bailout, said that, judging from what he had heard of Freedman, patrons of the game did not need to worry about the future of baseball in the big city.[7]

The honeymoon did not last long. Just weeks after buying control of the marquee franchise in the two-decade-old League, Freedman recommended jettisoning four of the circuit's 12 clubs. "The twelve-club league is an unwieldy affair and there is too much dead timber in it," he said. The new owner didn't specify which teams he would axe and which owners he would ruin financially, but he helpfully observed that "nearly every Eastern club that went to Louisville last season did so at a loss," and asserted that "only Sunday games were profitable for teams visiting Chicago and St. Louis."[8]

Ticket sales on July 4, which traditionally draws the season's biggest crowds, made Freedman eat his words—or at least they would have if he ever acknowledged a mistake. Chicago drew 14,000 spectators to its morning game and 22,391 to a second game in the afternoon. Pittsburgh attracted 15,000 and 18,000. New York, by contrast, attracted 6,000 paying customers at its morning game; the afternoon game was rained out.[9]

The New York magnate soon took to publicly insulting his fellow owners by name. Why, he asked, are John Brush of Cincinnati and Charlie Byrne of Brooklyn allowed to rub shoulders with "the real businessmen" of the League? "Who ever heard of Brush putting up a dollar?" he said of the thrifty former department store owner. Freedman also renewed his attack on western ballclubs, which he blamed for the League denying him a position on any committee. "I feel confident of giving some of those western magnates a lesson they will not relish before long," he said.[10]

Players—even future Hall of Fame members like the fireball pitcher Amos Rusie—were not off limits to the pugnacious Tammany man. He once fined Rusie $100 for breaking curfew in Baltimore, although players' contracts limited fines to $25 for first offenses. When Rusie asked him to reconsider, Freedman put him in to pitch despite a sore arm and fined him another $100 for losing the game, even though the League did not permit fines for bad play. Rusie refused to pay the fines or sign a contract to pitch for the Giants in 1896.[11]

Freedman's thin skin and short fuse also led him to clash with several baseball writers. For example, he had a *New York Journal* reporter, Charley Dryden, ejected from the Giants' training camp three weeks before Opening Day in 1898. He had taken umbrage at the scribe for referring to him as a "spurned magnate," even though Freedman had used those words to describe himself.[12]

The spurned magnate also publicly demeaned the venerable baseball writer Henry Chadwick, a longtime advocate for the sport, the inventor of the box score, and considered "the father of baseball" by many. Freedman initially was upset that Chadwick found fault with New York's third baseman, "Scrappy Bill" Joyce, but he loudly erupted when Chadwick dared to criticize Freedman himself for being discourteous to Cincinnati newspapermen at the Polo Grounds.

In a fine example of his hot-headed and uncouth retort to any questions about his baseball management skills, Freedman sent Chadwick an open letter that accused him of "the most miserable case of ingratitude I know of." Freedman apparently reckoned that since the League—no doubt encouraged by Chadwick's longtime friend, Spalding—paid the writer a $600 annual pension, Chadwick should treat players and owners obsequiously in print. "Your conduct of biting the hand that feeds you is too contemptible for me to give further utterance," the Giants owner wrote. Chadwick invited Freedman to withhold New York's share of his pension if he found the writer's candor to be off-putting. Other teams offered to make Chadwick whole if Freedman didn't pay, but the irascible executive never replied.[13]

Demonstrating his ability to hold a grudge, Freedman sucker-punched one writer, E. B. Hurst, twice in three years. The first was in 1896 at the Polo Grounds, and the second was in 1899 in a corridor of the Democratic Club in Manhattan.[14]

Spalding was appalled by Freedman's boorish behavior, which threatened to undo Spalding's long effort to make baseball a socially acceptable day out for genteel men and women by ridding it of brawlers, boozers, and bettors. He characterized Freedman as a "monstrous evil" and "the incarnation of selfishness supreme," an unrepentant bully who "would apply to other members of the league, in ordinary conversation, terms so coarse and offensive as to be unprintable." Nearing 50 and plumping up, Spalding postponed his retirement and returned to League politics because, he said, "those opposed to [Freedman] and to his methods pleaded with me to re-enter the field, urging that my presence was needed to force this undesirable magnate from the ranks."[15]

Spalding was not above editing history to make his nemesis look even worse than he was. In his book *America's National Game*, he recalled a Giants game against the visiting Orioles of Baltimore in which a former Giant outfielder, James William "Ducky" Holmes, struck out in the fourth inning of a tied game. As he returned to the dugout, a Giants fan yelled: "Holmes, you're rotten! That's what you left here for?" Holmes shot back that he was happy that he no longer had to put up with Freedman, whom he referred to by using an anti-Semitic slur. Freedman, who was Jewish, leapt out of the stands and raced up to the umpire to demand that Holmes be ejected, but the umpire said he didn't hear what Holmes had said. With no penalty forthcoming, Freedman pulled his team from the field and forfeited the game. He played all games against the Orioles under protest for the rest of the year.[16]

When Spalding quoted a newspaper account of the incident in his book, the slur or any reference to it was nowhere to be found. Without at least referring to the hateful word, Spalding made Freedman seem plain crazy.[17]

That is not to say that Freedman was a pleasant colleague or supportive employer. He was neither. Indeed, the baseball historian Brian Di Salvatore crowned Freedman "the most loathsome team owner in baseball history."[18]

* * *

Walter Spalding joined the Giants' board of directors in 1890, to help the club get back on its feet after a lack of patronage during the Brotherhood War nearly caused the flagship franchise to collapse. He intended to step down when Freedman bought the club in 1895 but stayed on at the new president's request. However, the erratic Freedman soon made clear that he would not take advice from Walter or any other director and they would have no influence in anything to do with the way the club was run or the way players were managed.

The Giants were winning, so the board accepted this and left Freedman to his own devices, figuring that he would at least do something in exchange for the $10,000 salary he paid himself. They later regretted giving him such a wide berth when the team sank to the bottom of the standings and directors had the unpleasant task of defending Freedman in public.

Walter's tolerance snapped after they both boarded the same Sixth Avenue elevated train on an unseasonably warm day in March and began talking about baseball.

"He said he would show them how strong he was," Walter recalled. "He told me that he didn't care whether the New York team lost money or not, that he didn't care what became of it. He said he would get even with those opposed to him by killing the game in New York. I hardly believed he meant what he said, but he continued to talk.

"Mr. Freedman declared he would not only refuse to buy good players with which to strengthen the team," the younger Spalding continued, "but he would substitute cheap men for the good ones now playing with New York if the club failed to make money. I protested against any such 'rule or ruin' policy, but he said that the fight was on and he would see it through." Walter later heard that Freedman said as much to others and concluded that he was in earnest, so he submitted a letter of resignation on March 14.[19]

Walter left the Giants board just as his older brother was dealing with newspaper articles in Chicago and New York that revealed his plan for the bicycle trust. Spalding was aware of the New York problem, but he had to remain focused on the trust if he wanted to collect his fee for arranging the deal. Too much money was at stake. Freedman would have to wait.

Charles Comiskey and Byron Bancroft Johnson did not wait. In the autumn of 1899, they changed the name of their minor-level Western League to the American League. If the new name alone did not signal their ambitions clearly enough to the NL moguls, Comiskey's decision to move his St. Paul Saints to Chicago ought to have done so. While the American would remain a top-level Class A minor league in 1900, its leaders unquestionably were gearing up to challenge the National League's monopoly on major-league ball.

Spalding spent most of 1900 in Europe, in Britain for a track meet and France for the Olympics, and then traveling with Elizabeth on an extended tour of the Continent, stopping in Italy, Greece, and Germany. The couple returned to the United States aboard the Hamburg America liner *Deutschland*. The four-funnel steamship, which was launched at the beginning of the year, was pummeled by a violent storm while crossing the Atlantic, delaying its arrival at Hoboken Piers in New Jersey on November 3, 1900.[20]

A friend who met Spalding in Hoboken said one of the first things Spalding asked about upon his return from Europe was why baseball seemed to have lost so much of its popularity. Spalding said the League needed a strong, scrupulous, and experienced leader to get the League back on track, by which he meant back to the way it was when he was actively involved; Spalding was thinking of Abraham G. Mills, League president from 1882 to 1884 (and then vice president of the Otis Elevator Company), but he could have been talking about himself—if he hadn't just built and moved into a lavishly decorated octagonal house in San Diego.

The American League's surprising strength in the first year of competition with the National League was not sufficiently alarming to pull Spalding back into baseball. While the new circuit sold almost 1.7 million tickets in 1901, National League teams sold more than 1.9 million tickets, almost 5 percent more than a year earlier. The revenue gap was even wider because AL teams sold all tickets for 25 cents while NL members could charge as much as 50 cents. American League teams collected a little less than $424,000 in gate receipts, compared with approximately $613,000 by National League clubs.[21]

What finally convinced Spalding to return was Freedman's reaction to the American League. While the new league did not locate a team in New York in 1901, Freedman said he could never tolerate a second circuit of major-league teams, even though the clubhouse scuttlebutt was that his team posted a profit "in the neighborhood of $60,000" in 1901. So, at the end of November 1901 he and his allies on the NL board—Brush, Robison, and Soden of Boston, along with Barney Dreyfuss of Pittsburgh—met privately at Freedman's country home in Red Bank, New Jersey. The agenda was brief: find a way to protect their baseball investments from the increased competition of the upstart American League and prepare to introduce it at the League's winter meeting a few days later.[22]

The National League's 1901 winter meeting, the most momentous in league history up to that point, began on a cold and rainy Tuesday in a parlor room of the Fifth Avenue Hotel in New York City. The organization was once again preparing to fight for survival against an aspiring usurper. The new American League had already established ballclubs in four of the National League's eight markets, acts that intentionally abrogated the National Agreement and with it the reserve clause. There was nothing to prevent American League clubs from accelerating their raids on National League rosters.

Brush pitched the radical idea he and Freedman hatched, which would reorganize the National League as a trust corporation that would buy and own all National League clubs as well as their grounds, gear, and players' contracts. The trust's president, characterized as the "supreme leader" in one newspaper, would be given a free rein to unilaterally transfer players among teams. The goal was to equalize rosters and make games more exciting. Freedman, naturally, would be the inaugural president and Brush his lieutenant; after they served for an unspecified term, a "board of regents" would choose their successors.[23]

The proposal was not well received. "It would destroy every vestige of the sporting character of the game," one newspaper opined, "make a so-called contest for a pennant a farce, and drag the national sport down to the level of a mere spectacular show, about as different from a real contest as an exhibition of bag-punching is from a real prize fight."[24]

More opprobrium was heaped on the obviously self-serving ownership and profit-sharing of the Freedman and Brush proposal. The new corporation, the National League Baseball Trust, would buy the teams' property using its own common stock. Freedman and his supporters on the board were to receive the four largest allocations of trust stock (and any dividends to come) while his opponents were to receive the four smallest.

It was difficult not to conclude that Freedman was, in best Tammany Hall fashion, trying to enrich himself at the expense of others. The allocations didn't reflect any club's performance at the turnstile or ticket booth. For example, Freedman and Brush proposed allocating 30 percent of the trust's stock to owners of the New York club, even though the Giants accounted for only 24 percent of League-wide gate receipts and 16 percent of tickets sold in the season just ended. (The number of tickets sold and amount of cash collected do not match because some clubs priced all tickets at 50 cents, others at 25 cents, and some priced tickets according to seat location.)[25]

The proposal also called for the trust to issue preferred stock that paid a 7 percent annual dividend to the National League "as a body." Freedman and Brush did not say how many shares the trust would authorize to be issued, how the League would distribute the preferred dividends, or how the players' salaries would be decided. When a vote on the proposal was called, the only "aye" came from Robison of St. Louis, a member of what was shaping up as the Freedman bloc. Representatives of five teams, including Soden and Jim Hart of Chicago, voted against a trust. Freedman and Brush abstained.[26]

Before the owners moved on to the next order of business, the election of officers, Spalding asked to address the magnates privately. That privilege was reserved for owners, and Spalding no longer had an ownership stake in any club. However, when he sold his shares in the Chicago club a decade earlier, the League made him an honorary member for life, in recognition of his contributions to the professional game.

Spalding told the assembled magnates that he was surprised to hear so much doom-mongering about the League. As someone who was in the room when the League was born and had spent much of his adult life monitoring its welfare, he would appreciate being the circuit's president if it truly was going to die. However, he did not think it was in extremis. He said the League was suffering from poor leadership decisions, most recently and most harmfully not fighting to prevent the abrogation of the National Agreement. "I told them that the abrogation of the National Agreement was the most damnable outrage that was ever perpetrated in baseball," Spalding recalled. Without the compact, the minor leagues were vulnerable to roster raids that would strip them of their best players and leave no reason for them to carry water for the NL. The League muffed the minor leagues' support just when it needed allies for the coming confrontation with the American League.

It was a stirring speech, one that appeared to be intended to vault Spalding into the League president's office. When he finished, a motion was made for the election of officers. After another long discussion the question was called and a vote was taken. It failed on a tie vote, indicating that Spalding's candidacy was not as strong as it appeared.[27]

Brush saw an opportunity to resurrect his trust idea. The Freedman bloc consisted of four clubs, and by voting together they could stop any motion put to the board, including the election of officers. Brush thought that would allow him to hold Spalding's presidential ambitions hostage until the board adopted his trust scheme.

A second attempt to elect National League officers for the next year was scheduled for the afternoon of Friday the 13th. Spalding and the longtime incumbent, Nicholas E. Young, were on the ballot and seeking not only to become president but secretary and treasurer as well. Each man received four votes, with Freedman and his allies voting en bloc for Young.

A second ballot was called for, this time with a third candidate, former president Abraham Mills, to try to break the deadlock. Again, the vote was tied four to four. A third ballot produced the third tie; another ballot had the same result. And so it went through the 25th ballot well past midnight. Neither candidate could win, but neither would quit.[28]

Shortly before one o'clock in the morning, the Freedman faction called it a night, left the parlor and returned to their rooms in nearby hotels to sleep. Arthur Soden of Boston put Nick Young in the chair; he quickly decided there was no quorum and departed for his hotel. The four remaining club presidents elected one of their own, Col. John I. Rogers of the Philadelphia Phillies, as the new chair, and he called for another ballot. Once again, club presidents from Brooklyn, Chicago, and Pittsburgh joined Rogers in voting for Spalding, but when Rogers called the names of Freedman and his supporters there were no responses.[29] The chair declared Spalding the unanimous choice.[30]

Three club presidents backing Spalding—Hart, Reach, and Rogers—called his hotel room to wake him and inform him of his election. Being elected with four votes after not being elected with four votes in 25 previous ballots "seemed to me a huge joke," Spalding wrote a decade after the event. "If I was President-Secretary-Treasurer—the Pooh-Bah of the League, certainly I was entitled to the records, the treasures, the archives of that body," he wrote. At about four o'clock in the morning, the 51-year-old businessman walked back to the Fifth Avenue Hotel, where Young was staying, and knocked on the door of his suite.

Young's son Robert answered the knock and told Spalding that his father was asleep in the next room; Spalding had the boy fetch his father. When the groggy Young appeared at the door, Spalding declared, in a tone one would use to serve a search warrant: "I have been elected president, secretary, and treasurer of the National League of Professional Baseball Clubs and I have the authority to demand the papers and archives in your possession." The possibly ex-president said he could not surrender the documents until he had confirmed Spalding's news. Spalding knew he had to seize the moment, so he dragooned a burly hotel porter, returned to Young's suite, and had the porter snatch a large trunk in which Young kept the paperwork and whisk it out of the hotel, with Spalding at his heels.[31]

Later that day, Spalding said he accepted the call to serve as the League's president under one condition: "Andrew Freedman must get out of baseball absolutely and entirely. He must be wiped off the baseball map." He called Freedman "a traitor and a marplot" and said "he has done more to ruin baseball than any other four forces that have existed in the history of the game."[32]

The club presidents were scheduled to reconvene that afternoon to make committee assignments, but the men from New York, Boston, Cincinnati, and St. Louis did not turn up. At least one of them, Brush, was reported to be on his way home to Indianapolis. Men from the other four clubs, the ones allied with Spalding, did arrive. Freedman, understandably interested in what his nemesis was up to, sent the New York club's secretary, Frederick R. M. Knowles, to monitor the goings on.

After spotting Knowles loitering at the door, Spalding asked to be called to the chair and identified Knowles as a representative of the New York club and declared a quorum. Spalding and his allies proceeded to unilaterally make committee appointments. Freedman received no appointments. Freedman was not amused, but Spalding later made light of his parliamentary prank. "Mr. Knowles, it is true, was on the scene only to watch the progress of affairs for Mr. Freedman and I may have been wrong in counting him as present," he said with a smile. "Anyway, I wrote Mr. Freedman thanking him for sending a representative in order to expedite business."[33]

Freedman kept to himself during the day Saturday, but at six o'clock that evening he issued a statement in the friendly confines of the Democratic Club. He dismissed Spalding's election as "farcical and illegal," and Spalding himself as "hysterical." He said he would take legal steps to rectify the situation "when the proper time comes and when other clubs feel they care to participate."[34]

He derided Spalding's high-minded speechifying about saving baseball from money-grubbing owners, claiming Spalding himself had made a fortune by making baseballs for 20 cents apiece and selling them to the League for $1.20. Freedman then described Spalding's disrespect of Anson over the years. Anson for years had been devoted to Spalding and the Chicago Club, never faltering in his loyalty, no matter how great the offers of money to betray his trust, Freedman said. "Anson saved a few thousand dollars from his work in baseball and invested it in baseball stock controlled by Spalding," he added, "but never was he given the opportunity to sell this stock, nor was he given any accounting of it. This is the disinterestedness of Mr. Spalding to a player who has been more faithful than any other club manager in the league."

Indeed, Anson owned 13 percent of the Chicago club but never received a dividend on his investment in 10 years.[35] Embarrassingly for Spalding, Anson also owned $5,000 of stock in the New York club, which had, under Freedman, paid Anson dividends of 5 percent, 6 percent, and 10 percent. Spalding claimed the Chicago shares in Anson's possession had been a gift but did not explain why that would negate Anson's right to dividends.[36]

The Chicago club's opaque finances, at least when it came to Anson, were illustrative of the cavalier way Spalding and his brother treated the captain whose teams had won five pennants and finished in second place four times in 13 seasons to that point.

In the first two decades he owned stock in the Chicago Baseball Club, Anson was not invited to a single shareholders meeting. When the organization finally did invite him to an annual meeting, the only attendees were Anson and Hart, his pockets bulging with proxies from the Spaldings, John Walsh, and others. When Anson asked to see the books, Hart said they were not in the office at the time. When Anson asked for the names of club employees, Hart said the club did not keep such a list but surmised that Spalding might have one. At his New York office. If he is there.

In 1889, Spalding persuaded Anson to "invest" $1,500 in the round-the-world tour when the worldly business titan knew or should have known that the excursion was no more than a money-losing promotion for his company's sporting goods.

Anson resented that Spalding chose Jim Hart to handle money and pay bills on the tour, at least as far as San Francisco. Hart was paid his usual salary plus expenses, and as the tour prepared to sail out of San Francisco, Spalding took up a collection to buy Hart a pair of diamond "cuff buttons." It was almost too much for Anson to bear when Spalding asked him to contribute. Cap made plain that he did not wish to chip in and could not understand why Hart warranted such a large bonus.

While steaming home at the end of the tour, Spalding induced Anson to sign a new contract that would last 10 years and promised Anson 10 percent of the team's net profit. Of course, there was no profit in 1890 because of the Brotherhood revolt—and Spalding, who had promised the profit sharing, resigned as president early in 1891, to be succeeded by Jim Hart, Anson's rival.

Spalding sent Anson a long letter in which he assured his captain that Hart was a mere figurehead, that Spalding would really run things, and that as long as Spalding had any connection with the Chicago club Anson was safe.

Considering his long association with the club, the fact that Spalding himself had recruited him to play in Chicago, and his steady delivery of pennants, Anson remembered, "I could see no reason for doubting his word, though subsequent events have shown me differently."

The Chicago Ball Club reorganized as the Chicago League Ball Club in 1893, and Anson was given a new contract "which I signed without reading, and which was only for five years instead of six." He discovered the discrepancy that evening, when he finally read the contract in full. "Having still the most implicit confidence in Mr. Spalding," Anson wrote, "I said nothing about it, relying on his promise to protect my interests."[37]

That confidence shattered when Spalding gave Cap an option to buy the Chicago club, and then persuaded financiers not to help him raise enough money to turn his 130 shares into a majority. Anson finally concluded the option was offered in bad faith, to let him down easily.[38]

Spalding's treatment of Anson over the years—not only disrespecting him but also financially defrauding him—highlights the magnate's willingness to put his personal gain ahead of friendship and loyalty.

* * *

On the Monday after the fractious National League meeting, Freedman's attorneys persuaded a New York State justice, David Leventritt, to issue a preliminary injunction that temporarily voided Spalding's election and enjoined the magnate from acting as president, secretary, treasurer, or any other officer of the National League. Leventritt also scheduled a hearing on December 19 to decide whether to keep the injunction in force until Freedman's lawsuit against Spalding was heard.

Before the court could serve Leventritt's injunction on Spalding, the magnate stood before a mass of ballclub executives, players, and newspapermen in the Fifth Avenue Hotel and theatrically proclaimed: "As President of the National League and the American Association of Professional Base Ball Clubs, I declare Andrew Freedman *out*. I defy him to attend any future meetings of the League while I am president." He urged shareholders in the New York ballclub to "take the final step" and vote Freedman out. He did not elaborate on how they might do that, even if they wanted to, since Freedman still owned most of the club's stock.[39]

When the injunction finally caught up to him that evening, Spalding jubilantly shouted, "It's too late!" He added, with mock rectitude, "but from now on, I bow to the majesty of the law."[40]

Spalding and his lawyer, Alfred W. Kiddle, outfoxed Freedman and his attorney, De Lancey Nicoll, at the hearing about whether to make the temporary injunction permanent. As soon as the hearing was gaveled to order, Kiddle rose and said his client would not object to keeping the injunction in place until Freedman's lawsuit could be heard. Kiddle then requested that the injunction be amended to allow his client to retain possession of the League's papers until the trial. Nicoll, the opposing lawyer, popped up and said he would never consent to that. Kiddle mildly withdrew the idea and said Spalding would return the papers to Young.[41]

What appeared at first to be a setback for Spalding was quickly recognized as a sly win. The court's calendar was so full that it would be next to impossible to schedule a trial before the 1902 season was expected to start, and the injunction gave no one authority to draft a schedule. However, it did not forbid the four National League teams in Spalding's corner from jumping to the American League and leaving the Freedman faction stranded.[42]

This, they hoped, would ratchet up pressure on Freedman to drop his suit.

Spalding, meanwhile, appeared immune to pressure and talked about the League's scrapping, including Freedman's lawsuit, with sangfroid. If his side lost in court, he coolly said, "I will retire, and retire gracefully. I didn't seek the office. I offered to serve without compensation and I really don't see that I can lose anything personally by being defeated on the matter."[43]

While vacationing in South Carolina over the holidays, Spalding sent an "informal" letter to some acquaintances, who just happened to be the owners or presidents of the eight League clubs. In it, he mentions that he bumped into Edward B. Talcott, a former president of the New York club, in Washington, DC, and they naturally got to talking about baseball and Spalding's tangle with Freedman. After nodding to the court order forbidding him to conduct League business, Spalding noted in his letter that Talcott had rekindled his interest in baseball in New York "and if the stockholders of the New York club are disposed to sell their holdings at a reasonable price, I think he and his friends might be induced to join in uplifting our national game." Spalding added that he would not buy shares in the New York club.[44]

Arriving back in New York a week later, Spalding said that five clubs had responded to his letter about Talcott's interest in buying the Giants. Since Spalding's opponents were unlikely to acknowledge his letter much less respond to it, many observers jumped to the conclusion that the five responses meant that five of the eight clubs now backed Spalding. He gave reporters copies of four of the letters, from known allies in Brooklyn, Chicago, Philadelphia, and Pittsburgh, but withheld the fifth missive, to honor Soden's request to keep the letter confidential.[45]

It was a foolish falsehood, and Soden exposed it by calling Freedman to give him the accurate gist of his letter to Spalding: He had taken no side in the feud and pledged to abide by the court's decision on the validity of Spalding's election. A gleeful Freedman rounded up some newspapermen and shared what Soden had said. "No wonder he did not want to make it public," he said of Soden's letter.[46]

When a New York judge at the end of March denied Spalding's motion to throw out Freedman's lawsuit on a technicality, it became clear that postponing League business as Opening Day drew near had backfired. Freedman had demonstrated that he had the will and the resources to wait out less-wealthy owners.[47]

Spalding threw in the towel a few days later. In a resignation letter handed out at the League's spring meeting in New York, he said "conditions" made it "impossible at this time" to enact reforms necessary to achieve his goals as president. The *Sporting News* asserted that he stood down after the Freedman faction threatened to make a competitor the supplier of the official league ball, a decision that could have taken a considerable bite out of the Spalding company's profit.[48]

His letter included what amounted to a pre-emptive rebuttal to such allegations. "I wish to emphatically declare that I am prompted in this action solely by the belief that prolonging a factional political warfare into the playing season would be distasteful to the public, injurious to the National League in particular, and to professional baseball in general," he said.[49]

Five months later, Freedman announced he had turned over control of the New York club to Brush and would elect him president at the club's annual meeting in November. Freedman said his other business interests, notably financing construction of New York's first subway system, the Interborough Rapid Transit Company, made it impossible for him to give the ballclub the time and attention it needed to succeed.[50]

With Freedman gone and National League owners willing to make peace with the American League, Spalding finally left the baseball business.

Chapter 17

Final Innings

After relocating to San Diego, Spalding sold his house in Chicago for $45,000 and his beach cottage in New Jersey for $125,000.[1] Both transactions went smoothly until, after several months, the buyer of the New Jersey estate stopped paying on two mortgages he had taken out on the property.

The process to foreclose and retake possession was complicated by the fact that the buyer was not who he said he was. The name on the deed was that of the brother-in-law of the true buyer, David Lamar, a twice-convicted securities fraudster who was the first con man to be called "the Wolf of Wall Street."[2]

Fresh off fleecing John D. Rockefeller Jr. of a million dollars in a stock scam, Lamar had the resources required for a prolonged court fight that he was counting on to exhaust Spalding's savings or his wits.[3]

The court case dragged on for five years, requiring more than a hundred court dates and an argument before the US Supreme Court.[4] In the drama's final act, the legal battle threatened to escalate into a gun battle between private detectives working for Lamar and Monmouth County sheriff's deputies enforcing a court order requiring Lamar to vacate the premises. Axe-wielding lawmen eventually broke through the mansion's barricaded doors to flush out Lamar's men and secure the property.[5]

Spalding followed the case from 2,500 miles away, in his new seaside home in the Theosophy Society settlement near San Diego. His decision to settle in the Point Loma property, commonly referred to as Lomaland, puzzled Easterners unfamiliar with the area's natural beauty, Mediterranean climate, and lovely beaches. Elizabeth, often labeled an "ardent" Theosophist, was suspected of using undue influence to induce her husband to move to Lomaland and become more involved in the group.[6]

Spalding, who was never particularly spiritual and whose mother once referred to a devout neighbor as a religious fanatic, told inquirers that he was not a Theosophist but was sympathetic to their work, especially in teaching children. "I find here at Point Loma many educated, cultured, refined, and most genial people," he said, "certainly the equal and perhaps superior to any I ever met anywhere."[7]

He spent less time studying Theosophy than he did planning a private nine-hole golf course on his Point Loma property and driving a primitive steam-powered Locomobile he had shipped from Chicago.[8] Retirement was not all fun and games, however. Spalding received shocking news on consecutive days toward the end of 1905.

On December 16, he learned that three Chicago banks owned by J. R. Walsh, a former business partner, had been taken over by regulators after they collapsed under the weight of bad loans to other Walsh-owned businesses, including a quarry, coal mine, and railroad. Walsh, who owned a large stake in the Chicago Baseball Club when Spalding ran the show, was arrested for filing false bank returns, convicted of 54 counts, and sentenced to U.S. Penitentiary Leavenworth in Kansas.[9]

On December 17 came news that Spalding's brother and business partner, Walter, had his skull fractured and lost his right eye in a horrific collision while driving American friends from Paris to Florence, Italy, where he had a summer home. A segment from Lyons to Avignon took longer than the party expected and, in the gloaming, the chauffeur did not see a pair of railroad grade-crossing gates until their vehicle smashed into them. The automobile, a Panhard made in France, came to rest on the tracks just as trains approaching the scene sounded their horns. The chauffeur grabbed the limp form of Walter Spalding and dragged him into a ditch just as the trains—the northbound *Riviera Rapide* and southbound *Mediterranean Express*—collided with the car. Spalding was so gravely injured that initial reports from the nearby town of Mondragon said he had died. Indeed, French doctors did not dare take him to a hospital in Avignon, roughly 30 miles away. They kept him in a farm outbuilding for five days until his condition was stable, and then transferred him to a hospital on a special train.

* * *

Spalding filled some of his retirement good-naturedly feuding with his friend Henry Chadwick, an Englishman and seminal baseball writer who insisted in article after article that baseball was not an American invention but a descendant of rounders, a children's game from England.

Chadwick crossed the rhetorical Rubicon in 1903, when he wrote an article for the *Spalding Guide* he edited. "There is no doubt whatever as to baseball having originated from the two-centuries-old English game of rounders," he stated. The only truly American field sport, he added, was lacrosse, invented by indigenous people long before Europeans stumbled across America.[10]

Spalding recognized a good publicity stunt and picked up the gauntlet. In the 1905 edition of the guide, he published a six-page essay to suggest that Sullivan, president of the Amateur Athletic Union as well as the American Sports Publishing Company, assemble "all possible facts, proofs, interviews, etc." that might shed more light on the origins of baseball and then submit his findings to a committee of distinguished sportsmen to settle the issue. Chadwick agreed and Spalding asked Mills—former National League president and current US senator from Connecticut—to be the chairman. The rest of the committee consisted of two other former League presidents, two ex-players, a retired club executive, and Sullivan.[11]

Spalding considered the origin question to be a lark. In a letter to Chadwick praising the 1905 guide, Spalding referred to the dispute and investigation to be "harmless rounder agitation" that might turn up new information about very early baseball. What it did turn up were two letters from a mining engineer in Denver, Abner Graves, who claimed he was a classmate of Abner Doubleday's at Green's Select School in Cooperstown in 1839 or '40 and saw Doubleday lay out a diamond-shaped playing field for a game called baseball. Graves said he played the game with other schoolboys under Doubleday's direction.[12]

Commissioners accepted Graves's tale despite its chronological inconsistencies and dubious assertions. For example, in the summer of 1839, Doubleday turned 20 and Graves was 5 years old, making it unlikely they would be classmates, much less teammates. Doubleday that summer was a cadet at the US Military Academy at West Point, more than a hundred miles from Cooperstown. There was no mention of Green's Select School in Otsego County before Graves made his claims in two letters, the first to a newspaper in Akron, Ohio, and the second to Spalding. Doubleday was never known to have played baseball and did not mention the game in personal papers left after his death.[13]

Spalding eventually conceded that Doubleday, while a fine US Army officer, had not invented baseball (which, as we have seen, didn't stop Major League

Baseball from affirming the Doubleday myth at the opening of the Hall of Fame). However, he never accepted Chadwick's notion that America's national pastime descended from English rounders. Instead, he concluded that baseball evolved from a bat-and-ball game called one old cat.[14]

* * *

In 1907, Spalding joined other leading San Diego businessmen— department store owner George W. Marston, newspaper publisher E. W. Scripps, and real estate and railroad baron John D. Spreckels—to buy the plot where the Spanish missionary Junípero Serra had founded San Diego in 1769. Marston later built the Serra Museum on the property, and he founded the San Diego Historical Society.[15]

Two years later, Spalding, along with Spreckels and Scripps, was appointed to a new County Highway Commission to use the proceeds of a $75,000 bond sale to grade and pave hundreds of miles of the county's rutted dirt roads, which were inhibiting the adoption of bicycles and automobiles. The roads happened to pass by properties owned by each man, making them considerably more valuable.[16]

His businesslike approach to public works projects attracted San Diego Republicans who were looking for a candidate to enter the party's primary to fill a US Senate seat in 1910. Spalding agreed to run only if he could cap campaign expenses at $7,500, all from his own pocket. A trustee chosen by him would oversee spending; he selected his wife's uncle, William Page, a newspaper editor from Indiana. Spalding pledged to publish a full accounting of campaign expenses. "Thus would the people of California be enabled to determine the cost of a senatorial campaign and be able to decide whether or not the position of United States Senator for California had been purchased," he said.[17]

While he shared many of the values of Republican progressives determined to break the iron grip of corruption that the Southern Pacific Railroad's Political Bureau had on the Legislature, he lacked the support of the Lincoln-Roosevelt Club, which ran the Progressive movement and had chosen its own candidate for the primary, John D. Works, a Los Angeles lawyer and former associate justice of the California Supreme Court.

Spalding was the top vote-getter in most of California's counties, but narrowly lost the statewide count by 1.2 percent of the votes cast, 64,757 to 63,182. In any case, balloting was only advisory; in the state capitol, Work received 92 legislators' votes versus 21 for Spalding. This was the last time that state legislators selected US senators.[18] He evidently did not make public the promised accounting of his campaign spending, perhaps because he was not going to take office.

Denied a seat in the Senate, he took one in the president's office at the San Diego Securities Company, which he founded to develop several miles of ocean frontage on San Diego Bay and more than 1,000 acres of land overlooking the Pacific Ocean at Point Loma. Working with other wealthy San Diegans who owned real estate in the area, Spalding lobbied for federal road-building funds and endorsed the sale of government bonds that raised enough money to build 500 miles of roads in San Diego County.

About this same time, Spalding completed a project that was particularly dear to him: a history of baseball and his role in it to that point. He had long urged Chadwick to write the book, but he was too old and ill to take on the project. When Chadwick died, aged 83, in 1908, Spalding stepped up. *Baseball: America's National Game* attracted widespread attention at the time, according to one contemporary account, but it predated reliable nationwide sales data required to compile best-seller lists.[19]

As he approached his 65th birthday, Spalding chose to give rather than receive a present. Hiring workmen under the direction of a Japanese landscape architect, one of Spalding's last acts was the creation of "Spalding Park" on beachfront property he owned. He spent $1.5 million on the area, which he called Sunset Cliffs, and donated it to the city of San Diego for use by the public. The park stretched over a mile of beach and included a saltwater pool carved into the rock; high tides washed it clean twice a day. Stairs cut into the rock provided access to natural caves carved by the ocean. Overhead, Japanese-style bridges bounded from one outcropping to the next and visitors could rest on benches shaded by palm trees. Unfortunately, the city did not maintain the park, and there is little evidence of it now.[20]

Spalding died at his home on the evening of September 9, 1915, after suffering a stroke. The news triggered a tsunami of testimonials for the man the Baseball Hall of Fame would one day christen the "organizational genius" of professional baseball in its infancy.

"For more than 40 years the name of A. G. Spalding was before the public, and he proved his ability to win success in three fields of endeavor—baseball, commerce, and politics," opined the *Boston Globe*. "It would be difficult to say in which of the three his achievements were most remarkable."[21]

The *St. Louis Post-Dispatch* focused on his zeal for spreading the gospel of baseball all over the globe. "That there should ever be another man who would stand in exactly the same relation to the people of the United States as the late A. G. Spalding is impossible," the paper said in an editorial. "After a connection with the evolution of the national game in this country that made his title, 'Father of Baseball,' an accurate one, he familiarized the people of other countries with its merits."[22]

While Spalding's death sparked a public outpouring of admiration, it also ignited a family feud. On the night he died, Elizabeth broke the news to his relatives back east with a telegram: "Albert died of apoplexy tonight. Please notify all the family. I am broken-hearted. Remains will be cremated day after tomorrow at 2 p.m."

The widow's message enraged Spalding's son Keith, not for what it said but what it didn't say. "We were not asked if we wished to come on," he wrote in an open letter to his stepmother. "We were simply told that the funeral would take place on the day following our receipt of the telegram and we all concluded upon consultation to submit rather than engage in an unseemly dispute at such a solemn hour.

"They know well enough," he added, presumably meaning Elizabeth and Tingley, "that short of three or four days at the least, it would be impossible for any of us to get to San Diego from the East, and, knowing this, they set the time of the funeral and made all their plans to carry the thing through without us."[23]

The family schism widened when Elizabeth, whom Spalding had chosen as the executor of his estate, estimated her late husband's wealth at a suspiciously low $600,000 and announced that he left $100,000 to each of his children—Keith, his son with his first wife; Albert Jr., his son with Elizabeth; and Durand Churchill, her son from her first marriage. She added that Keith had already been given $65,000 while his father was alive and thus would get only $35,000 from the estate; Durand also would receive only $35,000, for the same reason; Albert Jr. had sought only $1,000 in advance and would receive $99,000. The remainder would go to Elizabeth.[24]

Keith did not believe either the size of the estate or his father's desire to deduct from the brothers' inheritances. "Do you suppose my father, in his right mind, would have deducted from my inheritance money spent on my college education and the present of $30,000 which he gave me when I was married?" he asked.

The brothers, led by Keith, contested the will as soon as the magnate's widow filed it in court. They contended it was obtained through some "undue influence" Elizabeth and Katherine Tingley had over their allegedly enfeebled father, and the women intended to use the Spalding fortune to finance the Universal Brotherhood and Theosophical Society.

Doubt about Elizabeth's statement that Spalding's estate amounted to only $600,000 was affirmed in early October as John W. Carrigan, state inheritance attorney, said his quick survey found that it was worth more than $1 million. "It may go as high as $2 million," he added.[25]

While the estate battle dragged on, tragedy struck two of the three heirs contesting the will. In April 1916, Elizabeth secured a court order to commit her son Durand to the Livermore Sanitarium, a private psychiatric hospital east of San Francisco. He was admitted after a Superior Court judge found him to be incompetent following a breakdown over concerns about a company he and Keith Spalding owned; Churchill died in the hospital on September 11, 1935, aged 58. A few weeks later, another will contestant, Albert Jr., was killed in action on the first day of the Battle of the Somme in France. He had enlisted in the British army while working for his father in Europe. He died two weeks shy of his 26th birthday.

Keith and Elizabeth settled the legal battle over Spalding's estate the following summer, almost two years after Albert Sr. had died. A lawyer representing Keith said his client agreed to accept five-twelfths, about 42 percent, of the estate. Elizabeth received the rest.[26] The litigants did not disclose the size of Spalding's fortune, but in October, when California calculated the inheritance tax levy, the state appraiser Thomas O'Hallaran valued Spalding's estate at precisely $1,550,550.62, or approximately $49 million in 2024 purchasing power.[27] Most of that wealth was in A. G. Spalding & Bros. stock.

The company survived Albert Sr.'s passing and benefited from growing interest in golf and tennis throughout the prosperous 1920s. The stock market crash in 1929 and subsequent economic depression severely tested Spalding & Bros. To cope with drastically reduced sales of athletic goods, which had plummeted by about 60 percent nationwide at their lowest ebb, the Spalding company desperately reorganized its finances in 1934. The enterprise stayed solvent but was slow to recover. In 1955, long after the Depression ended, A. G. Spalding &

Bros. reported net sales of $23.2 million, which was still 10 percent *below* 1927 sales of $26.0 million; net profits in 1955 were less than half of those before the Depression. Even the cornerstone of Spalding's business—supplying the official ball used in the National League—had become a millstone around the company's neck. It reported that in 1955 it had sold 20,170 dozens to professional baseball leagues at its list price of $21.60 per dozen or $435,672; in fact, it received only $137,798 for the baseballs, about 57 cents apiece.[28]

So, the company revived a business strategy that had worked well for it in the past: It bought a competitor. Rawlings Manufacturing Co. of St. Louis was, at the time, the fourth-largest sporting goods company in the United States—just big enough to vault second-place Spalding ahead of industry leader Wilson Athletic Goods Manufacturing Co. Unlike in the freewheeling Gilded Age, however, in 1955 there were laws against monopoly behavior and government prosecutors willing to enforce them. The Federal Trade Commission reviewed the deal, and in 1960 ordered Spalding & Bros. to sell Rawlings.[29] A group of private investors bought it in 1963, reportedly paying roughly $10 million. Spalding bought it for $5.8 million eight years earlier.[30]

The loss of scale, relentless price pressure from competitors in low-wage countries, and far edgier advertising by Nike and other entrants to the market rewrote the rules of making and selling sporting goods. Spalding struggled to address these problems while burdened by hundreds of millions of dollars in debt that a Wall Street private-equity firm in 1996 borrowed on behalf of the company so it could take control of the company.[31] The financiers' anticipated boom in golf among Baby Boomers was a bust, and payments on the debts soon grew to twice the company's operating profit.[32] In April 2003, Spalding Sports Worldwide, as the company was called by then, announced it had thrown in the towel on basketball, football, and other sports and sold the Spalding brand name for $65 million to Russell Corp., a manufacturer of sweatshirts and other athletic wear.[33]

Spalding said its decision would help it to focus on its Top-Flite, Ben Hogan, and Strata golf products, which at the time accounted for about 70 percent of its sales. Company executives soon jettisoned the Spalding name and christened the enterprise Top-Flite Company. A month later, still groaning under the debts of previous owners, Top-Flite filed for bankruptcy protection and agreed to be acquired by a competitor, Callaway Golf.[34]

Albert Spalding's empire has fallen, as empires inevitably do. But the disappearance of his name and countenance in public and in the media does nothing to diminish his influence—for good and ill—not only on major-league baseball but also on professional sports in general and, to a lesser degree, commerce and politics. Even contemporaries with whom he disagreed and fought acknowledged his pivotal role in sports and business and the business of sports.

"When the grim reaper took Albert G. Spalding, he removed forever from the domain of sport an [*sic*] heroic figure, and from the National game the greatest man, in some respects, it ever produced—one who wrote his name large and indelibly upon every page of its history," stated the weekly *Sporting News*, a frequent critic. "He was a big man, mentally, morally and physically, and he did big things in such a broad, generous, and efficient way that he produced colossal and permanent results. He possessed all the elements of true greatness—the vision to conceive, the capacity to execute, the courage to defend, the sagacity to guide and preserve, and the resourcefulness to control, great projects. To whatever he turned his mind and hand he brought these qualities of success in full measure, and in whatsoever field he labored he was invariably first."[35]

Acknowledgments

This long-gestating project owes much to many. To start, there is the pantheon of baseball historians—John Betts, Fred Ivor-Campbell, Harold Seymour, John Thorne, and David Voigt—who brought academic rigor to the once-disdained subject and still told compelling stories. Anyone who enters this field stands on their shoulders.

I also owe a debt to previous Spalding biographers, Arthur Bartlett in 1951 and Peter Levine in 1985, and Mark Lamster, who in 2006 zeroed in on the world tour.

Many archivists and librarians offered their remarkably well-informed assistance, starting with the staff of the A. Bartlett Giamatti Research Library in the Hall of Fame, principally Claudette Scrafford, Freddy Berowski, and Rachel Wells. At the other repository of Spalding material, the New York Public Library, I tip my hat to Cara Dellatte.

Others who went out of their way to help: Nancy Adgent at the Rockefeller Archive Center in Sleepy Hollow, New York; Adam Burkhart at San Diego State University; Kimberly Gyorkos of the Byron Public Library in Byron, Illinois; Liam Hegarty and Paul Doherty at the Larchmont Public Library in Larchmont, New York; Mary Hussey, research archivist for the Monmouth County Clerk in Manalapan, New Jersey; Amber Kresol and Jean H. Lythgoe at the Rockford Public Library in Rockford, Illinois; Jacqueline T. Lynch of the Chicopee Historical Society in Chicopee, Massachusetts; Jeffrey L. Monseau at Springfield College in Springfield, Massachusetts; Glenn Porter of the Hagley Museum and Library in Wilmington, Delaware; and Catherine Uecker at the University of Chicago.

I thank Meredith Dias and Joshua Rosenberg at Globe Pequot and was honored to work with its amazingly patient executive editor, Rick Rinehart. Nancy Miller and Miriam Altshuler provided the impetus for this project, my agent Chris Rogers found it an excellent home, my friend Jonathan Putnam gave freely of his sage counsel, and my extraordinarily talented wife Alina Tugend carried me across the finish line. If, despite my best effort, there are any errors, they are all mine.

Notes

Preface: A Place in the Pantheon

1. Nicholas F. Weber, *The Clarks of Cooperstown: Their Singer Sewing Machine Fortune, Their Great and Influential Art Collections, Their Forty-Year Feud* (New York: Alfred A. Knopf, 2007).

2. Victor Salvatore, "The Man Who Didn't Invent Baseball," *American Heritage*, Vol. 34, no. 4 (June/July 1983).

3. "Hall of Fame and Doubleday Field Fittingly Dedicated," *Otsego Farmer*, June 16, 1939, 1; "Baseball Pageant Thrills 10,000 at Game's 100th Birthday Party," *New York Times*, June 13, 1939, 1.

4. "Old Pros Put One Over Collegians," *Boston Herald*, September 25, 1908, 4.

5. Leroy A. Wright, "Mixed Senatorial Question," *Lawyer & Banker and Bench & Bar Review* (Tacoma, WA), Vol. 3, no. 5 (October 1910); Franklin Hichborn, "The California Senatorial Situation," *Lawyer & Banker and Bench & Bar Review* (Tacoma, WA), Vol. 3, no. 6 (December 1910).

6. Press Reference Library, *Notables of the West: Being the Portraits and Biographies of Progressive Men of the West Who Have Helped in the Development and History Making of This Wonderful Country* (New York: International News Service, 1915), 129–30.

Chapter 1: An Unbaked Country Boy

1. *History of Ogle County, Illinois* (Chicago: H. F. Kett & Co., 1878), 590.

2. Henry C. Bradsby, *History of Bradford County, Pennsylvania: With Biographical Selections* (Chicago: S. B. Nelson & Co., 1891), 504–5.

3. Illinois State Archives, Illinois Public Domain Land Tract Sales.

4. R. David Edmunds, "Prairie Potawatomi Removal of 1833," *Indiana Magazine of History*, Vol. 68, no. 3 (September 1972), 240–53.

5. Edmunds, "Prairie Potawatomi Removal."

6. *History of Ogle County*, 589–92.

7. *History of Ogle County*, 589–92; Harriet Spalding, *Reminiscences of Harriet I. Spalding* (East Orange, NJ: privately published, 1910), 12–14.

8. F. W. Beers, *Gazetteer and Biographical Record of Genesee County, N.Y., 1788–1890* (Syracuse, NY: J. W. Vose & Co., 1890), 26; William Seaver, *Historical Sketch of the Village of Batavia* (Batavia, NY: Seaver & Son, 1849), 189.

9. Harriet Spalding, *Reminiscences*, 12–14.

10. Albert Clayton Beckwith, *History of Walworth County, Wisconsin* (Indianapolis: B. F. Bowen & Co., 1913), 528.

11. Ardis L. Sherman, *Reflections, Byron, Illinois, 1835–1976* (Byron, IL: Village of Byron, 1976), 43–44.

12. Harriet Spalding, *Reminiscences*, 48.

13. Harriet Spalding, *Reminiscences*, 70.

14. Harriet Spalding, *Reminiscences*, 67.

15. 1870 Census.

16. *Water-Cure Journal*, September 1856, 69.

17. Harriet Spalding, *Reminiscences*, 57.

18. Harriet Spalding, *Reminiscences*, 70.

19. Albert G. Spalding, *Baseball: America's National Game* (New York: American Sports Publishing Co., 1911), 510.

20. Spalding, *Baseball: America's National Game*, 510.

21. Charles Warren Spalding, *The Spalding Memorial: A Genealogical History of Edward Spalding of Virginia and Massachusetts Bay and His Descendants* (Chicago: American Publishers Assoc., 1897), 928–29.

22. Congressional Medal of Honor Society website (https://www.cmohs.org/recipients/edward-b-spalding).

23. *Rockford Republic*, March 18, 1922, 1 and 10.

24. John L. Molyneaux, "The Amateur Years of the Forest City Baseball Club, 1865–1867," *Nuggets of History*, Rockford Historical Society, Vol. 45, no. 1 (March 2007), 2.

25. Harriet Spalding, *Reminiscences*, 82.

26. Spalding, *Baseball: America's National Game*, 121.

27. Molyneaux, "Amateur Years of the Forest City Baseball Club."

Chapter 2: A Nationwide Sensation

1. Dominic A. Pacyga, *Slaughterhouse: Chicago's Union Stock Yard and the World It Made* (Chicago: University of Chicago Press, 2015), 42–43.

2. *Louisville Courier*, July 29, 1867, 3.

3. *Chicago Tribune*, July 25, 1867, 4.

4. John Thorn, "The Most Important Game in Baseball History?" in *Inventing Baseball: The 100 Greatest Games That Shaped the 19th Century*, ed. by Bill Felber et al. (Phoenix: Society for American Baseball Research, 2013).

5. Louise Carroll Wade, *Chicago's Pride: The Stockyards, Packingtown, and Environs in the Nineteenth Century* (Champaign: University of Illinois, 1987), 10.

6. *Chicago Tribune*, July 25, 1867, 4; Grossman, "Bands, Early and Golden Age" entry, in James R. Grossman, Ann Durkin Keating, and Janice L. Reiff, eds., *The Encyclopedia of Chicago* (Chicago: University of Chicago Press, 2004); William T. Coggeshall, *Lincoln Memorial: The Journeys of Abraham Lincoln* (Columbus: Ohio State Journal, 1865), 271.

7. *Chicago Tribune*, July 23, 1867, 4.

8. There was no official count; newspaper estimates ranged from 2,500 (in Chicago's rival cities of Cincinnati and St. Louis) to 10,000 in the *New York Herald*, July 28, 1867, 8; and *Woodstock* (IL) *Sentinel*, August 1, 1867, 2.

9. *Inter Ocean* (Chicago), July 26, 1867, 5.

10. Seymour Roberts Church, *Base Ball: The History, Statistics and Romance of the American National Game from Its Inception to the Present Time, Volume 1, 1845–1871* (San Francisco: Seymour R. Church, 1902), 26–27.

11. Alfred Henry Spink, *The National Game*, 2nd ed. (Carbondale: Southern Illinois University Press, 2000 [reprint of 1911 edition]), 5–6.

12. Spalding, *Baseball: America's National Game*. 109.

13. *Chicago Tribune*, July 25, 1867, 4.

14. *Inter Ocean* (Chicago), July 25, 1867, 5; *Belvidere* (IL) *Standard*, July 26, 1867, 2.

15. Spalding, *Baseball: America's National Game*. 109.

16. Church, *Base Ball*, 42.

17. *Louisville Courier*, July 29, 1867, 4.

18. Harry Ellard, *Baseball in Cincinnati: A History* (Cincinnati: Johnson & Hardy, 1907), 123.

19. *Woodstock* (IL) *Sentinel*, August 8, 1867, 2.

20. *Belvidere* (IL) *Standard*, July 26, 1867, 2.

21. *Belvidere* (IL) *Standard*, July 30, 1867, 2.

22. Spalding, *Baseball: America's National Game*, 111.

23. Spalding, *Baseball: America's National Game*, 112. Spalding wrote that this incident occurred in the seventh inning, but contemporary accounts said Wright batted in the sixth and eighth innings but not the seventh.

24. Spalding, *Baseball: America's National Game*, 112.

25. *Belvidere* (IL) *Standard*, July 30, 1867, 2.

26. *Belvidere* (IL) *Standard*, July 26, 1867, 2.

27. *Brooklyn Eagle*, April 4, 1896, 11.

28. Peter Morris, "Al Barker," SABR Baseball Biography Project, Society for Baseball Research, http://sabr.org/bioproj/person/0ab52a39 (accessed April 7, 2025).

29. *Louisville Courier,* July 29, 1867, 2.

30. *Belvidere* (IL) *Standard*, July 30, 1867, 2.

31. *Chicago Times*, July 26, 1867, cited by Al Spink in *Lexington Herald-Leader*, March 30, 1922, 5.

32. *Brooklyn Eagle*, April 4, 1896, 11.

33. *National Republican*, July 31, 1867, 3.

34. *Belvidere* (IL) *Standard*, July 9, 1867, 3.

35. *Brooklyn Eagle*, April 4, 1896, 11.

36. *Evening Argus* (Rock Island, IL), July 27, 1867, 2.

37. *Evening Star* (Washington, DC), July 31, 1867, 1.

38. *Alton* (IL) *Telegraph*, August 2, 1867, 5.

39. *Chicago Tribune*, July 28, 1867.

40. *Evening Star* (Washington, DC), July 31,1867, 1.

41. *New York Tribune*, July 28, 1867, 8.

42. *Inter Ocean* (Chicago), July 27, 1867, 4.

43. *Chicago Tribune*, as quoted in Stephen Fox, *Big Leagues: Professional Baseball, Football, and Basketball in National Memory* (Lincoln: University of Nebraska Press, 1994), 195.

44. Henry Chadwick, *The Game of Base Ball: How to Learn It, How to Play It, and How to Teach It* (New York: George Munro & Co., 1868), 104.

45. *National Republican*, August 1, 1867, 3.

46. *Chicago Tribune*, July 29, 1867, as republished in the *Louisville Courier*, July 31, 1867, 1.

47. Frank Jones, "The National Base Ball Club of Washington," *St. Louis Globe-Democrat*, July 31, 1867, 4.

48. William H. Boyd, *Boyd's Directory of Washington and Georgetown* (Washington, DC: Boyd's Directory Co., 1867), 659.

49. Henry Chadwick, "The Washington National—Card from Mr. Chadwick," *St. Louis Globe-Democrat*, July 31, 1867, 4.

50. Chadwick, 105.

51. *Chicago Republican*, July 29, 1867, cited in the *National Republican*, August 1, 1867, 3.

52. Newspapers in other cities—particularly St. Louis and Cincinnati, which were competing with Chicago to be the leading metropolis of the West—piled on. The *Missouri Democrat* mocked the *Tribune*'s boasting editorial about the benefits of prairie winds and pure water, writing that "it could not . . . be reasonably expected that nine men who live on (barely seared, nearly raw) 'blue beef' and breathe the odors of the (offal-polluted) Chicago River, can compete in baseball with an equal number from a healthy country like the District of Columbia." The *Leader* in Cleveland joyfully said, "Chicago is in hysterics" over Excelsior's loss, adding that the team was fairly beaten despite Chicago's "brag and bluster" after the game.

53. *Chicago Daily Tribune*, July 30, 1867.

54. *Chicago Republican*, July 29, 1867, cited in the *National Republican*, August 1, 1867, 3.

55. *Chicago Tribune*, July 31, 1867.

56. *Belvidere* (IL) *Standard*, July 30, 1867, 2; *Daily Kansas Tribune*, July 30, 1867, 2.

57. *Rockford Register*, August 3, 1867, 4.

58. L. B. (Leonard Bisco) Starkweather, "Catch It on the Fly" (Chicago: Lyon & Healy, 1867) in the Lester S. Levy sheet music collection, Johns Hopkins University.

59. *Rockford Register*, August 3, 1867, 4.

60. *Brooklyn Daily Eagle*, April 4, 1896, 11.

CHAPTER 3: AN EDUCATION

1. Harold Kaese, *The Boston Braves, 1871–1953* (New York: G. P. Putnam's Sons, 1954), 7–8.

2. Jules Tygiel, *Past Time: Baseball as History* (New York: Oxford University Press, 2000), 6; "Baseball," *New York Clipper*, December 13, 1856, 4.

3. Spalding, *Baseball: America's National Game*, 119–20.

4. Spalding, *Baseball: America's National Game*, 121–22.

5. Spalding, *Baseball: America's National Game*, 123.

6. Harriet Spalding, *Reminiscences*.

7. "Baseball," *Detroit Free Press*, October 6, 1867, 1; "Baseball," *Chicago Tribune*, November 3, 1867, 1.

8. "Lake Street in Flames," *Chicago Tribune*, January 29, 1868, 4.

9. Spalding, *Baseball: America's National Game*, 512–13.

10. "The Game at Freeport," *Chicago Tribune*, September 28, 1867, 3.

11. John Molyneaux, "No Longer Amateurs: The Forest City Baseball Club in 1868," *Nuggets of History*, Vol. 46, no. 2 (June 2008), Rockford Historical Society.

12. Molyneaux, "No Longer Amateurs."

13. Spalding, *Baseball: America's National Game*, 123.

14. Bessie L. Pierce, *A History of Chicago, Volume II: From Town to City, 1848–1871*, 470; "Sporting. Baseball," *Chicago Tribune*, November 7, 1868, 4.

15. John Molyneaux, "The Eastern Tour: The 1870 Season of the Forest City Baseball Club," *Nuggets of History*, Vol. 47, no. 3 (September 2009), Rockford Historical Society.

16. John Clifford, "Frankly Speaking," *Rockford Register-Republic*, August 16, 1939, 10.

17. "Tour of the Champions," *New York Clipper*, August 22, 1868, 3.

18. "Baseball 30 Years Ago," *Lima* (OH) *News*, July 15, 1899, 5.

19. Preston D. Orem, ed., *Baseball 1845–1881: From the Newspaper Accounts* (Altadena, CA: self-published, 1961).

20. Molyneaux, "No Longer Amateurs."

21. Molyneaux, "No Longer Amateurs."

22. "Athletic vs. Forest City," *New York Clipper*, June 27, 1868, 3; "The Forest City Badly Whipped by the Athletics—Score 94 to 13," *Chicago Evening Post*, June 19, 1868, 4; "Visit of the Athletic Club to Chicago," *Chicago Tribune*, June 19, 1868, 4.

23. "The Tour of the Athletics," *New York Clipper*, June 27, 1868, 91; "Summer Sports," *Chicago Tribune*, June 25, 1868, 4; "Sports and Pastimes," *Brooklyn Union*, June 30, 1868, 1.

24. John Molyneaux, "We Can Beat the Spots Off the Best Club That Ever Lived: The Forest City Baseball Club in 1869," *Nuggets of History*, Rockford Historical Society, Vol. 46, no. 3 (September 2008); Molyneaux, "Eastern Tour."

25. Retro Seasons website, www.retroseasons.com/leagues/nabbp/1868/standings/; "Club Averages: Athletic Club of Philadelphia," *New York Clipper*, December 5, 1868, 5.

26. Aaron B. Champion, "The Original Reds," *Saxby's Magazine*, August 1877; Ellard, *Baseball in Cincinnati*, 85.

27. "Match Between the Excelsiors of Chicago and Forest City of Rockford," *Chicago Tribune*, June 13, 1868, 1.

28. "Sports and Pastimes," *Brooklyn Union*, December 11, 1868, 1; "The National Game," *New York Daily Herald*, December 13, 1868, 5; "The National Convention," *New York Clipper*, December 19, 1868, 5.

29. Orem, *Baseball 1845–1881*.

30. "The National Game," *New York Herald*, August 27, 1869, 5; "Baseball," *Buffalo Evening Post*, August 27, 1869, 2; "Baseball," *Daily Picayune*, August 31, 1869, 2.

31. James C. Nicholson, *The Notorious John Morrissey: How a Bare-Knuckle Brawler Became a Congressman and Founded Saratoga Race Course* (New York: Oxford University Press, 2016).

32. Lee Allen, *The Cincinnati Reds* (Kent, OH: Kent State University Press, 2006), 6; John Thorn, *Baseball in the Garden of Eden* (New York: Simon & Schuster, 2011), 145.

33. "The Rockford Boys at Cincinnati," *Chicago Tribune*, July 25, 1869, 1; "Cincinnati vs. Forest City, of Rockford, Ill.," *New York Clipper*, July 31, 1869, 3.

34. Champion, "Original Reds."

35. Orem, *Baseball 1845–1881*; "Expenses of a Ball Club," *Sporting News*, December 18, 1886, 4.

36. Charles A. Church, *History of Winnebago County* (Chicago: Munsell Publishing, 1916), 870–73.

37. https://www.threadsofourgame.com/login/.

38. Harriet Spalding, *Reminiscences*.

39. "Baseball Items," *Wisconsin State Journal*, May 31, 1870, 1.

40. "The Forest City's Tour," *New York Clipper*, June 18, 1870, 2.

41. "Sporting News," *Brooklyn Daily Times*, May 31, 1870, 3.

42. Clubs did not have exclusive nicknames in this era. Mutual of New York was the most widely known club with that name but there were at least nine others. There were four Forest City clubs: Rockford and Cleveland played against the same competitors—and sometimes each other. Forest Citys in Ithaca, New York, and Savannah, Georgia, were less likely to sow confusion. In any case, city names will be added when needed for clarity.

43. "Sporting News."

44. "The National Game: Mutual vs Forest City—Exciting Game," *New York Daily Herald*, May 31, 1870, 4.

45. "Great Contest Between the White Stockings and Forest Citys, of Rockford," *Chicago Tribune*, June 17, 1870, 4.

46. "Great Contest."

47. James Wood and Frank G. Menke, "Baseball of the Bygone Days," *Montgomery Times*, August 17, 1916, 6.

48. "Close and Exciting Contest Between the Forest Citys and Red Stockings," *Chicago Tribune*, July 12, 1870, 4; "Cincinnati vs. Forest City," *New York Clipper*, July 23, 1870, 5; Christopher Devine, *Harry Wright: The Father of Professional Base Ball* (Jefferson, NC: McFarland & Co., 2003), 74.

49. "Close and Exciting Contest."

50. "Defeat of the Red Stockings by the Rockford Forest Citys—Score 12 to 5—Six Home Runs Made in the Game," *Chicago Tribune*, October 17, 1870, 2.

51. "Defeat of the Red Stockings by the Rockford Forest Citys."

52. Marshall D. Wright, *The National Association of Baseball Players, 1857–1870* (Jefferson, NC: McFarland & Co., 2000).

53. "The Red Stockings: Have They Expired," *New York Clipper*, December 3, 1870, 3.

54. Elwood A. Roff, *Base Ball and Base Ball Players* (Chicago: E. A. Roff, 1912), 21.

CHAPTER 4: CHAMPION

1. David Quentin Voigt, *American Baseball: From the Gentleman's Sport to the Commissioner System, Volume 1* (Norman: University of Oklahoma Press, 1966), 538; *New York Star*, as quoted in Dave Nightingale, "Baseball Same Now as in 1870," *Rockford Morning Star*, June 7, 1959, B1.

2. "The Professionals of 1870," *New York Clipper*, February 11, 1871, 5.

3. Unidentified writer in the *Chicago Times*, quoted in "To Have Another Centennial," *Decatur* (IL) *Daily Review*, April 7, 1970, 10; in Arthur Bartlett, *Baseball and Mr. Spalding* (New York: Farrar, Straus, and Young, 1951), 37; and in Works Project Administration, *Baseball in Old Chicago* (Chicago: A. C. McClurg & Co., 1939), 17.

4. "The Rockford Boys at Cincinnati," *Chicago Tribune*, July 25, 1869, 1; "Cincinnati vs. Forest City, of Rockford, Ill.," *New York Clipper*, July 31, 1869, 3.

5. Kaese, *Boston Braves*, 8; Brian McKenna, "Asa Brainard," SABR Biography Series, https://sabr.org/bioproj/person/asa-brainard/ (accessed March 10, 2024).

6. "What the White Stocking Managers Are Doing," *Chicago Tribune*, December 25, 1870, 4.

7. Spalding, *Baseball: America's National Game*, 153.

8. "National Association of Professional Baseball Players," *New York Times*, March 18, 1871, 8; "National Baseball Association," *Chicago Tribune*, March 18, 1871, 4.

9. Kaese, *Boston Braves*, 8

10. L. L. Doggett, *History of the Boston Young Men's Christian Association* (Boston: YMCA, 1901), 88–89; Isabel C. Barrows, *Physical Training: A Full Report of the Papers and Discussions of the Conference Held in Boston in November 1889* (Boston: George H. Ellis, 1890), 30; Kaese, *Boston Braves*, 8.

11. "Our National Game," *Rockford Register*, April 29, 1871, 8.

12. "From the Rockford B.B.P.'s in Boston," *Rockford Register*, April 29, 1871, 8.

13. "1871–1872 Boston Red Stockings Archive," *Antiques Roadshow*, PBS, https://www.pbs.org/wgbh/roadshow/season/19/new-york-ny/appraisals/1871-1872-boston-red-stockings-archive--201407A12/ (accessed January 13, 2024).

14. "Indiana Items," *Indianapolis News*, May 5, 1871, 1.

15. "'The Red Stockings'," *New York Times*, May 6, 1871, 1.

16. "The Sporting World," *Chicago Tribune*, May 6, 1871, 4; "The National Game," *New York Daily Herald*, May 6, 1871.

17. H. W. to Nick Young, Harry Wright correspondence, Spalding Collection, New York Public Library.

18. H. W. to Nick Young.

19. Spalding et al. to Hiram Waldo, Harry Wright correspondence, Spalding Collection, New York Public Library.

20. Sources vary on the team's actual win/loss record. George Wright, *Record of the Boston Base Ball Club Since Its Organization* (Boston: Rockwell & Churchill, 1874) says 22 "legal" wins and 10 "legal" losses, citing the Championship Committee; Kaese, *Boston Braves,* and George V. Tuohey, *A History of the Boston Base Ball Club, Being a Public Testimonial to the Players of the 1897 Team in Recognition of the Magnificent Work of the Past Season; a Concise and Accurate History of Base Ball from Its Inception; Containing Biographical*

Sketches of Past Managers and Players, and of the Present Year's Boston Team (Boston: M. F. Quinn & Co., 1897), 34, agree with Wright; Troy Soos, *Before the Curse: The Glory Days of New England Baseball, 1858–1918* (Jefferson, NC: McFarland & Co., 2006), and Baseball-Reference.com both say 20 wins, 10 losses, and one tie.

21. "Professionals of 1871," *New York Clipper*, October 21, 1871, 5.

22. "Meeting of the Olympic Club," *Brooklyn Daily Eagle*, April 26, 1871, 2; "The Atlantic Opening Match," *Brooklyn Daily Eagle*, May 1, 1871, 9; "The National Game," *New York Herald*, May 2, 1871, 3; "Games and Pastimes," *Chicago Tribune*, June 16, 1871, 4.

23. "The Professionals in Council," *New York Clipper*, November 4, 1871, 5; "The Special Meeting of the Professional Association," *New York Clipper*, November 11, 1871, 2; "The Championship Question," *New York Clipper*, November 18, 1871, 2.

24. "Baseball," *Philadelphia Inquirer*, December 18, 1871, 2; "The Baseball Championship," *Chicago Evening Post*, December 20, 1871, 2.

25. Bessie L. Pierce, *A History of Chicago*, 3 vols. (New York: Alfred A. Knopf, 1937–1957).

26. "The Boston Baseball Club," *Boston Evening Transcript*, March 16, 1872, 8.

27. "The Northwest," *Chicago Evening Post*, April 17, 1872, 2.

28. "Red Stockings vs. Olympics," *Times Union*, May 2, 1872; "Baseball," *Boston Evening Transcript*, May 2, 1872, 4.

29. David Nemec, *The Great Encyclopedia of 19th Century Major League Baseball* (New York: Dutton, 1997), 16–19.

30. Nemec, *Great Encyclopedia of 19th Century Major League Baseball*, 16–19.

31. National Park Service, Boston Harbor Islands National Recreation Area, "Calf Island," https://www.nps.gov/boha/learn/historyculture/facts-calf.htm (accessed February 24, 2024); "Other Games," *Boston Globe*, July 8, 1872, 5; "Baseball," *Boston Globe*, July 17, 1872, 5; *New York Clipper*, as quoted in *Boston's First Nine: The 1871–75 Boston Red Stockings*, Bob LeMoine and Bill Nowlin, eds. (Phoenix: Society for American Baseball Research, 2016), 244.

32. "The Championship Record," *New York Clipper*, August 3, 1872, 3; "The Championship Question," *Boston Globe*, August 30, 1872, 8; Kaese, *Boston Braves*, 10.

33. "Close of the Championship (Professional) Season of 1872—The Boston Red Stockings Win the Whip Pennant," *Chicago Tribune*, November 6, 1872, 3.

34. "The Baseball Club Meeting," *Boston Globe*, December 5, 1872, 8; "Baseball Matters," *Boston Herald*, December 5, 1872, 1; "The Boston Baseball Club," *New York Clipper*, December 14, 1872, 2.

35. "Relief for the Red Stockings," *Boston Globe*, December 12, 1872, 8; "The Boston Club," *New York Clipper*, December 21, 1872, 5; Kaese, *Boston Braves*, 11.

36. "Mutual vs. Boston," *New York Clipper*, July 26, 1873, 4.

37. Elmus Wicker, *Banking Panics of the Gilded Age* (New York: Cambridge University Press, 2000) 16–31; Kaese, *Boston Braves*, 13.

38. Carroll D. Wright and Oren W. Weaver, "Bulletin of the Department of Labor," No. 18 (September 1898), 668.

39. Harry Wright Collection, quoted in Devine, *Harry Wright*, 74.

40. "About-Home Matters," *Boston Post*, January 19, 1874, 3; "Notes of the Day About Town," *Boston Globe*, January 20, 1874, 8; "Notes of the Day About Town," *Boston Globe*, February 7, 1874, 8; "The Foreign Baseball Tour," *Inter-Ocean* (Chicago), February 26, 1874, 2.

41. "Baseball," *Boston Post*, February 23, 1874, 3; "The American Game in England," *New York Clipper*, April 4, 1874, 3; "The Baseball Tour to England," *New York Clipper*, February 28, 1874, 2; "Baseball—America vs. England," *Forest and Stream*, March 5, 1874, 62.

42. "Baseball: The Coming Season—Preparations for Games in London by the Boston and Athletic Clubs," *Brooklyn Daily Eagle*, February 27, 1874, 2.

43. K. Martin Tebay, *Harry's Mission: An Account of the American Baseball Players Tour of the British Isles, 1874* (Blackpool, England: Red Rose Cricket Books, 2019); "The American National Game in England," *Brooklyn Union*, March 14, 1874, 2.

44. "An April Snow Storm," *Boston Post*, April 27, 1874, 2.

45. "Sporting News. The Great White Stocking Baseball Club Scoops the Boston Reds," *Inter Ocean* (Chicago), July 6, 1874, 9; "The Fourth. The White Stockings Proclaim Their Declaration of Independence," *Chicago Tribune*, July 5, 1874, 7.

46. "Splendid Sendoff," *Philadelphia Inquirer*, July 17, 1874, 2; "The Red Stockings' Trip to England," *Boston Journal*, August 10, 1874, 1.

47. "The Red Stockings' Trip to England."

48. "England," *Tribune* (Scranton, PA), July 29, 1874, 1; "Baseball in England," *Boston Journal*, August 10, 1874; "Murnane's Baseball Stories," *Boston Globe*, February 14, 1915, 36.

49. Spalding, *Baseball: America's National Game*, 179.

50. "Baseball in England," *Boston Herald*, August 1, 1874.

51. "The American Baseball Players," (London) *Standard*, July 29, 1874, 3.

52. *Manchester Weekly Times*, August 8, 1874; *Manchester Courier and Lancashire General Advertiser*, August 3, 1874.

53. *Journal* (Newcastle Upon Tyne, England), August 18, 1874, 4.

54. K. Martin Tebay, *Harry's Mission*, 19.

55. Devine, *Harry Wright*.

56. Quoted in Bartlett, *Baseball and Mr. Spalding*, 68.

57. "Baseball in Ireland," *Boston Herald*, September 7, 1874.

58. Andy Leonard diary for 1874, Heritage Auctions website, https://sports.ha.com/itm/baseball-collectibles/others/1874-andy-leonard-personal-diary-documenting-baseball-goodwill-tour-of-britain/a/7155-80040.s (accessed May 25, 2025).

59. "Sports," *Brooklyn Union*, September 12, 1874, 4.

60. "Our National Game," *Boston Herald*, September 13, 1874; The Inflation Calculator, dollar value from 1874 to 2023, https://westegg.com/inflation/ (accessed April 13, 2024); "Return of the Ball Players," *Brooklyn Daily Eagle*, September 15, 1874, 4.

61. Bartlett, *Baseball and Mr. Spalding*, 70–71.

62. Nemec, *Great Encyclopedia of 19th Century Major League Baseball*, 57–59.

63. Harry Clay Palmer, James Austin Fynes, and Francis C. Richter, *Athletic Sports in America, England and Australia* (New York: Union Publishing House, 1889), 47; Kaese, *Boston Braves*, 14.

64. Spalding, *Baseball: America's National Game*, 200.

65. *Chicago Tribune*, July 15, 1875, 5.

Chapter 5: A League of His Own

1. Quoted in William E. McMahon, "Albert Goodwill Spalding," in Frederick Ivor-Campbell, Robert L. Tiemann, and Mark Rucker, eds., *Baseball's First Stars* (Cleveland: Society for American Baseball Research, 1996), 154.

2. "The Boston Club—Annual Meeting—Election of Officers," *Boston Journal*, December 8, 1871, 1.

3. "Baseball Gossip," *St. Louis Globe-Democrat*, March 21, 1875, 4.

4. Spalding, *Baseball: America's National Game*, 190.

5. "Baseball. The White Stockings-Philadelphia Game," *Chicago Tribune*, June 26, 1875, 5.

6. "The Philadelphias and White Stockings," *Chicago Tribune*, June 25, 1875, 2; "The White Stockings-Philadelphia Game"; "Third Defeat of the Home Club by the Philadelphias; the Reasonable Conclusion Is That the Whites Had Better Disband," *Chicago Tribune*, June 27, 1875, 14.

7. "Boston and Athletic Tie. A Disgraceful Ending to the Game—Philadelphia Courtesy in a Bad Light," *Philadelphia Times*, June 29, 1875, 1; "Philadelphia and Suburbs. Baseball," *Philadelphia Inquirer*, June 29, 1875, 3; "Rowdyism. The City of Brotherly Love Disgraced," *Boston Globe*, June 29, 1875, 5.

8. "The Professional Player," *New York Times*, March 8, 1872, 4.

9. Spalding, *Baseball: America's National Game*, 190.

10. Spalding, *Baseball: America's National Game*, 190.

11. "Baseball: The Professionals in Council—The Philadelphia Meeting," *Brooklyn Daily Eagle*, March 2, 1875, 2; "Sporting News: Meeting of the National Association at Philadelphia," *Chicago Tribune*, March 7, 1875, 5; "The Judiciary Committee and Their Work," *New York Clipper*, March 13, 1875, 3.

12. "Harry Wright," *New York Clipper*, March 20, 1875, 3.

13. Bartlett, *Baseball and Mr. Spalding*, 73.

14. Spalding, *Baseball: America's National Game*, 201–3; Michael Haupert, "William Hulbert," SABR Biography Project, https://sabr.org/bioproj/person/william-hulbert/.

15. Lee Allen, *The National League Story* (New York: Hill & Wang, 1961), 5.

16. Spalding, *Baseball: America's National Game*, 203.

17. "Marriage of a Baseball Player," *Providence Evening Bulletin*, November 19, 1875, 1; "A Pleasant Wedding," *Rockford Weekly Gazette*, December 31, 1875, 4.

18. Michael Haupert, "Chicago Cubs Team Ownership History, 1876–1919," SABR Team Ownership History Project, https://sabr.org/bioproj/topic/chicago-cubs-team-ownership-history-part1/; Haupert, "William Hulbert"; Spalding, *Baseball: America's National Game*, 203.

19. Hulbert family papers, including William Ambrose Hulbert items, 1836–1875, Chicago History Museum; Don Jensen, ed., *Base Ball 12: New Research on the Early Game* (Jefferson, NC: McFarland, 2021), 114.

20. Haupert, "William Hulbert."

21. Harry Palmer, "America's National Game," *Outing*, July 1888, 354; "Minutes of the July 16, 1875, Meeting of the Board of Directors of the Chicago Baseball Association," Chicago Cubs Records, Box 4, Vol. 4, Chicago History Museum.

22. "Minutes of the July 16, 1875, Meeting."

23. "Minutes of the July 16, 1875, Meeting."

24. Frederick E. Long papers, Box 1, Folder 10, National Baseball Hall of Fame and Museum Archives.

25. "Baseball. The Nine for Next Year," *Chicago Tribune*, July 20, 1875, 5.

26. "Baseball. The Chicago Nine for 1876," *Chicago Tribune*, July 24, 1875, 2.

27. Hulbert family papers.

28. "A Strong Team for Chicago Next Year—Boston Will Suffer," *Boston Globe*, July 21, 1875, 5; "Local Summary," *Boston Post*, July 23, 1875; "Boston Baseball Club Changes," *Boston Globe*, July 23, 1875, 4.

29. Allen, *National League Story*, 6; Peter Golenbock, *Wrigleyville: A Magical History Tour of the Chicago Cubs* (New York: St. Martin's Griffin, 1999), 16; Spalding, *Baseball: America's National Game*, 206.

30. Chicago Cubs Records, Chicago History Museum, Box 1, Folder 6.

31. Spalding, *Baseball: America's National Game*, 520.

32. Adrian C. Anson, *A Ball Player's Career: Being the Personal Experiences and Reminiscences of Adrian C. Anson* (Chicago: Era Publishing, 1900), 41–43; "An Iowa Letter," *Chicago Evening Post*, September 1, 1868, 1.

33. Spalding, *Baseball: America's National Game*, 520–21.

34. "The Chicago Club," *New York Clipper*, November 13, 1875, 2.

35. "Personal," *Chicago Tribune*, November 22, 1875, 5; Bradford Kingman, *History of Brockton, Plymouth County, Massachusetts, 1656–1894* (Syracuse, NY: D. Mason & Co., 1895); "The Weather in Boston," *Boston Post*, November 20, 1875, 2.

36. *Rockford Weekly Register-Gazette*, December 3, 1875, 3.

37. "Miscellaneous," *Rockford Times*, December 1, 1875, 4; "Personal," *Chicago Tribune*, December 8, 1875, 5.

38. Spalding, *Baseball: America's National Game*, 207.

39. Spink, *National Game*, 18.

40. "Personal," *Chicago Tribune*, December 8, 1875, 5.

41. "The Professional Baseball Association—What It Must Do to Be Saved," *Chicago Tribune*, October 24, 1875, 12; Dean A. Sullivan, ed., *Early Innings: A Documentary History of Baseball, 1825–1908* (Lincoln: University of Nebraska Press, 1997), 92.

42. Charles E. Elstner, *The Industries of Louisville, Kentucky, and New Albany, Indiana* (Louisville: J. M. Elstner, 1886), 160; J. E. Findling, "The Louisville Grays' Scandal of 1877," *Journal of Sport History*, Vol. 3, no. 2 (Summer 1976), 176–87.

43. National League Meetings, Minutes, Conferences, and Financial Ledgers, BA MSS 55, National Baseball Hall of Fame and Museum Archives, 17; "Baseball. Conference at Louisville," *Chicago Tribune*, December 19, 1875, 13.

44. A. G. Spalding and Henry Chadwick, eds., *Spalding's Official Baseball Guide* (Chicago: A. G. Spalding & Bros., 1886), 8–9; "The Grand Central Hotel," *New York Herald*, August 24, 1870, 2.

45. *Spalding's Official Baseball Guide*, 1886, 8–9.

46. "Sporting News. Interview with Al Spalding, Captain of the Centennial Chicagos," *Chicago Tribune*, November 28, 1875, 13.

47. Tom Melville, *Early Baseball and the Rise of the National League* (Jefferson, NC: McFarland & Co., 2001), 79.

Chapter 6: A Baseball Emporium

1. "The Snow-Storm. How It Was Generally Greeted," *Chicago Tribune*, March 2, 1876, 8.

2. Bartlett, *Baseball and Mr. Spalding*, 118–19.

3. Albert Spalding, *Rise to Follow: An Autobiography* (New York: Holt, 1943), 20; Bartlett, *Baseball and Mr. Spalding*, 99.

4. Bartlett, *Baseball and Mr. Spalding*, 99.

5. Spalding, *Rise to Follow*, 20.

6. Harriet Spalding, *Reminiscences*.

7. Ira Gertrude Brown, *The Panic of 1873* (Berkeley: University of California Press, 1928); David Ames Wells, *Recent Economic Changes and Their Effects on the Production and Distribution of Wealth and the Well-Being of Society* (New York: D. Appleton & Co., 1898), 435.

8. J. R. Vernon, "Unemployment Rates in Post-Bellum America: 1869–1899," *Journal of Macroeconomics*, Vol. 16, issue 4 (Autumn 1994); Nathan S. Balke and Robert J. Gordon, "The Estimation of Prewar Gross National Product: Methodology and New Evidence," *Journal of Political Economy*, Vol. 97, no. 1 (February 1989); "U.S. Business Cycle Expansions and Contractions," National Bureau of Economic Research, https://www.nber.org/research/data/us-business-cycle-expansions-and-contractions.

9. "Baseball: The Growth of Sports," *This Sporting Life*, April 17, 1889, 10; "The Spalding Banquet," *New York Times*, January 24, 1896.

10. "The Chicago Club," *Chicago Tribune*, March 12, 1876, 16.

11. *Lakeside Annual Directory 1877–1878* (Chicago: Lakeside Publishing and Printing Co., 1877), 1124.

12. J. F. Marsters catalog, 1875, Library of Congress online archive, https://www.loc.gov/resource/gdcmassbookdig.catalogueofallki00mars/?sp=8&st=image&r=-1.259,0.114,3.519,1.602,0 (accessed August 10, 2024).

13. *The Boston Directory for 1872* (Boston: Sampson, Davenport & Co., 1872), 316, 774, 802.

14. *Chicago's First Half Century, 1833–1883* (Chicago: Inter Ocean Publishing, 1883), 32; Bartlett, *Baseball and Mr. Spalding*, 99; Bill Francis, "Diamonds to Dollars," in *Baseball Memories & Dreams* (Coral Gables, FL: Mango Publishing, 2022).

15. H. P. Burchell, ed., *Spalding's Official Lawn Tennis Annual* (New York: American Sports Publishing, 1908), 212; Henry Chadwick, ed., *Spalding's Baseball Guide and Official League Handbook* (Chicago: A. G. Spalding & Bros., 1890), 35.

16. "Games and Pastimes," *Chicago Tribune*, March 12, 1876, 16; Thorn, *Baseball in the Garden of Eden*, 178; "The Flying Ball," *Inter Ocean* (Chicago), April 21, 1876, 8; "Sporting News: Informal Opening of the Baseball Season in Chicago," *Chicago Tribune*, April 21, 1876, 8; "Good Enough! The Finest Game of Baseball Ever Witnessed in Louisville," *Courier-Journal* (Louisville, KY), April 26, 1876, 4.

17. "Sporting News: First Game of Chicago's Great Champion Baseball Club," *Chicago Tribune*, April 26, 1876, 1; "Good Enough!".

18. "Sporting News: Second Meeting Between the Chicago and Louisville Clubs," *Chicago Tribune*, April 28, 1876, 5; "Eleven Errors: How They Did the Business for the Louisville Nine Yesterday," *Courier-Journal* (Louisville, KY), April 28, 1876, 4.

19. James Charlton, *The Baseball Chronology: The Complete History of the Most Important Events in the Game of Baseball* (New York: Macmillan, 1991), 29.

20. Alan E. Foulds, *Boston's Ballparks and Arenas* (Lebanon, NH: University Press of New England, 2005).

21. George V. Tuohey, ed., *A History of the Boston Baseball Club: A Concise and Accurate History of Baseball from Its Inception* (Boston: M. F. Quinn & Co., 1897); "Chicagos, 5; Bostons, 1," *Boston Globe*, May 31, 1876, 1.

22. "Last Year's Bostons Defeat This Year's Bostons," *Boston Globe*, May 31, 1876, 1.

23. "Chicagos, 5; Bostons, 1."

24. "Jottings," *Boston Evening Transcript*, May 31, 1876, 4.

25. Career Leaders & Records for Earned Run Average, Baseball-Reference.com, https://www.baseball-reference.com/leaders/earned_run_avg_career.shtml.

26. www.baseball-reference.com.

27. *Spalding's Official Lawn Tennis Annual*, April 1909, 9.

28. Bartlett, *Baseball and Mr. Spalding*, 99; Francis, "Diamonds to Dollars."

29. "Baseball. Notes: News, Personals, and Correspondence," *Cincinnati Enquirer*, September 5, 1876, 8; Paul Pedersen et al., *Contemporary Sports Management* (Champaign, IL: Human Kinetics, 2010), 56–57; Thorn, *Baseball in the Garden of Eden*, 207.

30. Nathaniel Clark Fowler, *Fowler's Publicity: An Encyclopedia of Advertising and Printing* (New York: Publicity Publishing, 1897), 89.

31. Randy Roberts and Carson Cunningham, eds., *Before the Curse: The Chicago Cubs' Glory Years, 1870–1945* (Champaign: University of Illinois Press, 2011), 11; Chicago Cubs records, NUCMC MS 71-888, Chicago Historical Society, cash books 1875–76.

32. "Pastimes: Convention of Baseball Managers at Cleveland," *Chicago Tribune*, December 10, 1876, 7; "A Standard Ball Selected," *St. Louis Globe-Democrat*, December 11, 1876, 8; "Baseball: Convention of Managers at Cleveland," *Courier-Journal* (Louisville, KY), December 14, 1876, 3; "A New Ball Ordered," *Cincinnati Enquirer*, December 18, 1876.

33. Bartlett, *Baseball and Mr. Spalding*, 101–2.

34. "Pastimes"; "The National Game," *New York Daily Herald*, December 11, 1876, 10.

35. Harold Seymour, *Baseball: The Early Years* (New York: Oxford University Press, 1960), 87.

36. Voigt, *American Baseball*, 76.

37. *New York Clipper*, June 23, 1877, 3.

38. *New York Clipper*, June 23, 1877, 3; *1878 Constitution and Playing Rules of the National League of Professional Baseball Clubs* (Chicago: A. G. Spalding & Bros., 1878), 46.

39. *1878 Constitution and Playing Rules*, 43–44.

40. "Baseball: Reviewing the Season," *New York Clipper*, November 17, 1877, 2.

41. "Sporting: Baseball," *Chicago Tribune*, May 17, 1877, 5.

42. "Sporting: Baseball."

43. *Constitution and Playing Rules of the National League of Professional Baseball Clubs* (Philadelphia: Reach & Johnston, 1876); "Sporting: Chicago Ball Players Getting Up Muscular Development in Gymnasium Practice," *Chicago Tribune*, March 19, 1876, 9.

44. "Sporting Notes," *Inter Ocean* (Chicago), January 25, 1877, 8; *Constitution and Playing Rules of the National League*, 1876, 41; *Constitution and Playing Rules of the National League of Professional Baseball Clubs* (Chicago: A. G. Spalding & Bros., 1877), 46.

45. "Sporting: The League Book," *Chicago Tribune*, March 3, 1878, 7; "Official Baseball Guide," *Boston Globe*, March 4, 1878, 3; *Cincinnati Enquirer*, March 4, 1878, 8.

46. *Spalding's Official Baseball Guide*, 1879, 6.

47. *Constitution and Playing Rules of the National League of Professional Baseball Clubs*, 1876 (Chicago: A. G. Spalding & Bros., 1881)

48. *Spalding's Official Baseball Guide*, 1879, 49, 50.

49. *Spalding's Official Baseball Guide*, 1877, 2.

50. Chadwick, *Spalding's Baseball Guide and Official League Book for 1883*, 2.

51. A. G. Mills papers, National Baseball Hall of Fame and Museum Archives.

52. *Spalding's Baseball Guide*, 1880; *Spalding's Official Baseball Guide*, 1881, 5.

53. A. G. Mills papers.

54. Chadwick, *Spalding's Baseball Guide and Official League Book*, 1884, 4.

Chapter 7: The Big Mogul

1.˜ J. E. Findling, "The Louisville Grays' Scandal of 1877," *Journal of Sport History*, Vol. 3, no. 2, 176–87; Voigt, *American Baseball*, 76; "Sporting: Some Reasons Why the Chicago Club Could Not Retain the Championship," *Chicago Tribune*, October 28, 1877, 7.

2. "Out-Door Sports," *Boston Post*, September 2, 1878, 3; "Baseball: The Championship," *Inter Ocean* (Chicago), September 2, 1878, 4.

3. "2024 Major League Baseball Pitching Leaders," Baseball-Reference.com, https://www.baseball-reference.com/leagues/majors/2024-pitching-leaders.shtml (accessed June 12, 2025).

4. Bartlett, *Baseball and Mr. Spalding*, 122.

5. Crisfield Johnson, *History of Allegan and Barry Counties, Michigan, with Illustrations and Biographical Sketches of Their Men and Pioneers* (Philadelphia: D. W. Ensign & Co., 1880), 373.

6. Michigan Supreme Court, *Olney v. Brown*, 163 MICH 125 (1910): Record.

7. Transcript of Michigan Supreme Court case no. 159, October term, 1909, *Olney et al. v. Brown et al.*, 76–79.

8. Stephen Hardy, "Adopted by All the Leading Clubs," in *For Fun and Profit: The Transformation of Leisure into Consumption*, ed. Richard Butsch (Philadelphia: Temple University Press, 1990), 80.

9. "The Bat Business," *Northwestern Lumberman*, March 24, 1883, 6; "Baseball Bats," *Daily Republican* (Monongahela, PA), May 4, 1883, 2.

10. "Andrews Building," Chicagology, n.d., https://chicagology.com/rebuilding/rebuilding182/ (accessed April 13, 2025).

11. *Olney et al. v. Brown et al.*, 80.

12. "Fire at Hastings," *Saint Paul Globe*, August 13, 1886, 4.

13. Gary Richardson and Tim Sablik, "Banking Panics of the Gilded Age," Federal Reserve History website, https://www.federalreservehistory.org/essays/banking-panics-of-the-gilded-age (accessed April 13, 2025); *Olney et al. v. Brown et al.*, 79–84.

14. "Sports and Pastimes," *Brooklyn Eagle*, March 30, 1884, 4.

15. "The Fire Record: Spalding & Bros.' Sporting-Goods House Damaged to the Extent of $80,000," *Chicago Tribune*, October 27, 1884, 6.

16. Edward Marshall, "The Psychology of Baseball," *New York Times* magazine section, November 13, 1910, 41.

17. "The Fire Record."

18. Hearings Before a Subcommittee on Interstate and Foreign Commerce, US House of Representatives, November 30, 1938, to January 6, 1938, 234–35; Bartlett, *Baseball and Mr. Spalding*, 147; *Spalding's Official Baseball Guide 1889*, 4–5.

19. Norman L. Macht, *Connie Mack and the Early Years of Baseball* (Lincoln: University of Nebraska Press, 2007), 198.

20. "The Sporting Goods Trade," *New York Times*, September 1, 1889, 1; "A Great Baseball Deal," *Brooklyn Eagle*, September 1, 1889, 1.

21. "A. J. Reach Sells Out: A. G. Spalding Now Has a Monopoly in the Retail Sporting Goods Line," *Brooklyn Daily Times*, August 31, 1889, 1.

22. Absorbed by Spalding," *Inter Ocean,* September 1, 1889, 2.

23. "Spalding's Sporting Goods Monopoly," *Kansas City Times*, September 1, 1889, 3.

24. "Hub Happenings," *Sporting Life*, February 27, 1892, 9; "Henry Ditson Dropped Dead," *Boston Globe*, November 16, 1891, 5; "Change in Sporting Goods Trade," *New York Times*, March 5, 1894, 8; "Removal" advertisement: *New-York Tribune*, March 5, 1894, 3.

25. James B. Dill, *The General Corporation Act of New Jersey* (New York: Baker, Voorhis & Co., 1903), 128–30.

26. "Baseball Briefs," *Pittsburgh Press*, February 6, 1892, 5.

27. "Spalding's Bomb," *Sporting Life*, January 18, 1896, 15.

28. "Duffey to Lose Records," *New-York Tribune*, October 29, 1905, 9; Joseph M. Turrini, *The End of Amateurism in American Track and Field* (Urbana: University of Illinois Press, 2010), 26; "Biography: Arthur Duffey," International Olympics Committee website, olympics.com/en/athletes/arthur-duffey (accessed April 13, 2025).

29. "Duffey, Sprinter, Goes to Court," *Montreal Star*, February 22, 1906, 2; "Duffey Loses Suit Against A.A.U.," *Baltimore Sun*, June 24, 1906, 10.

30. "Yale and Michigan Won," *Daily Nonpareil* (Council Bluffs, IA), April 30, 1905, 4; "Discus Was of Aluminum," *Saginaw* (MI) *News*, May 1, 1905, 4.

31. "Maroons Swamp Michigan Men in Conference Meet," *Inter Ocean* (Chicago), June 4, 1905, 9.

32. "Garrels' Discus Record Not Allowed," *New York Times*, June 27, 1905, 5; "Garrels Again Robbed of Honors, A.A.U. Refusing World's Records," *Detroit Free Press*, June 28, 1905, 9.

33. *Spalding's Official Athletic Almanac for 1904*, 200; *Spalding's Official Athletic Almanac for 1905*, 148 and 173.

34. Charles J. P. Lucas, "Commercializing Amateur Athletics," in *The World To-Day*, Vol. 10, no. 3 (March 1906), 281–85.

35. "Eckersall Is Under the Ban," *Chicago Tribune*, August 27, 1903, 4.

36. "Newsy News," *Transcript-Telegram* (Holyoke, MA), October 10, 1893, 3; "Chicopee: Business with the Lamb Company," *Springfield* (MA) *Daily Republican*, October 11, 1890, 6; Bruce D. Epperson, *Peddling Bicycles to America: The Rise of an Industry* (Jefferson, NC: McFarland, 2010), 88.

37. W. Jett Lauck, *The Causes of the Panic of 1893* (Boston: Houghton Mifflin, 1907), 110–22.

38. Epperson, *Peddling Bicycles to America*, 157; "That Bicycle War," *Holyoke* (MA) *Daily Transcript*, March 19, 1894, 4; "Big Bicycle War," *Journal* (Meriden, CT), June 19, 1894, 3.

39. "Newsy News."

40. "For a Few Days Only," *Berkshire Eagle*, March 23, 1894, 1; Epperson, *Peddling Bicycles to America*, 157; "New Victor Bicycles $85," advertisement in *Dixon* (IL) *Evening Telegraph*, March 27, 1894, 1.

41. "Overman Company Brings Suit," *Hartford Courant*, April 3, 1894, 1.

42. "May Show the True Cost of Bicycle," *Chicago Tribune*, June 16, 1894, 1; "Bicycle Makers at War," *Passaic* (NJ) *Daily News*, June 16, 1894, 8; "Big Bicycle War."

43. "Victor Men Change," *Springfield* (MA) *Daily Republican*, February 28, 1918, 7; "Overman Wheel Co. Affairs: The Assignment Due to the Need of Money," *Weekly Plain Dealer* (Cleveland, OH), December 31, 1897, 2.

Chapter 8: League Leader

1. "Base-Ball: The Death of William A. Hulbert," *Cincinnati Enquirer*, April 11, 1882, 2; "William A. Hulbert, President of the Chicago Base-Ball Club and of the National League," *Chicago Tribune*, April 11, 1882, 6; "Signal Service," *Chicago Tribune*, April 11, 1882, 2.

2. "The National League," *Buffalo Courier Express*, December 9, 1881, 4.

3. "The Late William A. Hulbert," *Chicago Tribune*, April 12, 1882, 3; "The City: Personal and General," *Chicago Tribune*, April 27, 1882, 8.

4. Walter Besant and James Rice, *The Seamy Side: A Story* (New York: Dodd, Mead, 1888), 180; first serialized in *Appleton's Journal, a Magazine of General Literature*, May 1879 through April 1880; Bartlett, *Baseball and Mr. Spalding*, 146.

5. "Base-Ball: Meeting of the Conference Committees of the Rival Associations," *Chicago Tribune*, February 18, 1883, 3.

6. "The National Game," *New York Times*, August 30, 1881, 4.

7. Amos Alonzo Stagg and Wesley Winans Stout, *Touchdown!* (New York: Longmans, Green, 1927), 105.

8. Frederick G. Lieb, *The Baseball Story* (New York: G. P. Putnam's Sons, 1950), 77.

9. "The Chicago Baseball Grounds," *Harper's Weekly*, May 12, 1883, 299; William J. Hagenah, *Report on the Investigation of the Chicago Telephone Company Submitted to the Committee on Gas, Oil, and Electric Light* (Chicago: Henry O. Shepard Co., 1911); Lieb, *Baseball Story*, 97.

10. The White Stockings vacated the site and Lakefront Park was torn down after a court ruled in 1885 the grounds were US government property and thus improperly leased to a private, profit-making business. Spalding built a new West Side Park at the intersection of Congress and Throop Streets.

11. Spalding, *Baseball: America's National Game,* 523–24.

12. Spalding, *Baseball: America's National Game,* 526.

13. "Baseball," *Kansas City Star*, July 23, 1886, 2.

14. Spalding, *Baseball: America's National Game*, 526.

15. Marshall, "Psychology of Baseball," 13.

16. "The Naughty Chicago Boys," *Cleveland Leader*, May 22, 1884, 3.

17. "In Trouble," *St. Louis Post-Dispatch*, May 30, 1884, 5.

18. Thorn, *Baseball in the Garden of Eden*, 201.

19. "The World's Champions," *St. Louis Post-Dispatch*, October 25, 1886, 5.

20. Bartlett, *Baseball and Mr. Spalding*, 165; "Blood Money for the Browns," *St. Louis Globe-Democrat*, October 31, 1886, 11; Lieb, *Baseball Story*, 98.

21. Lieb, *Baseball Story*, 99–100.

22. "Dalrymple for Pittsburg," *Sporting Life*, December 1, 1886, 1; "News Notes," *Sporting Life*, December 1, 1886, 4; "The Kelly Deal," *Sporting Life*, February 23, 1887, 1; Bartlett, *Baseball and Mr. Spalding*, 168; "The Great Twirler Here," *Pittsburgh Post*, April 30, 1887, 6; "Want McCormick Bad," *Pittsburgh Post*, April 19, 1887, 6.

23. "Chicago Ball Men," *Philadelphia Times*, January 16, 1887, 11.

24. "Another Good Man Signed," *Pittsburgh Post*, January 18, 1888, 6.

25. "A Vile Attack," *Sporting Life*, April 27, 1887, 1.

26. Spalding, *Baseball: America's National Game*, 515.

27. "A Vile Attack."

28. "Johnson Seeks Better Scoring," *Chicago Tribune*, February 4, 1911, 12; "Official Baseball Scorer," *Boston Globe*, December 2, 1920, 10; "Woman Aspires to Be Mayor," *Baltimore Sun*, December 3, 1920, 9.

29. "The Chicago Row," *Sporting Life*, September 7, 1887, 3.

30. Robert F. Burk, *Never Just a Game: Players, Owners, and American Baseball to 1920* (Chapel Hill: University of North Carolina Press, 1994), 62–64; "Base-Ball: Meeting of the Conference Committees of the Rival Associations," *Chicago Tribune*, February 18, 1883, 3.

31. "Sporting Matters," *Inter Ocean* (Chicago), December 1, 1883, 3.

32. "In and Outdoor Sports," *Cleveland Plain Dealer*, November 4, 1879, 1.
33. "Baseball: The Shreveports Defeat the Nolans and Challenge the Brennans," *Times-Picayune*, October 3, 1883, 8.
34. "Base Ball," *Saint Paul Globe*, January 2, 1884, 5.
35. "New Association," *Sporting Life*, September 17, 1883, 3.
36. Dan Schlossberg, *The Baseball Almanac* (Chicago: Triumph Books, 2002).
37. "Another New Association Movement," *Sporting Life*, September 3, 1883, 6; "New Associations," *Sporting Life*, September 17, 1883, 3.
38. "The New Association," *Sporting Life*, October 1, 1883, 3.
39. "Base Ball Wreckers," *Sporting Life*, October 1, 1883, 3.
40. The condescending tone is like an open letter Spalding wrote earlier to rebut an allegation that he had undermined an early minor league, the International Association. A cofounder of that circuit, L. C. Waite of St. Louis, accused Spalding of "secretly" proposing a League-affiliated minor league just days before leaders of the International movement—so named because it included several Canadian clubs—were to hold a formative meeting in Pittsburgh. Why would Spalding, a leading figure in the National League, bother to harass a smaller and weaker rival? "He desires to monopolize baseball patronage in this country," was Waite's succinct reply.
41. "Pastimes: 'Spalding's Plan' Defended by Its Author," *Chicago Tribune*, January 28, 1877, 7.
42. Letter to A. G. Spalding, February 9, 1884, A. G. Mills papers, Baseball Hall of Fame.
43. "The Union Association," *Sporting Life*, August 13, 1884, 6; "Base Ball Players Desert," *Sporting Life*, August 13, 1884, 6.
44. "Dissolution of the Union Association," *St. Louis Post-Dispatch*, January 16, 1885, 2; "Disbandment of the Union Association," *Cincinnati Enquirer*, January 16, 1885, 2.

Chapter 9: Color Line Blind

1. "News of the Day," *Alexandria* (VA) *Gazette*, December 13, 1867, 2.
2. David L. Fleitz, *Cap Anson: The Grand Old Man of Baseball* (Jefferson, NC: McFarland, 2005), 111–12.
3. Howard W. Rosenberg, "Recapping a Bit of Toledo's History," *Blade* (Toledo, OH), November 8, 2006, 3.
4. John R. Husman, "August 10, 1883: Cap Anson vs. Fleet Walker," Society for American Baseball Research, https://sabr.org/gamesproj/game/august-10-1883-cap-anson-vs-fleet-walker/ (accessed April 13, 2025).
5. *Kentucky State Journal*, August 25, 1881, 2.
6. John Brown to C. H. Morton, April 11, 1884, Chicago Baseball Club records, Chicago Historical Society, quoted in Steven A. Riess, *Touching Base: Professional Baseball and American Culture in the Progressive Era* (Urbana and Chicago: University of Illinois Press), 1999, 195.
7. "The Colored Ball Players Distasteful," *Toronto World*, May 27, 1887, 2.
8. "Base Ball Notes," *Sporting News*, June 1, 1887, 10.
9. "Baseball Notes," *Philadelphia Times*, July 17, 1887, 14; "International League Meeting," *Sporting News*, July 20, 1887, 1.

Chapter 10: Are Player Chattels?

1. *Spalding's Official Baseball Guide*, 1884, 8–9.

2. *Spalding's Official Baseball Guide*, 1885, 9.

3. "Harmony Is the Outcome," *Sporting Life*, September 2, 1885, 1.

4. *Spalding's Official Baseball Guide*, 1884, 41–42.

5. "The Salary Question," *Sporting Life*, September 2, 1885, 4.

6. "Baseball: The Great Meeting," *Sporting Life*, October 21, 1885, 1; "The League-Association Conference," *St. Louis Globe-Democrat*, October 17, 1885, 7; "Tough on Ballplayers: An Agreement That Is Worse Than the Reserve Rule," *Cincinnati Enquirer*, October 18, 1885, 2; "The Baseball Convention," *New York Times*, October 18, 1885, 2.

7. "Return of the Giants," *New York Times*, October 19, 1885, 8.

8. "From the Hub," *New York Clipper*, October 24, 1885, 9.

9. "Ball Players Combine," *Kansas City Times*, August 6, 1886, 2.

10. Thorn, *Baseball in the Garden of Eden*, 200; *Spalding's Official Baseball Guide*, 1890, 19–20.

11. "Personals," *Cincinnati Enquirer*, May 15, 1876, 5.

12. "Spalding and the Chicago Club," *St. Louis Post-Dispatch*, August 5, 1885, 5.

13. "Diamond Dust," *San Francisco Examiner*, June 20, 1887, 3; Burk, *Never Just a Game*, 64; "Baseball Notes," *Cincinnati Enquirer*, April 6, 1884, 13.

14. "Baseball Brotherhood," *Cincinnati Post*, August 23, 1887, 2.

15. "Reforms Proposed by the Brotherhood," *Chicago Tribune*, August 29, 1887, 2; "The Players' Brotherhood," *Cincinnati Enquirer*, August 24, 1887, 2; "The Baseball Players' Brotherhood," *Indianapolis Journal*, August 29, 1887, 5.

16. "From Chicago," *Sporting Life*, September 7, 1887, 3.

17. "League and Brotherhood," *Boston Globe*, September 26, 1887, 5.

18. "League and Brotherhood."

19. "Traffic Throttled: The Gould System at the Mercy of the Knights of Labor," *St. Louis Post-Dispatch*, March 8, 1886, 1.

20. Seymour, *Early Years*, 223.

21. "League and Brotherhood."

22. "Ball Players' Brotherhood," *New York Times*, October 2, 1887, 3.

23. "League and Brotherhood."

24. "Ball Players' Brotherhood."

25. "Is the Ball-Player a Chattel?" *Lippincott's*, August 1887, 310–19.

26. "League Meeting," *Sporting News*, November 23, 1887, 2.

27. "What They Accomplished," *Sun* (New York), November 20, 1887, 11.

28. "How the Boston Men Look at It," *Sun* (New York), November 20, 1887, 11.

Chapter 11: The World Tour

1. *Spalding's Base Ball Guide and Official League Book*, 1888, 2–3.

2. Harry Clay Palmer, *Sights Around the World with the Base-Ball Boys* (Philadelphia: Edgewood, 1892), 12.

3. "Spalding's Australia Enterprise," *Cincinnati Enquirer*, March 25, 1888, 10; "Base-Ball in Australia," *Chicago Tribune*, March 25, 1888, 2.

4. "Spalding's Australian Tour," *Inter Ocean* (Chicago), March 25, 1888, 5.

5. Baseball was first played in Australia on February 28, 1857, at Carleton Garden in Melbourne between two teams chosen from the members of the Melbourne Base Ball Club, according to *Bell's Life*, an Australian publication. One team, called Collingwood, won the first three-inning game by a score of 250 to 230. The other team, the Richmonds, came back and took the second three-inning contest by a score of 171 to 141. The Melbourne Base Ball Club was next heard from 31 years later, as part of the Melbourne Cricket Club, apparently reconstituted in anticipation of the American tour.

6. "On to Australia: Spalding Has a Gigantic Scheme on Hand," *Saint Paul Globe*, March 25, 1888, 7.

7. "Baseball," *Sydney Mail*, April 28, 1888, 919.

8. "To Australia: A Base Ball Invasion by Spalding," *Sporting Life*, March 28, 1888, 1.

9. "To Australia."

10. "No Game in Philadelphia," *Chicago Tribune*, October 14, 1888, 11.

11. Spalding, *Baseball: America's National Game*, 157.

12. "Off for Australia," *Meriden* (CT) *Journal*, October 13, 1888, 1.

13. "Getting Ready for Australia," *Chicago Tribune*, October 18, 1888, 7; "Base Hits," *Morning Call* (Paterson, NJ), November 1, 1888, 3.

14. "Spalding Will Pitch," *Chicago Tribune*, October 20, 1888, 6.

15. "The Farewell Game," *Inter Ocean* (Chicago), October 21, 1888, 6; "Chicago 11, All-America 6," *Sunday Tribune* (Minneapolis), October 21, 1888, 2.

16. "The All-America Are Beaten in Their First Game with Chicago," *San Francisco Chronicle*, October 21, 1888, 9.

17. Palmer, *Sights Around the World*, 109.

18. "Spalding's Australian Base Ball Tour Itinerary," *Inter Ocean* (Chicago), October 21, 1888, 6.

19. "On the Diamond," *San Francisco Chronicle*, November 5, 1888, 7.

20. "Ball in Two Cities," *San Francisco Examiner*, November 9, 1888, 8.

21. "Sporting Events," *Oakland Tribune*, November 10, 1888, 4.

22. "Farewell Game"; "Baseball Gossip," *San Francisco Chronicle*, November 4, 1888, 14.

23. "Oceanic Steamship Company," *San Francisco Examiner*, November 9, 1888, 3; "Better Than the Stars," *San Francisco Examiner*, November 19, 1888, 5; "Off for Australia," *San Francisco Examiner*, November 19, 1888, 5.

24. "Bombshell in Baseball: Fancy Prices for Fancy Players Ruled Out," *New York Times*, November 23, 1888, 2; "Ball Rules for 1889," *Washington Post*, November 23, 1888, 1.

25. "On a Business Basis: The League Puts a Stop to the High Salary Nonsense," *Plain Dealer* (Cleveland, OH), November 23, 1888, 1.

26. Francis C. Richter, *Richter's History and Records of Base Ball, the American Nation's Chief Sport* (Philadelphia: F. C. Richter, 1914), 62.

27. "The Graded Salary System," *Philadelphia Times*, November 25, 1888, 2; Palmer, *Sights and Sounds Around the World*, 65.

28. "John M. Ward Signed," *Washington Post*, November 25, 1888, 2.

29. "Baseball Business Done," *New-York Tribune*, November 23, 1888, 3; "To Improve the Batting," *New York Times*, November 21, 1888, 2; "John M. Ward Signed," *Washington*

Post, November 25, 1888, 2; "Helen Dauvray's Wedding," *Evening World* (New York), October 12, 1887, 1; Thorn, *Baseball in the Garden of Eden*, 233.

30. Palmer, *Sights Around the World*, 68–74.

31. Spalding, *Baseball: America's National Game*, 255–56.

32. Palmer, *Sights Around the World*, 85–86.

33. Bartlett, *Baseball and Mr. Spalding*, 186.

34. "The American Baseball Team," *Otago* (New Zealand) *Witness*, December 14, 1888, 23; "Baseball," *New Zealand Mail*, December 14, 1888, 16.

35. "America's National Game," *New Zealand Herald*, December 10, 1888, 5; "The American National Game: Spalding's Baseball Teams," *Auckland* (New Zealand) *Star*, December 10, 1888, 8.

36. Palmer, *Sights Around the World*, 12–13.

37. Palmer, *Sights Around the World*, 64–65.

38. Palmer, *Sights Around the World*, 96–97.

39. "The Ball Tourists: They Will Probably Make a Trip Around the World," *Philadelphia Times*, November 25, 1888, 2; Palmer, *Sights Around the World*, 135.

40. "Profits of Baseball," *Evening Star* (Thames, New Zealand), December 19, 1888, 4.

41. "Baseball: The Americans' Final Match," *Herald* (Melbourne, Australia), January 5, 1889, 3; "Football and Baseball Matches on the Melbourne Cricket Ground," *Age* (Melbourne, Australia), January 7, 1889, 6.

42. Palmer, *Sights Around the World*, 157–58.

43. Palmer, *Sights Around the World*, 171–73.

44. "Baseball Before the Sphinx by American Players," *Buffalo Courier Express*, February 12, 1889, 6.

45. "Spalding's Party at Brindisi," *Times-Democrat* (New Orleans), February 19, 1889, 2.

46. "Mr. Ward's Return Home," *Chicago Tribune*, March 14, 1889, 2.

47. "Ball Tossers en Route from Egypt," *Chicago Tribune*, February 15, 1889, 1.

48. "Our Baseballists Abroad. Shocking the People of Italy by Sacrilegious Propositions," *San Francisco Examiner*, February 15, 1889, 1; "Sporting: The American Teams at Naples," *St. Louis Globe-Democrat*, February 19, 1889, 8.

49. "Sporting: American Teams at Naples"; "Our Baseball Teams," *Wilmington* (NC) *Messenger*, February 26, 1889, 1.

50. "Williamson's Injury: The Great Infielder Describes it and Also Speaks of the Trip," *Sporting Life*, April 3, 1889, 1; "Ball-Players Overjoyed," *Inter-Ocean* (Chicago), April 7, 1889, 3.

51. "Ed Williamson Talks," *Cleveland Leader*, May 30, 1889, 3.

52. "Williamson's Injury."

53. Williamson worried that he was not only being left behind but left alone to pay the doctor's bill. He said as much when Spalding and Anson visited him before boarding the ship; he was not put at ease by their replies. "All I know is that Spalding told me that when I got ready to work, I would be satisfied with the arrangements made," Williamson said. What if he could never play professional ball again? "He told me I could depend on him for necessary expenses," the shortstop said. "Of course, I would have been better satisfied if he had signed me. We had agreed on terms last fall."

54. "Ed Williamson Talks."

55. "Baseball: Stray Sparks from the Diamond," *New York Clipper*, June 8, 1889, 8; "Amateur League Ball," *Inter Ocean* (Chicago), July 14, 1889, 3; "Players There in Force," *Chicago Tribune*, November 4, 1889, 2.

56. "Sporting Notes," *Detroit Free Press*, May 11, 1889, 8.

57. "Base Ball Notes," *Boston Globe*, May 18, 1889, 3; "Chadwick's Chat," *Sporting Life*, May 29, 1890, 2.

58. Spalding, *Baseball: America's National Game,* 261–63; "In Royalty's Presence," *Chicago Tribune*, March 13, 1889, 1.

59. "Sporting World," *Plain Dealer* (Cleveland, OH), April 7, 1889, 9; "Return of the Round-the-World Tourists," *Indianapolis Journal*, April 7, 1889, 7.

60. "Home Again," *Brooklyn Eagle*, April 6, 1889, 1.

61. "Many Ovations," *Sporting Life*, April 17, 1889, 1; Palmer, *Sights Around the World,* 272–78; "Lots of Errors," *Brooklyn Eagle*, April 8, 1889, 1; Richter, *Richter's History*, 112.

Chapter 12: Breaking Point

1. Seymour, *Early Years*, 225.
2. "Pugnacious Ball Players," *New York Times*, December 20, 1888, 2.
3. "End of a Big Baseball Trouble," *Sun* (New York), July 7, 1889, 2.
4. Seymour, *Early Years*, 225.
5. "Downed by the Hoodoos," *Chicago Tribune*, April 25, 1889, 3.
6. Baseball-Reference.com.
7. Thorn, *Baseball in the Garden of Eden*, 236.
8. "The League Meeting," *Sporting Life*, November 20, 1889, 2.
9. Steven A. Riess, *Sport in Industrial America 1850–1920* (Wheeling, IL: Harlan Davidson, 1995).
10. Riess, *Sport in Industrial America*; "Meeting of the Players' Brotherhood in New York," *Los Angeles Times*, November 5, 1889, 1.
11. William Anderson, "Creating the National Pastime: The Antecedents of Major League Baseball Public Relations," *Media History Monographs*, Vol. 4, no. 2 (2000–2001), 1–26.
12. *Chicago Tribune*, July 13, 1889, 3; *Evening World* (New York), July 13, 1889, 3.
13. "Spalding's Little Plan," *Chicago Tribune*, July 13, 1889, 3; "Classify Them," *Evening World* (New York), July 13, 1889, 1.
14. *St. Louis Post-Dispatch*, July 14, 1889, 8.
15. "Classification of Players," *New York Times*, July 14, 1889, 3.
16. Robert P. Gelzheiser, *Labor and Capital in 19th Century Baseball* (Jefferson, NC: McFarland & Co., 2005).
17. See, for example, "Johnson's Great Scheme," *Indianapolis Journal*, September 8, 1889, 7; "The Latest Scheme," *Pittsburgh Dispatch*, September 9, 1889, 6; "Buying Up Ball Players," *Philadelphia Inquirer*, September 12, 1889, 6.
18. "Is a Players' Rebellion Coming?" *Sporting News*, September 11, 1889, 1.
19. "A Great Baseball Trust," *Chicago Tribune*, September 22, 1889, 9.
20. "Spalding's View," *St. Louis Globe-Dispatch*, September 24, 1889, 4; "Day, Brush, Glasscock, and Ward," *Chicago Tribune*, September 24, 1889, 6.

21. "Young Laughs It All to Scorn," *Chicago Tribune*, September 24, 1889, 6.

22. "The League Meeting," *Sporting Life*, November 20, 1889, 2.

23. Boston, which finished just one game behind the Giants in 1889, attracted 147,000 spectators, 22,250 of whom paid an extra 25 cents to sit in the grandstand. Gross ticket revenue alone was $169,750. Harry Palmer, a journalist, estimated that Boston's surplus, after deducting salaries, travel, and other expenses, was more than $100,000. In Brooklyn, the American Association champion Brooklyn Bridegrooms drew a record 353,690 fans that year.

24. "Von Der Ahe's Plans," *New York Times*, October 25, 1899, 9; "Von der Ahe Talks," *Sporting Life*, October 30, 1889, 5.

25. "They Are Two to One," *Chicago Tribune*, October 24, 1889, 1.

26. "May Not Enjoin Them," *Pittsburgh Dispatch*, October 28, 1889, 6.

27. "A Confession," *Sporting Life*, October 9, 1889, 6.

28. "The Players' League," *Evening World* (New York), October 29, 1889, 1.

29. "Position of the Players," *Detroit Free Press*, November 5, 1889, 3; "Meeting of the Players' Brotherhood in New York," *Los Angeles Times*, November 5, 1889, 1.

30. "Spalding's Plain Talk," *Sporting Life*, October 31, 1889, 5.

31. "Monday's Brotherhood Meeting," *Chicago Tribune*, November 3, 1889, 4.

32. "All on the List," *Boston Globe*, October 31, 1889, 5.

33. "The Last Day's Work," *Sporting Life*, November 20, 1889, 2.

34. Spalding, *Baseball: America's National Game*, 273–279.

35. "How Players View It," *Pittsburgh Dispatch*, November 22, 1889, 6.

36. The Freight Bureau Scheme involved bribing railroad clerks to deny legitimate claims for lost or damaged freight, then having co-conspirators buy the claims from aggrieved shippers at steep discounts and resubmitting the documents to the crooked clerks for full compensation. When the swindle was exposed in March, Spalding denied knowing about the bribery and fraud but conceded that he had invested $15,000 in the scheme, which he said he had withdrawn before beginning his world tour.

37. "A Sharper's Dupes," *South Bend* (IN) *Tribune*, March 16, 1889, 1.

38. "Sporting Notes," *Pittsburgh Post*, January 3, 1890, 6.

39. Baseball-Reference.com (the players who left for the Players' League were Charlie Bartson, Charlie Bastian, Dell Darling, Hugh Duffy, Frank Dwyer, Charles "Duke" Farrell, Fred Pfeffer, Jimmy Ryan, John Tener, George Van Haltren, and Ned Williamson).

40. "The League," *Sporting Life*, April 2, 1890, 2.

41. "Stray Sparks from the Diamond," *New York Clipper*, November 2, 1889, 571.

42. Carl Zollmann, "Baseball Peonage," *Marquette Law Review*, Vol. 24, no. 3 (April 1940), 139–45.

43. Edmund P. Edmonds, "Arthur Soden's Legacy: The Origins and Early History of Baseball's Reserve System," *Albany Government Law Review*, Vol. 5, no. 1 (2012), 38–89; "Baseball Comment," *Philadelphia Inquirer*, March 16, 1890, 6.

44. "Carroll and the Players," *Pittsburgh Post*, January 3, 1890, 6.

45. "They Are Two to One," *Topeka State Journal*, November 8, 1889, 2.

46. "What Spalding Had to Say," *Pittsburgh Post*, November 16, 1889, 6; "Magnates Declare War," *Chicago Tribune*, November 16, 1889, 3.

47. Florence Peterson, "Strikes in the United States 1880–1936," US Department of Labor, Bulletin No. 651, August 1937.
48. "Spalding's Talk," *Pittsburgh Dispatch*, November 22, 1889, 6.
49. "A Review of Sports," *Pittsburgh Dispatch*, November 24, 1889, 6.

Chapter 13: Brotherhood War

1. The city in 1977 changed the name of Eighth Avenue north of Central Park to Frederick Douglass Boulevard to honor the 19th-century abolitionist, author, social reformer, and public speaker who was enslaved for the first 20 years of his life.
2. "National League," "Players' League," and "The Association," *Sporting Life*, April 26, 1890, 2, 3, and 13.
3. "Now Comes the Tug of War," *Sun* (New York), April 20, 1890, 5; "A King in the Box," *Pittsburgh Press*, April 20, 1890, 6; "The Race Fairly Started," *Pittsburgh Press*, April 20, 1890, 4.
4. "They Play With Anson," *Chicago Tribune*, April 20, 1890, 28; "Opening Games," *Sporting Life*, April 26, 1890, 2; "Chicago 5; Cincinnati 4," *Inter Ocean* (Chicago), April 20, 1890, 2; "Chicago 5, Cincinnati 4," *Chicago Tribune*, April 20, 1890, 2.
5. "National League," *Sporting Life*, April 26, 1890, 2.
6. "Changing the Schedule," *Pittsburgh Press*, April 27, 1890, 6.
7. "There Will Be No Change," *Chicago Tribune*, April 28, 1890, 6.
8. "Those Protested Notes," *Sporting Life*, August 16, 1890, 1.
9. Jonathan Fraser Light, *The Cultural Encyclopedia of Baseball* (Jefferson, NC: McFarland & Co., 2005), 733.
10. "League Men Sued," *Pittsburgh Post*, May 7, 1890, 6; "Pittsburgh Affairs," *Sporting Life*, May 10, 1890, 1.
11. "General Sporting Notes," *Pittsburgh Press*, May 7, 1890, 5.
12. "About the Diamond," *Pittsburgh Press*, May 11, 1890, 6; "Base Ball Notes," *Boston Globe*, May 11, 1890, 5.
13. "No Compromise," *Pittsburgh Dispatch*, May 11, 1890, 7.
14. Spalding, *Baseball: America's National Game*, 179.
15. "Brooklyn Budget," *Sporting Life*, April 26, 1890, 6.
16. "Chicago Gleanings," *Sporting Life*, April 26, 1890, 10.
17. "Chicago Gleanings."
18. "Conflicting Dates," *Sporting Life*, May 3, 1890, 5.
19. "Day Infusing Courage," *Sporting Life*, April 26, 1890, 10.
20. "On the Base Ball Field," *Sun* (New York), May 10, 1890, 4; "Tiernan to the Front," *Sun* (New York), May 13, 1890, 4.
21. MLB Attendance Data, Baseball Almanac website, https://www.baseball-almanac.com/baseball_attendance.shtml (accessed April 13, 2025).
22. "Some Rumored Changes," *Chicago Tribune*, May 7, 1890, 6.
23. Spalding, *Baseball: America's National Game*, 185.
24. "The Trouble and the Remedy," *Sporting Life*, May 10, 1890, 4.
25. "Spalding Criticized," *Sporting Life* quoting the *Detroit Journal*, May 31, 1890, 6.
26. "Something in the Wind," *Louisville Courier-Journal*, May 8, 1890, 7.
27. "Brunell Can Prove It," *Boston Globe*, May 13, 1890, 7.

28. The *Globe* said the National League and Players' League combined drew 256,015 spectators to championship games played through mid-May in 1890: 58 games in the National League and 55 in the Players' League. Only 90,684 people had watched National League games to that point in 1890 compared with 176,266 at its first 58 games in 1889. Exhibition games were not included.

29. "Attendance Figures," *Boston Globe*, May 12, 1890, 5.

30. "Ward's Reply," *Sporting Life*, May 31, 1890, 8.

31. "Death of J. Palmer O'Neil," *New York Times*, January 8, 1908, 9.

32. "Magnates Confer," *Sporting Life*, May 10, 1890, 1.

33. "Spalding on the Situation," *Philadelphia Times*, May 10, 1890, 2.

34. "Notes and Gossip," *Sporting Life*, August 16, 1890, 4.

35. "Spalding Is Defiant," *Chicago Tribune*, May 11, 1890, 3.

36. "News Notes and Comments," *Sporting Life*, August 16, 1890, 5.

37. "Still Another Reply," *Pittsburgh Post*, May 12, 1890, 6.

38. "More from Spalding," *Pittsburgh Dispatch*, May 24, 1890, 6.

39. "Too Sweeping by Far," *Sporting Life*, May 17, 1890, 1.

40. "Latest Ball Rumors," *Pittsburgh Dispatch*, July 1, 1890, 6.

41. "John B. Day Wants to Quit," *Chicago Tribune*, July 3, 1890, 6.

42. "Day at Home Again," *New York Evening World*, July 1, 1890, 1.

43. "More from Spalding."

44. Anderson, "Creating the National Pastime."

45. Burk, *Never Just a Game*, 111; Peter Levine, *A. G. Spalding and the Rise of Baseball* (New York: Oxford University Press, 1985), 67.

46. "League Affairs," *Sporting News*, July 12, 1890, 8.

47. "Here's the News for You," *St. Louis Globe-Democrat*, August 19, 1890, 9.

48. "What Will Become of the Old Athletic Club?" *Philadelphia Times*, September 14, 1890, 14; "Final Chapter in the Old Athletic History," *Philadelphia Times*, September 21, 1890, 14.

49. "Base Ball Notes," *Sun* (New York), July 15, 1890, 4.

50. "Al May Buy the Giants," *Chicago Tribune*, July 12, 1890, 6.

51. "President Day's Significant Trip," *Philadelphia Inquirer*, July 29, 1890, 3; "Spalding and the New Yorks," *Chicago Tribune*, July 29, 1890, 6.

52. "More Presidential Views," *Sporting Life*, July 19, 1890, 1.

53. "Notes of the Ball Field," *Minneapolis Journal*, quoted in *Brooklyn Eagle*, July 20, 1890, 2.

54. "The League Accused of Tampering With Players," *Sporting Life*, August 2, 1890, 1.

55. "Another League Failure," *Sporting Life*, August 9, 1890, 5.

56. Spalding, *Baseball: America's National Game*, 296–97.

57. "Another League Failure."

58. "Brunell's Views," *Sporting Life*, August 2, 1890, 1.

59. "Figures Will Lie," *Sporting Life*, August 9, 1890, 1.

60. "Figures Will Lie."

61. "Young on the Brotherhood Attendance," *Chicago Tribune*, August 14, 1890, 6.

62. "Spalding and Munson," *Philadelphia Inquirer*, August 6, 1890, 3; *Indianapolis Journal*, August 6, 1890, 5.

63. "Spalding and Munson."
64. "Spalding's Admission," *Sporting Life*, August 9, 1890, 1.
65. "Figures Will Lie."
66. "News Notes and Comments," *Sporting Life*, August 16, 1890, 5.
67. "Ewing Not a Traitor," *Sporting Life*, August 16, 1890, 8.
68. "Base Ball Notes," *Chicago Tribune*, August 14, 1890, 6.
69. "Notes of the Ball Field," *Brooklyn Eagle*, August 9, 1890, 1.
70. "Doc's Dotlets," *Sporting Life*, August 16, 1890, 3.
71. "Periodical Palaver," *Newsdealer* (San Francisco), June 1890, 1.
72. "Are We in the Game?" *Indianapolis News*, May 29, 1890, 2; "Wanted—a Compromise," *World* (New York), August 7, 1890, 7.
73. "Peace Talk," *Sporting Life*, August 16, 1890, 1, quoting the *St. Louis Star-Sayings*.
74. "President Nimick Sued," *Chicago Tribune*, August 14, 1890, 6.
75. "Will Give Up the Fight," *Sporting Life*, September 6, 1890, 5.
76. "May Cause Its Collapse," *Chicago Tribune*, July 3, 1890, 6.
77. "Syracuse Not Likely to Have Any More Sunday Games," *Philadelphia Times*, July 27, 1890, 14; "Base-Ball Notes," *Chicago Tribune*, August 14, 1890, 6.
78. "The Cincinnati Club," *Cincinnati Enquirer*, September 19, 1890, 2.
79. "Too Much: The Price for the Cincinnati Club," *Cincinnati Enquirer*, September 23, 1890, 1.
80. "That Sensation Is Sprung," *Pittsburgh Post*, September 22, 1890, 6.
81. "Notes and Gossip," *Sporting Life*, September 13, 1890, 4.
82. "Hub Happenings," *Sporting Life*, September 20, 1890, 3.
83. "Spalding Wants the War Ended," *Chicago Tribune*, October 9, 1890, 6.
84. "The Base Ball Conference," *Philadelphia Inquirer*, October 9, 1890, 3.
85. "All In Favor of Peace," *New York Times*, October 10, 1890, 3.
86. "All In Favor of Peace."
87. "World of Sport," *St. Louis Post-Dispatch*, December 21, 1890, 24.
88. "Ready to Make Peace," *Chicago Tribune*, October 10, 1890, 6.
89. "Stormy Conference," *Indianapolis Journal*, October 23, 1890, 5.
90. "Still Negotiating for Peace," *Chicago Tribune*, October 24, 1890, 6; "Looks a Little Brighter," *Pittsburgh Dispatch*, October 25, 1890, 6; "Mr. Spalding Talks," *Inter Ocean* (Chicago), October 28, 1890, 2.
91. "May Compromise but Not Amalgamate," *Chicago Tribune*, October 10, 1890, 6.
92. Spalding, *Baseball: America's National Game*, 288.
93. "Spalding on the Compromise," *New York Times*, October 29, 1890, 8.
94. "May Not Consolidate," *Chicago Tribune*, November 3, 1890, 7.
95. "No Consolidation for Boston," *Chicago Tribune*, November 1, 1890, 6; "Not in It," *Cincinnati Enquirer*, October 30, 1890, 4.
96. "The Players Are Determined," *Sun* (New York), November 1, 1890, 4.
97. "The First Meeting," *Sporting Life*, November 1, 1890, 2.
98. "Base Ball Men Confer," *Inter Ocean* (Chicago), November 2, 1890, 3; "Spalding Is Stubborn," *Inter Ocean* (Chicago), November 4, 1890, 3; "There May Be War Yet," *St. Louis Post-Dispatch*, November 4, 1890, 8; "Will Be No Compromise," *Chicago Tribune*, November 6, 1890, 12.

99. "Players' League Troubles," *Philadelphia Inquirer*, November 5, 1890, 5; "Traitors and Deserters," *Pittsburgh Post*, November 7, 1890, 6.

100. "Crowds in Attendance," *Chicago Tribune*, November 8, 1890, 6.

101. "Meeting of the Magnates," *Pittsburgh Post*, November 12, 1890, 6.

102. "Coming Back to the Fold," *Pittsburgh Post*, November 13, 1890, 6.

103. "Coming Back to the Fold."

104. "The Players' League," *Pittsburgh Post*, November 13, 1890, 6.

105. "Sale of a Baseball Club," *New York Times*, November 14, 1890, 3.

106. "Playing a Game of Bluff," *Pittsburgh Post*, November 17, 1890, 6.

107. "Base Ball Comment," *Philadelphia Inquirer*, September 14, 1890, 7; "Base Ball Comment," *Philadelphia Inquirer*, December 28, 1890, 3.

108. "Bygones, Be Gone," *Boston Globe*, December 14, 1890, 6; "An Option on Syracuse," *Sun* (New York), December 14, 1890, 10.

109. Seymour, *Early Years*, 245.

110. "Spalding Protected the Players," *World* (New York), December 30, 1890, 2; "Spalding Owns Both," *Chicago Tribune*, December 30, 1890, 5; "Taken in by Spalding," *Boston Globe*, December 30, 1890, 4.

111. "Pfeffer and Spalding Agree," *Chicago Tribune*, December 31, 1890, 6.

Chapter 14: Private Passions

1. "Local News," *Fort Wayne News and Sentinel*, June 21, 1890, 8.

2. "Shipping and Mail News," *Birmingham Post*, August 19, 1890, 8.

3. "Spalding Goes to Sea," *Boston Globe*, August 9, 1890, 7.

4. Thorn, *Baseball in the Garden of Eden*, 215; Emmett A. Greenwalt, *The Point Loma Community in California 1897–1942: A Theosophical Experiment* (Berkeley: University of California Press, 1955), 101.

5. "Today's Sailings," *Liverpool Mercury*, October 1, 1890, 8; Thorn, *Baseball in the Garden of Eden*, 216; "Pith of the News," *Inter Ocean* (Chicago), October 9, 1890, 1.

6. "Local News," *Fort Wayne Sentinel*, October 22, 1890, 4.

7. US Census Bureau, Historical Marital Status, Table MS-2, Estimated Median Age at First Marriage, by Sex: 1890 to Present.

8. Charles A. Church and H. H. Waldo, *Past and Present of the City of Rockford and Winnebago County, Illinois* (Chicago: S. J. Clarke Publishing, 1905), 109; "Parlor Concerts," *Rockford Journal*, January 23, 1875, 10; "Mayer-Churchill," *Rockford Weekly Gazette*, January 28, 1875, 8.

9. "Baltimore's Many Ballparks," *Baltimore Sun*, April 9, 1981, 52.

10. "Happenings," *Fort Wayne Daily News*, April 19, 1876, 1; "Local Lines," *Fort Wayne Sentinel*, July 27, 1882, 1; "Gutted at Last," *Fort Wayne Daily News*, April 6, 1885, 1; Thorn, *Baseball in the Garden of Eden*, 208; *History of Walworth County, Wisconsin* (Chicago: Western Historical, 1882), 883.

11. Thorn, *Baseball in the Garden of Eden*, 208.

12. "Local News," *Fort Wayne News and Sentinel*, June 23, 1888, 4.

13. "Voice Culture," *Fort Wayne Daily News*, July 29, 1887, 1; "Parties and Picnics," *Fort Wayne Journal Gazette*, June 24, 1888, 2.

14. "Both Dead: Fiendish Murder in Fall River," *Boston Globe*, August 4, 1892, 1.

15. "Universal Brotherhood," *San Diego Sun*, April 10, 1899, 1.

16. "Disaster on the Cornish Coast," *Newcastle* (England) *Daily Chronicle*, May 22, 1899, 5; "A Liner's Miraculous Escape," *Uttoxeter* (England) *New Era*, May 31, 1899, 3.

17. "Steamship Paris Goes Aground," *New York Times*, May 22, 1899, 1

18. "Mrs. A. G. Spalding Dead," *Asbury Park* (NJ) *Press*, July 10, 1899, 1.

19. "Died in St. Louis," *Fort Wayne News and Sentinel*, April 29, 1902, 1.

20. "Monmouth County Orphans Court," *Daily Standard* (Red Bank, NJ), June 15, 1901, 2.

21. "Spalding Likes Tingley Creed," *Chicago Tribune*, March 30, 1903, 15.

Chapter 15: Bicycle Boom and Bust

1. W. F. Grew, *The Cycle Industry: Its Origins, History, and Latest Developments* (London: Sir Isaac Pitman and Sons, 1921), 14.

2. Levine, *A. G. Spalding and the Rise of Baseball*, 90; "Wheel Notes," *Sporting Life*, November 2, 1887, 7.

3. "Hampden County," *Springfield* (MA) *Daily Republican*, October 11, 1890, 6; Advertisement, *Philadelphia Inquirer*, March 28, 1891, 3.

4. *Springfield* (MA) *Daily Republican*, February 13, 1890, 6.

5. Norman L. Dunham, "The Bicycle in American History" (Ph.D. diss., Harvard University, 1956), 468.

6. Census Office, *Twelfth Census.*

7. Arthur S. Dewing, "The American Bicycle Company," in *Corporate Promotions and Reorganizations* (Cambridge, MA: Harvard University Press, 1914), 249–68; George Pope, "American Bicycle Company," *Report of the Industrial Commission on Trusts and Industrial Combinations, Vol. xii* (Washington, DC: Government Printing Office, 1901), 689.

8. *Cycle Age*, June 1, 1899, 113.

9. Pope, "American Bicycle Company," 688–91.

10. Pope, "American Bicycle Company," 689.

11. Pope, "American Bicycle Company," 689.

12. "Fast Riders Suspended," *Sun* (New York), November 28, 1895, 4.

13. "Wheelmen's Final Acts," *New York Times*, February 14, 1896, 6.

14. "Newsy News."

15. A. G. Spalding advertisement, *Chicago Tribune*, March 26, 1894, 11.

16. A. G. Spalding advertisement, *Inter Ocean* (Chicago), April 15, 1894, 8.

17. "Big Bicycle War," *Meriden* (CT) *Journal*, June 19, 1894, 3; "Hum of the Wheel," *Brooklyn Citizen*, June 16, 1894, 3; "Pot Pourri of Trade Items," *Cycle Age*, June 29, 1899, 217.

18. Victor Sporting Goods advertisement, *Sporting Life*, June 2, 1894, 5; "Hum of the Wheel."

19. "The Overman Failure," *New York Times*, December 29, 1897, 4; "Bicycle Makers Fail," *News* (Paterson, NJ), December 28, 1897, 3.

20. "Cycle Board of Trade," *St. Louis Post-Dispatch*, February 2, 1895, 8.

21. Frank Presbrey, *The History and Development of Advertising* (Garden City, NY: Doubleday, Doran & Company, 1929), 361–62.

22. Dewing, "American Bicycle Company," 252.

23. "Gimbels Buy Out Spalding," *Philadelphia Times*, February 10, 1898, 6; "Spaldings Retire," *Philadelphia Inquirer*, February 10, 1898, 5.

24. Stephen Hardy, "Entrepreneurs, Organizations, and the Sport Marketplace: Subjects in Search of Historians," *Journal of Sport History*, Vol. 13, no. 1 (Spring 1986), 14–33.

25. "American Bicycle Company," *Commercial and Financial Chronicle*, May 1899, 974.

26. "Coleman Organizes New Combine," *Cycle Age*, May 11, 1899, 1.

27. "Bicycle Trust," *Minneapolis Daily Times*, May 14, 1899, 3; "Hitch in the Bicycle Trust," *Hartford Courant*, May 22, 1899, 5.

28. "Commence to See the Light," *Cycle Age*, June 1, 1899, 112.

29. "Commence to See the Light."

30. "Giant Bicycle Trust Formed on New Lines with Forty Millions of Capital," *Baltimore Sun*, July 19, 1899, 8.

31. The cash was provided by an underwriting syndicate headed by the United States Mortgage and Trust Company of New York and Lee, Higginson & Company of Boston, in exchange for bonds. The bonds were 20-year gold debentures—unsecured debt—that paid 5 percent interest annually in US gold coins. The preferred stock paid an annual dividend of 7 percent.

32. "Spalding's Early Plans," *Cycle Age*, June 1, 1899, 111.

33. Pope, "American Bicycle Company," 689.

34. "New Bicycle Company," *New York Times*, May 13, 1899, 7; *The Economist Investors' Supplement*, Chicago 1899; "Giant Bicycle Trust Formed."

35. Dewing, "American Bicycle Company," 254.

36. "Spalding Resigns," *Pittsburgh Press*, January 23, 1900, 5; "Revolt in A. B. C. Management," *Cycle Age*, January 29, 1900, 1.

37. "The Latest and Greatest Cycle Show," *Brooklyn Citizen*, January 21, 1900, 5.

38. "Bicycle Trust Defaults," *New York Times*, September 3, 1902, 2; "Cycle Trust Punctured," *Chicago Tribune*, September 3, 1902, 1.

39. Lawrence W. Fielding and Lori K. Miller, "The ABC Trust: A Chapter in the History of Capitalism in the Sporting Goods Industry," *Sport History Review*, Vol. 29, issue 1 (1998), 44–88.

40. "Colonel Pope Takes Hold," *Boston Evening Transcript*, May 14, 1903, 5.

Chapter 16: Trust Buster

1. "Appointment of A. G. Spalding," *New-York Tribune*, April 22, 1900, 16; "Spalding Appointed Director," *Sun* (New York), April 22, 1900, 33; Walter C. Kelly, "World's Championship Events," *Buffalo Courier*, April 29, 1900, 30.

2. "How Our Men Were Shut Out," *Brooklyn Citizen*, August 9, 1900, 3; "French Sporting Methods at International Games," *Buffalo Enquirer*, August 18, 1900, 4.

3. John V. Grombach, *The Olympics* (New York: Ballantine Books, 1960), 12.

4. "James E. Sullivan Home," *Jersey Journal*, August 17, 1900, 8.

5. "Al Spalding Touted as Nick Young's Successor in the National," *Cincinnati Enquirer*, October 30, 1901, 4.

6. "Mr. Freedman a Magnate," *New York Times*, January 17, 1895; "New York Baseball Club Bought Up," *Chicago Tribune*, January 17, 1895, 11; "New York Club Sale," *Baltimore Sun*, January 18, 1895, 6; "To Control Giants," *Inter Ocean* (Chicago), January 17, 1895, 4.

7. "Baseball Brevities," *New York Times*, February 7, 1895, 7.

8. "Says Four Clubs Will Be Dropped," *Courier-Journal* (Louisville, KY), March 16, 1895, 5.

9. "Gossip of the Diamond," *Sunday News* (Wilkes-Barre, PA), July 14, 1895, 5.

10. "Anson's Debut," *Boston Globe*, December 9, 1895, 7.

11. "Amos Rusie's Demand," *Indianapolis Journal*, April 10, 1896, 8.

12. "Freedman a Scrapper," *Dayton* (OH) *Herald*, March 14, 1899, 6.

13. "A Spurned Magnate," *Times Leader* (Wilkes-Barre, PA), March 25, 1898, 8.

14. "The Giants Go to Pieces," *Philadelphia Inquirer*, April 22, 1896, 5; "Freedman's Club May Discipline Him," *World* (New York), March 15, 1899, 8.

15. Spalding, *Baseball: America's National Game*, 302–3.

16. "Another Baseball Row," *Sun* (New York), July 26, 1898, 4.

17. Spalding, *Baseball: America's National Game*, 304.

18. B. Di Salvatore, *A Clever Base-Ballist: The Life and Times of John Montgomery Ward* (New York: Pantheon, 1999), 362.

19. "Spalding Can Stand Freedman No Longer," *World* (New York), March 16, 1899, 8.

20. "Deutschland In with Many Americans Aboard," *Chicago Tribune*, November 4, 1900, 7.

21. "Comparative Figures," *Sporting Life*, April 12, 1902, 9.

22. "National League Will Take Action," *Buffalo Review*, November 15, 1901, 10.

23. "Much at Stake," *Boston Globe*, December 10, 1901, 4.

24. "Brush Scheme Fails," *Baltimore Sun*, December 12, 1901, 6.

25. "Comparative Figures."

26. "Comment," *Philadelphia Times*, December 12, 1901, 12. "Brush Scheme Fails."

27. "No Trust in Baseball," *New York Times*, December 12, 1901, 10.

28. "A Sensation in Baseball," *Louisville Courier-Journal*, December 14, 1901, 6.

29. "Spalding President of Baseball League," *New York Times*, December 14, 1901; "Spalding Elected (After Many Deadlocks) to Succeed Young," *St. Louis Republic*, December 14, 1901, 4; "Baseball War Is On In Earnest," *Boston Post*, December 15, 1901, 5.

30. Rogers explained that he declared Spalding the winner based on House Speaker Thomas B. Reed's decision on a parliamentary question in Congress. The essence was that members who leave the House without permission should be recorded as present but not voting.

31. "Spalding Gets League Papers," *Chicago Tribune*, December 15, 1901, 17; Spalding, *Baseball: America's National Game*, 318–9.

32. "A Sensation in Baseball."

33. Sam Crane, "Shrewd Move of Spalding," *Pittsburgh Press*, December 15, 1901, 22; "Want Peace in Baseball," *New York Times*, December 27, 1901.

34. "Magnates Adjourn; Spalding in Control," *Brooklyn Eagle*, December 15, 1901, 52.

35. The club issued 1,000 shares: Spalding and his banker, John R. Walsh, owned 320 shares each; Anson, William Brown, and Walter Spalding 130 each; and Hart 83. The remaining 17 were in the hands of small investors.

36. "Freedman Flays Spalding," *New York Times*, December 15, 1901, 13; "Anson Replies to A. G. Spalding," *Chicago Tribune*, December 16, 1901, 6.

37. Anson, *Ball Player's Career*, 307–9.

38. "Cap Anson as Author," *Inter Ocean* (Chicago), April 29, 1900, 25–26.

39. "Spalding Enjoined," *Boston Globe*, December 17, 1901, 4.

40. "Freedman Now Dead Issue with Me; Off Baseball Map, Says Spalding," *Philadelphia Inquirer*, December 17, 1901, 10.

41. "Baseball Injunction Stands," *New York Times*, December 21, 1901, 7.

42. "Freedman's Temporary Victory," *New-York Tribune*, December 21, 1901, 5.

43. "Want Peace in Baseball."

44. "Baseball Hopes Rise," *New York Times*, January 5, 1902, 17; "Talcott to Replace Freedman," *Brooklyn Citizen*, January 5, 1902, 4.

45. "Boston Shift: Triumvirs May Desert Andrew Freedman," *Boston Globe*, January 7, 1902, 2.

46. "Soden Ready to Sell Out," *Boston Globe,* January 11, 1902, 1; "Freedman Feels Happy," *Saint Paul Globe*, January 12, 1902, 8.

47. "Freedman Wins First Round," *Chicago Tribune*, March 30, 1902, 9; "Baseball Case Decided," *New York Times*, March 30, 1902, 11.

48. W. A. Phelon, "Chicago Gleanings," *Sporting Life*, April 12, 1902, 9.

49. "New Baseball President," *New York Times*, April 3, 1902, 10.

50. "Freedman Fades," *Sporting Life*, October 4, 1902, 7.

Chapter 17: Final Innings

1. "$250,000 for Corner," *Inter Ocean* (Chicago), December 4, 1901, 9; "Rumson Property Sold," *Daily Standard* (Red Bank, NJ), April 20, 1901, 3.

2. "Lamar, Wall Street Wolf, Found Dead," *Daily News* (New York), January 14, 1934, 3C.

3. Ron Chernow, *Titan: The Life of John D. Rockefeller, Sr.* (New York: Random House, 1998), 356.

4. "David Lamar Must Move," *Freehold* (NJ) *Transcript* and *Monmouth* (NJ) *Inquirer*, November 30, 1906, 3.

5. "Spalding Wins Case," *Boston Globe*, February 15, 1907, 7.

6. "Spalding a Theosophist," *Ogdensburg* (NY) *News*, April 1, 1903, 4.

7. "Leaves Baseball for Mysticism," *San Francisco Examiner*, March 29, 1903, 27.

8. "Al Spalding Becomes a Citizen of San Diego," *San Diego Sun*, February 22, 1901, 4.

9. "Walsh's Banks Are Insolvent," *Chicago Tribune*, December 18, 1905, 1; "Chicago Banks to Liquidate," *Boston Globe*, December 18, 1905, 1; "J. R. Walsh Arrested for False Bank Return," *New York Times*, March 3, 1906, 1; "J. R. Walsh Guilty; Ridgely Pleased," *New York Times*, January 19, 1908, 28;

10. "The History of Baseball," article in *Spalding's Official Baseball Guide*, 1903, 3–7.

11. In addition to Mills and Sullivan, the commission's lineup included Morgan Bulkeley, Arthur Gorman, Al Reach, George Wright, and Nick Young.

12. Walter R. Littell, "The History of Cooperstown from 1886 to 1929," in *A History of Cooperstown* (Cooperstown, NY: Freeman's Journal Co., 1929).

13. "Origin of Baseball Finally Settled by a Commission," *St. Louis Post-Dispatch*, March 21, 1908, 6.

14. "Oldest Fan Talks of Baseball from 'One Old Cat' Period Down to Game They're Playing Today," *Evening World* (New York), October 9, 1911, 15.

15. "Three Edifices on the Way," *Los Angeles Times*, May 5, 1929, 84.

16. "Good Roads for San Diego County," *San Diego Sun*, July 8, 1907, 1.

17. Mark Souder, "The Guide to Spalding: San Diego, 1900–15," in *The National Pastime: Pacific Ghosts*, ed. Cecilia M. Tan (Phoenix: Society for American Baseball Research, 2019), 10–11; "Spalding for Senator," *Hanford* (CA) *Sentinel*, June 30, 1910, 2.

18. Levine, *A. G. Spalding and the Rise of Baseball*, 141.

19. Richard Crawford, "Sporting Goods Tycoon Left Mark on City," *San Diego Union-Tribune*, April 5, 2008, CZ.3; "History of Baseball," *Boston Globe*, October 30, 1911, 5.

20. Kathy Blavatt, *San Diego's Sunset Cliffs Park: A History* (Charleston, SC: History Press, 2020).

21. "Spalding's End Was Sudden," *Boston Globe*, September 10, 1915, 12.

22. "A. G. Spalding's Unique Career," *St. Louis Post-Dispatch*, September 12, 1915, 2.

23. "Keith Spalding Issues Reply to Stepmother," *San Diego Sun*, October 27, 1915, 7.

24. "Will of A. G. Spalding—Estate Set at $600,000," *Boston Globe*, September 15, 1915, 8.

25. "Spalding Estate Is Over Million," *New York Times*, October 2, 1915, 4.

26. "Spalding Heirs End Will Contest," *San Francisco Bulletin*, July 13, 1917, 1.

27. "Baseball Mask Machine Turns Out Gas Masks, So Spalding Estate Grows," *Sun* (San Diego), October 11, 1917, 7.

28. *A. G. Spalding & Bros., Inc., Petitioner, v. Federal Trade Commission, Respondent*, 301 F.2d 585 (3d Cir. 1962) https://law.justia.com/cases/federal/appellate-courts/F2/301/585/28707/#fn22_ref.

29. "Spalding Co. Undecided on Appeal of FTC Ruling," *Republican* (Chicago), April 20, 1960, 26.

30. "Spalding Sells Rawlings to Group of Investors," *Morning Union* (Springfield, MA), August 17, 1963, 2.

31. "Analysts Assess KKR Investment in Spalding," *Republican* (Springfield, MA), August 18, 1996, H1.

32. Steven Syre, "Trouble Off the Tees," *Boston Globe*, July 3, 2003, E1.

33. "Spalding Sells Sporting Goods Unit to Russell," *Los Angeles Times*, April 18, 2003, 41.

34. "Callaway Golf Announces Acquisition of Top-Flite," company press release, June 30, 2003, https://www.topgolfcallawaybrands.com/news-releases/news-release-details/callaway-golf-announces-acquisition-top-flite (accessed June 2, 2025).

35. "Albert Goodwill Spalding," *Sporting News*, September 18, 1915, 4.

Bibliography

Books

1878 Constitution and Playing Rules of the National League of Professional Baseball Clubs. Chicago: A. G. Spalding & Bros., 1878.

Abrams, Roger I. *The Money Pitch: Baseball Free Agency and Salary Arbitration.* Philadelphia: Temple University Press, 2000.

Album of Genealogy and Biography, Cook County, Illinois, with Portraits. Chicago: La Salle Book Co., 1900.

Alexander, Charles C. *Our Game: An American Baseball History.* New York: MJF Books, 1991.

Alexander, Charles C. *Turbulent Seasons: Baseball in 1890–1891.* Dallas: Southern Methodist University Press, 2011.

Allegrini, Robert V. *Chicago's Grand Hotels*. Charleston, SC: Arcadia, 2005.

Allen, Lee. *100 Years of Baseball: The Intimate and Dramatic Story of Modern Baseball from the Game's Beginnings Up to the Present Day*. New York: Bartholomew House, 1950.

Allen, Lee. *The Cincinnati Reds*. Kent, OH: Kent State University Press, 2006.

Allen, Lee. *The National League Story*. New York: Hill & Wang, 1961.

Alpern, Andrew. *Luxury Apartment Houses of Manhattan: An Illustrated History*. New York: Dover Publications, 1992.

Anderson, George B. *History of New Mexico, Volume 2: Its Resources and People*. Los Angeles: Pacific States Pub. Co., 1907.

Andreas, Alfred Theodore. *History of Chicago*, 3 vols. Chicago: A. T. Andreas Publishing Co., 1885.

Andreas, Alfred Theodore. *History of Cook County, Illinois: From the Earliest Period to the Present Time*. Chicago: A. T. Andreas Publishing Co., 1884.

Anson, Adrian C. *A Ball Player's Career*. Chicago: Era Publishing, 1900.

Appel, Marty. *Slide, Kelly, Slide: The Wild Life and Times of Mike "King" Kelly, Baseball's First Superstar*. Lanham, MD: Scarecrow Press, 1996.

Appletons' Illustrated Railway and Steam Navigation Guide. New York: D. Appleton & Co., June 1867.

Arcidiacono, David, and William J. Ryczek. *Major League Baseball in Gilded Age Connecticut: The Rise and Fall of the Middletown, New Haven and Hartford Clubs*. Jefferson, NC: McFarland & Co., 2009.

Ashcraft, W. Michael. *The Dawn of the New Cycle: Point Loma Theosophists and American Culture*. Knoxville: University of Tennessee Press, 2002.

Bachin, Robin F. *Building the South Side: Urban Space and Civic Culture in Chicago, 1890–1919*. Chicago: University of Chicago Press, 2004.

Bakker, Pamela A. *Eyes on the Sporting Scene, 1870–1930: Will and June Rankin, New York's Sportswriting Brothers*. Jefferson, NC: McFarland & Co., 2013.

Bales, Jack. *Before They Were Cubs: The Early Years of Chicago's First Professional Baseball Team*. Jefferson, NC: McFarland & Co., 2019.

Barkow, Al. *The Golden Era of Golf: How America Rose to Dominate the Old Scots Game*. New York: Thomas Dunne Books, 2000.

Barnard, F. A. *American Biographical History of Eminent and Self-Made Men: Michigan Volume, Part 1*. Cincinnati: Western Biographical Publishing Co., 1878.

Barrows, Isabel C. *Physical Training: A Full Report of the Papers and Discussions of the Conference Held in Boston in November 1889*. Boston: George H. Ellis, 1890.

Bartlett, Arthur. *Baseball and Mr. Spalding*. New York: Farrar, Straus and Young, 1951.

Bateman, Newton, and Paul Selby. *Historical Encyclopedia of Illinois and History of Winnebago County*, Vol. 2. Chicago: Munsell Publishing Co., 1916.

Bateman, Newton, Paul Selby, Horace G. Kauffman, and Rebecca H. Kauffman, eds. *Historical Encyclopedia of Illinois and History of Ogle County*, Vol. 2. Chicago: Munsell Publishing Co., 1909.

Batesel, Paul. *Players and Teams of the National Association*. Jefferson, NC: McFarland & Co., 2012.

Bauer, Robert Allan. *Outside the Lines of Gilded Age Baseball: Alcohol, Fitness, and Cheating in 1880s Baseball*. Grayland, WA: Rob Bauer Books, 2018.

Bauer, Robert Allan. *Outside the Lines of Gilded Age Baseball: Gambling, Umpires, and Racism in 1880s Baseball*. Grayland, WA: Rob Bauer Books, 2018.

Bauer, Robert Allan. *Outside the Lines of Gilded Age Baseball: The Finances of 1880s Baseball*. Grayland, WA: Rob Bauer Books, 2020.

Bauer, Robert Allan. *Outside the Lines of Gilded Age Baseball: The Origins of the 1890 Players League*. Grayland, WA: Rob Bauer Books, 2018.

Beckwith, Albert Clayton. *History of Walworth County, Wisconsin*. Indianapolis: B. F. Bowen & Co., 1913.

Beers, F. W. *Gazetteer and Biographical Record of Genesee County, N.Y., 1788–1890*. Syracuse, NY: J. W. Vose & Co., 1890.

Besant, Walter, and James Rice. *The Seamy Side: A Story*. New York: Dodd, Mead & Co., 1888 (originally published as a serial in 1879).

Betts, John Rickards. *America's Sporting Heritage: 1850–1950*. Reading, MA: Addison-Wesley Publishing Company, 1974.

Bevis, Charlie. *Tim Keefe: A Biography of the Hall of Fame Pitcher and Player-Rights Advocate*. Jefferson, NC: McFarland & Co., 2015.

Biographical Directory of the State of New York. New York: Biographical Directory Co., 1899.

A Biographical History with Portraits of Prominent Men of the Great West. Chicago: Manhattan Publishing Company, 1894.

The Biographical Record of Ogle County, Illinois. Chicago: S. J. Clarke Publishing Co., 1899.

Birmingham, Stephen. *Our Gang: The Great Jewish Families of New York*. New York: Harper, 1967.

Blavatt, Kathy. *San Diego's Sunset Cliffs Park: A History*. Charleston, SC: History Press, 2020.

Block, David, and Tim Wiles. *Baseball Before We Knew It: A Search for the Roots of the Game*. Lincoln: University of Nebraska Press, 2005.

Blume, Kenneth J. *Historical Dictionary of the U.S. Maritime Industry*. Lanham, MD: Scarecrow Press, 2012.

Bond, Gregory. *Jim Crow at Play: Race, Manliness, and the Color Line in American Sports, 1876–1916*. Madison: University of Wisconsin, 2008.

Bostock, Frances, and Geoffrey Jones. "Foreign Multinationals in British Manufacturing, 1850–1962." In *The Making of Global Enterprise*, edited by Geoffrey Jones. London: Frank Cass & Co., 1994.

Bowdidge, John S. "Toys and Sporting Goods." In *Manufacturing: A Historical and Bibliographical Guide*, edited by David O. Whitten and Bessie Emrick Whitten. Westport, CT: Greenwood Press, 1990.

Boyd, William H. *Boyd's Directory of Washington and Georgetown*. Washington, DC: Boyd's Directory Co., 1867.

Bradford, J. R. *The Stranger's Guide to the City of Chicago*. Chicago: Southard & Cullaton, 1873.

Bradsby, Henry C. *History of Bradford County, Pennsylvania: With Biographical Selections*. Chicago: S.B. Nelson & Co., 1891.

Brooks, Noah. *Our Base Ball Club and How It Won the Championship*. New York: E. P. Dutton, 1884.

Brown, Ira Gertrude. *The Panic of 1873*. Berkeley: University of California Press, 1928.

Brown, Warren. *The Chicago Cubs*. New York: G. P. Putnam Sons, 1946.

Burchell, H. P., ed. *Spalding's Official Lawn Tennis Annual*. New York: American Sports Publishing, 1908.

Burk, Robert F. *Never Just a Game: Players, Owners, and American Baseball to 1920*. Chapel Hill, NC: University of North Carolina Press, 1994.

Butsch, Richard. *For Fun and Profit: The Transformation of Leisure into Consumption*. Philadelphia: Temple University Press, 1990.

Caillault, Jean-Pierre. *A Tale of Four Cities: Nineteenth Century Baseball's Most Exciting Season in Contemporary Accounts*. Jefferson, NC: McFarland & Co., 2003.

Carlisle, Rodney P., ed. *Encyclopedia of Play in Today's Society*. Thousand Oaks, CA: SAGE Publications, 2009.

Carnegie, Andrew. *The Gospel of Wealth*. New York: Century Co., 1902.

Carter, Scott Sigmund, Susan B. Carter, Michael R. Haines, Alan L. Olmsted, Richard Sutch, and Gavin Wright, eds. *Historical Statistics of the United States, Earliest Times to the Present*. New York: Cambridge University Press, 2006.

Cash, Jon David. *Before They Were Cardinals: Major League Baseball in Nineteenth-Century St. Louis*. Columbia: University of Missouri Press, 2002.

Chadwick, Henry. *The Game of Base Ball: How to Learn It, How to Play It, and How to Teach It*. New York: George Munro & Co., 1868.

Chadwick, Henry, ed., *Spalding's Baseball Guide and Official League Handbook.* Chicago: A. G. Spalding & Bros., 1890.

Chance, Joseph E., ed. *My Life in the Old Army: The Reminiscences of Abner Doubleday from the Collections of the New-York Historical Society*. Fort Worth: Texas Christian University Press, 1998.

Chandler, David Leon. *Henry Flagler: The Astonishing Life and Times of the Visionary Robber Baron Who Founded Florida*. New York: Macmillan, 1986.

Charlton, James, ed. *The Baseball Chronology: The Complete History of the Most Important Events in the Game of Baseball.* New York: Macmillan, 1991.

Chernow, Ron. *Titan: The Life of John D. Rockefeller, Sr.* New York: Random House, 1997.

Chetwynd, Josh. *Baseball in Europe: A Country-by-Country History*. Jefferson, NC: McFarland & Co., 2008.

Chetwynd, Josh. "Great Britain: Baseball's Battle for Respect in the Land of Cricket, Rugby and Soccer." In *Baseball Without Borders: The International Pastime*, edited by George Gmelch. Lincoln: University of Nebraska Press, 2006.

Chicago's First Half Century. Chicago: Inter Ocean Publishing Co., 1883.

Chicopee Illustrated, 1896. Holyoke, MA: Transcript Publishing Co., 1896.

Church, Charles A. *History of Rockford and Winnebago County Illinois: From the First Settlement in 1834 to the Civil War*. Rockford, IL: New England Society of Rockford, IL, 1900.

Church, Charles A. *History of Winnebago County*. Chicago: Munsell Publishing, 1916.

Church, Charles A. *Past and Present of the City of Rockford and Winnebago County, Illinois.* Chicago: S. J. Clarke Publishing, 1905.

Church, Seymour Roberts. *Base Ball: The History, Statistics and Romance of the American National Game from Its Inception to the Present Time, Volume 1, 1845–1871*. San Francisco: Seymour R. Church, 1902.

Churchill, Gardner Asaph, and Nathaniel Wiley Churchill. *The Churchill Family in America*. Privately published, 1904.

Clark, Ira G. *Water in New Mexico: A History of Its Management and Use*. Albuquerque: University of New Mexico Press, 1987.

Clark, Victor S. *History of Manufactures in the United States, Vol. II*. Washington, DC: Carnegie Institution, 1916.

Coggeshall, William T. *Lincoln Memorial: The Journeys of Abraham Lincoln*. Columbus: Ohio State Journal, 1865.

Commercial and Agricultural Chicago. Chicago: G. W. Orear, 1887.

Conant, Charles A. *A History of Modern Bank Issue, With an Account of the Economic Crises of the Present Century*. New York: G. P. Putnam's Sons, 1902.

Cook, Sir Theodore Andrea. *The Olympic Games of 1908 in London: A Reply to Certain Criticisms*. London: Amateur Athletic Association, 1908.

Cook, William A. *The Louisville Grays Scandal of 1877: The Taint of Gambling at the Dawn of the National League*. Jefferson, NC: McFarland & Co., 2005.

Corcoran, Dennis. *Induction Day at Cooperstown: A History of the Baseball Hall of Fame Ceremony*. Jefferson, NC: McFarland & Co., 2010.

Crawford, Richard W. *San Diego Yesterday*. Charleston, SC: History Press, 2013.

Cremin, Dennis H. *Grant Park: The Evolution of Chicago's Front Yard*. Carbondale: Southern Illinois University Press, 2013.

Crocchiola, Stanley Francis Louis (F. Stanley, pseud.). *The Deming, New Mexico, Story*. Texas: Pantex, 1962.

Cronon, William. *Nature's Metropolis: Chicago and the Great West*. New York: Norton, 1991.

Crown, Judith, and Glenn Coleman. *No Hands: The Rise and Fall of the Schwinn Bicycle Company, an American Institution*. New York: Henry Holt & Co. 1996.

Currey, Josiah Seymour. *Chicago: Its History and Its Builders*. Chicago: S. J. Clarke Publishing Company, 1912.

Danzig, Allison, and Joe Reichler. *The History of Baseball: Its Greatest Players, Teams and Managers*. Englewood, NJ: Prentice Hall, 1959.

Davis, Susan O'Connor. *Chicago's Historic Hyde Park*. Chicago: University of Chicago Press, 2013.

Derby, George, and James Terry White. *National Cyclopædia of American Biography, Volume 14*. New York: James T. White & Co., 1910.

Devine, Christopher. *Harry Wright: The Father of Professional Base Ball*. Jefferson, NC: McFarland & Co., 2003.

Dewing, Arthur Stone. "The American Bicycle Company." In *Corporate Promotions and Reorganizations, Volume 10*. Cambridge, MA: Harvard University Press, 1914.

Di Salvatore, Bryan. *A Clever Base-Ballist: The Life and Times of John Montgomery Ward*. New York: Pantheon Books, 1999.

Dickey, Glenn. *The History of National League Baseball Since 1876*. New York: Stein & Day, 1979.

Dill, James B. *The General Corporation Act of New Jersey*. New York: Baker, Voorhis & Co., 1903.

Doggett, Laurence L. *History of the Boston Young Men's Christian Association*. Boston: YMCA, 1901.

Dorsey, Edward Bates. *English and American Railroads Compared*. New York: John Wiley & Sons, 1887.

Dyreson, Mark. *Crafting Patriotism for Global Dominance: America at the Olympics*. London: Routledge, 2009.

Dyreson, Mark. *Making the American Team: Sport, Culture, and the Olympic Experience*. Urbana: University of Illinois Press, 1998.

Edie Hill, Thomas. *The New Revised Hill's Manual of Social and Business Forms: A Guide to Correct Writing*. Chicago: W. B. Conkey, 1897.

Elders, James E. *The Tour to End All Tours: The Story of Major League Baseball's 1913–1914 World Tour*. Lincoln: University of Nebraska Press, 2003.

Ellard, Harry. *Baseball in Cincinnati: A History*. Cincinnati: Johnson & Hardy, 1907.

Elstner, Charles E. *The Industries of Louisville, Kentucky, and New Albany, Indiana*. Louisville: J. M. Elstner, 1886.

Enright, Jim. *Chicago Cubs: Baseball's Great Teams*. New York: Collier Books, 1975.

Epperson, Bruce D. *Peddling Bicycles to America: The Rise of an Industry*. Jefferson, NC: McFarland & Co., 2010.

Farrington, S. Kip, Jr. *Fishing the Pacific, Offshore and On*. New York: Van Rees Press, 1953.

Felber, Bill, Mark Fimoff, Len Levin, and Peter Mancuso, eds. *Inventing Baseball: The 100 Greatest Games That Shaped the 19th Century*. Phoenix: Society for American Baseball Research, 2013.

Field, Russell, ed. *Playing for Change: The Continuing Struggle for Sport and Recreation*. Toronto: University of Toronto Press, 2015.

Findlay, James F. *Dwight L. Moody, American Evangelist, 1837–1899*. Chicago: University of Chicago Press, 1969.

Findling, John E., and Kimberly D. Pelle. *Historical Dictionary of the Modern Olympic Movement*. Westport, CT: Greenwood Press, 1996.

Fisher, Charles Eben. *The Story of the Old Colony Railroad*. Taunton, MA: C. A. Hack & Son, 1919.

Fitzgerald, Robert Allan. *Wickets in the West: or, The Twelve in America*. London: Tinsley Brothers, 1873.

Fleitz, David L. *Cap Anson: The Grand Old Man of Baseball*. Jefferson, NC: McFarland & Co., 2005.

Fleitz, David L. *Ghosts in the Gallery at Cooperstown: Sixteen Forgotten Members of the Hall of Fame*. Jefferson, NC: McFarland & Co., 2004.

Foster, F. Apthorp, ed. *Vital Records of West Bridgewater Massachusetts to the Year 1850*. Boston: New England Historic Genealogical Society, 1911.

Fox, Stephen. *Big Leagues: Professional Baseball, Football, and Basketball in National Memory*. Lincoln: University of Nebraska Press, 1994.

Francis, Bill. "Diamonds to Dollars." In *Baseball Memories & Dreams*. Coral Gables, FL: Mango Publishing, 2022.

Freeman, W. B., and R. H. Bolster. *Surface Water Supply of the United States Part VIII, Western Gulf of Mexico*. Washington, DC: Government Printing Office, 1911.

French, John Homer. *Gazetteer of the State of New York*. Syracuse, NY: R. Pearsall Smith, 1860.

Friss, Evan. *The Cycling City: Bicycles and Urban America in the 1890s*. Chicago: University of Chicago Press, 2015.

Frommer, Harvey. *Old Time Baseball: America's Pastime in the Gilded Age*. Lanham, MD: Taylor Trade Publishing, 2006.

Frommer, Harvey. *Primitive Baseball: The First Quarter Century of the National Pastime*. New York: Atheneum, 1988.

Frost, Mark. *The Greatest Game Ever Played: Harry Vardon, Francis Ouimet and the Birth of Modern Golf*. New York: Hyperion, 2002.

Foulds, Alan E. *Boston's Ballparks and Arenas*. Lebanon, NH: University Press of New England, 2005.

Furst, R. Terry. *Early Professional Baseball and the Sporting Press: Shaping the Image of the Game*. Jefferson, NC: McFarland & Co., 2014.

Gabrielan, Randall. *Red Bank, Vol. III*. Mount Pleasant, SC: Arcadia Publishing, 1998.

Gabrielan, Randall. *Rumson: Shaping a Superlative Suburb*. Mount Pleasant, SC: Arcadia Publishing, 2003.

Gagnon, Cappy. *Notre Dame Baseball Greats: From Anson to Yaz*. Mount Pleasant, SC: Arcadia Publishing, 2004.

Garraty, John A., and Mark C. Carnes. *American National Biography*. Oxford: Oxford University Press, 1999.

Gelzheiser, Robert P. *Labor and Capital in 19th Century Baseball*. Jefferson, NC: McFarland & Co., 2005.

Gems, Gerald R. "The Gilded Age and the Progressive Era, 1865–1920." In *A Companion to American Sport History*, edited by Steven A. Riess. Hoboken, NJ: John Wiley & Sons, 2014.

Gems, Gerald, Linda Borish, and Gertrud Pfister. *Sports in American History: From Colonization to Globalization*. Champaign, IL: Human Kinetics, 2008.

Gershman, Michael. *Diamonds: The Evolution of the Ballpark*. Boston: Houghton Mifflin, 1993.

Gilbert, James B. *Perfect Cities: Chicago's Utopias of 1893*. Chicago: University of Chicago Press, 1991.

Gilbert, Thomas W. *How Baseball Happened: Outrageous Lies Exposed! The True Story Revealed*. Boston: David R. Godine, 2020.

Gilbert, Tom. *Baseball and the Color Line*. New York: Franklin Watts, 1995.

Ginsburg, Daniel E. *The Fix Is In: A History of Baseball Gambling and Game Fixing Scandals*. Jefferson, NC: McFarland & Co., 1995.

Glazier, Willard. *Peculiarities of American Cities*. Philadelphia: Hubbard Brothers, 1883.

Gmlech, George, ed. *Baseball without Borders: The International Pastime*. Lincoln: University of Nebraska Press, 2006.

Goddard, Stephen B. *Colonel Albert Pope and His American Dream Machines: The Life and Times of a Bicycle Tycoon Turned Automotive Pioneer*. Jefferson, NC: McFarland & Co., 2000.

Gold, Eddie, and Art Ahrens. *The Golden Era Cubs, 1876–1940*. Chicago: Bonus Books, 1985.

Goldstein, William. *Playing for Keeps: A History of Early Baseball*. Ithaca, NY: Cornell University Press, 1989.

Golenbock, Peter. *Wrigleyville: A Magical History Tour of the Chicago Cubs*. New York: St. Martin's Griffin, 1999.

Goodspeed, Weston A., and Daniel D. Healy. *History of Cook County, Illinois, Volume 2*. Chicago: Goodspeed Historical Association, 1909.

Goodwill, Thomas J. *Three Hundred Years in America: A History of the Goodwill Family*. Self-published, 1985.

Gore, James Howard. *American Legionnaires of France: A Directory of the Citizens of the United States on Whom France Has Conferred Her National Order the Legion of Honor*. Washington, DC: W. F. Roberts, 1910.

Graham, Frank. *The New York Giants: An Informal History of a Great Baseball Club*. New York: G. P. Putnam's Sons, 1952.

Green, James. *Death in the Haymarket: A Story of Chicago, the First Labor Movement and the Bombing That Divided Gilded Age America*. New York: Pantheon, 2006.

Greenwalt, Emmett A. *The Point Loma Community in California 1897–1942: A Theosophical Experiment*. Berkeley: University of California, 1955.

Grew, W. F. *The Cycle Industry: Its Origins, History, and Latest Developments.* London: Sir Isaac Pitman and Sons, 1921.

Griswold, Bert J. *The Pictorial History of Fort Wayne, Indiana: A Review of Two Centuries of Occupation of the Region About the Head of the Maumee River, Volume 1.* Chicago: Robert O. Law Co., 1917.

Griswold, Kenneth. *Baseball in Rockford.* Mount Pleasant, SC: Arcadia Publishing, 2003.

Grobani, Anton. *Guide to Baseball Literature*. Detroit: Gale Research Co., 1975.

Grombach, John V. *The Olympics*. New York: Ballantine Books, 1960.

Grossman, James R., Ann Durkin Keating, and Janice L. Reiff, eds. *The Encyclopedia of Chicago*. Chicago: University of Chicago Press, 2004.

Grow, Nathaniel. *Baseball on Trial.* Champaign: University of Illinois Press, 2014.

Gunmann, Allen. *The Games Must Go On: Avery Brundage and the Olympic Movement.* New York: Columbia University Press, 1984.

Guschov, Stephen D. *The Red Stockings of Cincinnati: Base Ball's First All-Professional Team and Its Historic 1869 and 1870 Seasons.* Jefferson, NC: McFarland & Co., 1998.

Gustaitis, Joseph. *Chicago's Greatest Year, 1893: The White City and the Birth of a Modern Metropolis.* Carbondale: Southern Illinois University Press, 2013.

Hager, Louis P., and Albert D. Handy. *History of the Old Colony Railroad.* Boston: Hager & Handy, 1893.

Hamilton, Neil A. *American Business Leaders: From Colonial Times to the Present, Volume 2.* Santa Barbara, CA: ABC–CLIO, 1999.

Hample, Zack. *The Baseball: Stunts, Scandals and Secrets Beneath the Stitches.* New York: Random House, 2011.

Hannan, Caryn. *Illinois Biographical Dictionary.* St. Clair Shores, MI: Somerset Publishers, 2008.

Hardy, James D., Jr. *The New York Giants Baseball Club: The Growth of a Team and a Sport, 1870–1900.* Jefferson City, NC: McFarland & Co., 1996.

Hardy, Stephen. "Entrepreneurs, Structure, Sportgeist," "James E. Sullivan (1860–1914)," and "Albert Goodwill Spalding (1850–1915)." In *Essays on Sport History and Sport Mythology*, edited by Donald G. Kyle and Gary D. Stark. College Station: Texas A&M University Press, 1990.

Harrison, Mitchell C. *New York State's Prominent and Progressive Men*, vol. II. New York: New York Tribune, 1900.

Hart, William. *East Orange in Vintage Postcards.* Mount Pleasant, SC: Arcadia Publishing, 2000.

Hefter, Natalie, ed. *Hilton Head Island.* Mount Pleasant, SC: Arcadia Publishing, 1998.

Helyar, John. *Lords of the Realm: The Real History of Baseball.* New York: Ballantine Books, 1994.

Henderson, Robert W. *Ball, Bat and Bishop: The Origin of Ball Games.* New York: Rockport Press, 1947.

Hetrick, J. Thomas. *Chris Von der Ahe and the St. Louis Browns*. Lanham, MD: Scarecrow Press, 1999.

Heverly, C. F. *History of the Towandas, 1770–1886*. Towanda, PA: Reporter–Journal Printing Co., 1886.

Hinton, Richard J. *The Hand-Book to Arizona: Its Resources, History, Towns, Mines, Ruins, and Scenery*. San Francisco: Payot, Upham & Co., 1878.

The History of Ogle County, Illinois. Chicago: H. F. Kett & Co., 1878.

History of Walworth County, Wisconsin. Chicago: Western Historical Co., 1882.

Horrall, Andrew. *Popular Culture in London c. 1890–1918: The Transformation of Entertainment*. Manchester: Manchester University Press, 2001.

Horton, Ralph L., ed. *Spalding Baseball Guides 1876–1905*. St. Louis: Horton Publishing Co., 1987 reprint.

Hotchkiss, George Woodward. *History of the Lumber and Forest Industry of the Northwest*. Chicago: George W. Hotchkiss & Co., 1898.

Huot, Leland, and Alfred Powers. *Homer Davenport of Silverton: Life of a Great Cartoonist*. Bingen, WA: West Shore Press, 1973.

Hurd, D. Hamilton, ed. *History of Plymouth County, Massachusetts*. Philadelphia: J. W. Lewis & Co., 1884.

Hutchison, Ray, "Capitalism, Religion and Reform: The Social History of Temperance in Harvey, Illinois." In *Drinking: Behavior and Belief in Modern History*, edited by Susanna Barrows and Robin Room, 184–216. Berkeley: University of California Press, 1991.

An Illustrated History of New Mexico. Chicago: Lewis Publishing Co., 1895.

Inter-Collegiate Prohibition Association of the United States. *The Plutocrat, and Eleven Other Orations, Delivered at the National Contest of the Inter-Collegiate Prohibition Convention at Harvey, Illinois, June 30, 1893*. Springfield, IL: Inter-Collegiate Co., 1893.

Ivor-Campbell, Frederick. "The Many Fathers of Baseball." In *The American Game*, edited by Lawrence Baldassaro and Dick Johnson. Carbondale: Southern Illinois University, 2002.

Ivor-Campbell, Frederick, Robert L. Tiemann, and Mark Rucker, eds. *Baseball's First Stars*. Cleveland: Society for American Baseball Research, 1996.

James, Bill. *The Bill James Guide to Baseball Managers from 1870 to Today*. New York: Scribner, 1997.

Jenkins, Rebecca. *The First London Olympics: 1908*. London: Hachette Digital, 2008.

Jensen, Don, ed. *Base Ball 12: New Research on the Early Game*. Jefferson, NC: McFarland & Co., 2021.

Jensen, Don. *The Timeline History of Baseball*. New York: Palgrave McMillan, 2005.

Jentz, John B., and Richard Schneirov. *Chicago in the Age of Capital: Class, Politics, and Democracy During the Civil War and Reconstruction*. Urbana: University of Illinois Press, 2012.

Johnson, Clifton. *Hampden County, 1636–1936*. New York: American Historical Society, 1936.

Johnson, Crisfield. *History of Allegan and Barry Counties, Michigan, with Illustrations and Biographical Sketches of Their Men and Pioneers*. Philadelphia: D. W. Ensign & Co., 1880.

Joiner, Thekla Ellen. *Sin in the City: Chicago and Revivalism, 1880–1920.* Columbia: University of Missouri Press, 2010.

Jones, Eliot. *The Trust Problem in the United States*. New York: Macmillan, 1921.

Josephson, Matthew. *The Robber Barons: The Great American Capitalists, 1861–1901*. New York: Harcourt Brace, 1962.

Kaese, Harold. *The Boston Braves, 1871–1953*. New York: G. P. Putnam's Sons, 1954.

Kane, Thomas P. *The Romance and Tragedy of Banking: Problems and Incidents of Governmental Supervision of National Banks*. New York: Bankers Publishing Co., 1923.

Keating, R. K. *Wheel Man: Robert M. Keating, Pioneer of Bicycles, Motorcycles and Automobiles*. Jefferson, NC: McFarland, 2014.

Kelly, Michael J. *Play Ball: Stories of the Diamond Field and Other Historical Writings About the 19th Century Hall of Famer*. Boston: Emery & Hughes, 1888 (Jefferson, NC: McFarland & Co., 2006 reprint).

Kett, H. F. *The History of Winnebago County, Ill.* Chicago: H. F. Kett Co., 1877.

King, Moses. *King's Handbook of New York City*. Boston: Moses King, 1893.

King, Moses. *King's Photographic Views of New York*. Boston: Moses King, 1895.

Kingman, Bradford. *History of Brockton, Plymouth County, Massachusetts, 1656–1894*. Syracuse, NY: D. Mason & Co., 1895.

Kirsch, George B. *Baseball in Blue & Gray: The National Pastime During the Civil War*. Princeton, NJ: Princeton University Press, 2003.

Kirsch, George B., Othello Harris, and Claire Elaine Nolte. *Encyclopedia of Ethnicity and Sports in the United States*. Westport, CT: Greenwood, 2000.

Knowles, Richard George, and Richard Morton. *Baseball*. London: George Routledge & Sons, 1896.

Koehler, A. E. *New Mexico the Land of Opportunity*. Albuquerque: Albuquerque Morning Journal, 1915.

Koszarek, Ed. *The Players League: History, Clubs, Ballplayers and Statistics*. Jefferson, NC: McFarland & Co., 2006.

Kuhn, Alvin Boyd. *Theosophy: A Modern Revival of Ancient Wisdom*. New York: H. Holt, 1930.

Lamb, Chris. *Conspiracy of Silence: Sportswriters and the Long Campaign to Desegregate Baseball*. Lincoln: University of Nebraska, 2012.

Lamster, Mark. *Spalding's World Tour: The Epic Adventure that Took Baseball Around the Globe—and Made It America's Game*. New York: Public Affairs, 2007.

Langtry, Albert Perkins, ed. *Metropolitan Boston: A Modern History*, vol. 2. New York: Lewis Historical Publishing Co., 1929.

Lauck, William Jett. *The Causes of the Panic of 1893*. Boston: Houghton Mifflin & Co., 1907.

Leitner, Irving A. *Baseball: Diamond in the Rough*. New York: Criterion Books, 1972.

LeMoine, Bob, and Bill Nowlin, eds. *Boston's First Nine: The 1871–75 Boston Red Stockings*. Phoenix: Society for American Baseball Research, 2016.

Leonard, John W. *Who's Who in Chicago: The Book of Chicagoans, a Biographical Dictionary of Leading Living Men and Women of the City of Chicago and Environs*. Chicago: A. N. Marquis & Co., 1905.

Leonard, William J. *Sea Bright, Rumson Road, Oceanic, Monmouth Beach, Atlantic Highlands, Leonardville Road, Navesink, Water Witch Club: Concerning Summer Homes Along the Shores of Monmouth County New Jersey*. Sea Bright, NJ: The Sentinel, 1903.

Leventhal, Josh. *A History of Baseball in 100 Objects*. New York: Black Dog & Leventhal, 2015.

Levine, Peter. *A. G. Spalding and the Rise of Baseball: The Promise of American Sport*. New York: Oxford University Press, 1985.

Levitt, Daniel R. *The Battle That Forged Modern Baseball: The Federal League Challenge and Its Legacy*. Lanham, MD: Ivan R. Dee, 2012.

Lewis, Edward, ed. *An Illustrated History of New Mexico: From the Earliest Period of Its Discovery to the Present Time*. Chicago: Lewis Publishing Co., 1895.

Lieb, Frederick G. *The Baseball Story*. New York: G. P. Putnam's Sons, 1950.

Lieb, Frederick G. *The Pittsburgh Pirates*. New York: G. P. Putnam's Sons, 1948.

Light, Jonathan Fraser. *The Cultural Encyclopedia of Baseball*. Jefferson, NC: McFarland & Co., 2005.

Littell, Walter R. "The History of Cooperstown from 1886 to 1929." In *A History of Cooperstown*. Cooperstown, NY: Freeman's Journal Co., 1929.

Lomax, Michael E. *Black Baseball Entrepreneurs, 1860–1901: Operating by Any Means Necessary*. Syracuse, NY: Syracuse University Press, 2003.

Long, Clarence D. *Wages and Earnings in the United States, 1860–1890*. Princeton, NJ: Princeton University Press, 1960.

Lowenfish, Lee. *The Imperfect Diamond: A History of Baseball's Labor Wars*. Lincoln: University of Nebraska Press, 1980.

Lucas, Charles J. P. *The Olympic Games, 1904*. St. Louis: Woodward & Tiernan, 1905.

Lucas, John. *The Modern Olympic Games*. New York, A. S. Barnes, 1980.

Lundin, Jon W. *Rockford: An Illustrated History*. Chatsworth, CA: Windsor Publications, 1989.

Macdonald, Neil W. *The League That Lasted: 1876 and the Founding of the National League of Professional Base Ball Clubs*. Jefferson, NC: McFarland & Co., 2004.

Macht, Norman L. *Connie Mack and the Early Years of Baseball*. Lincoln: University of Nebraska Press, 2007.

Magee, David, and Philip Shirley. *Sweet Spot: 125 Years of Baseball and the Louisville Slugger*. Chicago: Triumph Books, 2009.

The Manufacturing Interests. Chicago: Goodspeed Publishing Co., 1894.

Markham, Jerry. *A Financial History of the United States*. Armonk, NY: M. E. Sharpe, 2002.

Masteralexis, Lisa Pike, Carol A. Barr, and Mary A. Hums. *Principles and Practice of Sports Management*. Sudbury, MA: Jones & Bartlett Learning, 2011.

Matthews, George R. *America's First Olympics: The St. Louis Games of 1904*. Columbia: University of Missouri Press, 2005.

Matthews, George, and Sandra Marshall. *St. Louis Olympics 1904*. Mount Pleasant, SC: Arcadia Publishing, 2003.

McCoy's Rockford City Directory, 1920. Rockford, IL: McCoy Directory Co., 1920.

McCulloch, Ron. *Baseball Roots: The Fascinating Birth of America's Game and the Amazing Players That Were Its Champions*. Lynchburg, VA: Warwick House, 2000.

McCulloch, Ron, and Ron M. Warwick. *From Cartwright to Shoeless Joe: The Warwick Compendium of Early Baseball*. Lynchburg, VA: Warwick House, 1998.

McGraw, Blanche S. *The Real McGraw*. New York: Van Rees Press, 1953.

McNeil, William F. *The Evolution of Pitching in Major League Baseball*. Jefferson, NC: McFarland & Co., 2006.

Melville, Tom. *Early Baseball and the Rise of the National League*. Jefferson, NC: McFarland & Co., 2001.

Miller, Donald L. *City of the Century: The Epic of Chicago and the Making of America*. New York: Simon & Schuster, 1997.

Miller, Patrick B., and David K. Wiggins, eds. *Sport and Color Line: Black Athletes and Race Relations in the Twentieth Century*. New York: Routledge, 2004.

Minan, John H., and Kevin Cole. *The Little White Book of Baseball Law*. Chicago: American Bar Association, 2009.

Moreland, George L. *Balldom, the Britannica of Baseball: Comprising the Growth of the Game in Detail*. New York: Balldom Pub. Co., 1914.

Morris, Charles, ed. *Men of the Century: An Historical Work Giving Portraits and Sketches of Eminent Citizens of the United States*. Philadelphia: L. R. Hammersly & Co., 1896.

Morris, Peter. *But Didn't We Have Fun? An Informal History of Baseball's Pioneer Era, 1843–1870*. Lanham, MD: Ivan R. Dee, 2010.

Morris, Peter. *A Game of Inches: The Stories Behind the Innovations That Shaped Baseball*. Lanham, MD: Ivan R. Dee, 2006.

Morris, Peter, William J. Ryczek, and Jan Finkel, eds. *Baseball Pioneers, 1850–1870: The Clubs and Players Who Spread the Sport Nationwide*. Jefferson, NC: McFarland & Co., 2012.

Morse, J.C. *Sphere and Ash*. Boston: J.F. Spofford & Co., 1888.

Moyal, Monique. "From Spalding Through Beane: A Study of Economic Trendsetters in Baseball." In *Baseball/Literature/Culture: Essays, 2006–2007*, edited by Ronald E. Kates and Warren Tormey. Jefferson, NC: McFarland & Co., 2008.

Mullin, Bernard J., Stephen Hardy, and William A. Sutton. *Sport Marketing*. Champaign, IL: Human Kinetics, 2007.

Naismith, James. *Basketball: Its Origins and Development*. New York: Association Press, 1941.

Names, Larry D. *Bury My Heart at Wrigley Field: When the Cubs Were the White Sox*. Neshkoro, WI: Sportsbook Publishing Company, 1990.

Nasaw, David. *Going Out: The Rise and Fall of Public Amusements*. New York: Basic Books, 1993.

Nash, Jay Robert. *People to See: An Anecdotal History of Chicago's Makers and Breakers*. Lanham, MD: Rowman & Littlefield, 1981.

Nelson, William, ed. *The New Jersey Coast in Three Centuries: History of the New Jersey Coast, Volume 2*. New York: Lewis Publishing Co., 1902.

Nemec, David. *The Beer and Whisky League: The Illustrated History of the American Association—Baseball's Renegade Major League*. Guilford, CT: Lyons Press, 2004.

Nemec, David. *The Great 19th Century Encyclopedia of Major League Baseball*. New York: Dutton, 1997.

Nemec, David. *Major League Baseball Profiles, 1871–1900, Volume 1: The Ballplayers Who Built the Game*. Lincoln: University of Nebraska Books, 2011.

Nemec, David. *The Official Rules of Baseball Illustrated*. Guilford, CT: Lyons Press, 2006.

Nemec, David. *The Rank and File of 19th Century Major League Baseball: Biographies of 1,084 Players, Owners, Managers and Umpires*. Jefferson, NC: McFarland & Co., 2012.

Nicholson, James C. *The Notorious John Morrissey: How a Bare-Knuckle Brawler Became a Congressman and Founded Saratoga Race Course*. New York: Oxford University Press, 2016.

The North Western Reporter, vol. 78. St. Paul: West Publishing Co., 1899.

Nutt, John J. *Newburgh: Her Institutions, Industries and Leading Citizens*. Newburgh, NY: Ritchie & Hull, 1891.

Orem, Preston D., ed. *Baseball 1845–1881: From the Newspaper Accounts*. Altadena, CA: Self-published, 1961.

Origin, Growth, and Usefulness of the Chicago Board of Trade. New York: Historical Publishing Co., 1886.

Pacyga, Dominic A. *Slaughterhouse: Chicago's Union Stock Yard and the World It Made*. Chicago: University of Chicago Press, 2015.

Palmer, Harry Clay. *Sights Around the World with the Base-Ball Boys*. Philadelphia: Edgewood Publishing Co., 1892.

Palmer, Harry Clay, James Austin Fynes, and Francis C. Richter. *Athletic Sports in America, England and Australia*. New York: Union Publishing House, 1889.

Pasdermadjian, Hrant. *The Department Store: Its Origins, Evolution and Economics*. London: Newman Books, 1954.

Patten, William, and Joseph Walker McSpadden, eds. *The Book of Baseball: The National Pastime from Its Earliest Days*. New York: P. F. Collier & Sons, 1911.

Paullin, Charles O., and John K. Wright. *Atlas of the Historical Geography of the United States*. Washington, DC: Carnegie Institution of Washington and the American Geographical Society of New York, 1932; online version by the Digital Scholarship Lab at the University of Richmond, dsl.richmond.edu/historicalatlas/.

Pauly, Thomas H. *Zane Grey: His Life, His Adventures, His Women*. Chicago: University of Illinois Press, 2005.

Pearson, Daniel Merle. *Baseball in 1889: Players vs. Owners*. Madison, WI: Popular Press, 1993.

Pedersen, Paul, Janet Parks, Jerome Quarterman, and Lucie Thibault. *Contemporary Sports Management*. Champaign, IL: Human Kinetics, 2010.

Pernot, Laurent. *Before the Ivy: The Cubs' Golden Age in Pre-Wrigley Chicago*. Champaign, IL: University of Illinois Press, 2015.

Peterson, Florence. *Strikes in the United States 1880–1938*. Washington, DC: Government Printing Office, 1938.

Peterson, Scott D. *Reporting Baseball's Sensational Season of 1890: The Brotherhood War and the Rise of Modern Sports Journalism*. Jefferson, NC: McFarland & Co., 2015.

Petryshyn, Jaroslav. *Made Up to a Standard: Thomas Alexander Russell and the Russell Motor Car Company*. Burnstown, ON: General Store Publishing, 2000.

Picturesque Kenwood, Hyde Park, Illinois: Its Artistic Homes, Boulevards, Drives, Scenery and Surroundings. Chicago: Craig & Messervey, n.d.

Pierce, Bessie L. *A History of Chicago*, 3 vols. New York: Alfred A. Knopf, 1937–1957.

Pietrusza, David. *Major Leagues: The Formation, Sometimes Absorption and Mostly Inevitable Demise of 18 Professional Baseball Organizations, 1871 to Present*. Jefferson, NC: McFarland & Co., 1991.

Plan of Re-Numbering: City of Chicago. Chicago: Chicago Directory Co., 1909.

Platt, Harold L. *Shock Cities: The Environmental Transformation and Reform of Manchester and Chicago*. Chicago: University of Chicago Press, 2005.

Pope, Steven W. *Patriotic Games: Sporting Traditions in the American Imagination, 1876–1926*. New York: Oxford University Press USA, 1997.

Porter, David L., ed. *Biographical Dictionary of American Sports: Q–Z*. Westport, CT: Greenwood Press, 2000.

Porter, Dilwyn. "Entrepreneurship." In *Routledge Companion to Sports History*, edited by S. W. Pope and John Nauright. Abingdon, England: Routledge, 2010.

Portrait and Biographical Record of Winnebago and Boone Counties, Illinois. Chicago: Biographical Publishing Co., 1892.

Potter, W. W., Ford Hicks, and Edward Butler. *History of Barry County, Michigan, with Biographical Sketches of Prominent Men*. Grand Rapids, MI: Reed-Tandler Co., 1912.

Powers, Albert Theodore. *The Business of Baseball*. Jefferson, NC: McFarland, 2003.

Presbrey, Frank. *The History and Development of Advertising*. Garden City, NY: Doubleday Doran & Co., 1929.

Press Reference Library. *Notables of the West: Being the Portraits and Biographies of Progressive Men of the West Who Have Helped in the Development and History Making of This Wonderful Country*. New York: International News Service, 1915.

Rader, Benjamin G. *Baseball: A History of America's Game*. Urbana: University of Illinois Press, 2018.

Rae, John. *American Automobile Manufacturers: The First Forty Years*. New York: Chilton Co., 1959.

Reisler, Jim. *Igniting the Flame: America's First Olympic Team*. Guilford, CT: Lyons Press, 2012.

Representative Men and Old Families of Southeastern Massachusetts: Containing Historical Sketches of Prominent and Representative Citizens and Genealogical Records of Many of the Old Families, vol. 1. Chicago: J. H. Beers, 1912.

Richter, Francis C. *Richter's History and Records of Base Ball, the American Nation's Chief Sport*. Philadelphia: F. C. Richter, 1914.

Riess, Steven A. *City Games: The Evolution of American Society and the Rise of Sports.* Champaign: University of Illinois Press, 1989.

Riess, Steven A., ed. *A Companion to American Sport History*. Hoboken, NJ: Wiley-Blackwell, 2014.

Riess, Steven A. *Encyclopedia of Major League Baseball Clubs*. Santa Barbara, CA: ABC–CLIO/Greenwood Publishing Group, 2006.

Riess, Steven A. *Sport in Industrial America 1850–1920.* Wheeling, IL: Harlan Davidson, 1995.

Riess, Steven A. *Touching Base: Professional Baseball and American Culture in the Progressive Era*. Champaign: University of Illinois Press, 1999.

Riess, Steven A., and Gerald R. Gems, eds. *The Chicago Sports Reader: 100 Years of Sports in the Windy City*. Champaign: University of Illinois Press, 2009.

Ring, Jennifer. *Stolen Bases: Why American Girls Don't Play Baseball.* Champaign: University of Illinois Press, 2009.

Rinker, Kimberly A. *Chicago's Horse Racing Venues*. Mount Pleasant, SC: Arcadia Publishing, 2009.

Ritter, Lawrence S. *The Glory of Their Times: The Story of the Early Days of Baseball Told by the Men Who Played It*. New York: Harper Perennial, 1966.

Roberts, Randy, and Carson Cunningham, eds. *Before the Curse: The Chicago Cubs' Glory Years, 1870–1945*. Champaign: University of Illinois Press, 2011.

Robertson, Darrel M. *The Chicago Revival, 1876: Society and Revivalism in a Nineteenth-Century City*. Metuchen, NJ: Scarecrow Press, 1989.

Rockford City Directory and County Gazetteer for 1869. Rockford, IL: Kauffman & Burch, 1869.

Rockford To-Day: Historical, Descriptive Biographical. Rockford, IL: Rockford Morning Star, 1903.

Roff, Elwood A. *Base Ball and Base Ball Players*. Chicago: E.A. Roff, 1912.

Rosenberg, Howard W. *Cap Anson 3: Muggsy John McGraw and the Tricksters—Baseball's Fun Age of Rule Bending*. Arlington, VA: Tile Books, 2005.

Rosenberg, Howard W. *When Captaining a Team Meant Something: Leadership in Baseball's Early Years*. Arlington, VA: Tile Books, 2003.

Ross, Robert B. *The Great Baseball Revolt: The Rise and Fall of the 1890 Players League*. Lincoln: University of Nebraska Press, 2016.

Rossi, John P. *The National Game: Baseball and American Culture*. Lanham, MD: Ivan R. Dee, 2001.

Rowe, Ford F. *Rockford Streamlined, 1834–1941*. Rockford, IL: Graphic Arts Corp., 1941.

Royce; Charles C., and Cyrus Thomas. *Indian Land Cessions in the United States*. Washington, DC: Government Printing Office, 1899.

Ruble, Blair A. *Second Metropolis: Pragmatic Pluralism in Gilded Age Chicago, Silver Age Moscow, and Meiji Osaka.* Cambridge: Cambridge University Press, 2001.

Rucker, Mark, and John Freyer. *19th Century Baseball in Chicago*. Mount Pleasant, SC: Arcadia, 2003.

Ryczek, William J. *Baseball's First Inning: A History of the National Pastime Through the Civil War*. Jefferson, NC: McFarland & Co., 2009.

Ryczek, William J. *Blackguards and Red Stockings: A History of Baseball's National Association, 1871–1875*. Jefferson, NC: McFarland & Co., 2016.

Ryczek, William J. *When Johnny Came Sliding Home: The Post–Civil War Baseball Boom, 1865–1870*. Jefferson, NC: McFarland & Co., 1998.

Rydell, Robert W. *All the World's a Fair: Visions of Empire at American International Expositions, 1876–1916*. Chicago: University of Chicago Press, 1984.

Sackett, William E., ed. *Scannell's New Jersey's First Citizens*. Paterson, NJ: J. J. Scannell, 1917.

Scannell, John James, and William Edgar Sackett. *Scannell's New Jersey's First Citizens: Biographies and Portraits of the Notably Living Men and Women of New Jersey, Vol. 2*. Paterson, NJ: J. J. Scannell, 1919.

Scharchburg, Richard P. *Carriages without Horses: J. Frank Duryea and the Birth of the American Automobile Industry*. Warrendale, PA: Society of Automotive Engineers, 1993.

Schiff, Andrew J. *The Father of Baseball: A Biography of Henry Chadwick*. Jefferson, NC: McFarland & Co., 2008.

Schlossberg, Dan. *The Baseball Almanac*. Chicago: Triumph Books, 2002.

Schmidt, Christopher W. "John Montgomery Ward: The Lawyer Who Took On Baseball." In *Then & Now: Stories of Law and Progress*, edited by Lori Andrews & Sarah Harding, 44–50. Chicago: IIT Chicago-Kent College of Law, 2013.

Scott, Franklin William. *Newspapers and Periodicals of Illinois, 1814–1879*. Chicago: Lakeside Press, 1910.

Scully, Gerald W. *The Business of Major League Baseball*. Chicago: University of Chicago Press, 1989.

Sears, Edward S. *Running Through the Ages*. Jefferson, NC: McFarland, 2015.

Seaver, William. *Historical Sketch of the Village of Batavia*. Batavia, NY: Seaver & Son, 1849.

Sewall, May Wright, ed. *The World's Congress of Representative Women, Volumes 1–2*. Chicago and New York: Rand, McNally & Co., 1894.

Seymour, Harold. *Baseball: The Early Years*. New York: Oxford University Press, 1960.

Seymour, Harold. *Baseball: The People's Game*. New York: Oxford University Press, 1990.

Shannon, W. W. *Journal of the Assembly During the Thirty-Eighth (Extra) Sessions of the Legislature of the State of California, 1910*. Sacramento, CA: State Printing Office, 1911.

Sherman, Ardis. *Reflections, Byron, Illinois, 1835–1976*. Byron, IL: Village of Byron, 1976.

Shiffert, John. *Base Ball in Philadelphia: A History of the Early Game, 1831–1900*. Jefferson, NC: McFarland & Co., 2006.

Shlakman, Vera. *Economic History of a Factory Town: A Study of Chicopee, Massachusetts*. New York: Octagon Books, 1969.

Smith, Robert. *Heroes of Baseball*. Cleveland: World Publishing Co., 1952.

Smith, Robert. *A Social History of the Bicycle*. New York: American Heritage Press, 1972.

Snyder, John. *Cubs Journal: Year-by-Year and Day-by-Day with the Chicago Cubs Since 1876*. Cincinnati: Clerisy Press, 2008.

Sobel, Robert. *Panic on Wall Street: A History of America's Financial Disasters*. Washington, DC: Beard Books, 1999.

Soos, Troy. *Before the Curse: The Glory Days of New England Baseball, 1858–1918*. Jefferson, NC: McFarland & Co., 2006.

Spalding, Albert. *Rise to Follow: An Autobiography*. New York: Henry Holt and Company, 1943.

Spalding, Albert G. *Baseball: America's National Game*. New York: American Sports Publishing Co., 1911.

Spalding, A. G., and Lewis E. Meacham, eds. *Spalding's Official Baseball Guide*. Chicago: A. G. Spalding & Bros., various years.

Spalding, Charles Warren. *The Spalding Memorial: A Genealogical History of Edward Spalding of Virginia and Massachusetts Bay and His Descendants*. Chicago: American Publishers Assoc., 1897.

Spalding, Harriet. *Reminiscences of Harriet I. Spalding*. East Orange, NJ: privately published, 1910.

Spatz, Lyle. *Historical Dictionary of Baseball*. Lanham, MD: Scarecrow Press, 2013.

Sperling, John G. *Great Depressions: 1837–1844, 1893–1898, 1929–1939*. Chicago: Scott, Foresman, 1966.

Spink, Alfred Henry. *The National Game*, 2nd ed. Carbondale: Southern Illinois University Press, 2000 (reprint of 1911 edition).

Stagg, Amos Alonzo, and Wesley Winans Stout. *Touchdown!* New York: Longmans, Green & Co., 1927.

Stevens, David. *Baseball's Radical for All Seasons: A Biography of John Montgomery Ward*. Lanham, MD: Scarecrow Press, 1998.

Stevens, Walter Barlow. *St. Louis, the Fourth City, 1764–1909, Volume 2*. Chicago-St. Louis: S. J. Clarke Publishing, 1909.

Stewart, Estelle May, and Jesse Chester Bowen. *History of Wages in the United States from Colonial Times to 1928*. Washington, DC: Government Printing Office, 1934.

Stout, Glenn, and Richard A. Johnson. *The Cubs: The Complete Story of Chicago Cubs Baseball*. New York: Houghton Mifflin, 2007.

Stratman, Linda. *Fraudsters and Charlatans: A Peek at Some of History's Greatest Rogues*. Stroud, England: History Press, 2010.

Sullivan, Dean A., ed. *Early Innings: A Documentary History of Baseball, 1825–1908*. Lincoln: University of Nebraska Press, 1997.

Sullivan, J. E., ed. "Review of the Olympic Games of 1904." In *Spalding's Official Athletic Almanac for 1905*. New York: American Sports Publishing Co., 1905.

Sutter, L. M. *New Mexico Baseball: Miners, Outlaws, Indians and Isotopes, 1880 to the Present*. Jefferson, NC: McFarland & Co., 2010.

Swanson, Krister. *Baseball's Power Shift*. Lincoln: University of Nebraska, 2016.

Szetela, Thaddeus M. *History of Chicopee*. Chicopee, MA: Szetela & Rich, 1948.

Tan, Cecilia, ed. *The National Pastime: Pacific Ghosts*. Phoenix: Society for American Baseball Research, 2019.

Tebay, K. Martin. *Harry's Mission: An Account of the American Baseball Players Tour of the British Isles, 1874*. Blackpool, England: Red Rose Books, 2019.

Thorn, John. *Baseball in the Garden of Eden: The Secret History of the Early Game*. New York: Simon & Schuster, 2011.

Thorn, John. "The Most Important Game in Baseball History?". In *Inventing Baseball: The 100 Greatest Games That Shaped the 19th Century*, edited by Bill Felber et al. Phoenix: Society for American Baseball Research, 2013.

Thornley, Stewart. *Land of the Giants: New York's Polo Grounds*. Philadelphia: Temple University Press, 2000.

Thornton, Patrick K. *Legal Decisions That Shaped Modern Baseball*. Jefferson, NC: McFarland & Co., 2012.

Thurston, John Henry. *Reminiscences, Sporting and Otherwise, of Early Days in Rockford, Ill.* Rockford, IL: Press of the *Daily Republican*, 1891.

Tiffany, Nelson Otis. *The Tiffanys of America: History and Genealogy*. Buffalo, NY: privately published, 1901.

The Town of Harvey, Illinois, Manufacturing Suburb of Chicago, Aged Two Years. Chicago: Harvey Land Association, 1892.

Tuohey, George V. *A History of the Boston Base Ball Club, Being a Public Testimonial to the Players of the 1897 Team in Recognition of the Magnificent Work of the Past Season; a Concise and Accurate History of Base Ball from Its Inception; Containing Biographical Sketches of Past Managers and Players, and of the Present Year's Boston Team.* Boston: M. F. Quinn & Co., 1897.

Turrini, Joseph M. *The End of Amateurism in American Track and Field*. Urbana: University of Illinois Press, 2010.

Tweit, Susan J. *Barren, Wild, and Worthless: Living in the Chihuahuan Desert*. Albuquerque: University of New Mexico Press, 1995.

Tygiel, Jules. *Past Time: Baseball as History*. New York: Oxford University Press, 2000.

Vincent, Ted. *The Rise and Fall of American Sport: Mudville's Revenge*. Lincoln: University of Nebraska Press, 1994.

Vlasich, James A. *A Legend for the Legendary: The Origin of the Baseball Hall of Fame*. Bowling Green, OH: Bowling Green State University Popular Press, 1990.

Voigt, David Q. "Serfs vs. Magnates: A Century of Labor Strife in Major League Baseball." In *The Business of Professional Sports*, edited by Paul D. Staudohar and James A. Mangan, 95–114. Urbana: University of Illinois Press, 1991.

Voigt, David Quentin. *American Baseball: From the Gentleman's Sport to the Commissioner System, Volume 1*. Norman: University of Oklahoma Press, 1966.

Voigt, David Quentin. *America Through Baseball*. Chicago: Nelson-Hall, 1976.

Voigt, David Quentin. *The League That Failed*. Lanham, MD: Scarecrow Press, 1998.

Wade, Louise Carroll. *Chicago's Pride: The Stockyards, Packingtown, and Environs in the Nineteenth Century*. Champaign: University of Illinois, 1987.

Wadlin, Horace G. *Labor and Industrial Chronology of the Commonwealth of Massachusetts*. Boston: Wright & Potter, 1900.

Walker, Moses Fleetwood. *Our Home Colony: A Treatise on the Past, Present and Future of the Negro Race in America*. Steubenville, OH: Herald Printing Company, 1908.

Ward, John Montgomery. *Base-Ball: How to Become a Player, with the Origin, History and Explanation of the Game*. Philadelphia: Athletic Pub. Co., 1888.

Waterman, A. N. *Historical Review of Chicago and Cook County and Selected Biography*. Chicago: Lewis Publishing, 1908.

Watson, Edward B., and Edmund V. Gillon Jr. *New York Then and Now*. Mineola, NY: Dover Publications, 1976.

Weber, Nicholas F. *The Clarks of Cooperstown: Their Singer Sewing Machine Fortune, Their Great and Influential Art Collections, Their Forty-Year Feud*. New York: Alfred A. Knopf, 2007.

Wells, David Ames. *Recent Economic Changes and Their Effects on the Production and Distribution of Wealth and the Well-Being of Society*. New York: D. Appleton & Co., 1898.

Whalen, Thomas J. *When the Red Sox Ruled: Baseball's First Dynasty*. Lanham, MD: Ivan R. Dee, 2011.

White, James Terry. *National Cyclopaedia of American Biography*. New York: James T. White & Co., 1893.

White, Richard. *It's Your Misfortune and None of My Own: A History of the American West*. Norman: University of Oklahoma Press, 1991.

White, Richard. *The Republic for Which It Stands: The United States During Reconstruction and the Gilded Age*. New York: Oxford University Press, 2017.

Whitten, David O., and Bessie E. Whitten, eds. *Manufacturing: A Historiographical and Bibliographical Guide*. Westport, CT: Greenwood, 1990.

Whitten, David O., and Bessie Emrick Whitten, eds. *Handbook of American Business History: Manufacturing*. Westport, CT: Greenwood, 1990.

Wicker, Elmus. *Banking Panics of the Gilded Age*. New York: Cambridge University Press, 2000.

Wilbert, Warren N. *The Arrival of the American League: Ban Johnson and the 1901 Challenge to National League Monopoly*. Jefferson, NC: McFarland & Co., 2007.

Wilbert, Warren N. *A Cunning Kind of Play: The Cubs-Giants Rivalry, 1876–1932*. Jefferson, NC: McFarland & Co., 2002.

Works Project Administration. *Baseball in Old Chicago*. Chicago: A.C. McClurg & Co., 1939.

Works Project Administration. *Rockford*. Rockford, IL: Graphic Arts Corp., 1941.

Wright, George. *Record of the Boston Base Ball Club, Since Its Organization: With a Sketch of All Its Players for 1871, '72, '73 and '74, and Other Items of Interest*. Boston: Rockwell & Churchill, 1874.

Wright, Marshall D. *The National Association of Base Ball Players, 1857–1870*. Jefferson, NC: McFarland & Co., 2000.

Wright, Marshall D. *Nineteenth Century Baseball: Year-by-Year Statistics for the Major League Teams, 1871 through 1900*. Jefferson, NC: McFarland & Co., 2004.

Zang, David W. *Fleet Walker's Divided Heart: The Life of Baseball's First Black Major Leaguer*. Lincoln: University of Nebraska Press, 1995.

Zeiler, Thomas W. *Ambassadors in Pinstripes: The Spalding World Baseball Tour and the Birth of the American Empire*. Lanham, MD: Rowman & Littlefield Publishers, 2006.

Zimmerman, Sarah, Neill DePaoli, Arthur J. Krim, Peter Stott, and James W. Bradley. *Historical & Archaeological Resources of the Connecticut River Valley*. Boston: Massachusetts Historical Commission, 1984.

Journal/Magazine Articles, Reports, and Other Sources

"1871–1872 Boston Red Stockings Archive." *Antiques Roadshow*, PBS, https://www.pbs.org/wgbh/roadshow/season/19/new-york-ny/appraisals/1871-1872-boston-red-stockings-archive--201407A12/ (accessed January 13, 2024).

Ackerly, Neal W. "Review of the Historic Significance of and Management Recommendations for Preserving New Mexico's Acequia Systems." Report for the Historic Preservation Division, September 1996.

Anderson, William. "Creating the National Pastime: The Antecedents of Major League Baseball Public Relations." *Media History Monographs*, Vol. 4, no. 2 (2000–2001), 1–26.

Annual Reports of the Department of the Interior for the Fiscal Year Ended June 30, 1906. Washington: Government Printing Office, 1906.

Applin, Albert. "From Muscular Christianity to the Marketplace: The History of Men's and Boys' Basketball in the United States, 1891 to 1957." Ph.D. diss., University of Massachusetts, 1982.

Ashcraft, Jennifer K., and Craig A. Depken II. "The Introduction of the Reserve Clause in Major League Baseball: Evidence of Its Impact on Player Salaries During the 1880s." Working Paper No. 07-10, International Association of Sports Economists, April 2007.

Baker, Ray Stannard. "An Extraordinary Experiment in Brotherhood: The Theosophical Institution at Point Loma, California." *American Magazine*, Vol. LXIII, no. 3 (1907).

Balke, Nathan S., and Robert J. Gordon. "The Estimation of Prewar Gross National Product: Methodology and New Evidence." *Journal of Political Economy*, Vol. 97, no. 1 (February 1989).

Bauer, Robert Allan. "Outside the Lines of Gilded Age Baseball: Profits, Beer, and the Origins of the Brotherhood War." Ph.D. diss., University of Arkansas, Fayetteville, 2015.

Bauer, Robert Allan. "Spring Training in Hot Springs." *Arkansas Historical Quarterly*, Vol. 77, no. 1 (Spring 2018), 1–20.

Beaver, Daniel C. "Baseball, Modernity, and Science Discourse in British Popular Culture, 1871–1883." *Historical Journal*, Vol. 1, no. 23 (2021).

Betts, John Rickards. "The Technological Revolution and the Rise of Sport, 1850–1900." *Mississippi Valley Historical Review*, Vol. 40, no. 2 (September 1953), 231–56.

Bloyce, D. "Just Not Cricket: Baseball in England 1874–1900." *International Journal of the History of Sport*, Vol. 14, no. 2 (1997), 207–18.

Bloyce, D. "'That's Your Way of Playing Rounders, Isn't It'? The Response of the English Press to American Baseball Tours to England, 1874–1924." *Sporting Traditions*, Vol. 22, no. 1 (2005), 81–98.

Bloyce, D. "A Very Peculiar Practice: The London Baseball League, 1906–1911." *Nine: A Journal of Baseball History and Culture*, Vol. 14, no. 2 (2006), 118–28.

Bloyce, D., and P. Murphy. "Baseball in England: A Case of Prolonged Cultural Resistance." *Journal of Historical Sociology*, Vol. 21, no. 1 (2008), 120–42.

Carter, Gregg Lee. "Baseball in Saint Louis, 1867–1875: An Historical Case Study in Civic Pride." *Missouri Historical Society Bulletin*, Vol. 31 (1975), 259.

Casey, Harry. "The Story of Baseball: A Brief History of the National Game," three parts. *Baseball Magazine*, February–April 1912.

Caylor, O. P. "Baseball's Contribution to the Economy." *Harper's Weekly*, May 3, 1890, 204–5.

Champion, Aaron B. "The Original Reds." *Saxby's Magazine*, August 1877.

Chadwick, Henry, ed. "Origins of Baseball." In *Spalding's Official Base Ball Guide* (New York: American Sports Publishing Co., 1908).

Connolly, James B. "The Capitalization of Amateur Athletics." *Metropolitan Magazine*, July 1910, 443–54.

Davies, Ross E. "Along Comes the Players Association: The Roots and Rise of Organized Labor in Major League Baseball." *NYU Journal of Legislation and Public Policy*, Vol. 16, no. 2 (Spring 2013), 321–49.

Dunham, Norman L. "The Bicycle in American History." Ph.D. diss., Harvard University, 1956.

Dyreson, Mark. "America's Athletic Missionaries: Political Performance, Olympic Spectacle and the Quest for an American National Culture, 1896–1912." *Olympika: The International Journal of Olympic Studies*, Vol. 1 (1992), 70–91.

Dyreson, Mark. "The Emergence of Consumer Culture and the Transformation of Physical Culture: American Sport in the 1920s." *Journal of Sport History*, Vol. 16, no. 3 (Winter 1989), 261–81.

Edmonds, Edmund P. "Arthur Soden's Legacy: The Origins and Early History of Baseball's Reserve System." *Albany Government Law Review*, Vol. 5, no. 1 (2012), 38–89.

Edmunds, R. David. "Prairie Potawatomi Removal of 1833." *Indiana Magazine of History*, Vol. 68, no. 3 (September 1972), 240–53.

Emery, John M. "For Prosperity's Sake, Buy an Automobile: Car Dealers and Consumer Demand in Depression-Era Cooperstown." *New York History*, Vol. 88, no. 1 (Winter 2007), 97–117.

Epperson, Bruce D. "'The Finances Stagger These Fellows': The Great American Bicycle Trust, 1899–1903." *International Journal of the History of Sport*, Vol. 28, no. 18 (2011), 2633–52.

Fielding, Larry, and Lori K. Miller. "The Foreign Invasion: The Sporting Goods Industry between 1950 and 1975." Presentation to North American Society for Sport History, Auburn, AL, 1996.

Fielding, Larry, Paul Pedersen, and Elizabeth Gregg. "From Market Directed Flows to Management Directed Flows: The Bicycle Industry Experience 1890–1900." Presentation to North American Association for Sport History, Glenwood Springs, CO, 2006.

Fielding, Lawrence W., and Lori K. Miller. "The ABC Trust: A Chapter in the History of Capitalism in the Sporting Goods Industry." *Sports History Review*, Vol. 29, no. 1 (Spring 1998), 44–58.

Findling, J. E. "The Louisville Grays' Scandal of 1877." *Journal of Sport History*, Vol. 3, no. 2 (Summer 1976), 176–87.

Findling, John E. "Chicago Loses the 1904 Olympics." *Journal of Olympic History*, Vol. 12, no. 3 (October 2004), 24–29.

Freedman, Stephen. "The Baseball Fad in Chicago, 1865–1870: An Exploration of the Role of Sport in the Nineteenth-Century City." *Journal of Sport History*, Vol. 5, no. 2 (Summer 1978).

Gates, Paul Wallace. "Large-Scale Farming in Illinois, 1850 to 1870." *Agricultural History*, Vol. 6, no. 1 (January 1932), 14–25.

Gelber, Steven M. "'Their Hands Are All Out Playing:' Business and Amateur Baseball, 1845–1917." *Journal of Sport History*, Vol. 11, no. 1 (Spring 1984).

Godley, Andrew, and Scott R. Fletcher. "International Retailing in Britain, 1850–1994." *Service Industries Journal*, Vol. 21, no. 2 (2001).

Goebel, Thomas. "The Uneven Rewards of Professional Labor: Wealth and Income in the Chicago Professions, 1870–1920." *Journal of Social History*, Vol. 29, no. 4, 749–77.

Gordon, Sloane. "Putting 'em Over." *Pearson's Magazine*, Vol. 26, no. 2 (August 1911), 195–201.

Hagenah, William J. *Report on the Investigation of the Chicago Telephone Company Submitted to the Committee on Gas, Oil, and Electric Light*. Chicago: Henry O. Shepard Co., 1911.

Hagerty, J. E. "Experiences of an Early Marketing Teacher." *Journal of Marketing*, Vol. 1, no. 1 (July 1936), 20–27.

Hardy, Stephen. "Entrepreneurs, Organizations, and the Sport Marketplace: Subjects in Search of Historians." *Journal of Sport History*, Vol. 13, no. 1 (Spring 1986), 14–33.

Hardy, Stephen, John Loy, and Douglas Booth. "The Material Culture of Sport: Toward a Typology." *Journal of Sport History*, Vol. 36, no. 1 (Fall 2009), 129–52.

Hartford, William J., ed. "Albert Goodwill Spalding: Every Schoolboy Reveres the Name—the Foremost Sportsman of the World—Successful in Sports and Business." *Successful American*, Vol. 1, no. 5 (May 1900), 26–27.

Hartford, William J., ed. "William Thayer Brown: Head of the Most Extensive Sporting House in the World." *Successful American*, June 1903, 408–10.

Hay, Robert. *Final Geological Reports of the Artesian and Underflow Investigation Between the Ninety-Seventh Meridian of Longitude and the Foothills of the Rocky Mountains*, Vol. III. Washington, DC: Government Printing Office, 1893.

Hichborn, Franklin. "The California Senatorial Situation." *Lawyer & Banker and Bench & Bar Review* (Tacoma, WA), Vol. 3, no. 6 (December 1910).

Hylton, J. Gordon. "The Historical Origins of Baseball Grievance Arbitration." *Marquette Sports Law Review*, Vol. 11, no. 2 (2001), 185–94.

Jaffa, Nathan, *Report of the Secretary of the Territory 1909–1910 and Legislative Manual*. Santa Fe: New Mexican Printing Co., 1911.

Kearney, Joseph D., and Thomas W. Merrill. "Private Rights in Public Lands: The Chicago Lakefront, Montgomery Ward, and the Public Dedication Doctrine." *Northwestern University Law Review*, Vol. 105, no. 4 (2011), 1417–1530.

Kirsch, George B. "The Creation of American Team Sports: Baseball and Cricket, 1838–72." *American Historical Review*, Vol. 95, no. 5 (December 1990), 1627–28.

Knopf, Philip. *Official Proceedings of the Board of Commissioners of Cook County Illinois for the Year 1897–98.* Chicago: J. M. W. Jones Stationery and Printing Co., 1898.

Levine, Peter. "Business, Missionary Motives Behind 1888–89 World Tour." *Baseball Research Journal*, Vol. 30, no. 1 (1984), 25–41.

Llewellyn, Matthew P. "The Battle of Shepherd's Bush." *International Journal of the History of Sport*, Vol. 28, no. 5 (2011), 688–710.

Lucas, Charles J. P. "Commercializing Amateur Athletics." *The World To-Day*, January 1906.

Lucas, John. "American Preparations for the First Post World War Olympic Games, 1919–1920." *Journal of Sports History*, Vol. 10, no. 2 (Summer 1983).

Lucas, John. "The Hegemonic Rule of the American Amateur Athletic Union 1888–1914: James Edward Sullivan as Prime Mover." *International Journal of the History of Sport*, Vol. 11, no. 3 (December 1994), 355–71.

Mallory, Patrick. "The Game They All Played: Chicago Baseball, 1876–1906." Unpublished dissertation, Loyola University of Chicago, 2013.

McMahon, Joseph J., Jr., and John F. Rossi. "A History and Analysis of Baseball's Three Antitrust Exemptions." *Villanova Sports and Entertainment Law Forum*, 1995, 213–59.

Miller, Lori K., and Larry W. Fielding. "Retail Price Maintenance: A Historical View of Its Impact on the Sporting Goods Industry." *Journal of Legal Aspects of Sport*, Vol. 5, no. 1 (1995), 1–27.

Molyneaux, John L., *Nuggets of History* series on baseball in Rockford, Rockford Historical Society, various issues, 2005–2008.

Moore, Glenn. "The Great Baseball Tour of 1888–89: A Tale of Image-Making, Intrigue and Labor Relations in the Gilded Age." *International Journal of the History of Sport,* Vol. 11, no. 3 (December 1994), 431–56.

Moore, Glenn, "Ideology on the Sportspage: Newspapers, Baseball, and Ideological Conflict in the Gilded Age." *Journal of Sport History*, Vol. 23, no. 3 (Fall 1996).

Morris, Peter. "Al Barker." SABR Baseball Biography Project, Society for Baseball Research, sabr.org/bioproj/person/0ab52a39 (accessed July 10, 2016).

Moser, Zachary. "Problems in Traditional Integration Narratives: The Construction of Cap Anson's Color Line Villainy." *Black Ball: New Issues in African American Baseball History* Vol. 9 (2017), 17–39.

"The New Spalding Policy Explained and Defended by A. G. Spalding." *Iron Age*, January 12, 1899, 38–43.

Paxson, Frederic L. "The Rise of Sport." *Mississippi Valley Historical Review*, Vol. 4, no. 2 (September 1917), 143–68.

Peterson, Florence. "Strikes in the United States 1880–1936." US Department of Labor, Bulletin No. 651, August 1937.

Proceedings of the National Association of Professional Base Ball Players. Washington, DC: Beresford, 1871.

Pruter, Robert. "Youth Baseball in Chicago, 1868–1890: Not Always Sandlot Ball." *Journal of Sport History*, Vol. 26, no. 1 (Spring 1999), 1–28.

Reiskind, Michael, and Kenneth A. Perkins. "Baseball in Jamaica Plain." Jamaica Plain Historical Society, http://www.jphs.org/victorian/baseball-in-jamaica-plain.html.

Report of the Industrial Commission on the Chicago Labor Disputes of 1900, vol. 3. Washington, DC: Government Printing Office, 1901.

Richardson, Gary, and Tim Sablik. "Banking Panics of the Gilded Age." Federal Reserve History website, https://www.federalreservehistory.org/essays/banking-panics-of-the-gilded-age (accessed April 13, 2025).

Riess, Steven A. "The Baseball Magnates and Urban Politics in the Progressive Era: 1895–1920." *Journal of Sport History*, Vol. 1, no. 1 (1974), 41–62.

Ross, Robert B. "We Are the People: Geographies of the Industrial Production of Culture and the Rise and Fall of the 1890 Players National League of Professional Base-Ball Clubs." Dissertation, Syracuse University, 2007.

Salvatore, Victor. "The Man Who Didn't Invent Baseball." *American Heritage*, Vol. 34, no. 4 (June/July 1983).

Sarachek, Bernard. "American Entrepreneurs and the Horatio Alger Myth." *Journal of Economic History*, Vol. 38, no. 2 (June 1978).

Spalding, Albert G. "Report of the Director of Sports." In *Report of the Commissioner-General for the United States to the International Universal Exhibition, Paris, 1900*, Vol. 1 (Washington, DC: Government Printing Office, 1901).

Spence, Vina E. "Industrial History of Chicopee." M.A. thesis, Clark University, 1930.

Starkweather, Leonard Bisco. "Catch It on the Fly" (song). Chicago: Lyon & Healy, 1867, in the Lester S. Levy sheet music collection, Johns Hopkins University.

Tarr, Joel A. "J. R. Walsh of Chicago: A Case Study in Banking and Politics, 1881–1905." *Business History Review*, Vol. 40, no. 4, 451–66.

Thirteenth Annual Report of the Factory Inspectors of Illinois: Year Ending December 15, 1905. Springfield: Illinois State Journal Co., 1906.

Tobin, Gary Allan. "The Bicycle Boom of the 1890s: The Development of Private Transportation and the Birth of the Modern Tourist." *Journal of Popular Culture*, Vol. VII, issue 4 (Spring 1974), 838–49.

United States Circuit Court of Appeals Reports. Rochester, NY: Lawyers' Co-Operative Publishing Co., 1908.

United States Industrial Commission, Report of the U.S. Industrial Commission on Trusts and Industrial Combinations, vol. 2. Washington, DC: Government Printing Office, 1901.

"U.S. Business Cycle Expansions and Contractions." National Bureau of Economic Research, https://www.nber.org/research/data/us-business-cycle-expansions-and-contractions.

Van Pelt, Armond. "Two Strikes on Hitler." *Sporting Goods Dealer*, April 1943.

Vernon, J. R. "Unemployment Rates in Post-Bellum America: 1869–1899." *Journal of Macroeconomics*, Vol. 16, issue 4 (Autumn 1994).

Voigt, David Quentin. "The Boston Red Stockings: The Birth of Major League Baseball." *New England Quarterly*, December 1970.

Walters, William D. "Selling Location: Illinois Town Advertisements 1835–1837." Normal: Illinois State University, 2010.

Ward, John M. "Notes of a Baseballist." *Lippincott's Monthly Magazine*, August 1886, 212–20.

Ward, John M. "Is the Base-Ball Player a Chattel?" *Lippincott's Monthly Magazine*, August 1887.

Ward, John M. "Our National Game." *The Cosmopolitan*, October 1888, 443–46.

Weir, Robert. "'Take Me Out to the Brawl Game:' Sports and Workers in Gilded Age Massachusetts." *Historical Journal of Massachusetts*, Vol. 37, no. 1, 29–47.

White, Marjorie. "Spalding Called Father of Pro Baseball." *Sundial*, the Sunday magazine of *El Paso Times*, August 3, 1969.

Wright, Carroll D., and Oren W. Weaver. "Bulletin of the Department of Labor," No. 18 (September 1898), 668.

Wright, Leroy A. "Mixed Senatorial Question." *Lawyer & Banker and Bench & Bar Review* (Tacoma, WA), Vol. 3, no. 5 (October 1910).

Zollmann, Carl. "Baseball Peonage." *Marquette Law Review*, Vol. 24, no. 3 (April 1940), 139–45.

Index

Note: Photo insert images indicated by *p1, p2, p3,* etc.